How to Take Skepticism Seriously

How to Take Skepticism Seriously

ADAM LEITE

OXFORD
UNIVERSITY PRESS

Oxford University Press is a department of the University of Oxford. It furthers the University's objective of excellence in research, scholarship, and education by publishing worldwide. Oxford is a registered trade mark of Oxford University Press in the UK and certain other countries.

Published in the United States of America by Oxford University Press
198 Madison Avenue, New York, NY 10016, United States of America.

© Oxford University Press 2024

All rights reserved. No part of this publication may be reproduced, stored in a retrieval system, or transmitted, in any form or by any means, without the prior permission in writing of Oxford University Press, or as expressly permitted by law, by license, or under terms agreed with the appropriate reproduction rights organization. Inquiries concerning reproduction outside the scope of the above should be sent to the Rights Department, Oxford University Press, at the address above.

You must not circulate this work in any other form
and you must impose this same condition on any acquirer.

CIP data is on file at the Library of Congress

ISBN 978–0–19–769117–5

DCI: 10.1093/oso/9780197691175.001.0001

Printed by Integrated Books International, United States of America

For Jonathan and Abe

Contents

Preface ix

PART I. FINDING OUR FOOTING: SKEPTICISM AND METHOD

1. Getting Located 3
2. Why Moore Matters 17
3. Stroud's Question 38
4. Austin, Dreams, and Skepticism 56

PART II. WHAT IS OUR EVIDENCE?

5. Reclaiming Our Evidence 97
6. Evidence and Method 132
7. Epistemic Asymmetry 156
8. Methodological Interlude: Four Moments in Contemporary Epistemology 189

PART III. ON "THE SENSORY BASIS OF OUR KNOWLEDGE OF THE WORLD"

9. Skepticism and Perception 229
10. What Is the Global Priority Thesis? 256
11. Seeking an Argument I: Regress Arguments and the Global Priority Thesis 277
12. Seeking an Argument II: The Global Priority Thesis and the Explanation of Belief 295

PART IV. TAKING STOCK

13. Enough Is Enough . . . 315

Bibliography . . . 333
Index . . . 339

Preface

I have been thinking about external world skepticism for a very long time. During my sophomore year of college a desultory philosophical conversation was taking place via graffiti on a bathroom stall in UC Berkeley's Moses Hall. I found myself thinking that the participants weren't making comments that really *mattered*. I have written on a bathroom stall only once in my life. I wrote, "But seriously folks, what are we going to do about Descartes' Evil Demon?"[1]

In those early years, my engagement with skepticism was nurtured by my teachers at UC Berkeley. Barry Stroud's epistemology lecture course and then-recent masterpiece *The Significance of Philosophical Scepticism* helped me discover a way to do philosophy that I found meaningful. I still find the book exemplary of serious philosophical engagement with fundamental issues, even as I have come to disagree with many of Stroud's arguments and conclusions both there and in his subsequent work. His recent death is the loss of a philosophical giant. Janet Broughton advised my senior honors thesis on external world skepticism, and I would like to thank her for that formative experience. And I am deeply grateful to the late Wally Matson, long-time member of the UC Berkeley philosophy department, for his generous support and enthusiasm about my philosophical aspirations. He kindly read the completed honors thesis and wrote approximately ten pages of comments. One of these—"It was like *Hamlet* without the Prince, since you never explained *how* we can know we are not dreaming"—set one of the key questions of my PhD dissertation. When he read my dissertation in 2001 or so, Wally sent me unpublished transcripts of J.L. Austin's lectures given at UC Berkeley in the late 1950s. These lectures differ significantly from Warnock's redaction published as *Sense and Sensibilia*. As Wally saw, the view of skepticism that I had arrived at in the dissertation was very much the position that Austin had articulated in the Berkeley lectures. This realization has shaped

---

[1] I am struck now by the recognition that Eli Hirsch's hilarious and profound philosophical play *Radical Skepticism and the Shadow of Doubt* is set in a restroom.

my thinking in fundamental ways. I am sad that Wally is no longer living. I would like to share this book with him.

At the Harvard department in the 1990s I found an intellectual milieu that fit my philosophical sensibilities well. This was before the days of rankings and incessant online chatter, and there was a sense that members of the department were trying in their various ways to find a path forward in philosophy. Meta-philosophical issues were still very much in the air, though Goodman was no longer active, Quine was no longer teaching, and Rawls taught his last graduate course during my first year. Among my early teachers, Stanley Cavell was especially important to me, though I never found a way to make full use of what he offered; my analytic philosopher's sensibilities left me intellectually lost and impatient both during his lectures and while reading his work. Nonetheless, he held out for me the prospect of a way of doing philosophy that aspires to honesty.

While this book bears very little resemblance to my PhD dissertation, I think that the central motivating idea remains, perhaps now in even clearer focus and defended in much greater detail. My dissertation supervisors were, for me, the perfect combination for a project on external world skepticism, and I remain profoundly grateful to all three. Warren Goldfarb's work on the later Wittgenstein was a lodestar, as was his cautious stance towards much contemporary theorizing in metaphysics and epistemology. One of his comments about my dissertation prospectus—"So on your view skepticism is an empirical problem"—crystallized a key aspect of what I was arguing. Dick Moran arrived and joined my committee just before I defended my prospectus, providing unceasing support for my work and a much-appreciated humanistic orientation in epistemology and philosophy of mind. And Jim Pryor, who joined my committee shortly after finishing his PhD at Princeton, forced me to pay careful attention to contemporary analytic epistemology. I remember talking with him at length about comments I had given him on a very early draft of his paper "The Skeptic and the Dogmatist"; in retrospect I can now see just how helpful it was to have a generous young faculty member on my dissertation committee, especially one enthusiastic about the topic of my research.

I have been fortunate to discuss these issues with many wonderful colleagues at Indiana University over the years, including especially Mark Kaplan, Gary Ebbs, Kirk Ludwig, Joan Weiner, Katy Abramson, Fred Schmitt, and—before he left for Arizona—Jonathan Weinberg. Mark has been especially important to my philosophical and professional development. While we share a fundamentally Austinian orientation, our wide areas of agreement have served to sharpen our disagreements. Since his retirement I have greatly missed our frequent conversations. He has read drafts of a very significant portion of this material, and it is much improved thanks to his astute comments. Katy Abramson has been my co-author, philosophical interlocutor, and family friend for many years. Without her, none of this would have come into anything like its current form.

I am especially thankful to Penelope Maddy and Eli Hirsch for their critical engagement with my work on skepticism. In addition to asking hard and valuable questions, they have helped me maintain my sense that this work might actually matter to other thinkers. Finally, I would like to express my gratitude to many colleagues in other departments who have offered me helpful feedback and useful conversation over the years. I would especially like to thank Al Casullo and Jon Kvanvig (for APA comments on an ancestor of Chapter 5), Annalisa Coliva, Branden Fitelson, Richard Fumerton, Peter Graham, Hilary Kornblith, Krista Lawlor, Berislav Marušić, John McDowell, Ram Neta, Duncan Pritchard, Ernie Sosa, Matthias Steup, Jonathan Vogel, Mike Williams, and finally Timothy Williamson for one brief but important conversation. (There are surely others whose names belong on this list, and I apologize for its incompleteness.) One of the things that I appreciate about our discipline is that it encourages intellectual friendships despite disagreement and direct criticism, and I hope that everyone whose work I discuss in this book will understand my critical engagement as an expression of respect and gratitude. I hope I will have an opportunity to receive their critical engagement in the same spirit.

I would like to thank OUP's editorial team, especially Peter Ohlin and project editor Chelsea Hogue, and project manager Lavanya Nithya. Thanks to Caroline McDonnell for the cover design, Elizabeth Bortka for copy-editing, Emily Manvel Leite for help with the proofs, Alex Webb for work on the bibliography and proofs, and Nate Logsdon for assistance with indexing. Thanks, too, to the organizers and audiences at various events where portions of this material were presented, including the UC Irvine Conference on Skepticism (2018), the 2018 Pacific Division APA author meets criticism session on Penelope Maddy's work, the 2018 Brandeis University Conference in honor of Eli Hirsch, the University of Geneva Conference on Epistemic Justification (2009), the 2009 Pacific Division APA, the University of Fribourg (Switzerland) Conference on Inferential Internalism (2008), the Midwest Epistemology Workshop (2008), the Inland Northwest Philosophy

Conference "Knowledge and Skepticism" (2004), and departmental colloquia at the University of East Anglia, the University of Massachusetts–Amherst, and the University of Wisconsin–Milwaukee. Work on this project was supported by fellowships from the Indiana University College of Arts and Sciences Arts and Humanities Institute and by the Indiana University sabbatical leave program.

Chapters of this book derive from the following publications. I am grateful to the publishers for permissions to reuse this material.

Chapter 4: "Austin on Dreams and Scepticism," in *The Philosophy of J.L. Austin*, edited by M. Gustafsson and R. Sorli (Oxford University Press, 2011), 78–113.

Chapter 5: "How to Take Skepticism Seriously," *Philosophical Studies* 148, no. 1 (2010): 39–60 (published by Springer Nature), and to a lesser extent "That's Not Evidence; It's Not Even True!", *Philosophical Quarterly*, 63, no. 250 (2013): 81–104 (published by Oxford University Press).

Chapter 6: "The Plain Inquirer's Plain Evidence Against the Global Skeptical Scenarios," *International Journal for the Study of Skepticism* 8, no. 3 (2018): 208–222 (published by Brill Academic Publishing), part of a symposium on Penelope Maddy's *What Do Philosophers Do?*

Chapter 7: "Skepticism and Epistemic Asymmetry," *Philosophical Issues: Epistemology*, edited by L. Miracchi and E. Sosa, 29 (2019): 184–197 (published by John Wiley & Sons).

Chapter 12: "That's Not Evidence; It's Not Even True!," *Philosophical Quarterly* 63, no. 250 (2013): 81–104 (published by Oxford University Press).

PART I
FINDING OUR FOOTING
Skepticism and Method

1
Getting Located

1. Skepticism and Epistemological Theorizing

The topic of this book is a form of external world skepticism that has been widely discussed in analytic philosophy for many decades. This form of skepticism makes a global claim: that no one knows or can even have good reason to believe anything about the world around us. This claim is intended to conflict with many of the epistemic claims and assessments that we make in ordinary life. And this form of skepticism understands itself to arise from within our best epistemic practices and commitments; its aspiration is to show that skepticism inevitably follows from principles of epistemic assessment to which we are already committed in the proper conduct of everyday life and science. In this way it purports to show that our own best commitments lead to disaster.

This form of skepticism is not merely the expression of a yearning for complete certainty. Some skeptical arguments raise in pointed fashion the question of how we can have knowledge on the basis of defeasible evidence. They function by highlighting a possibility that is incompatible with the truth of one's belief and yet compatible with all of one's evidence, a possibility that one has done nothing special to eliminate. "You don't know you are seeing a goldfinch in the garden, a real goldfinch," it might be said, "since all of your evidence, strong as it is, is compatible with the possibility that it is just a stuffed fake." Such worries fall by the wayside once we recognize that fallibilism is true. As is shown by our best scientific practice as well as ordinary life, we can know things even if our evidence is compatible with various possibilities of error. We know that smoking tobacco causes cancer, though our evidence doesn't entail that it does. Likewise, it is enough that in addition to all of the evidence that the thing in the garden is a goldfinch, nothing tells in favor of the suggestion that it is just a stuffed fake and a great deal indicates that it isn't one. (The situation would be different if one's neighbor had a penchant for decorating the neighborhood with stuffed birds.) If the question were simply whether fallibilism is true, skepticism would be of much less interest than it is.

My discussion will accordingly be framed by fallibilism. The skeptical arguments that are my focus aim to cut more deeply. They do not merely demand complete certainty or raise a question about how we can have knowledge on non-entailing grounds. They aim to challenge whether we can have any good reason at all to believe anything about the world around us.

These skeptical arguments appeal to certain scenarios—Descartes' deceiving Evil Demon, the Brain-in-a-Vat, the possibility that all of one's sensory experience is just a very life-like dream—to raise a fundamental question about our epistemic relation to the world around us. They claim that if we cannot acquire adequate evidence against these scenarios, then we lack not only knowledge about the world around us, but even good reason to believe that there is a world anything like we take there to be. And they claim that it is in principle impossible to acquire good evidence against these scenarios. They consequently conclude that we have no good reason to believe that there is a world anything like we take there to be. They thus purport to show that we are ourselves committed to epistemic principles that lead to a deeply unsettling conclusion about our relation to reality.

My overriding question is whether this form of skepticism is true. But this inquiry also has a meta-philosophical aim. I want to understand something about the nature of certain venerable philosophical puzzles and their relation to everyday life. An important tradition of twentieth century philosophy, exemplified by G.E. Moore and including in their different ways J.L. Austin and the later Wittgenstein, maintained that at least some central philosophical problems can be resolved without the development of much, if any, philosophical theory. On this view the materials already present in ordinary life are enough to enable us to fully satisfactorily treat certain philosophical questions. One primary goal of this book is to test this view. Can we show that the materials already available in ordinary epistemic life (by which I mean to include everything involved in science) suffice to stop the skeptical argument from so much as getting started? If we can, then we don't need to develop a philosophical theory of knowledge, or of our epistemic relation to the world, in order to reject skepticism. We already had everything we needed all along.

To test this approach, we need to remain non-committal about many philosophical issues. As discussions in analytic philosophy unfolded over the latter part of the twentieth century, there was a tendency to see debatable philosophical theories even in the "therapeutic" aspect of Austin and Wittgenstein's approaches to traditional epistemological problems. As a result, discussions of their writings often spawned philosophical debates in their own right. For instance, some philosophers have claimed—inspired by Wittgenstein's "private language argument," among other things—that the skeptic is committed to a view of thought content that is impossible, incoherent, or unintelligible. But others find it possible, perfectly coherent, and intelligible, and rather than resolving the debate on a basis to which we are all committed in ordinary life, we are launched on the high seas of philosophy. That can be fun, interesting, even exciting. But it isn't the goal of this book.

Similar points apply to the suggestions that the skeptical argument's scenarios—the Evil Demon, the Brain-in-a-Vat, and the like—aren't really possible, or that nothing is being said if someone attempts to assert or deny them (or asserts that one knows or doesn't know them), or that the philosophical investigations culminating in skepticism are a "no claim" context (Cavell 1979). It is a pretty widespread thought in recent philosophy that such suggestions lead straight to debates in the philosophy of language, modality, and the like, debates that are hardly resolvable on the basis of the commitments of ordinary life. Too many people find it perfectly intelligible to consider whether one is being deceived by an evil demon to claim that it is *just obvious* that the suggestion is impossible (and not merely false), or that the suggestion is not intelligible, or that one is not really saying or asking anything.

My approach will accordingly be concessive in a very important respect. I grant for the sake of argument that the skeptical scenarios are conceptually or in some sense metaphysically possible. I grant for the sake of argument that something is being asked if we wonder, "Am I being deceived by an evil demon?" I grant that something is being asserted—something that conflicts with much of what we ordinarily take to be the case—if we declare, "I am being deceived by an evil demon." And something is likewise being asserted—something that comports with much of what we ordinarily say and believe—if we declare "I am not being deceived by an evil demon, and I know that I am not."

Within the framework set by these concessions, I want to ask: Do the commitments evident in the proper conduct of everyday epistemic life and science already suffice by themselves, without the development of an epistemological theory, to license rejection of the skeptical argument and its devastating conclusion? The aim of this book is to show that they do.

I make no claim that we must approach external world skepticism in the way I propose. I'm willing to grant for the sake of argument that perhaps some clever philosopher will someday construct a fully general theory of knowledge, evidence, and the like, or a general theory of our epistemic relation to the world, that both secures widespread acceptance and refutes external world skepticism. Still, there are four major reasons to adopt the approach that I am recommending.

First, all significant versions of external world skepticism purport to show that in ordinary life and science we are already committed to principles of epistemic assessment that lead to skeptical catastrophe. That claim is directly put to the test by the approach urged here. If it turns out to be false, then those skeptical views fail.

Second, ordinary life and science are in fact where we *do* begin. We live our lives committed to a host of claims about what we do and don't know, to various principles of epistemic evaluation, and the like—commitments that (to speak from within them) are both reasonable and right on the whole. A philosopher might offer an argument that we should put some or all of that on hold and adopt some very different commitments. The crucial question, then, would be whether that argument, whatever it is, can give us good reason to change our view. So far as I can see, the best way to test that out is to start where we really are when we first confront skeptical argumentation (if, that is, we don't get ahead of ourselves): namely, standing within the commitments of ordinary life.

Third, this sort of approach looks more secure than the alternative, at least for those of us who are prepared to treat the epistemic commitments of ordinary life and science as the main *prima facie* data for epistemological theorizing. If the data already suffice to refute some claim, and nothing indicates any problem with the data, then why appeal to contestable theory to reject the claim?

Finally, it is worth keeping in mind that despite squabbles over various matters of detail and methodological debates in science, at a big picture level the epistemic commitments of ordinary life and science form a broad area of agreement even among epistemologists who diverge widely in their philosophical views. In this respect, too, a refutation of skepticism based on these commitments is on firmer ground.

At the end of the day, then, I am recommending an approach. I am inviting you to try it out. And I am inviting you to consider your honest response to this question: *If, when we have reached the end of this book, we agree that the epistemic commitments evident in the proper conduct of ordinary life and science succeed in undermining skeptical argumentation, is anything more really needed for a fully satisfactory rejection of external world skepticism*? You might still be curious about whether a convincing general epistemological theory can be developed. But that's not the question. The question is whether any such thing would still be needed for the purposes of a satisfactory rejection of skepticism. If you agree with me that it isn't, then my approach is vindicated. The proof of the pudding is in the eating, and the defense of this approach is no shorter than the argument of the book.

Even if it is successful, this approach will not, by itself, yield a full argument for an antitheoretical position. That would require showing in addition that philosophical theorizing can't satisfactorily do what we thought was needed and that when we try to develop the theory with clear eyes we lose our grip both on what we are trying to do and even on what the problem was supposed to be. (I take both claims to be part of the burden that Wittgenstein shoulders when he considers various moves toward philosophical theorizing in the *Philosophical Investigations*.) However, my aim here is antitheoretical in another familiar sense. I aim to show that philosophical theorizing is not necessary for a satisfactory resolution of an enduring philosophical problem.

In itself, my appeal to the commitments of ordinary epistemic life is not extraordinary. Many contemporary epistemologists understand themselves to be developing theories that capture our ordinary epistemic concepts, practices, or language (or, in a more metaphysical key, the properties and relations picked out by our ordinary epistemic concepts, practices, or language).[1] Still, the approach I am urging is hardly the norm these days. The epistemological literature offers a familiar pattern. An epistemologist offers a sophisticated new theory of knowledge, of the semantics of "knows," of perceptual justification, of thought content, of our epistemic relation to the world, and so on, and then shows how the theory can be used to defeat the skeptic. What might be said for this tight linkage between epistemological theory and critical engagement with skepticism? Is there a good reason for proceeding in this way?

Here's one common thought: we need to build an epistemological theory in order to satisfactorily respond to the skeptic, because such a theory would enable us to see *why* we are entitled to reject skepticism and accept the claims of ordinary life. Perhaps the most famous approach of this sort is Descartes'

---

[1] I am grateful here to an anonymous referee for the press.

project in the *Meditations*. However, the underlying thought lives on even in the work of many contemporary epistemologists who have given up both Descartes' specific justificatory aspirations and his way of framing the skeptical problem. Robert Nozick, for instance, writes:

> Granting that we do know, how *can* we? Given these other possibilities [the skeptic] poses, how is knowledge possible? In answering this question, we [seek] to formulate hypotheses about knowledge and our connection to facts that show how knowledge can exist even given the skeptic's possibilities. These hypotheses must reconcile our belief that we know things with our belief that the skeptical possibilities are logical possibilities. (1981, 167, italics in original)

Nozick foregoes any aspiration to convince the skeptic, but here he nonetheless takes it that no response to skepticism will be satisfactory without an explanatory theory that shows how knowledge is possible. Despite Nozick's emphasis on "explanation" rather than "proof," this is still epistemological theorizing in a vindicatory key.

A similar thought seems to be implicit in Jim Pryor's elaboration of Moore's "Proof of an External World." Pryor describes his aim this way:

> [T]he skeptic can present us with arguments from premises we find intuitively acceptable to the conclusion that we *cannot* justifiably believe or know such things [as "here is a hand"]. So we have a problem.... The modest anti-skeptical project attempts to diagnose and defuse those skeptical arguments: to show how to retain as many of our pretheoretical beliefs about perception as possible, without accepting the premises the skeptic needs for his argument. (2000, 517, italics in the original)

To provide a reason for rejecting the skeptic's key premises—to show us *why* we should reject those premises—Pryor offers a distinctive epistemological theory. According to this theory, merely having an experience as of a hand provides immediate *prima facie* justification for believing that there is a hand in front of you, quite apart from any other justified beliefs or justifications you have (Pryor 2000). This theory is no mere supplement or add-on for Pryor. Rather, it provides a needed argument in support of a Moorean stance. "If we're to have a satisfying philosophical response to skepticism, it will consist in that supporting argument, not in the reasoning that Moore's argument articulates" (2004, 370). Again, the thought seems to be that our rejection of the skeptic's argument requires shoring up with an epistemological theory that explains *why* we can be content with the claims of ordinary life.

Here's a second common thought that may lie behind the familiar tight linkage between discussions of skepticism and epistemological theorizing: A satisfactory resolution of external world skepticism will have significant payoff in the form of epistemological theory. As John Greco puts it,

> Skeptical arguments are useful and important because they drive progress in philosophy. They do this by highlighting plausible but mistaken assumptions about knowledge and evidence, and by showing us that those assumptions have consequences that are unacceptable. *As a result we are forced to develop substantive and controversial positions in their place.* (Greco 2000, 2–3, italics added)

Epistemological theory, on this line of thought, is a benefit forced upon us by an encounter with skepticism, even if ordinary life does not stand in need of vindication from philosophy.

Here's a third thought. Maybe our best hope for coming to terms with skepticism is to show that while it presents itself as arising from materials found within our ordinary epistemic commitments, it actually rests upon substantial theoretical assumptions (as Michael Williams argued [1996]). On this approach, the first task is to identify the skeptic's distinctive theoretical commitments. Then we need to consider their plausibility and defend an alternative view. However, as Williams puts it, "ordinary practice [may] underdetermine its theoretical interpretation" (1996, 41). If that is so, then—on the assumption that the skeptical argument rests upon substantial theoretical presuppositions—the question of skepticism's truth must await the conclusion of debates in epistemological theory that cannot be resolved on the basis of the commitments and procedures of ordinary epistemic practice.

Many contemporary epistemologists seem to understand their engagement with skepticism in something like these last terms. But I find myself wondering: If the epistemic principles and procedures that we are committed to—and think we are right to be committed to—in the conduct of everyday life and science really do underdetermine the choice between affirming and denying skepticism, on what basis could the decision be made in a convincing way? When it comes to such an important matter as whether we actually know or have good reason to believe anything about the world around us, do you really want to await resolution of a debate understood in such terms? Wouldn't it be better if there were a viable alternative?

My aspiration is to put into practice a very different kind of approach. If we find that we can satisfactorily reject skeptical argumentation using only the commitments of ordinary epistemic life, then there wouldn't be any need to develop an epistemological theory to counter any theoretical assumptions behind the skeptic's arguments; skepticism's self-understanding would already have been shown to be false. Moreover, if we are standing within the perspective of ordinary epistemic life, then the relation between epistemological theorizing and external world skepticism will look rather different than many philosophers assume. Epistemological theory would not be needed for a satisfactory reply to the skeptic, since the commitments of ordinary epistemic life would already suffice. No special philosophical vindication would be needed.[2] Nor would an epistemological theory necessarily be a pay-off of the encounter, since the aspects of ordinary epistemic life that undo the skeptic will probably underdetermine the choice between many rival anti-skeptical epistemological theories. And there will be no need to develop "substantive and controversial positions" in epistemology, since all the crucial work will be done by truisms of ordinary life. Recognizing those truisms will likely aid reflective understanding of our ordinary lives, but they won't add up to a theory. Looking at matters from a vantage point within the commitments of ordinary epistemic life, those truisms will provide prima facie constraints and data for subsequent theorizing, if we want to engage in it.

Here's what we should expect from the sort of approach I'm urging. We will carefully scrutinize skeptical arguments to see what requirements they impose, and we will consider whether those requirements are among the commitments of ordinary epistemic life and science. To do this we might do such things as articulate epistemic claims and principles to which we are committed in ordinary life and science, reflectively describe those commitments and what they involve, reflectively describe aspects of our ordinary epistemic practices, utilize clear examples to show that particular requirements or principles are not correct, draw certain kinds of generalizations from such examples, put two and two together to reach a more general description, summarize the results of all of this, and the like.

---

[2] For more on this, see Chapter 2.

How does all of this differ from epistemological theorizing? Consider some standard approaches. Some epistemologists claim not to put much or even any stock in the commitments and practices of ordinary epistemic life, instead attempting to develop epistemological theories on some other basis. Obviously, that would be a very different sort of endeavor from what I am proposing. Some epistemologists have thought that certain questions raised in light of our everyday commitments can't be fully resolved by them, so that something else, some further form of theorizing, is required. A major contention of this book is that nothing of the sort is needed in order to satisfactorily reject skepticism. Some epistemologists who seek to understand the practices, concepts, and language of ordinary epistemic life (or the properties and relations picked out by them) still have aspirations that go beyond anything I described in the above paragraph, because they seek *theories*: accounts that are fully general, systematic, and explanatory.[3] In the standard case, they seek general, systematic, and explanatory accounts of such things as 'what knowledge is,' 'what evidence is,' 'what justification is,' and the like—theories that aim to explain the truth of the claims and assessments to which we are committed in everyday life (or else to explain some and explain the rest away). For the purposes of the project I am proposing, we do not demand, develop, offer, or utilize any such theory. It would not even matter if no such theory were possible.

Another familiar type of epistemological theorizing takes a slightly different form. It attempts to meet a distinctive felt need that can be seen by thinking about a simplified, schematic depiction of our relation to skeptical argumentation. Before we first encounter skeptical argumentation, we are going along happily in ordinary life. Then we encounter the skeptical argumentation, and we are pitched out of ordinary life: it seems that nothing available in ordinary life will resolve the problem. We feel the need for something different, and we look to philosophy to provide some special reasoning or argumentation that will help us regain our ordinary position: for instance, a transcendental argument showing that the existence of the external world is a condition of the possibility of our having experience at all, or a demonstration that the very possibility of contentful mental states requires that our beliefs are largely true, or a proof deriving the necessary falsehood of the skeptical scenarios from causal constraints on reference, or an argument that the best explanation of the pattern of our sensory experience (described as

---

[3] In characterizing the aim in this way I am indebted to a referee for the press.

the skeptic would describe it) is that there is a world of objects largely as we take it to be. (Depending on their aspirations, such projects may or may not appeal only to premises the skeptic would accept.)

Again, the approach that I am proposing does not depend on any such undertaking. Instead, it focuses on an earlier stage: the moment when the skeptical argumentation supposedly forces us to look to something other than the obvious commitments of ordinary life. It asks whether that has really happened. It proposes that we don't need any special philosophical argumentation here; rather, the skeptical problem is satisfactorily resolved when we recognize that it doesn't even get started. In a crucial sense, everything was already in order as it was.

I want to stress that in thus distinguishing my approach from those that appeal to epistemological theorizing, I do not regard the commitments of ordinary epistemic life as inviolable or unrevisable. We have found reason to revise and develop them over time, and this very well might continue. Historically, science has been an important part of this story. Many significant revisions have come from science in its ongoing process of development, as it both corrects itself and corrects and extends pre-scientific ways of thinking. When I use phrases such as "our ordinary position," "the epistemic commitments of ordinary life," and the like, I mean to be including all of that. I am happy to bring scientific theories or practice into play if they are needed to respond to the specifics of a particular skeptical argument or to illustrate a relevant claim.[4]

One further very important point needs to be particularly stressed regarding the approach I am urging. I propose to conduct the inquiry from a distinctive position. Unlike many epistemologists, I will work resolutely from within the commitments of ordinary life. That is to say: for the purposes of this investigation we will not stand outside those commitments, hold them at arm's length, and describe them from that external position. Instead, we will stand within them, articulate what we are in fact committed to, and confront

---

[4] A quick aside on the relation between scientific and philosophical theorizing: Someone might hypothesize that a case could perhaps arise in which we need to appeal to theorizing in the borderlands between science and philosophy to satisfactorily refute some skeptical argument. It might be wondered: would such a situation comport with my approach, or rather tell against it? Since nothing like any such case has actually arisen, I am content to leave the issue to be adjudicated in a way that responds to the details of the particular case when and if it actually arises. It is no part of my approach to offer a completely sharp demarcation line in advance that renders a fully determinate verdict for every possible case. Indeed, the demand for such a thing is of a piece with the kind of theorizing that I eschew for the purposes of this project.

the skeptical argumentation on that basis. As will become apparent, this stance is absolutely fundamental to the method I am exploring.

If this approach succeeds, the pay-off will be significant.

First, we will learn a very important lesson. To put it minimally, external world skepticism presents no threat to our ordinary position. To put it more forcefully and in a way that will be defended over the course of the book: skepticism is false. To put it even more bluntly: the problem of skepticism can be put to rest.

Second, we will thereby identify the minimal resources needed to resist skepticism. If we can't get skepticism going from within our ordinary position, then from the ordinary position the reasonable thing to do is to reject it as false. In thus rejecting it, we highlight the aspects of ordinary epistemic life that suffice to do the trick.

Third, we will come to understand more about key features of our epistemic lives. This won't be by way of the development of an epistemological theory, however. As I have highlighted, it is central to my approach that we have to distinguish the question, "Is there any reason to think that skepticism is true?" from the question, "What's the best epistemological theory of our knowledge of the world?" The goal of my approach is to answer the first question without yet taking much of a stand on the second. Epistemological theorizing would then be a downstream enterprise. But through our encounter with skepticism—through finding the minimal pretheoretical resources necessary for rejecting skepticism—we will deepen our understanding of how knowledge, evidence, and the like actually work. We will thereby gain reflective self-understanding of a different sort than is promised by epistemological theory. Where we had been confused about or puzzled by certain aspects of our ordinary lives, we will now know our way about. And should we wish to go on to try to develop an epistemological theory that does justice to all of this, we will have found data to which that theory should, prima facie, be true.

What are the prospects for this approach? That is a primary focus of this inquiry. And since G.E. Moore set us on this path, that is where we will begin.

2. The Nature of the Work

This book invites you to engage in a distinctive form of philosophical inquiry—distinctive, at least, in relation to contemporary epistemology.

We in analytic philosophy have grown used to considering philosophical questions from a position that is, in a certain sense, divorced from our real commitments. We consider a question, sketch an answer, ask what someone might say in objection, and then try to adjudicate the issue as if from a fully neutral position. This is a salutary approach in many respects. It exhibits the virtues of open-mindedness, fairness to one's opponents, a willingness to reconsider one's own views, and the like.

For the purposes of the present inquiry, however, such a stance can be distorting. This is because the central questions here are *what we ourselves are actually committed to in real life* and *where those commitments lead us*. To explore such matters, it is not helpful to focus primarily on what some imagined objector might say, since someone with commitments very different from mine or yours might say all sorts of things. Nor is it helpful to try to adjudicate issues as if from a neutral position. The question is centrally what *you* want to say, and in particular *what you would actually be prepared to offer* as an expression of your commitments appearing in the proper conduct of ordinary life.

I will attempt to articulate my commitments in precisely this spirit. You may find that you disagree with some of the things that I say about what we know or have reason to believe, or about the principles, procedures, and commitments of ordinary epistemic life. Such disagreement opens important opportunities for discussion. But don't keep double books, saying one thing in the study and acting very differently in real life. I live by everything that I will say in the course of this encounter with skeptical argumentation. You should be prepared to do the same for your part. If you are, then there is the possibility of meaningful and significant conversation if we disagree (not the mere spinning of intellectual wheels). If you aren't, then our disagreement—disconnected as it is from the conduct of real epistemic life—is irrelevant to this inquiry.

This book also has a distinctive form. It does not offer the progressive development of a linear argument, the step-by-step construction of a theory, the critical history of an issue, or a collection of essays on a theme. Rather, its form is more like a spiral. Moore charts a course for us to follow, and so we begin in the first two chapters with his thought and its critical reception. In a sense, the remaining chapters aim to flesh out what Moore attempted. But this isn't just a matter of filling in details. Part of the task is to identify sources and progressive layers of resistance to what I am saying—and to dispel them. As a result, certain questions and themes will recur. Some claims will initially be stated somewhat baldly and without much support, inviting reservations from the reader and extensive exploration in later chapters. This is a matter of deepening—deepening our understanding of the issues at play and of the actual contours of our ordinary epistemic lives. As we will see, the deeper we press into our ordinary practices, the more resistant they look to the kinds of interpretations that would license the skeptical conclusion.[5]

We epistemologists have grown used to a certain way of engaging with skepticism. We are eager to launch into discussions of closure principles and warrant transmission, various internalisms and externalisms, counterfactual conditions for knowledge, the nature of perceptual justification or warrant, epistemological disjunctivism, theories of evidence, and the like. This anxiousness to begin with familiar theoretical debates is born of habits of mind that I think should be abandoned. By the time we get to Chapters 5 and following, issues near the heart of contemporary analytic epistemology will be at center stage. However, you probably won't fully understand what work those chapters are doing or how they are doing it if you don't start in the right place. A shift in perspective is first needed, and this shift is aided by the earlier chapters' exploration of crucial aspects of the *kind* of enterprise Moore, and later Austin, were engaged in.

While I do not offer an epistemological theory, I see this endeavor as philosophical—indeed, as part of a distinctive philosophical tradition. This tradition is paradigmatically exemplified in Moore's work at the roots of analytic philosophy. Its spirit appears at moments in American pragmatism, becomes increasingly central in the work of Austin and Wittgenstein, figures in different ways at important junctures in the work of Quine and Goodman, and most recently shows up in Maddy's delightful book, *What Do Philosophers Do?* (2017). The broad orientation of this tradition has deep historical roots (or so I am told by historians I trust) in moments of Aristotle, Cicero, Hume, Reid, and Early Moderns (such as Cavendish, Bayle, and Boyle) who relied significantly on the rising modern sciences. In his appeal to common sense Berkeley tried to work within this tradition, but he waffled in spite of himself. Johnson sought to capture its spirit when he kicked a stone and declared, of Berkeley's idealism, "I refute it thus." And Shaftesbury epitomized this orientation when he replied to Locke, "Philosopher, tell me something of moment to me."

---

[5] I'm grateful to Katy Abramson for highlighting this way of seeing my project.

It would be a mistake, however, to think that the animating spirit of this tradition is dismissiveness toward paradigmatic philosophical problems. Rather, it is a spirit of utmost seriousness. In the end, I am inviting us to give external world skepticism precisely the form of attention that we would give to any interesting and surprising claim that we take the time to consider in ordinary life or science. I am asking whether we should really accept it as true, and I want to bring to that question our best procedures and commitments—just as we would in any other serious inquiry in science or ordinary life. This, I think, is what it is to take skepticism seriously.

2
Why Moore Matters

> Dismissing without further investigation something that conflicts with what is already known is the very heart of rationality.
> —Barry Stroud, *Significance of Philosophical Scepticism*, 105

> The question whether we do ever know such things as [whether this is a finger], and whether there are any material things, seem to me ... questions which it is quite easy to answer, with certainty, in the affirmative.
> —Moore, "Some Judgments of Perception," *Philosophical Studies*, 228

1. Enter G.E. Moore

In their insistence upon the obvious truths of ordinary life, G.E. Moore's writings on external world skepticism can be philosophically chastening. They can leave us with the suspicion that by responding to skepticism with elaborate theory-building, epistemologists have been doing something rather silly—or at least something entirely unnecessary. I think this is the right reaction to have. Once we realize what Moore is up to, we see that his rejection of skepticism is a mark of the seriousness with which he takes it. He asks whether he should accept it as true, and he pursues that question just as he would any other serious inquiry in science or ordinary life. If he succeeds, Moore thus shows us, in broad outline, how to dispense with skepticism in a way that is both intellectually responsible and avoids constructive epistemological theory-building altogether. His approach thereby promises to reveal something very important about what it would take to satisfactorily resolve certain sorts of perennial philosophical problems.

To see why I say this, we must begin with the relation between epistemological theorizing and ordinary life. There is a familiar distinction—going back at least to Hume—between our ordinary, non-philosophical position and the position of philosophical reflection on human knowledge. In the ordinary, non-philosophical position we are committed to all sorts of claims about the world and about what we know and have reason to believe. This position involves commitment to various practices, rules of thumb, and principles of reasoning, inquiry, and epistemic assessment, including everything involved in the conduct of science. It is hardly unreflective; reflective summaries and reflective self-correction—as in methodological discussions in science—have a central place in it. However, it doesn't involve commitment to any fully general theories about such matters as what philosophers call "the structure of empirical justification," nor anything like a general account of the requirements one must meet in order to know things. It doesn't even involve a demand for such things. In this sense, it is a *pre-philosophical* position.

We don't need a theoretical characterization of philosophical theorizing in order to recognize either this distinction or the ordinary, pre-philosophical position. We epistemologists already implicitly recognize both in our practice. Consider, for instance, the fact that when we judge in ordinary life that people know things, we don't appeal to and can't state a fully general set of standards for knowledge, nor do we think any such thing necessary. Perhaps (it might be said) such an account nonetheless lies latent in our psychology and can be ferreted out. Perhaps it can instead be reconstructed as an interpretation of our practice. Or perhaps—as many would argue—no such theory can be derived from the procedures, principles, and rules of thumb of ordinary epistemic life at all, but rather must be discovered in some other way. All of these familiar approaches recognize a gap here. It is precisely because of this gap that some people find it of interest and importance to develop a general account of knowledge. The very enterprise of seeking a general account of knowledge thus presupposes recognition of an ordinary, pre-philosophical position: this is a position which we epistemologists inevitably recognize, and our theorizing presumes it. And as I just noted above, this is a position in which no such theorizing is demanded, a position in which it is perfectly appropriate to make epistemic claims and assessments, really thinking them true, even in the absence of anything like a fully general account of knowledge.

Moore did not explicitly articulate a conception of such a position, but he had a name for it: common sense. What his writings on skepticism vividly enact—and I use this word intentionally, as Moore does something in these writings beyond just offer arguments—is the recognition that an intellectual step is needed if we are to get from this position to the initial stages of skeptical reflection. We already have commitments before the encounter with skeptical argumentation, commitments to both factual claims and various practices of inquiry and epistemic assessment. These include such considerations as that there is a piece of paper before me, that I know there is, and that I see it. From within that position, this all looks quite reasonable on the whole. What, then, are we to *do* with all of that? Something has to happen, or to be done, to get us to distance ourselves from these commitments, if we are to get skeptical reflection going. Moore thus takes these commitments as his starting point. He insists that we stand with both feet firmly in that ordinary position and asks whether there is any good reason to shift our view. He then tries to show us that from within that starting point, external world skepticism doesn't even get going as an epistemological problem.

It might immediately be complained, "Suppose he succeeds. So what? Skepticism might still be *true*!" But notice that this complaint is voiced from a position that is already outside of Moore's starting position. There is a crucial difference between saying that within a certain position a given claim is regarded as correct or true, and saying—from within that position—that it is correct or true. If we are working from within Moore's starting position, we voice our commitments about what is the case, what we know, and what we have reason to believe. We engage in our familiar practices of inquiry and epistemic assessment and evaluation. We don't stand outside and describe what that position is committed to, but rather speak from within it, asserting that certain things are the case and that others aren't. If Moore is right, we find that we can't so much as get a plausible argument going for external world skepticism from within that position. We are thus left steadfast in our conviction that skepticism is false: we know and have good reason to believe all kinds of things about the world. This would already be enough to refute any form of external world skepticism that aspires both to arise from within our ordinary epistemic practices and to contradict our ordinary claims to know or have reason to believe lots of things about the world around us.

It can be tempting to redescribe this situation by saying, "Well, okay, we conclude from within our ordinary position that external world skepticism is false, but so what? Maybe that position is wrong. Why should we privilege it anyway?" However, to say something along these lines is *already* to have left the ordinary position. The same point applies if we say, "All you have done is appeal to what you *believe*. Why should the fact that you *believe* such-and-such count for anything, anyway?" To respond from within the position from which Moore is working, we would say this: Moore doesn't appeal to the fact that he or you believe that such and such, but to the facts (which he and you believe). Departures from our pre-philosophical position—shifts from claiming that *such-and-such is the case* to thinking about *one's belief that such-and-such* in a way that puts one's commitment to the claim on hold— are so familiar in epistemology as to be nearly invisible. The crucial question Moore's work raises is whether they are well motivated. This is a central, guiding question to which I shall return repeatedly in this and subsequent chapters.

My aim in this chapter is to bring out the general shape of what Moore attempted and to show where we would be left if we filled in the details. I begin (Section 2 of this chapter) by considering the reception of Moore's thought in recent epistemology, for here we find a failure of philosophical imagination—a failure to see the very possibility of an approach like Moore's. This discussion will lead us (Section 3) to the question of the relation between our ordinary position and epistemological theorizing, help us identify where Moore—and we—initially stand in our encounter with external world skepticism, and highlight the crucial question of what might motivate movement out of that position. As Moore sees it, no good motivation is to be found. Since no reasonable route to the skeptical conclusion appears, he consequently rejects skepticism.[1]

What would it take to show this to be an intellectually satisfying response? One tempting thought (highlighted in Chapter 1) is that here we need to appeal to epistemological theory, because otherwise we won't be able to see *why* it is appropriate and satisfying to engage with skepticism in this way. However, as I noted above, Moore aims to reply to external world skepticism in a way that makes use of no epistemological theorizing nor any philosophical underpinnings whatsoever. His is a minimalist response in this sense: it takes place before the work of philosophical theory-building begins. It would not be in the spirit of his response to appeal to philosophical theory at this juncture.

Fortunately, we don't have to. We see the success of Moore's response by enacting it, not by vindicating it through epistemological theorizing.

---

[1] While my reading of Moore differs considerably from the common understanding of the sort of enterprise Moore was engaged in, it is similar in important respects to that offered by Maddy (2017) and informed by Stroud's interpretation (1984). As Chapter 6 discusses in detail, Maddy and I diverge significantly on matters pertaining to the implementation of the Moorean approach.

If we pursue Moore's approach, we seek to show two things. First, that from the vantage point of our ordinary, pre-philosophical position, each attempt at skeptical argumentation has failings that keep it from getting off the ground. Second, that from this same starting point, we find no reason for dissatisfaction with this situation: we don't even find any reason to be discontented on the grounds that our ordinary, pre-philosophical position could just be wrong. If we succeed in showing both of those things, then we don't find any reason to give up anything that we started out committed to and we don't find any good objection to proceeding in this way. Nothing goes wrong, and no problems arise. *So we started out committed to such and such being the case, and that is where we end up. We don't find any reason to think or do anything differently.* This would be an intellectually responsible reply of a sort that is perfectly familiar in ordinary life. Nothing more is needed by way of vindication, given the vantage point from which we are working.

This may be an unfamiliar approach from the standpoint of contemporary epistemology. But if you are standing where Moore urges us to stand, what could be a better way to show a response to be intellectually satisfactory?

2. Moore's Standpoint and Contemporary Epistemology: A Misunderstanding

Let's begin by recalling what, exactly, Moore did.

Moore held up both hands, declaring while doing so, "Here is one hand, and here is another." He concluded, "So there are objects external to the mind" ("Proof," 1993d, 166). Since he certainly knew the premises, he said, he also knew the conclusion.[2] He likewise claimed in a lecture that he knew that he was not dreaming; he knew, he said, that he was standing up, and since he couldn't know this if he was dreaming, he must not be dreaming ("Certainty," 1993a, 191ff). He rejected a skeptical argument of Russell's in part on the ground that he did know that his current experience was not produced by a malicious demon ("Four Forms," 1993c, 224). And in response to several skeptical arguments he maintained that he could clearly reject the principles upon which these arguments were based, since he did after all know, for

---

[2] See, for instance, *Some Main Problems*, 1953, 126 (reprinted in Moore 1993e, 78). The point is strongly suggested but not explicitly stated in "Proof," 1993d, 166–167. (Here and in the main text of this chapter I use keywords from Moore's titles to aid quick identification of Moore's papers.)

example, that there was a pencil in front of him ("Four Forms," 19932c, 196–226; *Some Main Problems*, 1953, chapter 6 ["Hume's Theory Examined"]). In short: Moore responded to skepticism by appealing to considerations about the world and his knowledge of it.

In doing so, Moore did not merely offer argumentation; he engaged in rhetorical performance. "This, after all, you know, really is a finger: there is no doubt about it" ("Some Judgments of Perception," in Moore 1922, 228); "I *do* know that I held up two hands above this desk not very long ago. As a matter of fact, ... you all know it too. There's no doubt whatever that I did" ("Proof," 1993d, 168). These reminders and small turns of phrase place us, his audience, into a certain position in relation to skeptical argumentation. They maneuver us into a position in which, like Moore, we gladly make use of our knowledge about the world around us, and about how to go about inquiry and epistemic assessment, in order to dismiss both the skeptical claim and arguments in its favor.

There is nothing dialectically improper about this response. Granted, such an appeal is unlikely to convince an interlocutor who actually holds that we have no reason to believe anything about the world around us. But even if we were faced with such a person, there would be nothing objectionable about Moore's procedure. If you think that I know nothing about English history, I can perfectly appropriately reject your charge by pointing out something that I *do* know, such as that King Harold the Second lost the Battle of Hastings in 1066. And if you attempt to argue for your claim in a way that depends upon claims about English history that I know to be false, I can appropriately point that out as well.

Still, there is a deep-seated tendency in recent epistemology to think that Moore's responses are not adequate by themselves but need shoring up or vindication through substantive epistemological theory. For instance, Earl Conee writes,

> Does being some such common sense proposition confer any sort of epistemic merit, and if it does, what sort, how much, and why?
>
> Without answers to these questions, a reliance on this common sense to oppose skepticism is not fully reasonable. Satisfactory answers to these general epistemic questions will include general epistemic claims. In at least this way a proponent of common sense beliefs needs abstract epistemology in order to give that category of beliefs a telling role in philosophical arguments. (Conee 2001, 58–59)

This sort of complaint privileges epistemological theory in our encounter with external world skepticism. Rather than seeing us as standing in our ordinary position and asking what is to move us to a position in which we come to think the skeptical claim might well be right (and so feel the need for epistemological theory to ward it off), this approach sees our ordinary position as in need of vindication before we may stand in it and reply from there to skeptical concerns. This is a mistake, both as an interpretation of Moore and, I will argue, as a matter of getting a clear view of our relation to external world skepticism. Moore's performances do not depend, for either their legitimacy or success, on commentary from a developed epistemological theory.

To illustrate this point, I want to consider several recent approaches to Moore, beginning with an interpretation offered by John Greco (2002). Greco aims to provide a "defense" (his word) of Moore's "Proof of an External World" by showing it to "fit into" (546) the epistemological framework of Thomas Reid, which Greco deems to be "exactly right" (545). This underlying epistemological framework, Greco claims, both illuminates the point of Moore's procedures and secures their success.

Greco takes Moore to have adopted six principles from Reid.

"E1: Not everything we know is known by proof." (549)

"E2: External objects are known by perception, not by proof." (549)

"E3: The evidence of sense is no less reasonable than that of demonstration." (551)

"M1: One should not try to prove what is not known by proof." (552)

"M2: Rather than trying to prove that external things exist, or that we know that external things exist, we should take a close look at the sceptic's reasons for saying that we do not know this." (553)

"M3: Common sense has defeasible authority over philosophical theory." (554)

These principles can have the air of mere truisms dressed up in philosophical jargon. So understood, it is plausible enough that Moore would accept them. Moore clearly accepts M2 and M3, as can be seen in the way in which he responds to particular skeptical arguments by critically scrutinizing their premises (as in "Four Forms of Scepticism") and refuting them by appealing to his knowledge of the world. He would clearly accept E1, since he says at the end of "Proof of an External World" that though he can't prove "here is one hand and here is another," he knows it to be true (Moore 1993d, 169–170).

E1 follows from that claim. Moore would presumably accept something like E2 as well: a natural explanation of how he knows "here is a hand" is that he *sees it*, and since he seemingly takes it that adducing that latter fact, which he presumably knows perfectly well, would not constitute a proof then and there, it seems that he would be content enough to say that he knows "here is a hand" by perception (or something in that vein). E3 also seems to be something he'd be willing enough to endorse, at least on one plausible understanding of the phrase "the evidence of sense." If seeing things is a way of coming to know about them, then surely it is a route to highly reasonable beliefs. A similar point applies to M1's talk of "what isn't known by proof." If the phrase refers simply to the sort of case at hand, in which Moore thinks he can't prove something that he knows, then M1 would offer sound advice. If something is known but can't be proven, then there is no point in trying, nor is there any need.

However, these same forms of words can take on a very different significance depending upon how they are placed in a larger body of theory. Greco's Reid—and hence his Moore—is a *reliabilist foundationalist* who holds that we have a number of naturally reliable faculties (including, notably, sensory perception) which issue epistemologically basic beliefs—different sorts of beliefs for different faculties—that have positive epistemic status just in virtue of arising from those faculties and quite independently of the positive epistemic status of any other beliefs. These beliefs then provide the material starting points for demonstrative and non-demonstrative reasoning. Epistemological claims such as E1–E3, understood as Greco's Reid understands them, thus carry with them very specific epistemological commitments, for instance, about the justificatory structure and basis of our knowledge of contingent matters about the world around us. This faculty-based foundationalist picture is what gives specific content to talk in these principles of "what is known by proof" versus "what is known by perception," as well as to the phrase "the evidence of sense."

This picture thus shapes the correct understanding of M1–3 for Greco's Reid, and hence for his Moore. M1's "what is known by proof," is, on this understanding, what is arrived at by the naturally reliable operation of our faculty for demonstrative inference when it takes known inputs. Likewise, M3 is given its specific content because of its placement within this theory: "common sense" becomes those things that "we know immediately, by the natural operation of our cognitive powers, as opposed to that which is known only by special training or by reasoning" (Greco 2002, 554). The special epistemic authority of "common sense," so understood, thus arises from the *prima facie* favorable epistemic status of these beliefs in virtue of the way in which they—unlike the claims of philosophical theory—immediately arise from the natural operation of our cognitive powers. M2, too, takes its place within this larger picture: since "here is a hand" isn't "known by proof" in the sense of that phrase specified by the theory, one shouldn't try to prove it, and so one should instead consider how the arguments for skepticism might go awry.

Notice, however, how little of this picture one *has* to take on in order to proceed as Moore does. One can obviously endorse M2 and M3 without placing them within this theoretical framework. In fact, if one's concern is to understand whether and how one might be made to move from one's ordinary, pre-philosophical position to a genuine concern that external world skepticism might be true after all, then one would surely endorse M2 and M3; one would focus critically on the skeptic's arguments in a way that gives one's ordinary commitments defeasible authority. And while Greco's Reid gives content to talk of "common sense" by tying it to the deliverances of certain cognitive faculties, Moore never does any such thing. The phrase "common sense," in Moore's usage, simply amounts to a convenient summary or synoptic label that doesn't purport to capture anything about what these claims' defining characteristics are (or what gives them some special status) beyond the fact that they are part of the position from which we start when we encounter skeptical argumentation.

It might seem that Moore's claim to know things that he can't prove commits him to a substantial epistemological theory distinguishing what is "known by proof" from what is "known by perception." However, we can instead understand Moore's distinction simply as a summary statement of certain aspects of the commitments that are involved in our starting position. Here's why. Suppose that Moore is using "prove" and "perceive" in perfectly ordinary, pre-philosophical ways. He grants that in certain circumstances he could get "what might be called a proof" of "here is a hand." For instance, if there were reason to think that what was before him was merely an artificial mock-up of a hand, then, he says, "someone might be said to get a proof" by "coming up and examining the suspected hand close up, perhaps touching and pressing it, and so establishing that it really was a human hand" ("Proof," 1993d, 169). Given what Moore grants about this case, he could say that in the usual sort of case, in which no such fraud is suspected, it is simply unclear what would be wanted if one was asked to prove, say, that there is a table here.

What would it *be* to prove such a thing, if not simply to show the person the table? But of course, we might know there is a table there even if we would be entirely befuddled by a request to prove it. People can know things even though they wouldn't have the faintest idea how to prove them.

Moore recognizes, however, that within the context of a particular kind of epistemological project the request for proof gets construed in a very particular way. He writes, regarding the skeptically-inclined philosopher,

> What they really want is not merely a proof of these two propositions ("Here's a hand and here's another"), but something like a general statement as to how *any* propositions of this sort may be proved. This, of course, I haven't given; and I do not believe it can be given: if this is what is meant by proof of the existence of external things, I do not believe that any proof of the existence of external things is possible. ("Proof," 1993d, 169)

What Moore has in mind here is a general account revealing how any claims about the existence of external things—or about one's knowledge of such things—can be shown to be correct without presupposing either any such claims or that one knows any such claims. Such an account is precisely what the skeptic demands. But we don't demand any such thing in everyday life, which is Moore's starting position. Moore's insistence that he can know things "without proof" can thus be read as nothing theoretically thicker than this: he can know things even in cases in which he would be utterly nonplussed by the demand to "prove" them and even if it is not possible to provide the distinctive kind of vindication of his knowledge claims which the skeptic requires.

In short, then, while certain aspects of Moore's position could be expressed in the words appearing in Greco's principles, we can see these aspects not as arising from a substantial epistemological theory but rather as a manifestation of the fact that he is working from within his "ordinary," everyday certainties and epistemic practices *prior to and independently of underwriting by any particular philosophical theory* (even a theory that would seek to legitimate such a stance). This approach leads him to claim that he *does* after all know that he is standing, giving a lecture, and the like, even though he can't "prove" that these things are true or that he knows them: that he *does* know them would be, for Moore, among the initial commitments of the position from which the inquiry begins and to which it is accountable.

Greco isn't alone in missing the significance of this possibility. It is often suggested that Moore's "Proof of an External World" rests upon an incipient proto-externalist view according to which a mature adult can have a satisfactory epistemic position despite being incapable of providing anything by way of an answer to the question, "How do you know?" or "What reason do you have to believe that?"[3] However, Moore could perfectly well grant *both* that in the circumstances involved in his proof of an external world we can know that there is a hand here even if we can't prove it *and also* that something would be going badly wrong if a mature adult claimed to know that there is a hand here but could offer nothing whatsoever in favor of the belief (not even such things as, "Well, I can see it"). And once we see this point, we can see that his "Proof" need not depend on proto-externalism any more than it needs to presuppose a position like that of Greco's Reid. All it requires is a willingness to draw out and make explicit the commitments of our initial, pre-philosophical position—commitments which may not themselves add up to anything like a substantive theory of knowledge or reasonable belief.

A similar point applies to the "Moorean Dogmatist" approach to empirical justification. Pryor (2000) traces external world skepticism to the requirement, roughly, that in order to know or have good reason to believe anything about the external world, one must have *independent, antecedent reasons* for believing that one is not dreaming or being deceived by an evil demon—reasons that do not involve or depend upon any considerations about the external world. Pryor responds with a theory of perceptual justification according to which an experience as of *p* provides *prima facie* (defeasible), immediate justification for believing that *p*—a justification that depends solely upon that experience itself, not upon any of one's beliefs about the world or justifications one has for other beliefs about the world. This view denies the skeptical requirement, since on this view a person can have justification for believing that there is a hand in front of them merely in virtue of having an appropriate experience. In fact, Pryor (2004) defends a course of reasoning that runs as follows:

1. Experience as of a hand before me.
2. (Based on that experience): Here is a hand.
3. (Based on that belief): So, I am not a bodiless spirit being deceived by an evil demon.

---

[3] This has been suggested by Coliva in her discussion of Moore's Proof (2010, 47ff). Sosa (1999) has likewise suggested an externalist move for Moore, as has Baldwin, *G.E. Moore*, chapter 9.

As Pryor sees things, someone could explicitly reason in this way and thus come to know—for the first time—a claim like (3), thereby arriving at knowledge of the existence of an external world.

It is striking how little of this is part of Moore's responses to skepticism. To be fair, Pryor doesn't present his view as an interpretation of Moore. But he does present it as an interpretation of the *kind of thing* Moore is up to. And what I want to bring out is that this is to misunderstand the kind of engagement with skepticism that appears in Moore's texts.

Moore's own "Proof" doesn't include a step like that from (1) to (2), and Moore does not appeal to a theory of perceptual justification like Pryor's in his response to skepticism.[4] Nor does he need to. He doesn't even need to think that a mature adult could in principle come to know a claim such as (3) for the first time by making an explicit inference from a premise such as (2). All he needs is this: that one can reasonably believe (and know) things about the external world even if the best reasons one has for such claims as that there is an external world and that one is not dreaming (or being deceived by an evil demon) all unavoidably involve or depend upon considerations about the external world. And Moore did think this. He thought that he knew that there are external things, and he thought that he had no better reason in favor of the existence of such things than the one provided by the consideration that here is one hand and here is another.[5] He likewise thought that he knew that he was not dreaming, and he thought it perfectly appropriate to appeal to his knowledge of the world to dismiss the suggestion that he might be ("Certainty," 1993a, 191–194). These commitments do not require him to accept a view like Pryor's. If they are indeed part of our starting position when we encounter skeptical argumentation, then that will be enough; nothing "deeper" or philosophically "heftier" will be needed. Read this way, the burden of Moore's "Proof" isn't to reconstruct a line of reasoning by which we could gain knowledge for the first time that there are external things. It is,

---

[4] Moore does on occasion suggest such a theory, but that is in the very different context of trying to provide an account of our epistemological relation to the world via perception. For Moore, such theorizing does not underwrite the response to skepticism; rather, the response to skepticism comes first. (For more on this, see Section 3.)

[5] See his discussion of the sense in which he has provided a "proof," where he writes that "it is perhaps impossible to give a better . . . proof of anything whatever" ("Proof," 1993d, 166). In a closely related passage he writes, "And similarly, if the object is to prove *in general* that we do know of the existence of material objects, no argument which is really stronger can, I think, be brought forward to prove this than particular instances in which we do in fact know of the existence of such an object" (*Some Main Problems of Philosophy*, 1953, 126).

more simply, to indicate absolutely decisive evidence, of a sort we all possess, that it is true that there are external things.[6]

Methodological discussions likewise often seek a vindication of Moore through philosophical theorizing. Thomas Kelly, for instance, begins with a conception of a "Moorean fact" as a proposition which is "invulnerable" to being undermined by means of philosophical arguments (2005, 180). Kelly traces this conception to a view about belief revision.

> We should, I think, view the Moorean ... as one who thinks that, according to what are in fact the correct norms of belief revision, philosophical considerations are simply not the kind of thing which could undermine another select class of propositions, "the Moorean facts." (186–187)

Kelly's Moorean thus takes there to be two classes of propositions, "Moorean facts" and "philosophical considerations," which are related to each other in a certain way by the correct norms for belief revision. This is itself already a substantive epistemological position, and not one to which, on my reading, Moore is committed. For one thing (as we will see), Moore's approach allows that any given starting commitment could be overturned in the process of our encounter with skepticism. More importantly, Moore's approach does not require *any* view about general norms for belief revision governing a relation between two such classes of propositions. And perhaps most significantly, Kelly proposes to derive this norm for belief revision from a particular methodology for philosophical theory construction (196). Kelly thus aims to vindicate Moore's approach on the basis of epistemological theory, and the vindication ultimately depends upon the resolution of a debate about the proper methodology for philosophical theory construction. This is, again, an interpretation of Moore on which the philosophy comes first.

By contrast, I am proposing a way of reading Moore on which it would be a mistake to ask, "What particular epistemological theory underwrites Moore's responses to skepticism?," or to charge (as Conee does in the quote in Section

---

[6] This is fortunate, because Pryor's version of Moore's argument arguably runs into a problem from the point of view of our ordinary epistemic practices, summarized in Chapter 8, Section 3.2 below. For this reason it is all to the better if Moore's response to external world skepticism does not depend upon or require commitment to "Moorean Dogmatism." (Here my reading of Moore accords with Ram Neta's proposal that "By Moore's lights, his Proof is not intended to give us knowledge that we might not already have" (Neta 2007).

2 above) that Moore's responses must rest upon a framework of general epistemological principles. Such questions and complaints would miss the kind of work in which Moore is here engaged. Vindication of the approach would come, rather, through *seeing it work* when we steadfastly take it up.

William Lycan (2007) is one of the few commentators to have seen the possibility that Moore is working from a position that does not presuppose or require vindication through positive epistemological theorizing. According to Lycan, Moore's signal contribution rests in one of his signature rhetorical moves: asking whether it is more certain—or, as he sometimes puts it, more rational to believe—(a) that the premises of some deductively valid skeptical argument are true, or (b) that one does indeed know, for example, that there is a pencil here. As Lycan emphasizes, any deductively valid argument ultimately forces this sort of comparative judgment regarding the relative rational certainty of the premises versus the denial of the conclusion. On Lycan's reading, then, Moore simply deploys a familiar and inevitable procedure in his response to skepticism.

Still, I find Lycan's interpretation inadequate for two related reasons. Exploring them will help reveal the significance of the shift in perspective that Moore urges on us.

First, Lycan's version of Moore's anti-skeptical strategy invites Conee's question (above). As we might put it, "Why should we think it of any significance in this context that we find these particular propositions very certain? Don't we need an epistemological theory to explain why we should give any weight to our judgments of comparative certainty in our encounter with skeptical argumentation?" Lycan asserts that we don't (2007, 97–98), but he does not explain why not. To see why not, you need to make more thoroughly the shift that Moore encourages. You need to recognize that you are starting from within your ordinary, pre-philosophical commitments and that the question is precisely whether the skeptic can offer you any good reason to change your view.

Second, consider the standpoint from which the comparative judgment is made. If we start from a neutral position, without any of our ordinary commitments, and ask which is more certain—the premises of a skeptical argument or that we know that there is a pencil here—we have no ready basis on which to make the judgment. In fact, from a position in which you have suspended all of your ordinary commitments about the world and what you know of it, it is no longer obvious at all that it is more certain that there is a pencil here than that some skeptical principle is correct. We are stranded on the high seas of epistemology, contra Lycan's intent. If, by contrast, we are working within our ordinary, pre-philosophical position, then there are ample relevant considerations ready-to-hand, starting with the fact that I see the pencil right there. That is to say, it is the fact that we are standing, with Moore, in the ordinary, pre-philosophical position that leads to our ready agreement with his comparative judgments. But from that position, the judgment of comparative certainty does not do any essential work. It is sufficient to appeal (speaking now from within our ordinary, pre-philosophical position) to such facts as that this is a hand, that we aren't dreaming, and that I see a pencil right there. All the crucial work is already done when we appeal to the manifest facts.

As I said above, these two points are related. This is because once we see that what is doing the real work is that Moore is speaking from within the pre-philosophical position and asking what reason can be given for changing his view (the second point), we can also see that Conee's question (highlighted in the first point) lapses. From within the pre-philosophical position we say to the skeptic, in effect, "You've proposed that not-*p*. But that's clearly false, because it conflicts with X, Y, and Z, which are all true—and you've offered no good reason for thinking anything else." From within that position, there would be nothing more that needs to be said. So far, we would have been given no reason not to rest content with where we are.

This point raises a question of Moore interpretation. What was he *doing* with his comparative arguments? I think that it is best to read them rhetorically. Taken at face value, they are strikingly bad arguments. "X is more certain than Y, so X is certainly true and Y is clearly false" is a lousy argument. So is "It is more rational to believe X than to believe Y, so I should believe X and reject Y as false." As I have emphasized, Moore's rejection of skeptical arguments is best viewed as based instead on such facts as that *he manifestly knows that there is a pencil here*. From this viewpoint his comparative judgments function rhetorically to jolt us back into the pre-philosophical position if we begin to stray from it. "Right," one thinks, "There really is no doubt whatsoever that I know that there is a pencil here." And it is arguable that this is how Moore intended them to function. At one point he puts the comparative judgment this way:

> I think we can safely challenge any philosopher to bring forward any argument in favor either of the proposition that we do not know it, or of the proposition that it is not true, which does not at some point rest upon some

premise which is, *beyond comparison*, less certain than is the proposition which it is designed to attack. ("Some Judgments of Perception," in Moore 1922, 228, italics added)

The rhetorical force of the italicized words is to remind us that the proposition in question—that I know that this is a pencil here before me, for example—is *manifestly true* and *there is no doubt about it whatsoever*.

3. How Moore Does Epistemology

The structure of Moore's anti-skeptical position is revealed in some underappreciated aspects of his argumentative strategy.

"A Defence of Common Sense" (Moore, 1993b) begins with a list of claims or statements (Moore calls them "propositions"), including claims about things external to the mind, that he avers we all know with certainty. His "defense" amounts to this: he argues that those philosophers who would deny these propositions (or deny that we know them) contradict themselves or fall into incoherence *because of ways in which they are committed to precisely these very propositions*. Importantly, he does not provide a philosophical characterization of the class of "common sense" propositions and then offer a philosophical theory in defense of privileging them in philosophizing. Nor does he offer an epistemological theory on which the deliverances of some faculty called "common sense" are generally trustworthy. Rather, he reminds us that we too really are committed to his "common sense" propositions, and he argues that we can't reasonably get from this starting point to a position in which we deny them. This is a "defense" conducted from within our ordinary pre-philosophical position and without vindication through constructive philosophical theory-building.

The argumentative strategy of papers such as "Certainty" and "Four Forms of Scepticism" accords with this aspect of the "Defence." Moore scrutinizes the argumentation that is supposed to move us from our pre-philosophical position to the skeptical conclusion. He repeatedly confronts this argumentation with commitments drawn from our pre-philosophical starting position, commitments such as that he knows he is standing up ("Certainty," 1993a, 191), that he knows this is a pencil ("Four Forms," 1993c, 226), and that it isn't good reasoning to move from "A's may on occasion fail to be associated with B's" to "It is not known with certainty that this A is so associated"

("Four Forms," 220, 222, 224). The point, as he explicitly says, is to show that these arguments "do not give me any reason to abandon my view" ("Four Forms," 222). Once that is shown, he takes the anti-skeptical work to be done.

Of course, Moore did engage in philosophical theory-building. However, it is very important to see what he was up to. It may not be precisely what we might have thought. In particular, it is not the sort of enterprise that could serve the vindicatory aspirations of the interpretations canvassed above.

In section IV of the "Defence," Moore turns to the project of providing what he calls an "analysis" of propositions about external objects and our epistemological relation to them. It isn't entirely clear what he means by "analysis," but he is very clear about the contrast with the work accomplished earlier in the paper; in fact, he introduces this section by saying that he is turning to a question of "a very different order" ("Defence," 1993b, 127). Moore insists that we already understand these propositions independently of engaging in these "analytic" projects, and he maintains that they are quite certainly true, but he says that the question of how such propositions are "to be analysed is one to which no answer that has been hitherto given is anywhere near certainly true" ("Defence," 133). So, for Moore, this question is of a "different order" insofar as it concerns the "analysis" of claims that are (to speak within Moore's pre-philosophical position) *certainly true* and have *already been fully defended* in the earlier sections of the paper. Moore's equanimity in the face of ongoing uncertainty over multiple decades regarding the correct "analysis" of our epistemological relation to external objects (and of the nature of sense-data and their role in this relation) is a mark of this same attitude.

For Moore, then, skepticism is dealt with before the work of philosophical theory-building begins. What would give us reason to think skepticism correct is something about or in our starting position that points in that direction. A proposed analysis might appear to provide some such reason, but resolution of the issue would take place by considering more carefully the commitments of our pre-philosophical position. The fundamental question here is thus what happens when we attempt to attain reflective understanding of the commitments of ordinary epistemic life. Do we find anything that leads us to a skeptical conclusion or that gives us reason to discount or set aside some or all of the commitments that would block it? Moore makes no claim that this will not or could not happen. It is possible that we will find considerations that warrant downgrading or doubting some or all of our ordinary judgments about what we know or have reason to believe. It could be, for example, that we will find a fundamental conflict—for instance, that some principle of epistemic assessment to which we are committed has the consequence (given certain undeniable facts) that we can't know that there is a pencil here. Moore's crucial point is that nothing like any such reason in favor of skepticism has yet been identified. Given that this is so—and assuming that our survey has been exhaustive enough—there is nothing more that needs to be done. In this regard, the ordinary position does not require or await vindication by philosophical theory.

This pattern is particularly clearly displayed in the first seven chapters of Moore's 1910–11 lectures, *Some Main Problems of Philosophy* (Moore, 1953). The first chapter begins with a recitation of "common sense" beliefs which we all share. This passage is introduced with the phrase, "We certainly believe..." (2), but this wording is quickly dropped in favor of outright assertion of the relevant propositions and sometimes even the claim that we know them to be true. The rhetorical effect—with which we effortlessly go along—is that we are *speaking from within our view of the world*, stating manifest truisms. Moore then takes these as the starting points for his subsequent investigations of perception, sense-data, and knowledge. Rather than appealing to constructive epistemological theorizing in order to determine whether we know of the existence of external things, he proposes "to answer the principal objections of those philosophers who have maintained that we certainly do not" (1953, 27). The reply provided in chapter 6, "Hume's Theory Examined," is then conducted on the same plane as the "Defence of Common Sense." Moore highlights certain skeptical puzzles that arise from his account of perception when combined with certain epistemological principles—principles which have not been shown to arise from any "common sense" views. In response he makes use of his starting-point commitments, highlighting that because we do, after all, know that this is a pencil, and because no plausible reason has been offered in favor of the epistemological principles at play, we can reject these epistemological principles: "The strongest argument to prove that Hume's principles are false is the argument from a particular case, like this, in which we do know of the existence of some material object" (1953, 125–126). No reason has been found to give up our initial commitments or to change our view.

It is noteworthy that what has been interpreted as Moore's "particularism" in epistemological method (Chisholm 1973) is a *downstream consequence* of his starting point in our pre-philosophical position, not something which itself rests upon an epistemological-cum-methodological theory in the way we saw Kelly (2005) suggest. Moore does regard our ordinary, pre-philosophical judgments about what we know and don't know as providing a *prima facie* constraint for epistemological theorizing (*Some Main Problems*, 1953, 143).[7] This is because we *do* start with some commitments to particular judgments and to principles and practices of assessment, and the question—from where we are in fact standing—is whether we can find some good reason to call any of that into doubt. From this vantage point, a proposed epistemological thesis that would deny that we know, for example, that this is a pencil, is *ipso facto* suspect, because it conflicts with *manifest truths*. Admittedly, to put it this way is to speak from within our ordinary, pre-philosophical position at a particular stage in the inquiry. But that is precisely where Moore is standing. He has, so far, found no reason to stand anywhere else.

Of course, a philosopher might engage in various counterfactual exercises. Someone could suppose that some or all of these manifest truths are incorrect or in doubt and then consider where we would be left if that were so. Likewise, someone could imagine that they are in an initial position in which they reasonably suspend judgment on these matters. But if we keep our eye on the ball, it is clear that no such exercise could reach the conclusion, voiced with full commitment, that we do not have nor can have any knowledge or reasonable beliefs about the external world. The most that would be yielded is that *if* certain things were so, then we couldn't have knowledge or reasonable belief about the world, or that *if* certain things were so, then that is what we would be forced to conclude, or that *if* we suspended judgment about certain manifest truths, then we would be unable to see how we could have knowledge or reasonable belief about the world. But so what? Our actual position is one in which—to speak from within it—those things are not so. The crucial questions are whether we have good reason to *actually* regard these initial commitments with suspicion or worse, and whether we *actually* have good reason to suspend judgment about these manifest truths, so that what we should *actually* conclude would be shaped in these ways. Moore's crucial contention is that no such reason has emerged.

Moore's point requires a shift in perspective that can be very hard for philosophers to maintain. There is a tendency to demand that we take up a position, imagined as "neutral," in which we stand outside of ordinary life to

---

[7] He sometimes casts the point in simple inductivist terms (e.g., *Some Main Problems*, 1953, 143), but this is inessential. He likewise might well have noted that the judgments in question are defeasible.

argue that skepticism is false and thereby vindicate the beliefs of ordinary life. But why accede to this demand? The crucial question is whether there is any good reason, available to us in our pre-philosophical starting position, for taking up this "neutral" position and for thinking that what we find, if we do so, has any significance at all for whether we know anything about the world around us.

Whether there is any such reason is a genuine and important question. We will return to it. The essential point for now, however, is this. From Moore's point of view, the path to skepticism will be blocked if we can find, from within our ordinary starting position, no good reason for taking up this "neutral" position, and if we can show, from our ordinary starting position, that no good reason has been offered in skepticism's favor. We will then be left where we started, and we will declare that we do know a great deal about the world around us indeed. Moore's underlying approach will then have been vindicated on its own terms.

It might be objected that this approach must itself rest on some sort of controvertible epistemological theory, perhaps a principle that our beliefs and commitments are "innocent until proven guilty" or a general principle of epistemological conservatism.[8] But Moore's position doesn't depend upon any such thing. Our starting point is (to speak from within it) one in which we know all sorts of things and have good reasons in support of them—and in which we are perfectly reasonable in taking all that to be so. Moore's procedure, then, makes use of truistic everyday epistemic rules of thumb along the following lines: If you have good reasons for your view, then don't revise it without good reasons; knowing something often entitles you to reject things incompatible with it without further inquiry; if you know something, then you shouldn't accept something incompatible with it without very good reason; and the like. Something along these lines is surely part of the commitments of ordinary epistemic life. Might we have or find good reason to revise such commitments? Of course. But given where we are standing—the commitments and procedures we are working within and from—we shouldn't revise them unless we find what we can recognize from that position as good reasons for doing so. And of course, the skeptical arguments that are our focus don't depend upon rejecting such rules of thumb in any case.

There could be forms of skepticism that appeal to certain principles without purporting to ground them in anything arising from our pre-philosophical

---

[8] This charge was pressed on me by Eli Hirsch (personal communication).

position. They might appeal to "philosophical" justifications at odds with the commitments of everyday epistemic life and practice. Such views cannot be refuted on their own terms via an approach like Moore's, unlike forms of skepticism (my primary target) that purport to arise from within the commitments and principles of everyday epistemic life. However, such forms of skepticism can still be satisfactorily rejected via a procedure like Moore's. The crucial point is that *what we know* is the standard for rejecting such views, given our starting point. Here's why. We start in the ordinary, pre-philosophical position. To speak from within that position, we know all kinds of things—about the world, about our own epistemic status, about how to proceed in epistemic assessment, and the like. If the skeptical argument depends upon a principle that conflicts with all of that, and if it offers nothing that we can see as a compelling reason in favor of the principle, then the reasonable thing to do—reasonable from within the principles and procedures at play in our starting position—is to reject it. We would have no reason to do otherwise.

Is this objectionable dogmatism? Surely not. We are open to the possibility of revising our view, and we are giving full attention to any putative reasons for doing so. If good reasons come along, we will accept them. We are just insisting on working from within what is in fact our best going view. To speak from within the commitments of that position: that's not dogmatism, but rather good methodology.

Moore thus offers us a distinctive strategy for engaging with skepticism. On his approach we do not need a final response to external world skepticism once and for all—we do not need anything equivalent to a general account of perceptual knowledge or a transcendental argument showing the impossibility, unintelligibility, or instability of either the skeptic's distinctive scenarios or the skeptical position. Rather, we just engage in the patient, ongoing work of scrutinizing the reasons and arguments that are offered. As we will see, the lesson to learn from Moore is that this may well be enough.

3
Stroud's Question

1. The Challenge for the Skeptic

If we adopt the Moorean approach we focus on the earliest stages of skeptical reflection, the initiating moves that are supposed to get the whole thing going. In particular, we carefully scrutinize the relation between those initiating moves and ordinary life. Our focus is on this question: How are we supposed to get skeptical reflection started from within what I have called our pre-philosophical position—our ordinary practices, procedures, and commitments regarding inquiry and epistemic assessment?

To approach this question in a Moorean spirit, here's what you need to do. Stand squarely within the ordinary position. Start out with all of our ordinary commitments about what is the case, about what evidence we have for what, about what we know or have reason to believe, about when someone knows, is justified, or has good reason to believe something, and about how we should proceed when assessing people's knowledge, defending our views, and deciding what to believe. Working from within that position, ask: can we somehow be moved in a reasonable way to accept the conclusion that we know far less about the world around us than we initially thought, or that we can't even have any reason to believe anything about the world? Address this question by freely making use of the commitments of our ordinary position to respond to the key assumptions, principles, and early moves of skeptical argumentation—unless and until you find some aspect of our ordinary commitments that blocks you from doing so.

Here, the would-be skeptic faces a crucial challenge.

A central commitment of the ordinary position is that we know many things about the world. To speak from within that position: I know that I am sitting in my study, that there is a table here with a computer, paper, and a pen on it. I also know that I am seeing the table, the computer, and the pen. I likewise know a great deal about the sorts of circumstances in which my sensory experience is reliable and the sorts of circumstances in which it isn't, and I know that it's reliable right now relative to the question of whether there is a table here. Moreover, I know a good deal about how the senses work, and about how the world works more generally. I know, for instance, that dream experience differs in certain identifiable respects from my experience of the world when I am wide awake, wearing my glasses, not under the influence of mind-altering substances, and the like. I also know a great deal about more general matters, such as the causal structure of the world. I know, for instance, that things don't happen as a result of the machinations of evil demons, since there aren't any evil demons.

Another thing that I am committed to as part of the ordinary position is that particular facts about the world frequently provide excellent evidence for other claims about the world. For instance, I might correctly appeal to the fact that my plants are drooping as evidence that they need water, given that it is 90 degrees out and hasn't rained. And I might likewise appeal to the fact that my plants are drooping as part of an answer to the question, "How do you know that they need water?"

All these commitments raise a straightforward problem for attempts to get skepticism going from within our ordinary position. Unless these commitments are somehow taken out of play, any skeptical argument will remain vulnerable to responses of the sort Moore urges: we will simply appeal to considerations about the world and our knowledge of it to rebut the standard skeptical scenarios, to provide evidence about the world, or to supply grounds for rejecting epistemological principles appearing in the skeptical argument. The key challenge, then, if we are to get skepticism going from within the ordinary position, is to show how—contrary to appearances—*materials already within that position* really do preclude such moves. If this limitation isn't established, then the skeptical argument won't even begin to get off the ground. The right thing to conclude—standing in our pre-philosophical starting position—would then be that whether we have knowledge, and what we know, is simply not revealed by what happens when we limit ourselves in the way the skeptical argumentation requires.

Of course, you might think, "Well, I'm just curious. If I limit myself in this way, where would I be left? Could I satisfactorily account for my knowledge of the world in these terms?" But if that is all you are doing, then there is no reason to think that the result tells you *anything* about whether and what you know about the world. For the exercise to be informative, there must be some good reason of the right sort for carving things up in that way. What might that reason be? Why, at the very beginning of our reflections, should we disallow our ordinary commitments about the world and our knowledge of it?

2. The Project of General Epistemic Assessment

One motivation might be suggested right off the bat. "There is an obvious good reason for leaving our ordinary, pre-philosophical position and temporarily suspending all of our ordinary commitments about the world and the extent of our knowledge: we want to find out whether all of that is *correct*." This thought underlies a fundamental objection to any anti-skeptical strategy that appeals, with Moore, to considerations about the external world and our knowledge of it. Such a strategy, it might be said, doesn't squarely address the question that was being posed. It simply misses the point.

Barry Stroud, for instance, sees an attempt to provide a fully general "assessment of all of our knowledge of the world" lying at the very beginning of the line of thought that leads to skeptical argumentation (1984, 111). What we want to know, he suggests, is whether we actually *do* know *any* of the things that we take ourselves to know about the world. To answer that question, Stroud says, "We cannot appeal to one thing known about the world in order to support another; all of it is meant to be in question all at once" (118). Stroud's suggestion, then, is that there is a distinctive question of assessment that, once raised, prevents us—in that context of inquiry—from acceptably making use of what we know about the world. It is this initiating question that places limitations upon us. As a result, a response like Moore's is blocked from the get-go.

How, from Moore's perspective, might we best respond to this suggestion? Considering this question will bring out some of the fundamental issues underlying resistance to Moore's response to skepticism. Before we get to that, however, we need to bring Stroud's question more clearly into view.

Mere generality does not have the effect that Stroud stresses. If I simply ask, "Do I know anything at all about the world around me?" *one* straightforward and seemingly appropriate (though obvious) answer would be to say "Yes" and to mention one of the many things I know. Still, I think that it is undeniable that we can feel the tug of Stroud's question. It is perhaps best thought of as a fully generalized version of a familiar sort of reflective, self-critical epistemic assessment. For instance, I can ask in a reflective moment, "What do I *really know* about the assassination of JFK?" In answering that question, I can't acceptably reflect, "Well, Kennedy was shot by Lee Harvey Oswald. So I *do* know something about the Kennedy assassination after all." That piece of knowledge isn't available to be used in that way in the course of the critical reassessment.

Stroud's thought, then, is that this familiar aspect of our epistemic practices can be generalized to apply to one's knowledge of external things as such. I can ask, in a reflective moment, "What, if anything, do I really know about the world external to my mind?," thereby raising a general question of critical epistemic self-evaluation. Once I've done that, Stroud suggests, I'm precluded from making use of my ordinary commitments about the world external to my mind or about what I know of that world. Those commitments become—relative to my inquiry—mere psychological facts about myself as soon as the question of reflective scrutiny gets applied to them, and so I must establish their credentials before I am entitled to work from within them. From this position, we wouldn't be able to respond to skeptical argumentation in the way that Moore proposes. Instead, the task would be to identify some basis upon which all of our knowledge of the world rests, and to show—in a way that presupposes no knowledge of the world—how that basis could suffice to yield knowledge. The demand for a vindicatory epistemological theory now appears irresistible.

From Moore's perspective, we need something that does the work that Stroud's question attempts to accomplish, if skeptical argumentation is even to have a hope of getting going. This is because from Moore's perspective the introduction in a critical mode of the skeptic's distinctive possibilities—that one is dreaming, being deceived by an evil demon, or just a brain in a vat—does not *by itself* have this effect. Moore was content to appeal to considerations about the world and his knowledge of it in order to dismiss skeptical arguments. So, without the framing provided by Stroud's question of general epistemic assessment, it would—from Moore's viewpoint—be perfectly in accord with the epistemic commitments of ordinary life to reject such possibilities by appealing to other considerations about the world. For instance, if someone said, "But you don't know that there is a pencil here, because for all you know you might be dreaming," Moore might (though he didn't) reply, "No, I do know that I am not dreaming, because my current experience is nothing like a dream. Dreams don't have certain features possessed by my current experience." If it is suggested that it is at least in some sense possible that one could have a dream that is phenomenologically identical to a waking experience, Moore might (though he didn't) accept the point and yet note that there is no reason to think that anything of the sort ever actually goes on. In both these replies, he would be making use of his background knowledge of what dream experience is like for creatures like us. And if it is suggested that Moore might be the victim of an evil demon's deceptions, he might (though he didn't) respond that he surely is not, since there are no evil demons. Likewise, he isn't a brain in a vat, since virtual reality hasn't been developed to that extent—not yet, at any rate. So, if a skeptical argument hopes to get anywhere by offering such possibilities, all the crucial action must already have taken place off-stage. Something must already have been done to preclude appealing to things we know about the world.

Stroud sometimes suggests that such appeals are rendered objectionably dogmatic simply by the fact that the skeptic puts forward the skeptical scenarios as a *criticism* of our ordinary claims to know (1984, 121). He offers the example of a detective's assistant who claims to know, on the basis of a list of people given to him by a murdered duke's social secretary, that only the butler could have done it. When the master detective points out that the social secretary could have been an accomplice and so the list cannot be trusted, the assistant cannot acceptably reply, "No, the social secretary must be trustworthy, and the list must be impeccable, since I know that the butler did it." Why, Stroud asks, should we be any more impressed by Moore's claim that he isn't dreaming, based as it is on things he takes himself to know about the world? Isn't Moore likewise simply insisting on his knowledge in the face of a well-placed objection (1984, 108, 113)?

The answer is this: the mere attempt at criticism doesn't always have such an effect. Suppose that in response to my comment that my son just graduated from high school, you suggest—in an attempt at criticism—that perhaps the principal was an accomplice and the whole thing a deception. Given that you have no reason whatsoever in favor of the objection, I can perfectly appropriately dismiss it out of hand. "Don't be ridiculous. I know he's just graduated from high school. I was there, and it wasn't a deception." Here I reiterate the very knowledge claim that you meant to criticize, and I do so in dismissing that very criticism.

This example differs in certain structural respects from the skeptic's dream scenario, and those structural features will be the focus of attention in later chapters. The important point here, however, is this: Stroud claims that *merely* introducing a possibility as criticism of a knowledge claim has the effect that we see in the assistant detective's case. What the graduation example shows is that this isn't so. The detective's assistant cannot acceptably dismiss the detective's objection by confidently reiterating that the butler did it. But in the graduation example, we *can* acceptably dismiss the poorly motivated objection by confidently reiterating what we know. The difference seems to be that while there is some reason to suspect that the assistant detective's list might be wrong, there is no reason whatsoever to suspect that my son's graduation was just a hoax. Stroud seems to be ignoring the way in which the efficacy of a criticism often depends upon the reasons that bear on the particular case.

Given these points, Moore—standing as he is with both feet in our ordinary, pre-philosophical position—might well find a fundamental disanalogy between the master detective's apt criticism and the familiar skeptical hypotheses: there is reason for suspicion that the secretary's list was not accurate, but there is no reason to suspect that I am dreaming right now or being deceived by an evil demon. The former case consequently can't be treated as a straightforward model for the latter, whatever else there is to say for or against Moore's approach. Stroud's example thus doesn't offer a telling objection to Moore's procedure of rejecting skeptical argumentation by appealing to considerations about the world and his knowledge of it.

Of course, we would have difficulty vindicating the claim to know that the skeptical possibilities don't obtain—and we will feel a consequent need to develop an epistemological theory to vindicate our claims to knowledge of the external world—if something has *already* been done to preclude us from making use of other things we know about the world. That is why something like Stroud's question of general assessment is so important. It aims to secure the needed limitation, blocking us from making use of anything we take ourselves to know about the world and thus providing the framing that is needed if the skeptical inquiry is to reach a negative conclusion. And it also appears to do so in a way that arises out of our ordinary, pre-philosophical starting point. Until Stroud's suggestion is addressed, then, no response like Moore's can be intellectually satisfying.

3. An Answer without Epistemological Theory

Stroud suggests that Moore simply didn't get it. "Moore gives the impression of having no idea what the skeptical philosopher really wants to say or do," (1984, 124). Clarke is even more blunt, suggesting that Moore writes as if he had had a "philosophical lobotomy" (Clarke 1972, 757). But why should Moore be seen as offering an inadequate response within a project of general critical reassessment that is already successfully underway? Perhaps Moore recognized what the skeptical philosopher was trying to do, but had some good reason available from within his starting position for rejecting the inquiry—and the limitations it imposes—altogether.

To begin, it should be acknowledged that Moore himself sometimes felt the allure of the position that results from the aspiration to critically assess all of one's knowledge of the world at once. "Four Forms of Skepticism" ends as follows:

> It seems to me *more* certain that I *do* know that this is a pencil and that you are conscious, than that any single one of [Russell's] four [skeptical] assumptions is true, let alone all four. . . . Nay more: I do not think it is *rational* to be as certain of any one of these four propositions, as of the proposition that I do know that this is a pencil. And how on earth is it to be decided which of the two things it is *rational* to be most certain of? (Moore 1993c, 222)

Until this point in the paper, Moore had been speaking from the pre-philosophical position, firmly rooted within his ordinary commitments. However, his final question—the final sentence of the paper—is not posed from that position. For in that position the question is readily answerable. Moore can say all sorts of compelling things in favor of the claim that he knows this is a pencil, beginning with the fact that he can see it, whereas from within the ordinary, pre-philosophical position there is nothing to be said in favor of the conjunction of Russell's four assumptions. Puzzlement such as Moore's only arises here if we think that we need to decide the question of rationality in a way that does not make use of all of our ordinary commitments—that is, when we attempt to appraise the relative rationality of believing these various propositions *after* taking up the standpoint Stroud's question aims to generate. Here, then, Moore is not merely alive to the pressures arising from Stroud's project; he is their victim.

Elsewhere, however, he explicitly resists temptation, even while recognizing full well the nature of that project. In "Proof of an External World," he writes (in a passage already highlighted) that what the skeptically-inclined philosophers "really want is not merely a proof of these two propositions ('Here's a hand and here's another'), but something like a general statement as to how *any* propositions of this sort may be proved." He continues,

This, of course, I haven't given; and I do not believe it can be given: if this is what is meant by proof of the existence of external things, I do not believe that any proof of the existence of external things is possible." (Moore 1993d, 169, italics in original)

A "general statement as to how *any* propositions of this sort may be proved" would amount to an account that would satisfy the constraints set by Stroud's question of general critical assessment. It would explain how we could, in principle, start from some evidential base that does not include any propositions about the world around us and, without presupposing or depending upon any propositions about the world around us, proceed in a rationally acceptable way to conclusions about external things, thereby gaining knowledge of external things for the first time. Moore thus shows he is perfectly aware of what the skeptical epistemologist wants to do and what it would take to satisfy the demands imposed by that inquiry. But he rejects in one sentence this project that has motivated legions of epistemologists since Descartes. He says, "It can't be done," and proceeds as if the fact that it can't be done *has no negative implications regarding our knowledge of the world around us.* He thus insinuates that his knowing things about the world doesn't require him to be able to do any such thing or even that it be possible.

Moore evidently thinks that in admitting that such an account isn't possible, he has not capitulated to the skeptic. He also thinks that this attitude is not objectionably dogmatic. But what could Moore say, given his overall position, in its defense?

To approach this question, let's ask what happens when someone clear-headedly standing in Moore's position considers Stroud's question of general assessment and the project it inspires.

First, let's get our ordinary, pre-philosophical position clearly in mind. Operating within this position, Moore is committed to a great many claims to know things about the world. In many of these cases he can vindicate these claims in accordance with (to speak from within that position) the proper principles and procedures of epistemic assessment. For instance, if he asks, "Do I really know that there is a pencil here in front of me? How do I know?," he can answer, "Yes, I do know there is a pencil in front of me. I see a pencil here now, I remember putting it here a while ago, and I haven't moved it since." If he asks himself how he knows it isn't a papier-mâché facsimile that someone slipped in while he wasn't looking, he can quite rightly point out that there is no reason in favor of any such suggestion, and he can even test the pencil by trying to write with it. If he then asks whether he really knows that he isn't dreaming or being deceived by an evil demon, he can likewise dismiss these suggestions in the ways I've already discussed. So, to speak from within the ordinary position, he has a great deal of evidence bearing on his various particular beliefs about the world, and he can use it well to vindicate many of his claims to know particular things.

Keeping this position clearly in mind, let's consider the line of thought Stroud suggests. We begin by asking, in a mode of critical reassessment, whether we really know anything that we take ourselves to know about the world. We take that question to preclude us from making use of, presupposing, or otherwise relying upon things that we take ourselves to know about the world, and so we demand a general account of how we could acceptably get from some sort of more restricted evidential base to knowledge of the external world. In considering what that evidential base could be, we see that it must be whatever the senses give us, described in a way that is not yet committal regarding anything about the external world. We then recognize that to have knowledge of the world on this basis we would have to be in a position to eliminate certain possibilities, such as that we are dreaming or deceived by an evil demon. But we find that this restricted evidential basis isn't sufficient—given our inability to rely on background knowledge of the world—to give us a good reason to think that these possibilities don't obtain. So, we close the inquiry by concluding that we can't really know anything about the world around us.

Imagine now that you are Moore, standing in the position of ordinary epistemic life and contemplating this line of thought.

To begin, suppose that someone says, "Limit your evidential base to include only the deliverances of the senses, described in a way that is not yet committal regarding anything about the world," and then proposes to follow out Stroud's reasoning from that point. Notice how odd it would be to close the inquiry by concluding that we don't know anything about the world! What we find is that if we utilize only that restricted evidential base, then we can't vindicate any particular claims to know things about the world. But if we are standing in Moore's starting position, we won't yet conclude that we don't know anything about the world. We will just conclude that if we choose to restrict our evidential base in that way, then we can't tell whether we know anything about the world. We have simply chosen to prescind from the materials we need in any given case.

Note, moreover, that this restriction in the evidential base appears arbitrary relative to the principles and procedures of epistemic assessment that are in play in our ordinary position. When we vindicate the claim to know that there is a pencil here, it is appropriate to make use of other things we know about the world. For this reason, a project like Stroud's appears to deprive Moore of epistemically appropriate resources in a way that is arbitrary relative to the relevant principles and procedures. The situation looks rather like a courtroom trial in which the evidence is limited—say, for reasons of political expedience—in ways that are arbitrary in relation to the question of guilt.

Of course, Stroud doesn't think the limitation is epistemically arbitrary: it is generated, he would tell us, by the initiating question of general assessment, "What, if anything, do I really know about the world around me?" And indeed, if this restriction in the evidential base is just a straightforward application of principles and procedures of epistemic assessment that are present in the pre-philosophical position, then far from being arbitrary, it is imposed by epistemic principles and procedures to which Moore is already committed.

Notice, however, how critical epistemic reassessment actually functions in ordinary life. If I ask, "What, if anything, do I really know about the assassination of John F. Kennedy?," there is indeed a great deal that I can't take for granted in answering the question. But not *everything* that I take myself to know about the assassination is thereby placed out of play.[1] I can, for instance, continue to make use of the fact, which I surely know, that John F. Kennedy was president of the United States. And I can continue to make use of my knowledge—which clearly concerns the Kennedy assassination—that certain things, such as certain autopsy reports, video recordings, and the like, *are* relevant evidence in relation to some of the questions that might be asked about how Kennedy died and who was responsible. Notice, moreover, that if I ask myself "Do I really know that Kennedy was president of the United States?," no task of showing how I could reach this conclusion from a restricted basis is imposed at all. No further inquiry is needed. The correct answer is, "Obviously, I do." The difference here concerns the epistemic reasons that bear on the case. When there is no reason whatsoever to suspect error, then the appropriate form of response to the question "Do I really know?" may be different from when there is some reason to suspect error. Given that one has all sorts of information that bears on the issue, restrictions

---

[1] This point is forcefully made by Mark Kaplan (2018).

are imposed in the evidential base only in the latter case. Of course, such questions can sometimes be a useful way of jogging one's thinking. I might ask, "Do I really know that Kennedy was president?" and realize that I have some prima facie reason to suspect that I might be wrong about this matter. But if I find not even a prima facie reason to suspect that I am wrong, I can quite properly respond simply, "Of course I know Kennedy was president." This is not an epistemologically arbitrary matter of practical expedience or the like. It is a matter of what the relevant reasons support. This is about as far from objectionable dogmatism as one can get.

To speak with Moore now, from within our ordinary position, we have no reason even to suspect that we are globally mistaken about the world around us, not even prima facie reason for concern. It is hence quite appropriate for us, given the operative principles and procedures of assessment, to dismiss Stroud's question of global assessment. "Of course I know all sorts of things about the external world." From Moore's standpoint in our ordinary position, the restriction in evidential base imposed by Stroud's project of global assessment is indeed epistemically arbitrary; the tribunal of Cartesian reflection is thus shown up as a kangaroo court. This is why when Moore says that it is not possible to give "a general statement as to how *any* propositions of this sort may be proved," he is neither capitulating to skepticism nor engaging in an objectionably dogmatic refusal to take it seriously. Rather, the remark highlights that such a project's failure is of no consequence whatsoever.

The point here isn't particularly about Stroud. It is about the restriction his question aims to impose. Do you have a better way to put that restriction in place? I mean this as a serious question. We will return to it repeatedly in the coming chapters.

4. The Concerns Behind Stroud's Question

It is time to take stock. The upshot of reflection on Moore's response to skepticism thus far appears to be this: there is—at least so far—no reasonable route to the skeptical conclusion from principles and procedures of epistemic assessment at play in the position of ordinary life. Merely trotting out the familiar skeptical hypotheses is ineffectual by itself, and Stroud's question of global assessment doesn't, as things are, impose the limitations that would be needed in order for a negative verdict to be reached. These considerations suggest that when we take seriously our real starting point, we cannot find any reason to prescind quite generally from our ordinary commitments about what we know and have reason to believe about the world. Nor do we find any reason to suspect that our most basic principles and procedures of epistemic justification and assessment are incorrect. We started out taking ourselves both to know all sorts of things concerning a world outside of our minds and also to be proceeding quite correctly in matters of epistemic assessment, and that is precisely where we end up. This isn't to deny that there might be a line of thought that does what the skeptic needs. But it would have to be provided, and any proposal would need to be scrutinized in the sorts of ways we have been considering.

Suppose, however, that no such line of thought meets the skeptic's needs. Where would that leave us? Getting clear about this at the big-picture level will help bring out the most fundamental lessons of Moore's response to skepticism, and it will help frame the project and task of the rest of this book.

Let's begin with the complaint—noted in the preceding chapter—that might be put like this: "Okay, I grant that if we begin resolutely within our ordinary position, then external world skepticism doesn't even get started as an epistemological problem. So what? Skepticism might still be *true*!" What should we make of this concern?

This much is true: everything could seem to us just as it does in the ordinary position—and we could say everything that I have said in Moore's defense—even if our beliefs were wildly out of touch with reality. Moore might go through his performances and quite properly claim to know all sorts of things about the world around him, and yet be radically, globally, deceived. However, this possibility does not present any epistemic threat given the principles and procedures of epistemic assessment that are operative in ordinary life. Here's why. To speak from within the position of ordinary life: we often know things even though there are—and we recognize that there are—perfectly imaginable scenarios in which things would seem just as they do and yet we would be wrong. For instance, as I write this I know that my spouse is in the United States. (We spoke earlier, and I consequently know a great deal about what she is up to.) I recognize that even if she had left the country earlier today, everything could seem to me just as it does right now—for instance, if she had intentionally misled me as part of an elaborate deception. But in fact there is no reason whatsoever even to suspect that something funny is going on, so I quite contentedly say, "I know she is in the U.S. She didn't leave the country today without telling me." This sort of position is completely satisfactory in ordinary life. The mere possibility that everything could seem just as it does and yet I could be completely mistaken is epistemically inert when there is no reason in its favor.

As this point reveals, our ordinary position is fallibilist in two subtly different senses. First, we are committed to allowing that we can know things even when we lack evidence that entails the truth of our beliefs. Second, we recognize that even when we have evidence that is incompatible with the falsity of our belief, it may still be possible that everything could seem to us just as it does and yet we might be completely mistaken. In neither regard do we take the mere possibility of error to be in any way epistemically troubling when there is no reason to suspect that it obtains. So, if we are truly considering skepticism from within our ordinary position, we should be prepared to accept that doing our level best is no iron-clad guarantee of getting things right. We might do everything as well as possible, quite reasonably arrive at the conclusion that skepticism is false, and nonetheless be wrong. That possibility is itself a consequence of the commitments of ordinary epistemic life, and it is a consequence of a kind with which we are ordinarily content. It is the sort of thing that we regard as perfectly compatible with actually knowing what we quite reasonably claim to know.

At this point we might expect an outburst. "But couldn't our ordinary position misrepresent the relevant epistemic principles and requirements—what knowledge requires, what is an instance of knowledge, when something constitutes a good reason or good evidence, what constitutes a reason for doubt or a reason to suspect that one is in error, what kind of grounds we need in order to have knowledge or reasonable beliefs about the world? Couldn't our ordinary position be wrong in allowing that we can possess knowledge of the world even if it isn't possible to complete the Cartesian project that Moore rejects?"

Suppose we grant for the sake of argument that this is all in some sense possible. So what? For reasons we have just seen, the mere possibility is inert if we can identify no reasons in its favor.

Let me walk up to that point more slowly. We are standing within our ordinary position, in which we are committed to the truth of certain epistemic principles and to the epistemic propriety of certain procedures of epistemic assessment. Within this standpoint we deploy the principles and procedures of epistemic justification and assessment to which we are committed, and we find that the mere possibility that everything could seem as it does even if we were completely mistaken is epistemically inert when there is no reason in its favor. We apply this point to our epistemic evaluations and to our commitments regarding epistemic assessment itself. The crucial question then is whether we have any reason to think that our principles and procedures of epistemic assessment are leading us fundamentally astray. We would have such a reason if we found them to be in fundamental conflict, for instance, or if we found that our ordinary practices of epistemic evaluation and assessment are fundamentally shaped by and pervasively responsive to non-epistemic factors (such as practical expedience) in ways that we regard as epistemically problematic. But so far no reason has emerged for any such concern. To speak again from our standpoint within our ordinary position, it is consequently correct—epistemically so—to retain our confident commitment to our principles and procedures of epistemic assessment.

This is not merely a point about what it is conversationally correct to say. Some philosophers have resisted the anti-skeptical appeal to our ordinary commitments by highlighting the broadly Gricean (1989) point that the mere conversational and practical propriety of our ascriptions of knowledge, good reasons, and the like in ordinary life is perfectly compatible with their falsehood. They suggest that this conceptual distinction should deter our easy acquiescence in the epistemic principles and procedures of our ordinary position. Stroud, for instance, writes,

> As long as it is even intelligible to suppose that there is a logical gap between the fulfillment of the conditions for appropriately making and assessing assertions of knowledge on the one hand, and the fulfillment of the conditions for the truth of those assertions on the other, evidence from usage or from our practice will not establish a conclusion about the conditions of knowledge. (1984, 64)

However, Stroud makes two mistakes here. First, he incorrectly takes entailing evidence—the complete absence of a "logical gap"—to be required in order to "establish a conclusion." We don't make any such demand in our ordinary position, which is where we, with Moore, are standing. Second, he fails to see that in our starting position we are working from *within* our commitments, giving voice to them and reasoning from them, not drawing conclusions from data about our usage. The relevant consideration isn't, for instance, that I am *inclined to say*, "I know that this is a pencil," nor even that saying this would be appropriate on occasion, but rather that (to speak from within the ordinary, pre-philosophical position) *I know that this is a pencil.* The mere conceptual distinction that Stroud points to, and the mere fact that the propriety of our epistemic verdicts does not entail their truth, does not yet give us any reason to suspect that our ordinary epistemic principles, procedures, or assessments are quite generally in error. Our commitments can thus countenance the Gricean distinction and remain intact.[2]

All this might leave one with a vertiginous sense of imprisonment in our ordinary position. One might now think something like this:

> For all that has been said, everything might seem just as it does and yet I might be radically deceived and fundamentally in error. I want to *get outside*—to see whether my beliefs about the world are actually correct and whether the principles and procedures I am committed to really are good ones. I take it that I know things about the world, have reasonable beliefs, that certain things are or are not reasons for believing, doubting, suspecting, other things—but am I right about *any* of this? That's what I want to know.

One might thus try to step outside the ordinary, pre-philosophical position, try to stand apart from all of one's initial commitments and attempt to get an external evaluation of them—despite having no reason to think them generally mistaken. What fuels this transition is the fear that one might just be unavoidably, irremediably, duped. This fear is distinct from a yearning for absolute certainty in the form of infallible grounds for one's beliefs about the world (though such a yearning might be an expression of this fear). What is sought here is not necessarily evidence entailing the truth of one's beliefs, let alone entailing evidence about which one could not possibly be in error, since even if one accepts that such things are not required for knowledge or reasonable belief, one might still feel that there is a question to be asked here about one's entire system of beliefs and epistemic principles and practices regarding the external world: Does that entire system actually give us what we want? If we are thus moved by the fear that we might just be duped, the fact that we can redescribe our entire position as one of *mere seeming* will itself seem enough to justify leaving our ordinary pre-philosophical position. We will then try to stand outside of it in its entirety and somehow evaluate it

---

[2] For further discussion of this point, see Leite 2004a, 234–235. What the objector needs here is some plausible argument that in the relevant cases conversational and practical factors shape the conditions of appropriate assertion in ways that we can recognize to be incompatible with the truth of our everyday epistemic verdicts. Until such an argument is offered, we have been given no reason not to continue to maintain our commitment to the truth of many of our ordinary claims to know things about the world.

from that external position. If we then find that the resulting limitation on the materials with which we may work leaves us incapable of showing that how things seem is how they really are, this may strike us as disaster. It might then seem reasonable to conclude that we cannot have knowledge or reasonable belief about the relevant matters.

This line of thought can plausibly be charged with various errors.

First, it arguably makes a mistake akin to a "level-confusion" (Alston 1980). It concludes that we lack knowledge or reasonable belief about the world, based on the discovery that we cannot show from a certain standpoint that we have knowledge or reasonable belief about the world. This is to confuse the requirements for having knowledge or reasonable belief with the requirements for showing from a certain perspective that we know or have reasonable belief.

Likewise, we might note—if we are standing within our ordinary position—that it is a distortion to use epistemic terms to describe both what this line of thought is after and what the negative result is. To speak from within the ordinary position, the right thing to say—right not just in pragmatic terms, but in relation to the relevant epistemic reasons—is that *we do know that we are not being duped*. The line of thought asks, "But am I right about any of this? That's what I want to know." And from within the ordinary position the answer is, "I am correct about a great deal of this, and I know that." I can move from established truth to established truth to vindicate my knowledge claims, and I can do so in ways that satisfy all of the relevant requirements concerning epistemic reasons. If the question is whether my beliefs about the world are formed in a truth-conducive way, that question can be readily answered as well, in the affirmative. And I quite properly take myself to know the truth of that answer—properly not just in pragmatic or conversational terms, but in terms of the epistemic reasons relevant to the case. From this perspective, then, the conclusion of the line of thought is just wrong.

It might be responded that none of this is to the point. Words are elastic. If you are struck by your inability to establish—from a standpoint outside all of your initial commitments—that how things seem is how they are, you might convey your dismay by lamenting, "So, we don't *really know* that we are not being radically duped." Such a response is not unintelligible; we can figure out what it is trying to convey. But recognizing this elasticity also highlights an important point. It is part of ordinary life that the denial of a competent knowledge claim on the basis of this impossible standard is itself properly criticizable in epistemic terms. For instance, someone is culpable—or else reveals that they don't really understand how responsible inquiry works—if they attempt to evade established climate science that easily. Competent climate scientists really do know that the earth is warming, and they really do know that they are not being duped. From our starting point in the ordinary position, then, we have yet to find a good reason against our ordinary commitments.

Still, if you find yourself feeling imprisoned in the ordinary position and worried it may be radically mistaken, if you consequently seek an external validation of your initial commitments, and if you despair upon discovering that no such thing can be had, then all of the responses I have offered are apt to look like mere quibbles. They do not assuage the worry that got the whole thing going, nor do they satisfy the aspiration to which it led. But that gap reveals precisely what we are dealing with when Stroud's question to Moore is pressed this far in spite of everything that's already been said. Given the lack of any reason to think anything is wrong, the worry does not show up as a fundamentally epistemic matter at all, but rather as an existential concern relating to our various vulnerabilities as fallible and limited creatures. It *is* always possible to redescribe our position simply in terms of how things subjectively seem, and once we have done that we can never establish—using only the remaining limited resources—that we have good reason to believe that things are as they seem. But it would be a mistake to take this to show that anything is going awry epistemically. If Moore is right, when we start out clearheadedly within the ordinary position we find no reason to think our ordinary epistemic commitments are generally incorrect and every reason to think them largely on track. We find no way to get a worry going in terms that are epistemically acceptable, and we likewise find no reason to think there is anything amiss with this situation. We don't even find reason to suspect that our most fundamental principles, standards, and procedures of epistemic assessment might be leading us astray. No such reason has been given.

What is required here is thus not philosophical theorizing, but reconciliation to our situation. As Stanley Cavell puts it,

> [The] experience I have called "seeing ourselves as outside the world as a whole," looking in at it . . . is an expression of what I meant when I said that we want to know the world as we imagine God knows it. And that will be as easy to rid us of as it is to rid us of the prideful craving to be God—I mean to *rid* us of it, not to replace it with despair at our finitude. (1999, 236–237)

This is where the underlying impetus of Moore's approach shows itself. Moore is neither blind to the skeptical philosopher's ambitions nor suffering from a philosophical lobotomy. Rather, one of his central goals is to show us how to be at home with ourselves.

Can that aspiration be carried through in detail? That is the overarching question of the remainder of this book.

4
Austin, Dreams, and Skepticism

"Some like Witters [Wittgenstein]," J.L. Austin reportedly declared, "but Moore is my man" (Grice 1989, 381).[1] Like Moore, Austin responds to skeptical concerns from within the standpoint of our ordinary, pre-philosophical position and without the development of epistemological theory. At the same time, he constantly has one eye on the aspects of our ordinary practice that he is exemplifying: he carefully describes key features and commitments of our pre-philosophical position to reveal precisely how a response to skepticism can arise out of them. His writings thus develop the Moorean methodology even as they put it into practice. The work is incremental, but the goal is radical: to reduce large intellectual edifices to rubble. As he puts it regarding certain sense datum theories, "the right policy" is not to offer an opposing theory, but rather "to go back to a much earlier stage, and to dismantle the whole doctrine before it gets off the ground" (1962, 142).

In his engagement with skepticism, Austin pays particular attention to the considerations about dreaming that figure centrally in Descartes' "First Meditation" (1984, 13). Descartes crucially depends on the claim that we cannot find any good grounds for thinking that we are not dreaming; "There are," he says, "no definitive signs by which to distinguish being awake from being asleep." On first encountering this argument it is natural to reply like this:

> Of course it would be completely unreasonable for me to believe that there is a piece of paper before me right now, if I granted that I don't know or have reason to believe this isn't a dream. But I do have good reason to believe that I'm not dreaming; I even know that I'm not. *This* is nothing like a dream.

---

[1] This chapter is derived from Adam Leite (2011). "Austin, Dreams, and Scepticism," in *The Philosophy of J.L. Austin*, edited by M. Gustafsson and R. Sørli (Oxford Publishing Limited, © the several contributors). Reproduced with permission of the Licensor through PLSclear.

As I will argue, Austin shows us—at least in outline—how this ordinary, pretheoretical response could succeed.

1. Austin on Dreaming

When we are awake and our faculties are functioning properly, can we tell that we are not asleep and dreaming? Austin's answer is unequivocal.

> There are recognized ways of distinguishing between dreaming and waking. (1979, 87)

> I may have the experience ... of dreaming that I am being presented to the Pope. Could it be seriously suggested that having this dream is "qualitatively indistinguishable" from *actually being* presented to the Pope? Quite obviously not. (1962, 48, italics in original)

> [W]e all know that dreams are *throughout un*like waking experiences. (1962, 42, italics in original)

As the lack of qualification in the last passage indicates, Austin's claim is a strong one: no dream is qualitatively indistinguishable from a waking experience had while one's faculties are functioning properly. If that is so, then it should be relatively straightforward to determine that one is not asleep and dreaming. Drawing on what "we all know" about dreams, a person who is awake and whose faculties are functioning properly should be able to determine from what her present experience is like that she is awake, not dreaming. And this has an important explanatory pay-off. We would think it bizarre for someone to raise the question, "Mightn't I be dreaming?" in the course of most everyday inquiry, reasoning, or epistemic appraisal. Austin can explain why that is so. If we all recognize that every competent adult in ordinary circumstances can plainly tell that they are not dreaming, then there is no point in bringing the issue up. That is why we don't bother to do so, and why doing so is silly even if knowledge or reasonable belief about the world requires adequate grounds for believing that one is not dreaming.

To see why Austin held this view, a fair bit of reconstruction is required.

The published version of *Sense and Sensibilia* was assembled by G.J. Warnock using notes from the various occasions on which Austin gave the lectures over several years. In the published version the second claim quoted above—the claim that it could not seriously be suggested that dreaming one is being presented to the Pope is qualitatively indistinguishable from the real thing—is immediately followed by this:

> After all, we have the phrase 'a dream-like quality'; some waking experiences are said to have this dream-like quality. . . . But of course, if the fact here alleged [that dreams are qualitatively indistinguishable from waking experiences] *were* a fact, the phrase would be perfectly meaningless. (1962, 49)[2]

On one natural interpretation, the argument here is as follows:

1. Our language contains the phrase, 'a dream-like quality,' and this phrase is linguistically meaningful.
2. If we could never distinguish dreams from waking experiences, then this phrase would have no meaning.
3. So, we must be able to distinguish some dreams from waking experiences.
4. We could not do that if dreams and waking experiences were always qualitatively indistinguishable.
5. So dreams and waking experiences must always be qualitatively different.

Step (2) of this argument obviously requires commitment to an objectionable verificationist theory of linguistic meaning, and many readers have found this sufficient reason to reject the argument. Even leaving this aside, however, the argument is patently inadequate. (5) manifestly doesn't follow from (3) and (4), because (3) and (4) only require that *some* dreams be qualitatively different from waking experiences, not that they *always* differ. This leaves it wide open that some dreams might be qualitatively indistinguishable from waking experiences.[3]

---

[2] In Austin's earlier paper, "Other Minds," the first passage quoted above is followed by a similar comment: "There are recognized ways of distinguishing between dreaming and waking (how otherwise should we know how to use and to contrast the words?)" (1979, 87).

[3] This failing is pointed out by Blumenfeld and Blumenfeld (1978, 238). It arises even if we interpret the argument as appealing instead to the weaker, non-verificationist idea that if there were never an aspect of dream experience that differed from waking experience, then there would be no *point* to the phrase 'a dream-like quality.'

Austin did not merely intend to establish the weaker claim that *some* or even *most* dreams can be distinguished from waking experiences. For one thing, the weaker claim doesn't do the work the argument would need it to do, since it doesn't support his confident claim that it "quite obviously" cannot seriously be suggested that dreaming one is being presented to the Pope is qualitatively indistinguishable from the real thing. Moreover, the weaker claim is irrelevant in the dialectical context. A.J. Ayer had offered a standard argument for sense-data beginning with the premise that "there is no intrinsic difference in kind between those of our perceptions that are veridical in their presentation of material things and those that are delusive" (1940, 5–6). What Ayer clearly meant—and all that he needed for the purposes of the argument—is that *some* "delusive" perceptions do not differ from "veridical" perceptions in what they are like from the relevant person's point of view; that is, that there are *some* cases in which it seems to the perceiver that she is in perceptual contact with objects around her, she isn't, and the situation is qualitatively indistinguishable by her from one in which she is. The suggestion on the table, then, is that some instances of dreaming are cases of this sort. It would simply be beside the point to reply by claiming that some or even most instances of dreaming *aren't* of this sort.[4]

Is Austin just guilty of poor argumentation from unmotivated verificationist premises? Some readers have thought so. However, it is noteworthy that Austin didn't actually think that his claim about dreams needed sophisticated philosophical defense. In his initial characterization of the failings of sense datum theories, he writes, "The fact is . . . that the facts of perception, as discovered by, for instance, psychologists but also as noted by common mortals, are much more diverse and complicated than has been allowed for" (1962, 3). His strategy, then, is in part to remind his readers of the relevant facts. He thought that an honest look would reveal that Ayer had simply gotten them wrong. Ayer's argument, he writes, "begins . . . with an alleged statement of fact. . . . Let us ask whether what is being alleged here is actually true. . . . Consider a few examples. . . ." (1962, 48). The dream of being presented to the Pope is offered as one such example. It is thus designed to

---

[4] This interpretation might be challenged on the ground that Austin later grants that there may be some cases in which "veridical perceptions" and "delusive perceptions" are qualitatively indistinguishable. (He goes on to argue that even this concession wouldn't require us to grant that we always perceive sense-data, since there is no reason why there shouldn't be cases in which perceiving one sort of thing is exactly like perceiving another [1962, 52].) However, the discussion of dreams appears at a moment in the text when the thesis of qualitative indistinguishability is itself under attack, and Austin's point there is that the example of dreams cannot be used to support this premise of the argument from illusion.

remind us of the relevant facts, to make vivid that Ayer is denying the "obvious fact that the 'experiences' are *different*" (1962, 50, italics in original). Evidently, Austin intended *the example itself* to carry the argumentative weight.

In the fall of 1958, Austin visited the University of California Berkeley and delivered what I understand to be his last revision of the lectures later published as *Sense and Sensibilia*. In this last, unpublished version of the lectures the argument from the meaningfulness of the phrase 'a dream-like quality' is conspicuously absent. In its place, Austin offers a list of particular ways in which dreams differ from waking experience:

> But there are differences, e.g., in temporal and spatial boundaries. And it is like being told a story: one cannot ask for completeness—e.g., what the weather was—if it wasn't given. Also—as another aspect of "having a dream-like quality"—things HAPPEN to the dreamer, often, rather than his doing these things. And not only is the sensuous balance different (e.g., few smells), but so also is the emotional balance quite different in dreams from that of real life. (1958, 8, Lecture VII.7)[5]

What Austin manifestly intended to be offering here are some of those facts that "we all know" about the ways in which dreaming is "*throughout un*like waking experiences." In hoping his example would carry conviction, he was banking on—and reminding us of—our knowledge of what dreams are like.[6]

This strand of Austin's argument is thus ultimately empirical. He appeals to a set of generalizations drawn from a lifetime of experiences with dreaming and with being told things about dreams. And it follows from those generalizations that no dream is qualitatively indistinguishable from

---

[5] From notes taken at the University of California, Berkeley, by R. Lawrence and W. Hayes. These notes—covering in detail the entirety of the twenty-nine lectures Austin delivered at Berkeley—were kindly brought to my attention by Wallace Matson, then Professor Emeritus of Philosophy at UC Berkeley. (Matson was present at the lectures and supplemented the Lawrence and Hayes typescript with his own notes.) I am in possession of a copy of the Lawrence and Hayes typescript and will gladly make it available to other researchers. I do not know whether other copies are in existence, as I have not had a chance to explore the Oxford Austin archives. According to Matson, the Lawrence and Hayes notes were at Warnock's disposal when he prepared the published edition of *Sense and Sensibilia*. I do not know Warnock's reasons for not including this passage in the published edition.

[6] Given the obvious failure of the argument in the published version of *Sense and Sensibilia* and its replacement in the Lawrence and Hayes notes by a set of empirical generalizations in support of the example, I'm inclined to think that the text of *Sense and Sensibilia* would look quite different had Austin lived to rework this material for publication. Archival work needs to be done to determine whether Austin had entirely abandoned the problematic argument by the time he prepared the Berkeley lectures. It is noteworthy, however, that the verificationist themes that sometimes sound in the published version of *Sense and Sensibilia* are largely missing from the Berkeley typescript.

veridical waking experiences. This underlying empirical argument is an instance of a style of argument that we all regard as unexceptionable in ordinary life and science. Given a wide enough experience with cats in a sufficient variety of circumstances, we can reasonably conclude that cats don't talk, that is, that *no* cat will talk. We might go on to allow that it is in some sense conceivable or possible (conceptually possible, logically possible, or whatever) for a cat to talk. But still, we might quite reasonably insist, the data show that it won't happen. So in arguing as he does, Austin is taking up a position within our ordinary practices, making use of a type of argument that we would all ordinarily accept without a blink.[7] To be sure, substantive questions might be raised. Are dreams really the right sort of phenomenon to be treated in this way? And do the facts actually support Austin's conclusion? So far as I can see, there is no serious empirical dispute about these matters. (Again, the mere conceivability or possibility—in some sense—of alternatives is irrelevant.) Those who feel the need for something more might profitably look at contemporary scientific work on dreaming.[8]

Even granting that Austin is right on this score, however, one might still have epistemological reservations about the further claim that by considering whether our current experience has (or lacks) certain features, we can tell that we are awake.

First, Austin would have to concede that our judgments about whether we are awake are fallible. He grants that while dreaming we are often incorrectly convinced that we are awake.[9] Moreover, on his view error should be possible regarding the presence or absence of relevant phenomenological features, since he holds that error is generally possible in our judgments about what our current experience is like (1962, 112–113; 1979, 90ff.).[10] And

---

[7] Of course, some philosophers have purported to raise doubts about whether such arguments actually support their conclusions, or have maintained that such arguments are not reasonable, etc. These challenges, and possible Austinian responses to them, are beyond the scope of this discussion.

[8] Around 2000, I did a survey of the relevant scientific literature. The results are reported in the paper from which this chapter is derived (Leite 2011a, fn. 10). A similar conclusion is reached by Owen Flanagan (2001).

[9] In the Berkeley notes he comments, regarding delirium tremens, "What produces the conviction is that the sufferer takes it for granted, in some odd sense (as in dreams), that this is a real experience" (1958, 8, Lecture VII.6). And the supplementary notes include this: "It is characteristic of dreams that *at the time* one thinks they are actual" (p. 8a note 2a). In this regard, Austin differs from thinkers such as Ernest Sosa (2005) who hold that while dreaming one does not judge or believe, and is not convinced, that one is awake (and indeed, that while dreaming a dreamer does not judge or believe, and is not convinced, of the truth of the content of the dream).

[10] This concession strongly suggests that Austin is committed to the possibility of one's current state having phenomenal features that one fails to recognize even when they are present. This possibility is crucial if we are to make sense of the idea that dreams have phenomenological features that distinguish them from waking experiences even though we often fail to recognize them or their

he would have to grant that even if we have determined that our current experience has (or lacks) the relevant features, this would not *entail* that we are not dreaming. However, Austin would not regard these concessions to our fallibility as blocking our ability to know or reasonably believe that we are not dreaming, since he holds in general both that our sometimes making mistakes does not preclude our ability to gain knowledge (1979, 98) and that evidence adequate for knowledge need not ensure against "outrages of nature" (1979, 88). Any fallibilist should be willing to follow him here.[11]

Two worries might nonetheless arise. First, it might be thought that if dreams have features that distinguish them from waking experiences, then we ought to recognize these features and their significance *while we are dreaming*. However, as Austin repeatedly stresses, the fact that under certain conditions we confuse two things does not show that we cannot distinguish them under *other* conditions (1962, 51). The trouble with dreaming is that while one is dreaming, one is (normally, often) not in a position to appreciate the relevant features. (It is worth noting that with training some people appear to be able to learn to appreciate them, at least on occasion. A key step in learning to "lucid dream" is learning to consider—while dreaming—whether one's state has certain phenomenological features that mark it as a dream.)

Second, it might be thought that the fact that we regularly get it wrong *when we are dreaming* raises a problem regarding our ability to tell that we are not dreaming *when we are awake*. However, this is not so. The following situation is perfectly familiar: there are two states, A (the good state) and B (the bad state); when one is in B, one is unavoidably convinced (incorrectly) that one is in A, but when one is in A, one can tell that one is in A, not in B.[12] For example, someone who is drunk may slur his speech and yet be entirely convinced (incorrigibly so) that he is not doing so. Still, someone who is not drunk and not slurring his words can tell, on the basis of how his speech sounds, that he is not doing so. In the bad state he fails to correctly register and appreciate the features that indicate that he is in the bad state, while in the

---

significance while we are dreaming. (I am grateful to Fred Schmitt for highlighting the importance of this issue for the Austinian position.)

[11] In Leite (2004a) I offer an Austin-inspired defense of a fallibilist view that I take to be similar to Austin's.

[12] This general point has been stressed by Williamson (2000). Bernard Williams (1978) highlighted the point with regard to dreaming in particular. I discuss the whole issue at length in Chapter 7.

good state he correctly registers and appreciates the presence of the features that indicate that he is in the good state and not in the bad one.[13]

Given these points, what evidence might we have—when we are awake and in full possession of our faculties—that we are not dreaming? Various phenomenological considerations will be relevant. But a striking consideration is brought out by Austin's comment that dreaming "is like being told a story: one cannot ask for completeness" (1958, 8): we cannot expect to be able to press deeply at a variety of points for further narrative details; dreams do not include anything like a reasonably full "backstory," an account of our recent and more distant history that enables us to make sense—in the way we generally can in waking life— of where we are, why we are there, how we got there, what we are doing, and how all that relates to our more distant past and ongoing activities.

This is the feature of dreams that Descartes appealed to at the end of the Sixth Meditation to explain his knowledge that he was not dreaming. Hobbes, like many readers, thought that this appeal failed. He wrote:

> My question is whether ... a man could not dream that his dream fits in with his ideas of a long series of past events. If this is possible, then what appear to the dreamer to be actions belonging to his past life could be judged to be true occurrences, just as if he were awake. (Hobbes [1641/2] 1984, 137)

Does Hobbes' objection succeed? We must distinguish two issues. Hobbes could be suggesting that one might have a dream that includes a full complement of relevant dream-generated nonveridical memories, or he could be suggesting that even without any such full complement of apparent memories, one might merely have a strong feeling, while dreaming, that one's current experience fits appropriately with one's past in a way that

---

[13] It might be objected that even when we are awake, we are not in a position to determine whether our experience has the relevant distinguishing features, because just as dreams can bring an incorrect conviction that one is awake, they can also involve incorrect convictions about what one's current subjective state is like. However, I might incorrigibly get it wrong when I am dreaming but still be able to determine that my experience has the relevant features when I am awake; this objection is a version of the objection just canvassed in the main text, and so is likewise mistaken in principle. (It is empirically dubious as well.) It is worth noting that Austin's position on this issue entails denial of Robert Nozick's (1981) "sensitivity requirement." Nozick maintained that one doesn't know that p unless the following condition is met: if p were false, one wouldn't believe that p. Austin's position requires denial of this requirement, since he holds that one can know that one is not dreaming *even though* if one were dreaming, one would still believe that one was not dreaming. (Nozick's requirement is vulnerable to pretty straightforward counterexamples [Williamson 2000; Sosa 2002; Leite 2004b]. See Chapters 5 and 7.)

renders one's present intelligible. The latter suggestion is quite plausible (I regularly have dreams of this sort), but it is irrelevant in this context, since it does not impugn one's position while one is awake. The former suggestion, by contrast, would be to the point, were there evidence in its favor. (Its mere imaginability is irrelevant in this context.) And as Austin stresses, the evidence with which we are all familiar goes the other way. Dreams never involve a full complement of apparent memories sufficient to render one's apparent current situation and activities intelligible in the way that they generally are when one is awake.[14]

Now if it is true that dreams at best involve a streamlined backstory, then one can unproblematically determine whether one is awake even if dreams can generate a wide variety of false convictions. Try to recount or call to mind a reasonably full, rich story about where you are, how you got there, what you are doing there, and the many links between features of your situation and the rest of your life. If you manage to recount or call to mind such a story, then that provides you with good grounds for concluding that you are not dreaming. Might you merely be *dreaming* that you are recounting or calling to mind such a story? No. If you are currently recounting an appropriately rich history, elaborating further details, then your current experience includes a backstory of the sort not found in dreams. Might your conviction that you are currently thinking about that history only be the product of a dream, and so be misleading? Again, no. For consider how the objection would have to go in detail. "Might I only be dreaming that I started today with a shower and breakfast, then went to the office and answered email, worked on the paper I started yesterday, taught a class, and am now listening to a song while revising yesterday's lecture notes and drinking the tea I bought last week—a song that I listened to while driving to Lake Superior thirty years ago on my honeymoon with my spouse, who used to like it and who still likes other songs I like, such as . . . [and so on]?" If you manage to consider an adequately ramified question like that then your current state involves thinking about an appropriately rich backstory, and so—the thought

---

[14] Contemporary research on the neurophysiology of dreaming, particularly on the REM-sleep functioning of brain systems associated with memory, might help explain why this would be. It is true that while awake, people sometimes (temporarily) find themselves seeming to remember doing something that they in fact only dreamed about doing. But this phenomenon doesn't support Hobbes' suggestion or suggest that dreams are at times indistinguishable from waking experiences; the phenomenon is straightforwardly explicable just given the familiar facts that (1) while dreaming we can acquire confused convictions and (2) confused convictions from whatever source can sometimes linger even when we could correct them after a moment's thought. (I am grateful here to a query from an anonymous referee for the press.)

goes—you are not dreaming. Of course, a wide range of other phenomenological considerations will be relevant here as well, as Austin stresses (see also Hobson 1999).

2. The Commitments of Our Ordinary Practice

Austin's proposal—that if we freely make use of our empirical background knowledge of what dreams are like, then we can readily determine that we are not dreaming—might give rise to a vague sense of epistemological unease. How could it be legitimate to make use of empirical background knowledge at this juncture? Isn't that knowledge placed out of play when we consider whether or not we are dreaming? Worries along some such lines can easily tempt us out of our ordinary confidence that we can tell that we are not dreaming. There is a concern emerging here that can arise from various sources. However, as I will argue in the following sections Austin can help us see that we shouldn't be too quick to leave our ordinary confidence behind.

To make this case, I will first lay out some of Austin's key points about the commitments of the ordinary position. This will occupy the remainder of Section 2. We will then return to our guiding question in Section 3.

First, a few words to orient the discussion. It is often assumed that Austin's main focus in epistemology is the use and meaning of epistemic terms such as 'knows.' This interpretation is not without some support. In "Other Minds," Austin does describe key aspects of our practice of making knowledge claims, objecting to them, and responding to those objections, and part of his aim appears to be to draw conclusions about the conditions under which a knowledge claim is true. However, it is a mistake to think that his focus is limited to such matters. His target is both broader and more fundamental. Whenever someone claims to know something, he says, they are "liable to be taken" to be claiming that they are able to prove it (1979, 85).[15] Much of his discussion consequently concerns the principles and procedures at play (when people are doing things right) when someone attempts to establish that something is true by articulating reasons to believe it and responding to objections. This will be the focus of my discussion. These commitments likewise appear when we attempt to defend a belief by providing reasons in

---

[15] Austin allows, however, that there can be cases in which someone knows that something is the case but can't prove that it is (1979, 86).

its favor, whether in response to another's queries or in solitary meditation. They play a central part when we are reasoning about what to believe.

Importantly, what Austin offers here isn't an epistemological theory. It is a reflective description of some key aspects of ordinary epistemic life from the standpoint of a committed participant.

2.1 Objections Involving Alternative Possibilities

Suppose that someone has offered or is considering a set of reasons in defense of a claim. As Austin notes, there are several points at which an objection could in principle be lodged. Objections could be raised regarding (1) the *adequacy* of the offered considerations (assuming they are true), (2) the *truth* of the offered considerations, or (3) the reasoner's *ability to determine* the adequacy or truth of the offered considerations or of the original claim.[16] In each case, the objection can take the form of a suggestion about how the world could be—a particular way in which the evidence could be inadequate, the alleged evidence false, or the person unreliable—and a request for good reasons for thinking that the world is not that way. Here, however, Austin draws a crucial distinction. He indicates it as follows:

> Enough is enough: it doesn't mean everything. Enough means enough to show that . . . it "can't" be anything else, there is no room for an alternative, competing description of it. It does *not* mean, for example, enough to show it isn't a *stuffed* goldfinch. (1979, 84)

Suppose that I have claimed that there is a goldfinch in the garden and have supported my claim by noting that the bird in question has a red head.[17] We all sense that in any ordinary situation there would be a significant difference between the objection, "But woodpeckers have red heads too. What shows it isn't a woodpecker?" and the objection, "Couldn't it just be stuffed?" The first must be taken seriously. The second is silly and shouldn't be. (For an even clearer example of the latter sort, consider the objection, "But couldn't it be an intergalactic spying device cleverly disguised to look like a goldfinch?")

---

[16] Austin's categories here are only roughly characterized. He identifies objections of the first sort in terms of cases in which one might respond, "But that doesn't prove it!" The second he calls "challenging our facts"; the third, challenging "the reliability of our alleged 'credentials'" (1979, 84, 86).

[17] Austin's familiar example involves a European goldfinch, not an American one.

Objections of the first sort are appropriately countered only by adducing specific additional evidence that things are not as the objection suggests they might be: for example, "It can't be a woodpecker, because of the gold on its wings." By contrast, objections of the second sort may be summarily dismissed, for example, by saying, "Don't be ridiculous. There's no reason to think that it is an intergalactic spying device cleverly disguised to look like a goldfinch!" In order to respond adequately to objections of this latter sort, one doesn't need to find or adduce additional specific evidence showing that things are not as the objection suggests they might be.

How should we understand this distinction? Regarding our knowledge of other minds, Austin writes,

> These special cases where doubts arise and require resolving, are contrasted with the normal cases which hold the field *unless* there is some suggestion that deceit, &c., is involved, and deceit, moreover, of an intelligible kind in the circumstances, that is, of a kind that can be looked into because motive, &c., is specially suggested. (1979, 113)

And again, regarding objections arising from human fallibility, he comments,

> Being aware that you may be mistaken doesn't mean merely being aware that you are a fallible human being: it means that you have some concrete reason to suppose that you may be mistaken in this case. Just as "but I may fail" does not mean merely "but I am a weak human being" . . . : it means that there is some concrete reason for me to suppose that I shall break my word. (1979, 98)

In both passages, Austin is concerned primarily with epistemic reasons for thinking that the suggested possibility obtains. The proposal appears to be that if one recognizes that there is no good reason in favor of a suggested possibility, then one may (and should) simply dismiss it, while if there is some adequate reason in its favor, then one may not do so. The presence or absence of relevant epistemic reasons is what is at center stage.[18]

---

[18] Our ordinary discourse in this regard involves a variety of related locutions. Austin himself uses a variety of expressions, and it is not at all apparent whether he means to distinguish them. As my preferred idiom, I will talk of there being or not being some reason in favor of a certain possibility (or in favor of the truth of a certain proposition). I will also occasionally use the word 'evidence' to do the same work. My talk of possibilities, propositions, and the like—that is, the things that can on

As the above passages make clear, on Austin's view the mere fact that a suggested possibility is compatible with one's evidence does not constitute a reason in its favor. A reason, in the relevant sense, is something that is the case and tells in favor of the suggested possibility. "It might be stuffed" or "he might be faking," by itself, is thus not a reason in the intended sense. To capture this notion, Austin talks of "specific" and "concrete" reasons. These formulations are also meant to capture an important additional distinction. That human beings are fallible and can make mistakes is not a consideration of the right sort; that one was not wearing one's glasses might well be, as might such considerations as that one frequently makes mistakes about relevantly similar matters in relevantly similar circumstances, that red-headed woodpeckers are not uncommon in the area, or that one's neighbor often puts fake birds in nearby yards. Austin does not provide a theory or principle to explain this additional distinction, and it is difficult to know how such a theory would best be elaborated. But all that's needed here is that a distinction of this sort is embedded in our practice. The suggestion that one might have made a mistake, since people do after all sometimes make mistakes, is often appropriately met with the rejoinder, "Yes, but what reason is there to think that I have made a mistake *now*?"

Austin's claim, then, is this. In a given context the possibilities that could in principle figure in objections to a given claim or argument can be divided into those that have no good epistemic reason in their favor and those that have some good reason in their favor, where a good reason is something that tells in favor of the possibility's obtaining and is appropriately specific and concrete. (There may be borderline or unclear cases, but nothing in this argument turns on that issue.) If there is sufficient good reason in favor of the suggested possibility, then to respond adequately one must obtain or provide additional reasons that defeat the reason(s) in question. If one recognizes there is no reason in favor of the suggested possibility, however, then of course one needn't find defeating reasons, since there is no reason to defeat; the possibility hasn't even made it onto the field, as it were. In the latter case one is already in a position to reject the suggested possibility if one recognizes that there are no reasons in its favor, and explicitly or implicitly indicating this recognition will constitute an adequate response. It is this latter sort of rejection that I have in mind when I talk of "summarily dismissing" a suggested

---

occasion have reasons in their favor—is similarly idiomatic rather than technical. Nothing more is needed in this context.

possibility and of "rejecting it out of hand." The difference in required response reflects at bottom a difference in the sort of reasons one must possess, a difference that arises from a difference in the reasons that bear on the issue.

Austin is thus offering us a characterization of a key commitment of our epistemic practice. The evidence necessary to substantiate the claim that there is a goldfinch in the garden must be sufficient to eliminate any "alternative, competing" possibility—that is, any alternative that has some adequate reason in its favor. What this requires is evidence defeating the reasons in favor of those competing possibilities. Such evidence—even in conjunction with positive evidence that it is a goldfinch—may not be enough to show (in one familiar sense of this word) that the bird isn't stuffed. But that doesn't matter. Since there is no reason in its favor, that latter possibility isn't on the table to begin with. That is why "enough is enough."[19]

It should be emphasized that Austin is not claiming that we may summarily dismiss an objection if we simply happen to lack any information in its favor. "Enough is enough," but you have to have something: ignorance is not so easily transmuted into epistemic strength. That is, the proposal is that *if your background information enables you to recognize that there is in fact nothing in a suggested possibility's favor*, then you may summarily dismiss it even if you lack additional specific evidence against it. Background ignorance would instead leave you unable to reach a reasonable conclusion about whether or not the suggested possibility may be thus dismissed.

It is hard to see how we could be in a position to treat a possibility in this way without also possessing background information that tells against the possibility's obtaining and in favor of some other. This background information may well fall short of what would be required to show (in one familiar sense of that word) that the possibility does not obtain. For instance, the facts that no one would have any interest in deceiving me by putting a stuffed facsimile in my back yard, that nothing like that has happened around here before, and that nothing was on the branch five minutes ago all help underwrite my judgment that there is no reason in favor of the suggestion that the

---

[19] What of Austin's phrase 'within reason and for present intents and purposes' in the sentence "Enough means enough to show that (*within reason and for present intents and purposes*) it 'can't be anything else'" (italics added)? I read this phrase as calling attention to the importance of the actual circumstances in which the particular course of reasoning is placed. Austin is here emphasizing that what will count as adequate grounds for the purpose of *this* course of reasoning—given the reasons that bear on the issue here and now—may not count as adequate grounds elsewhere. That was a view which he clearly held, and he could have held it even without thinking that practical considerations played any significant role in this regard.

seeming goldfinch is stuffed. But they hardly suffice to *show* that this possibility doesn't obtain. (Seeing the bird fly away would do so, as would cutting it open to reveal the usual mess.) However, knowing that something isn't the case needn't require an ability to show that it isn't. So I don't see anything to prevent Austin from holding that someone in such a position could thereby know that the bird isn't stuffed. (For more on this point, see Leite 2022).

2.2 Reliability Objections and Epistemic Priority

Before we return to our guiding question about our ability to tell that we aren't dreaming, it will be helpful if we look at a second key aspect of our ordinary epistemic practice. This concerns what might be termed "epistemic priority".

In any particular course of reasoning or argumentation certain considerations may be relied upon as premises or inference principles, and others may not. Some may not be so used until others have been established. For instance, suppose that (1) the fact that I am on the graduate faculty of my university is a good indication that I am entitled to serve on doctoral committees, and (2) the fact that I am entitled to serve on doctoral committees is a good indication that I am on the graduate faculty. If you know both these evidential relationships hold, it doesn't follow that you could equally well appeal to either fact to support the other. If you possess some reason to doubt that I am entitled to serve on doctoral committees, then (all else equal) it would be objectionable for you to reason from the claim that I am entitled to serve on doctoral committees to the conclusion that I am on the graduate faculty of my university. If it is certain that I am on the graduate faculty of my university, then you might be able to appeal to this fact to defeat that reason for doubt, arguing from this basis to the conclusion that I am entitled to serve on doctoral committees. But there may also be cases in which the reason for doubt precludes you from making use of *either* consideration in defense of the other: you would first have to defeat the reason for doubt by making use of some other considerations. To put the point generally, how you may acceptably reason or argue will depend upon the reasons that bear on the case.

Austin was aware of this point. Call the relations involved here *epistemic priority* relations, and the requirements and constraints on reasoning and argumentation that involve such relations *priority requirements* and *priority constraints*. Austin adamantly insisted that the epistemic priority relations and requirements that structure acceptable reasoning or argumentation in particular cases do not reflect a context- or circumstance-independent justificatory order amongst the relevant propositions.

[I]n general, *any* kind of statement could state evidence for any other kind, if the circumstances were appropriate. (1962, 116; cf. 111, 140)

[T]here *could* be no *general* answer to the questions what is evidence for what, what is certain, what is doubtful, what needs or does not need evidence, can or can't be verified [because these matters all depend on "the circumstances"]. (1962, 124)

Austin thus held that there are *no substantive circumstance-independent priority requirements*—no requirements stating such things as that in order to reasonably believe anything in a certain class, one must have independent reasons in support of some particular proposition *p* (or in support of some proposition(s) in some other specified class). He thus opposes epistemological views that hold that all of one's beliefs about the world must, as a group, rest upon an evidential basis of some other kind.

In these passages Austin doesn't specify what he means by "the circumstances," and his examples in *Sense and Sensibilia* do not clarify the issue. However, the passages earlier discussed from "Other Minds" indicate that by "the circumstances" Austin meant at least in part the reasons to which the particular course of reasoning or argumentation should be responsive. On Austin's view, then, epistemic priority requirements are always determined at least in part by the reasons that bear on the case on the particular occasion.

It bears repeating what sort of claim Austin is making here. His claim is intended as a general description of a key aspect of our best epistemic practice—of what commitments show up when we understand ourselves to be doing it right. The only way to test such a claim is by considering what we think it right to say and do when we are standing in the pre-philosophical position. I will offer some support for Austin's claim in later chapters. For now, however, I only want to elaborate some of its consequences.

One important type of priority requirement arises from considerations that challenge what Austin calls "the reliability of our alleged 'credentials'" (1979, 86), that is, considerations that challenge our possession of relevant authority, competence, or reliability (either in general or on a particular occasion). Suppose, for instance, that some consideration strongly suggests that I took a thoroughly inappropriate approach to solving a mathematical problem. In that case, I should not be fully convinced of my answer's truth until I have somehow defeated this reason, perhaps by asking an expert whether I proceeded properly. Under these circumstances, a priority requirement is in place: I am not entitled to bluntly declare my answer correct or to make use of it as a premise in further reasoning (aside from conditional or suppositional reasoning) unless and until I have identified or acquired independent grounds that defeat the evidence that I proceeded inappropriately.

Similar requirements can be imposed regarding entire domains of belief. Suppose that I have believed a certain person regarding a great many things. I now discover good evidence that this person is an inveterate liar with a desire to mislead me as much as possible. Under these circumstances I cannot reasonably believe on the basis of this person's say-so any of the things this person tells me unless and until I possess reasons that defeat the evidence that this person is lying to me. Such reasons cannot be provided by things that I believe only on the person's say-so, even if (as it happens) those things are in fact true and their truth decisively indicates that the person wasn't lying. A priority requirement is thus in place here regarding the entire class of things that I have believed on this person's say-so.

Can we generalize from this example to all possible cases? That is, are we committed to a principle something like the following?

General Reliability-Related Priority Requirement: In all possible cases, if p is a possibility that would undermine one's authority, competence, or reliability regarding a certain domain of beliefs—or if one recognizes that p is such a possibility—then one cannot reasonably believe anything in that domain unless one has adequate independent grounds for believing that p is not the case, where an independent ground is a ground not itself in that domain.

Austin would have said not. He denied that we are committed to substantive circumstance-independent priority requirements: "[I]n general, any kind of statement could state evidence for any other kind, if the circumstances were appropriate" (1962, 116; cf. 111, 140). He consequently would have held that any principle along these lines will fail to hold in some possible circumstances. In particular, there will be some possible circumstances in which (a) one does not need independent grounds against the possibility in order to reasonably believe things in the domain and (b) one can properly offer considerations in the domain as evidence against the possibility.

Which circumstances? The example we just considered had a crucial distinctive feature: it was an example in which one recognizes some good reason in favor of the possibility that would undermine one's authority, competence, or reliability in the relevant domain. So, Austin would likely say that the cases in which such a requirement doesn't hold will be some subset of those in which one does not recognize any reason in favor of the possibility in question. Of such cases, one's position will be strongest if there is not only no such reason, but one recognizes as much. So, if there are any cases in which such a priority requirement doesn't hold, it seems they should include at least some of these. And even if there are other conditions that must be met in these cases, it must be possible—on Austin's view—for those other conditions to be met, so that there are some possible cases in which the general reliability-related priority requirement does not hold.

That is to say, Austin suggests the following. Consider a proposition p and a set of propositions ß that are related as follows in one's actual circumstances:

1. If one recognized some adequately strong reason in favor of the truth of p, then one would possess grounds for a legitimate challenge to one's authority, competence, or reliability regarding propositions in ß, and
2. The truth of certain propositions in ß decisively indicates the falsity of p.

On Austin's view, the priority relations and requirements that apply when p and ß are related in this way will depend upon the actual circumstances—in particular, upon the relevant reasons. If one believes the relevant propositions in ß in a way that would be undercut if one recognizes some adequately strong reason in favor of the truth of p, and if one does recognize such a reason, then one cannot treat any considerations in ß as evidence for anything else unless one has some independent reasons that defeat one's evidence for p—reasons that are not provided by any considerations in ß. By contrast, however, if one recognizes that there is no reason in favor of p's being the case, then—assuming all other relevant requirements are met—one can perfectly well ineliminably rely upon considerations in ß in the course of dismissing the suggestion that p is the case.[20]

Notice that Austin's proposal only concerns priority relations. For this reason, it is perfectly compatible with the further claim that mature adults can't reasonably believe things in the domain unless they also reasonably

---

[20] A similar suggestion has been made more recently by Bergmann (2006, 199–200), though in the key of epistemological theory rather than description of our best practice.

believe—for any particular scenario that they recognize would render their beliefs unreliable in that domain—that it does not obtain. For instance, Austin's proposal is perfectly compatible with also granting that mature adults can't reasonably believe things about the world around them unless they also reasonably believe that they aren't dreaming. An objector might worry that if one's ability to recognize that there are no reasons in favor of the relevant possibility also depends upon having reasonable beliefs in the relevant domain, then objectionable circularity must be involved here. But this is not so. At most what would be involved is mutual dependence: one's possession of reasonable beliefs in the relevant domain would require recognizing that there is no reason in favor of the relevant possibility, and one's ability to recognize that there is no reason in favor of the possibility would require reasonably believing other things in the domain. This sort of mutual epistemic dependence is not inherently problematic. Admittedly, insuperable problems would be generated if one or both of the dependence relations necessarily involved a priority relation. But Austin's claim that there are no substantive circumstance-independent epistemic priority relations would lead him to deny that such priority requirements must always be involved. So on his view, there should be no insuperable difficulties along these lines.

Austin's key claim, then, is this:

Austin's Claim: In certain circumstances one can properly appeal to considerations within a domain to dismiss a way in which one might be unreliable about that domain, even if one lacks relevant independent reasons on the issue.

This claim is not a principle of epistemological theory grounded by abstract philosophical argumentation. It is intended as a summary characterization of what we are committed to in our ordinary epistemic practices. A key question, then, is this: what are our actual commitments regarding particular examples? For now, let us grant Austin's Claim for the sake of argument and see where it takes us. In later chapters I will consider whether the commitments of our ordinary, pre-philosophical position really do support Austin on this issue.

Our present concern is what happens when we apply Austin's Claim to the issue of dreams and skepticism. And the crucial upshot of the foregoing discussion is as follows: Coming to believe something as a result of a dream is not a reliable way of forming beliefs, since most of the beliefs that arise during dreams are false. So, on the one hand, if one recognizes some sufficient reason in favor of the possibility that one is dreaming, this will ground a reliability-based objection to a wide class of beliefs: one will not be able to acceptably utilize any beliefs in that class to provide evidence that one is not dreaming, and without adequate independent reasons for thinking that one is not dreaming, one would not be entitled to rely upon any of those beliefs for the purposes of any further reasoning. On the other hand, however, if one recognizes that nothing tells in favor of the possibility that one is dreaming, then on Austin's view one may dismiss that possibility out of hand—even if one could not be in a position to do so without relying upon empirical background beliefs.

3. Am I Dreaming?

3.1 Reducing the Worry to Rubble

Our guiding question is whether there is anything objectionable about Austin's appeal to empirical considerations to buttress the claim that we can tell that we are awake, not dreaming. We've seen that if Austin's description of the commitments of our ordinary practice is correct, then a key preliminary question is whether there is any reason to think we might just be dreaming. So let's begin with that.

Is there any good reason in favor of this possibility in the ordinary sort of circumstances? I'm inclined to think not. For the sake of argument, however, let's assume the worst and suppose the answer is "Yes." After all, the following line of thought has some plausibility:

> People (including me) sometimes have dreams which seem very much like waking experiences. While dreaming they are often convinced that they are awake, not dreaming. Right now I am in a state very much like a waking experience and am convinced that I am awake, not dreaming. Given these considerations, my situation regarding the question of whether I am dreaming is analogous to that of a birdwatcher whose neighbor is an ornithological taxidermist with a known penchant for practical jokes. Just as this birdwatcher has some reason in support of the possibility that the thing he observes on the branch might merely be stuffed, I have some reason in favor of the possibility that I am dreaming right now. It's not a very strong reason, not the sort I would have if I seemed to myself to have awakened in

the middle of the night in an extremely unusual, strange, and unexpected situation. But it is some reason nonetheless. Hence, for creatures like us, in the world as it currently is, there is always some pro tanto reason in favor of the possibility that one is asleep and dreaming.

The goal of this section is to show that even if this argument succeeds, Austin's explanation of how we can tell we're not dreaming would still work. To anticipate the key idea: we can't even specify what it is that we have reason to suspect might be the case—what, that is, the dreaming possibility really comes to—unless we make use of background empirical information about what dreams are like. For this reason, that same empirical information is likewise available when it comes to explaining why, all things considered, we have overwhelming reason to believe that we are awake, not dreaming.

This point arises from the consistent application of the commitments and procedures of our ordinary epistemic practice at its best. As Austin notes, the charge that someone's evidence is inadequate must be supported by some specification of the possibility that the evidence putatively fails to rule out.

> If you say "That's not enough," then you must have in mind some more or less definite lack. . . . If there is no definite lack, which you are at least prepared to specify on being pressed, then it's silly (outrageous) just to go on saying "That's not enough." (1979, 84)

However, not just any specification will do.

> The doubt or question "But is it a *real* one?" has always (*must* have) a special basis, there must be some "reason for suggesting" that it isn't real, in the sense of some specific way, or limited number of ways, in which it is suggested that this experience or item may be phony. Sometimes (usually) the context makes it clear what the suggestion is. . . . If the context doesn't make it clear, then I am entitled to ask "How do you mean? Do you mean it may be stuffed or what? *What are you suggesting*?" (1979, 87)

That is, when it is unclear what is being offered as an objection, you can quite appropriately respond by requesting a further specification. This is because different ways of elaborating the objection may call for very different forms of response. Does it suffice to note that there is no reason in the objection's favor? Are you instead required to offer specific evidence to defeat some reason that supports the objection? In the latter case, what defeating considerations are relevant? Everything depends on what exactly is being suggested. If your background information makes it appropriate to handle various elaborations of the objection differently, then further clarification or specification of the suggestion is legitimately demanded.

Apply these points to the issue at hand. If we consider the possibility that we are dreaming, what exactly are we suspecting might be going on? Austin would begin by distinguishing subcases in a way that is appropriately sensitive to his background information: "On the one hand, the suggestion may be that I am in a state occurring during sleep that involves lifelike phenomenological states, generates mostly false beliefs including an incorrect conviction that I am awake and perceiving the world, and *is phenomenologically indistinguishable from paradigmatic waking experiences*. On the other hand, the suggestion may be that I am in a state occurring during sleep that involves lifelike phenomenological states, generates mostly false beliefs including an incorrect conviction that I am awake and perceiving the world, and *differs phenomenologically from normal waking states in certain specified respects*."

Austin would then ask whether either of these possibilities has some good reason in its favor. Given his background information, he would conclude that there is no reason whatsoever in favor of the first possibility: dreams differ from waking experiences in certain phenomenological respects, and so there is no reason whatsoever to suspect that he is having a dream that is phenomenologically indistinguishable from paradigmatic waking experience. Austin would accordingly dismiss the first sub-possibility out of hand, and quite reasonably so, since, as he recognizes, there is no reason whatsoever for thinking it obtains and a great deal of reason to think it doesn't. Here, Austin would be proceeding entirely in accord with the lessons of Section 2 above.

Turning now to the second sub-possibility, we've granted that there is some reason to suspect that this might be the case. It is arguable that a priority requirement is consequently in place here; Austin cannot acceptably rely upon certain considerations in order to defeat the reasons in favor of this possibility. Notice, however, that this process of distinguishing subcases in response to background information has the consequence that empirical information is contained in the very specification of the subcase itself: it is characterized as one which phenomenologically differs in certain specified respects from paradigmatic waking experiences. This needn't be understood as a semantic matter. There is no need to claim here that 'dreaming' *means* a state that differs from paradigmatic waking experience in certain respects. The point is just that this background information has been relied upon to specify *what it is that has some reason in its favor*. As a consequence, this information is freely available to Austin in his reasoning. He can therefore reason as follows. "I have some reason to suspect that I am in a state that phenomenologically differs from normal waking experiences in certain specified respects. Can I nonetheless tell that I am not currently in such a state? Yes. My current experience has/lacks the relevant features."

In essence, what we have here is a point about relations amongst reasons. If Austin is attempting to establish that he is not dreaming, he should begin by adducing the total relevant evidence:

A. Fact: People are not infrequently in a state that:
   (i) is lifelike.
   (ii) involves a conviction that one is awake and perceiving the world.
   (iii) takes place during sleep.
   (iv) leads to many incorrect convictions about how things are in the world, including an incorrect conviction that one is awake and perceiving the world.
B. Fact: This state has phenomenological features that differ in certain specified ways from the phenomenological features characterizing standard cases of waking experience.
C. Fact: People are never in a state involving (i)–(iv) that is phenomenologically indistinguishable from standard cases of waking experience. That's not how we work.
D. Fact: I am now in a lifelike phenomenological state, convinced that I am awake and perceiving the world.

From this evidence he can appropriately reason as follows:

The Austinian Empirical Argument
1. There is no reason in favor of the possibility that I am in a non-waking state that is phenomenologically identical to standard waking experience. (from C)
2. There is some reason in favor of the possibility that I am now in a state that has features (i)–(iv) above and differs phenomenologically from standard waking experience in certain specified respects. (from A, B, D)

3. So, given this evidence so far, I might be in a state having features (i)–(iv) and differing phenomenologically from standard waking experience in the specified respects.
4. However, my current state does not differ from standard waking experience in the specified respects; it lacks the special features that characterize the state in question. (independent premise, drawn from consideration of his current state)
5. So, I am not in that state: I am not in a state that has features (i)–(iv) and differs phenomenologically from standard waking experience in the relevant respects.
6. So, since both suggestions have been defeated, I conclude that I am not dreaming now.

He thus reaches the advertised conclusion: he rejects the suggestion that he might be dreaming, and he relies upon empirical considerations to do so.

In sum, if Austin correctly captures how to proceed in inquiry and aptly characterizes the empirical facts, then he is right: we can tell that we aren't dreaming. And this remains so even if we grant that because people are sometimes convinced by dreams that they are awake, there is some pro tanto reason in favor of the suggestion that we are dreaming now.

3.2 Objections and Replies: Sorting through the Rubble

You might be satisfied with what has been said so far. If so, you may want to skip to the discussion of external world skepticism in section 4 below. If, however, you still remain unconvinced of the acceptability of the Austinian Empirical Argument, here are some objections and replies.

Objection 1. "The Austinian Empirical Argument, starting with Step 2, depends upon claim (B) above—that is, upon the claim that the relevant state differs from standard waking experience in certain specified respects. However, that claim is no longer available once you recognize the reason in favor of the possibility that you are in a state that has features (i)–(iv) above."

Response: If that claim is unavailable at that stage in the reasoning, it will have to be because the evidence that I have calls it into doubt by providing some reason against it. That's why, for instance, the claim that I am standing giving a lecture wouldn't be available to me at this juncture: since I have some reason in favor of the possibility that I am in the described misleading state, if am convinced that I am standing giving a lecture then there is some reason to suspect that I am *not* standing giving a lecture. But my evidence, (A)–(D) above, doesn't support the suggestion that the relevant state—the one that there is some reason to suspect that I am in—is phenomenologically indistinguishable from standard waking experience. It provides reason in favor of the possibility that I am in a state that *does* differ phenomenologically in certain respects from standard waking experience. And so I can determine that I am not in that state by checking whether my current experience has the relevant features.

Objection 2: "Considerations (A) and (D), taken by themselves, provide some reason in favor of the possibility that you are in a misleading non-waking state *without* specifying it as a state that differs phenomenologically from standard waking experience, and so they preclude you from relying on the fact that the state in question differs phenomenologically from standard waking experience."

Response: The objector is simply ignoring some of the relevant facts. To determine what actually has some reason in its favor, you have to look at all of the relevant evidence. The total evidence is such that there is some pro tanto reason in favor of the possibility that one is in a state having features (i)–(iv) and differing in certain phenomenological respects from standard waking experience; moreover, the total evidence is such that this reason is defeated. That is what we see when we insist on taking all of the relevant evidence into account. Of course, if you deprive yourself of certain background information at the outset, then this response will be unavailable. But we've been given no reason to do that.

Objection 3: "While these rejoinders are conversationally or dialectically appropriate, an underlying epistemological problem still arises from the structure of the relevant epistemic priority requirements. In particular, if we take all of the relevant reasons into account, and even if we grant that what they support is only the possibility that one is in a state that differs phenomenologically from standard waking experiences, still the resulting epistemic priority requirement will preclude Austin from relying on the empirical claim that the states in question differ phenomenologically."

Response: A priority requirement tracks rational relations amongst propositions in the circumstances. In the present case, what it captures is the fact that a good, sufficiently strong reason in favor of the suggestion that one is in a certain sort of misleading state also provides a good reason to doubt each of a wide range of one's convictions. It does this by providing good reason to suspect that the conviction is false or that one is not reliable regarding it. That is why each of these considerations is placed "out of bounds" by the priority requirement. The crucial question, then, is what the relevant reasons in the circumstances provide reason for or against.

Use "Φ" as a label for the type of state that there is some reason to suspect one is in. And grant, as this objection does, that the relevant considerations only provide reason for suspecting that one might be in a misleading state of a type that differs phenomenologically in certain specified respects from standard waking experiences. Now consider this proposition: *States of type Φ differ phenomenologically from standard waking experiences in the specified ways*. Suppose that you believe this proposition. Conjoin the fact (a) that you believe this proposition, with the fact (b) that there is some reason in favor of the possibility that you are in a state of type Φ, a state that involves features (i)–(iv) and differs phenomenologically in the specified ways. Do these two considerations (a) and (b), taken together, constitute any reason in favor of the possibility that it is *not* the case that states of type Φ differ phenomenologically from standard waking experiences in the specified ways? Do they give you any reason to doubt that states of type Φ differ phenomenologically from standard waking experience in the relevant ways? Obviously not. If what has reason in its favor were in fact the case, it would be true that states of type Φ differ phenomenologically from standard waking experiences in the specified respects, and you would be perfectly reliable about this. So the reasons in favor of the possibility that one is in a state of type Φ do not provide reason against the claim that states of type Φ phenomenologically differ in the specified respects from standard waking states. They do not provide such reason even when conjoined with the fact that one believes that states of type Φ and standard waking experiences so differ.

Given this consideration, we must reject the overhasty assumption that the priority requirement generated in these circumstances will place Austin's claim about the phenomenological features of dreams out of bounds. Properly formulated, the relevant priority requirement runs as follows, letting "ß" be the name for the set of propositions that have been called into doubt by the fact that there is some pro tanto reason in favor of the possibility that one is in a state of a type that involves features (i)–(iv) and differs phenomenologically in certain specified respects from standard waking experiences:

In order to warrantedly believe any of the propositions in ß, one must have independent evidence (not consisting of considerations in ß) adequate to defeat the reasons in favor of the possibility that one is in a state of a type characterized by features (i)–(iv) and differing phenomenologically in the specified respects from standard waking experience.

This requirement precludes most considerations about the world from constituting the needed defeating reasons, but it allows phenomenological considerations of the sort Austin appeals to. It does not preclude relying on the empirical fact that the state in question differs phenomenologically from standard waking experiences, because that fact is not in class ß (as defined above). And for this reason, it would be a mistake to think that by placing most of one's beliefs about the world out of play, the reasons for doubt would also remove the claim that dreams differ in certain respects from waking experiences. What there is reason to doubt—and so what is taken out of play—are the claims about which one would be unreliable if the possibility that has some reason in its favor were actual. Those do not include the claim about dreams. That's what the priority requirement, properly formulated, reflects.

Objection 4: "Whenever there is some reason in favor of a possibility characterized as Φ, there will also be some reason in favor of a possibility characterized using a less precise specification, Φ-, that is entailed by Φ. So, consider this specification of the possibility that you are dreaming: 'You are in a state occurring during sleep that involves very lifelike phenomenology and generates mostly false beliefs about the world as well as an incorrect conviction that you are awake and perceiving the world.' This specification simply leaves out any information about whether the state differs phenomenologically from normal waking states. However, the reasons in favor of the more precisely specified possibility distinguished above are also reasons in favor of the suggestion that you are in this less finely specified state. So even when we include all of the relevant evidence in our description of the circumstances, there is still some reason to suspect that you are in a misleading non-waking state not specified as one that differs phenomenologically from standard waking experience. This would seem to mean that there is also a priority requirement in place regarding this possibility, so specified, and it would seem that this priority requirement precludes us from relying upon the background empirical information about dreams that licenses treating phenomenological considerations as adequate evidence that we are not dreaming. It consequently still appears that Austin's argument fails."

Response: This is not so, as we can see when we take seriously the way in which priority requirements are related to the underlying relations amongst reasons. We are supposing that there is some pro tanto reason to suspect that one is in a misleading non-waking state that differs in certain specified phenomenological respects from standard waking states. There is no reason at all to suspect that one is in a misleading non-waking state that is phenomenologically indistinguishable from standard waking states. In these circumstances, there is reason to suspect that one is in a misleading non-waking state (where the specification simply says nothing at all about whether the state in question differs phenomenologically from standard waking states). But there is reason to suspect this only in virtue of there being reason to suspect that one is in a misleading non-waking state that differs phenomenologically from standard waking states. Consequently, nothing more is needed to defeat the former than is needed to defeat the latter; a more demanding priority requirement is not created.

To sum up the discussion so far: The dialectical moves that I have suggested on Austin's behalf amount to a demand that the objections and priority demands be formulated in a way that correctly reflects the actual reasons and priority relations that obtain in the circumstances. We began with the charge that if in ordinary circumstances there is pro tanto reason in favor of the possibility that we are dreaming, then the resulting priority requirement precludes Austin's empirical claim that dreams differ from waking experiences. We saw that Austin can avoid this charge by making obviously acceptable dialectical moves, namely, by demanding appropriately precise specifications of the suggested possibilities and insisting on taking appropriate account of all of the relevant evidence. We can now see that the appropriateness of these responses reflects the underlying facts regarding what has reasons in its favor, what doesn't, and what evidential relations obtain in the circumstances.

Still, despite these points it might be worried that Austin's response involves some form of objectionable circular reasoning.

Objection 5: "Once you're in doubt about whether you are dreaming, you won't be able to tell whether you are not dreaming unless you already believe that you aren't. So you are assuming the very thing that has been put into doubt."

Response: That is not so. At the stage in the deliberation at which we recognize that there is some pro tanto reason in favor of the possibility that we are dreaming, we can suspend our initial confidence that we are not dreaming—where that amounts to suspending our initial confidence that we are not in a lifelike, misleading state that differs from waking experience in certain specified respects. Even so, we will still be able to make use of the claim that dreams differ in certain phenomenological respects from waking experiences, for the reasons described above.

Objection 6: "But how could Austin respond to the suggestion that he might just be dreaming that dreams phenomenologically differ in certain specified respects from waking experiences?"

Response: "I'm not just dreaming that dreams differ phenomenologically in those ways from waking experiences, because I am not dreaming right now; my current experience is nothing like a dream." That's the right response, on Austin's view, because (a) it does not appeal to any of the considerations that would be placed out of bounds by relevant reasons for doubt, (b) it appeals to something that *is* good evidence that one is not dreaming, and (c) even if there is always some reason in favor of the possibility that one is dreaming, there is no reason in favor of the possibility that one is wrong in thinking that dreams and standard waking experiences differ in those ways.

Objection 7: "This last response is objectionably question-begging because it assumes that dreams and waking experiences differ in certain respects."

Response: There is no ground for objection here. As we've seen, even if there is always some pro tanto reason in favor of the possibility that one is dreaming, *that reason does not call into doubt the claim that dreams and waking experiences differ in certain respects.* So we have been given no reason to doubt that dreams and waking experience differ in these respects, and we have a great deal of empirical evidence that they do.

Objection 8: "But that assumption about the differences between dreams and standard waking experience would be wrong if you were having a dream that was phenomenologically indistinguishable from normal waking experience! And it is conceptually or metaphysically possible that you could have such a dream!"

Response: But if one recognizes that there is no reason whatsoever in favor of a certain possibility and ample evidence against it, one may dismiss it out of hand—and in doing so one may rely upon considerations about which one would be unreliable if that possibility were the case. *That was the whole point of the discussion of priority requirements in Section 2.2.* Since—as the empirical evidence shows—there is no reason whatsoever in favor of the possibility that one is having a dream that is phenomenologically indistinguishable from normal waking experience, one may summarily reject that suggestion. The same goes for the suggestion that perhaps one is merely dreaming that dreams and waking experiences differ.

Those are all of the objections I can think of. Is there something I've failed to take into account?

4. The Dream Argument for External World Skepticism: Demolishing the Doctrine

The global skeptical arguments that are my focus deploy hypotheses to the effect that one might just be dreaming, a brain in a vat, or the victim of a deceptive evil demon. They maintain that we cannot know or have good reason to believe that such conditions do not obtain, and that because this is so, we cannot know or have good reason to believe anything about the world. Such arguments have a long pedigree, but if the framework developed so far is correct, then Austin showed us how to counter them.

To have any hope of succeeding, a global skeptical argument must accomplish at least the following two things:

(1) It must establish an epistemological dependence: it must make it plausible that one can't have knowledge or good reasons for beliefs in the target class unless one possesses adequate evidence that one is not in a certain hypothesized state (dreaming, being deceived by an evil demon, etc.).

(2) It must preclude one from deploying considerations in the target class as evidence that one is not in the hypothesized state. That is, it must require independent grounds for thinking that one is not in that state.

Requirement (2) is crucial. For all requirement (1) says all by itself, it could be satisfied by knowledge in the target class. It leaves open that one could (with G.E. Moore) reply to arguments for external world skepticism by pointing out that one is standing giving a lecture (and so not dreaming), and similarly by highlighting that there are no deceptive evil demons and that technology does not currently exist to create brains in vats. The argument for external world skepticism must preclude us from appealing to empirical considerations about the world in this way. This is what requirement (2) would accomplish. A key question, then, that any compelling skeptical argument must answer is this: why can't we deploy empirical considerations about the world to dismiss the suggested possibility?

It might be thought that appealing to empirical considerations about the world in this way would simply beg the question, since the sceptic claims that one doesn't know or reasonably believe anything about the world. However, this account of the situation badly underestimates the challenge facing skeptical arguments. As Moore insisted, we confront skeptical arguments from an initial position in which we take ourselves to know and have excellent reasons for all sorts of claims about the world and so regard ourselves as free to make use of these claims for the purposes of reasoning and inquiry. The skeptical argument must somehow convince us, from that starting point, that we can't actually know or reasonably believe anything about the world. Starting where we do in confronting the argument, we quite reasonably take ourselves to be entitled to make use of empirical considerations about the world. Somehow, the early stages of the argument must *bring us to see* that we can't do that. The crucial question for any skeptical argument, then, is how this is to be accomplished.

In one of the most thoughtful and sensitive depictions of skepticism available, Barry Stroud offers an argument for external world skepticism that aims to respond to this concern (1984, chapter 1). His argument is built around the commonsensical claim that "knowing that one is not dreaming is a condition of knowing something [anything] about the world around us" (1984, 19, *passim*), or as he also puts it, that "we must know we are not dreaming if we are to know anything about the world around us" (1984, 30). Stroud argues that once we accept this requirement, we are forced to conclude that we cannot know that we are not dreaming: the requirement precludes its own satisfaction (1984, 19–23). His reasoning seems to be as follows: The requirement applies to *every* piece of knowledge "that goes beyond one's sensory experience" (1984, 22). Since the qualitative features of one's current experience are neutral on the issue (any qualitative feature of waking experience can equally well be dreamed [1984, 18]), any evidence that one is not dreaming will itself have to "go beyond one's sensory experience" to involve claims about the world around us. Likewise, the very claim that one is not dreaming is something that "goes beyond one's sensory experience." The requirement accordingly applies to one's knowledge of all these things as well. Consequently, Stroud concludes, one cannot satisfy the requirement. In order to know the things that enable one to know that one is not dreaming, one will have to know that one is not dreaming. And so, as a condition of knowing that one is not dreaming, one will have to know that one is not dreaming. But this is impossible (1984, 22–23).

Taken literally, this argument fails. Stroud's requirement, as he formulates it, only says that knowing that we aren't dreaming is a necessary condition of knowing things about the world (things that "go beyond one's sensory experience"). If we apply that condition to one's knowledge that one is not dreaming, we get this:

> A necessary condition of knowing that you are not dreaming is that you know that you are not dreaming.

This is a trivial logical truth with no skeptical upshot. More generally, Stroud's requirement—when taken literally—yields at most that if you know anything about the world around you, you must also know that you are not dreaming. But that requirement doesn't have the consequence that you cannot know that you are not dreaming, since it leaves open the possibility that the dependence relations run both ways and that things you know about the world come into the story of how you know you aren't dreaming.

What Stroud's argument needs is a requirement stating a *precondition* or a priority relation, a relation of asymmetric epistemic dependence. For readers who find formal specifications helpful: the requirement will have to be formulable using an irreflexive relational predicate such that the two demands

aRb and bRa

are not co-satisfiable when a is not identical with b. In what follows I will use the phrase 'antecedently know' to formulate this logical or structural feature of the requirement. The requirement would then read as follows:

> In order to know any proposition about the world at all, you must antecedently know that you are not dreaming.

To say that you must "antecedently know" that you are not dreaming is to say that you must know this on an *independent basis*. That is, you must know this—as a condition of knowing anything about the world—in a way that does not draw upon your knowledge of the world. Only a requirement with this structure will preclude the possibility that you know that you are not dreaming by virtue of knowing things about the world.

Here, then, is an argument built around a priority version of Stroud's requirement.

1. For anything about the world that you could come to believe merely as the result of a dream (which includes everything you believe about the world), you cannot now know or reasonably believe it unless you have adequate independent reasons for believing that you are not now dreaming.
2. Anything that you can do or experience during waking life can equally well be dreamed or the product of a dream.[21] (This includes qualitative features of your experience.)
3. So anything you could plausibly appeal to as a reason to believe you are not now dreaming is something that could equally well be dreamed or the product of a dream.
4. So any consideration that you might plausibly appeal to as a reason for believing that you are not now dreaming will either be neutral on the question or will fall under Step (1) above. In the latter case, in order to know or reasonably believe it you will still need an adequate independent reason for believing that you are not now dreaming.
5. Consequently, you cannot have an adequate independent reason for believing that you are not dreaming.
6. So, you cannot now know or even reasonably believe anything that you could come to believe about the world merely as the result of a dream (which includes everything you believe about the world).

This, I think, is the most plausible version of Stroud's dream argument. But despite its plausibility, Austin would regard it as a failure. We will need to do a little bit of work to see why. The key issue is a subtle one. It has to do with the interplay between the first two premises.

On Stroud's way of understanding the argument, the first premise—the priority requirement—is something like a conceptual truth that holds independently of the actual empirical circumstances, while the second premise merely states a conceptual, metaphysical, or "logical" possibility. If we understand the argument in this way, then we treat the mere possibility of having a dream that is phenomenologically indistinguishable from waking experiences as being enough to generate a priority requirement dictating that in order to know anything about the world around you, you must know

---

[21] Stroud explicitly appeals to a premise along these lines (1984, 18, 22).

on independent grounds that you are not dreaming. Austin, however, would have none of this. Whether an epistemic priority requirement like (1) holds will depend, he will say, upon the circumstances. We won't have reason to accept the requirement unless there is some reason in favor of the suggestion that we might be in the relevant state. On the current construal of the argument, the relevant state is one that perfectly mimics waking experience. And as we have seen, Austin denies that we have any reason to suspect that we are in such a state. That's not what human dreams are like. For this reason, and because he holds that priority requirements depend on the circumstances, Austin would deny the priority requirement stated in premise (1) when it is interpreted as concerning a non-waking state that perfectly mimics the phenomenology of waking experience. He would say that we can appeal to our knowledge of the world in order to dismiss the suggestion that we might be having a dream of this sort.

There is a second way of reading the argument, but it fares no better. On this reading, premise (1) is understood as a circumstance-relative priority requirement that happens to hold for us, in our circumstances. Now as we have seen, Austin could perfectly well grant that there is a circumstance-relative priority requirement in place to the effect (more or less) that in order to know or reasonably believe things about the world, you must have adequate independent reason to believe that you are not dreaming. This is because Austin could grant that even in ordinary circumstances there is some reason in favor of the possibility that we are dreaming. But as we have also seen, the possibility with some reason in its favor is that we are in a misleading non-waking state *that differs in certain key phenomenological respects from waking experience*. This is *not* the possibility that we are in a misleading non-waking state that is phenomenologically just like a waking experience. For this reason, Austin would deny the claim that any putative reason for thinking you aren't dreaming will either be neutral on the matter or subject to requirement (1) all over again. An adequate specification of the possible state figuring in the priority requirement will involve empirical claims about what dreams are like. Given this, we can have excellent grounds for judging that we are not in that state, as we saw in Section 3. So while we should grant there is a way of interpreting premise (1) on which Austin would perhaps find it acceptable, on that understanding of the argument Steps (3) and (4) won't follow. We will still have adequate grounds for believing that we are not dreaming.

Another way to see the failure of this second construal of the argument is to focus on Step (2), the claim that anything that you can do or experience during waking life can perfectly well be dreamed. Austin would reject this premise as either irrelevant or false. He would regard it as irrelevant if it is interpreted merely as a claim about "logical," conceptual, or metaphysical possibility, since on Austin's view the mere "logical," conceptual, or metaphysical possibility of a dream that perfectly mimics waking experience is not a reason in favor of one's being in such a state and consequently does not put a priority requirement like (1) in place. For reasons we have seen, on Austin's view we can eliminate that possibility by appealing to considerations about the world (including the fact that nothing like that happens to creatures like us). Alternatively, he would regard premise (2) as false if it is treated as an empirical claim about what human dream experiences are or might very well actually like, since the empirical evidence shows that standard waking experiences differ in certain phenomenological respects from dreams.

Putting all these pieces together, we can now see the crux of the issue. If anything like Stroud's argument is to be successful by Austin's lights, it would have to be the case that:

(A) an appropriate priority relation holds because there is some reason in favor of the possibility that one is dreaming,

and

(B) dreams are or might very well sometimes be phenomenologically indistinguishable from waking experiences.

But Austin would deny this conjunction. (B)—understood as a claim about what dream experience is actually like for creatures like us—is false. So, if there *is* a priority requirement here, it will be a circumstance-dependent one generated by the fact that there is some reason to suspect that we might now be in a misleading state that differs in certain phenomenological respects from waking experience. But as we have seen at length, *that* priority requirement does not preclude us from establishing that we are not in that state. We can perfectly well appeal to phenomenological considerations to do so. That was the whole point of the discussion in Section 3 of this chapter. From Austin's point of view, then, any plausibility Stroud's skeptical argument has is nothing but sleight of hand.

In the epistemological imagination, skepticism is a circumstance-independent problem. The skeptical result is supposed to follow from the mere concepts (or essences) of knowledge or reasonable or justified belief and the mere conceptual, metaphysical, or "logical" possibility that one is in a misleading state qualitatively indistinguishable from waking experience. For skepticism to arise in this way, the concept (or perhaps essence) of knowledge (or of reasonable or justified belief) would have to generate or involve a circumstance-independent priority requirement concerning the possibility in question. For Austin, however, there are no substantive circumstance-independent priority requirements to do the trick.

On Austin's view, then, skepticism is a contingent, ineliminably empirical matter. A successful skeptical argument would have to rest upon empirical background assumptions that both give us reason to accept an appropriate priority requirement and have the consequence that we cannot satisfy it. The argument would have to appeal to a hypothesis which (a) has some reason in its favor, (b) generates a priority requirement in relation to our beliefs about the world, and (c) cannot (given that priority requirement) be determined not to be the case. As things are, no such skeptical hypothesis arises. The dream argument can be rejected in the ways I have just sketched, and Austin's view allows an even quicker rejection of arguments appealing to the possibilities that we are brains in vats or victims of a deceiving evil demon. To put it succinctly, there are no deceiving evil demons, and technology isn't sufficiently advanced at present to create brains in vats. These replies are correct, on Austin's view, because these latter skeptical hypotheses have no reason whatsoever in their favor.[22]

5. Back to Our Real Ground (and No Further)

The above approach to arguments for external world skepticism assumes that only an appropriately structured epistemic priority requirement will preclude Austin's reliance on empirical background information. However, a number of epistemologists have suggested that there is a traditional epistemological project or question that, properly understood, puts all empirical claims about the world out of bounds (McGinn 1989; M. Williams 1996; Stroud 2002; Bonjour 2003).[23] Once that is accomplished, it might be suggested, some requirement such as Stroud's requirement—now understood as a mere

---

[22] I say "at present" to emphasize that on Austin's framework we could someday find ourselves facing skeptical problems of our own making, for instance if technologies for creating nonveridical experiences through brain stimulation become sufficiently advanced while being unscrupulously deployed.

[23] There is disagreement among Stroud, McGinn, and Williams about whether the result is properly understood as somehow casting doubt upon the truth of our ordinary claims to knowledge about the external world. Bonjour is less pessimistic than the others, since he holds that the project can be completed satisfactorily.

necessary condition—could do the needed work in generating the skeptical result, because from the perspective generated by the guiding question or project, we lack any means of determining that we are not dreaming.

In the preceding chapter we considered one version of this suggestion due to Stroud, a version focused on a question of global epistemic assessment. We saw that this suggestion failed to lay the groundwork for a successful skeptical argument. Another version of this approach focuses on certain kinds of explanatory questions. Stroud is an important source for this line of thought as well. He suggests that the traditional epistemologist wants to explain how anyone knows or justifiably believes anything about the world at all. The generality of this question, he claims, precludes us from appealing to any empirical background information about the world to provide the explanation (2002, 120). Laurence Bonjour suggests that a similar result follows from the question, "What good reasons do I have for any empirical beliefs about the world?" If I seriously attempt to answer that question, Bonjour claims, then I must put all empirical background information off the table and show, from that perspective, how I have good grounds for believing anything about the world (2003).

These projects are distinct from the project of global reflective assessment discussed in the previous chapter. They don't start by asking *whether* we know or have good reason to believe anything about the world, but rather by requesting a fully general account of whatever justification we have for believing things about the world. They claim that this request has the effect of placing our commitments about the world "off the table." When we then find that no such account can be provided, they conclude that we lack good reasons or knowledge about the world after all.

On Austin's view, we have no good reason to pursue any such project, nor any good reason to draw this conclusion from it. Austin maintains that the following are all circumstance-dependent matters, determined in part by contingent, empirical facts about the world: (1) what constitutes empirical evidence or reason for what, (2) which possibilities or objections have reason in their favor and which don't, (3) what is required in order to defeat the possibilities that have some reason in their favor, and (4) what priority requirements or constraints obtain regarding a particular claim. The circumstance-dependency of these matters has the consequence that if we are precluded from relying upon any empirical claims about the world, then we simply cannot determine what we have good reason to believe about the world or explain how we know the things we know about the world: the resources necessary to identify our epistemic position relative to any particular claim about the world will have been made unavailable. This is quite a different matter from finding that we don't have any good reasons or knowledge about the world. All it shows is that when we ask a certain kind of question, we are blocked from making use of the resources we need. That's perfectly compatible with our knowing and having good reason to believe things about the world, and also with our being able to identify some of those good reasons and things that we know. And in fact, we can identify many of those good reasons and things that we know, and we can explain how we know them. All we have to do is make use of other things we know about the world. It would consequently be nothing but a mistake to conclude from this project's failure that we have no knowledge or good reasons for believing anything about the world.

So if Austin is right about the circumstance-dependence of these matters, then he can help himself to the following line of thought. He can point out:

(i) The project inevitably fails for a purely structural reason that doesn't speak to whether we actually have good reasons for beliefs about the world. Its failure results simply from the fact that we have set things up in a way that blocks us from using the information we need in order to determine whether we have good reasons for our beliefs.
(ii) So the project's failure reveals nothing about the epistemic status of any of our beliefs.
(iii) There is another perfectly good way of explaining how we know what we know or what good reasons we have for our beliefs about the world—namely, by relying on our background information about the world in the course of providing the explanation.

From this perspective, the proposed project appears to be silly. It would be like trying to determine by sight whether there is any furniture in a completely dark room and then concluding—when we find we can't do what is being asked of us—that there isn't any furniture in the room or that there is no way to tell whether there is. It would be better to turn on the lights.[24]

This perspective sheds light on Austin's overriding methodological assumption that epistemological reflection begins from where we are, with the claims to which we are currently committed. Given Austin's claim regarding

---

[24] For detailed elaboration and defense of this line of argument, see my (2005).

the circumstance-dependence of evidence and epistemic priority relations, any episode of empirical inquiry, justification, or epistemic assessment must begin with a body of empirical background beliefs in place in order for the episode to proceed at all, since without them one cannot so much as determine what is in fact a good reason for what, which objections are to be taken seriously and which aren't, and so on. Any of these background materials can come under scrutiny or under fire in the course of the episode. But the objections will have to arise and be rebutted in ways that are appropriately related to that background information. Austin's methodology in relation to skepticism is thus of a piece with his understanding of the commitments of our pre-philosophical position.

I think that if Austin's overarching framework is correct, then he has shown us how to put the dream argument to rest. One crucial question, however, is whether what I have called Austin's Claim is actually correct. According to Austin, a key part of our pretheoretical commitments is that epistemic priority requirements depend upon the circumstances. In particular:

> *Austin's Claim*: If a certain suggested possibility would undercut one's reliability regarding a certain class of beliefs, one may nonetheless ineliminably rely upon beliefs in that class in dismissing the suggestion—provided one recognizes that it has no reason in its favor.

Is Austin right about that? Is that really a commitment of our ordinary, pre-philosophical position? That is one central question going forward. And a second is this. Austin's Claim focuses on just *one* way in which it might seem unacceptable to reply to skeptical argumentation by relying upon considerations about the world; are there other plausible ways of putting the necessary limitation into effect, ways properly related to our pre-philosophical starting point? These are the crucial issues facing any attempt to follow the path charted by Moore and Austin.[25]

---

[25] I first explored several of this chapter's central lines of thought in my Harvard University PhD dissertation (2000). At the time, I understood myself to be broadly inspired by Austin, but it was not until Wallace Matson pointed out the relevant passages in the Lawrence and Hayes notes that I realized that the position I had arrived at could be drawn out of Austin's writings. This chapter derives from my Leite (2011a). I am grateful to Oxford University Press for permission to reuse and rework this material.

PART II
WHAT IS OUR EVIDENCE?

5
Reclaiming Our Evidence

1. The Fundamental Question

Moore and Austin offer responses to external world skepticism that crucially depend upon their knowledge about the world.[1] From the vantage point of our ordinary, pre-philosophical position, is there anything objectionable or unsatisfactory about proceeding in this way? Taking skepticism seriously requires that we address this question head on.

The centrality of this issue can quickly be seen by considering the skeptical argument that has come to be known as "The Argument from Ignorance."[2]

1. I can't know (reasonably or justifiably believe) anything about the world around me (e.g., that there is a piece of paper here in front of me) unless I know (reasonably or justifiably believe) that I am not being deceived by an evil demon (not dreaming, not a brain in a vat (BIV) being fed misleading inputs).
2. But I don't know (reasonably or justifiably believe) that I am not being deceived by an evil demon (not dreaming, not a BIV being fed misleading inputs).
3. So, I don't know (reasonably or justifiably believe) anything about the world around me (including that there is a piece of paper here in front of me).

The argument can also be recast as a piece of first-person critical deliberation about what to believe.

---

[1] This chapter derives from Adam Leite (2010), "How to Take Skepticism Seriously," *Philosophical Studies* 148, no. 1, 39–60 (Springer Nature) and utilizes material from Adam Leite (2013), "That's Not Evidence; It's Not Even True!," *Philosophical Quarterly* 63, no. 250, 81–104 (Oxford University Press). I am grateful to both publishers for permission to reuse this material.

[2] The name was first used, I believe, in DeRose (1995).

Test claim for scrutiny: Here's a piece of paper before me.

Objection: But here's a possible scenario: I am the victim of an all-powerful evil demon who deceives me about what is going on around me.

Principle: If I can't provide an adequate response to this objection, in the form of some consideration that tells against this scenario, then I should not hold this belief.

Recognition: I can't provide an adequate response to this objection: There is nothing that I can appeal to against this possibility.

Conclusion: So, I should not believe that there is a piece of paper before me.

Generalization: This test case is just a stand-in for all the things I currently believe about the world around me. The same reasoning applies to each of them. So I should not believe any of those things.

These are relatively crude presentations, and there are lots of details about which one might fuss.[3] But I'm presenting matters this way so that I can easily highlight a fundamental issue: the second premise of the Argument from Ignorance and the moment (which I'm calling "Recognition") at which we supposedly find that there is nothing that we can appeal to in response to the suggestion that we are being deceived by an evil demon. How are we supposed to find ourselves in agreement with such claims?

For a parallel, consider the following argument:

(i) If we are in the twenty-first century, then the current year is after 1999.
(ii) But the current year is not after 1999.
(iii) So, we are not in the twenty-first century.

The correct response to this argument, given the principles and procedures of ordinary life, is this: "Valid argument, but (ii) is a clearly false premise." It would be *crazy* to treat this argument as giving you some reason to accept its conclusion. My question, then, is simply this: from the standpoint of ordinary life, why should I regard the skeptical arguments any differently?

---

[3] For instance, this presentation leaves aside possible concerns about degrees of belief or credence and works with an on/off notion of belief.

Consider the position we were starting from when we encountered the skeptical arguments. We started out with lots of convictions about the world and about our epistemic position in relation to it. The reasoning was supposed to move us from our ordinary position to the skeptical conclusion. But I cannot see how that has happened. Consider the Argument from Ignorance. Here are some of the things that I believed when the argument started: There are no evil demons. There are no brains in vats—not yet, at any rate. And as Austin stressed, dreams have certain distinctive features which my current experience lacks, so my current experience is nothing like a dream. Moreover, I started out taking myself to know these things and to have lots of good reasons for believing them. I could supply some of those reasons if asked to do so. Standing in the ordinary position, then, it looks as if I should simply reject the second premise of the Argument from Ignorance: I know that I'm not being deceived by an evil demon, because there aren't any evil demons. Likewise, standing in my ordinary position it seems that I ought to reject the step in the critical deliberation that I labeled 'Recognition.' Of course there's something I can appeal to against this hypothesis. It has nothing whatsoever in its favor: there are no evil demons. Those look to me like considerations that warrant dismissing the suggested hypothesis as ridiculous.

It is crucially important here that in ordinary life it is entirely acceptable to appeal to considerations about the world as evidence for or against other claims, as reasons for accepting or rejecting suggestions, proposed hypotheses, and the like. Not only is this perfectly acceptable. To speak from within our ordinary position: considerations about the world often constitute evidence on various issues. Saying this isn't yet to offer any sort of epistemological theory. To take just a few examples: it doesn't commit us to a direct realist theory of perception, or to epistemological disjunctivism (Pritchard 2012), or to the equation of our evidence with what we know (Williamson 2000). It is simply a truism that we all accept. For instance, the fact that the plants in my garden are drooping is evidence that they need water, and I might quite rightly appeal to it as such. It looks as though I am doing something straightforwardly parallel in rejecting Descartes' Evil Demon scenario by pointing out that I can't be an evil demon's victim, since there aren't any evil demons.

The same point applies to the Underdetermination formulation of the skeptical argument, which starts from the idea that our evidence is neutral between the hypothesis that we are being deceived by an evil demon and the hypothesis that there is a real world that is much as we take it to be. To claim that our evidence is neutral requires starting from the thought that our evidence is ultimately restricted to sensory experience, described in a way that doesn't commit us to anything about the world. From the pre-philosophical, ordinary position our response should be: "Wait. Why are you restricting my evidence that way? I've got all sorts of evidence that includes much more than that." Something has to be done to show that our ordinary position actually warrants restricting our evidence in that way. The key challenge, then, if we are to get skepticism going from within the ordinary position, is to show how *materials already available within that position* preclude us from appealing to considerations about the world to rebut the standard skeptical scenarios. So far as I can tell, that has never been done. Most people writing on skepticism today proceed as though they don't even recognize that it needs to be done.

Of course, according to the lore of our tradition we're not supposed to respond to the skeptical argument in the way I've been suggesting. But why not? Why can't we make use of considerations about the world at this juncture? All the crucial work must actually be done here. Do any principles or commitments of our ordinary epistemic practices preclude this sort of response?

Now, you might have an immediate knee-jerk reaction to what I am suggesting:

> But your evidence *just is* limited to how things seem to you, to your sensory experience characterized in a way that does not entail anything about the world! The whole task is to show how a rational being could make a rational transition from its sensory experience, so understood, to well-grounded beliefs and knowledge about the world!

Be patient. I know that this is a background thought presumed by a lot of skeptical argumentation. The crucial question is: how we are supposed to get there?

As we saw in Chapter 3, Stroud attempted to generate this limitation on our evidence by posing a question of general critical reassessment, "What, if anything, do I really know about the world?" If successful, Stroud's approach would have provided the background framing needed by the Argument from Ignorance. As we saw, however, Stroud's approach failed to impose the needed limitation on our evidence from within our ordinary, pre-philosophical position. The aim of this chapter is to begin to consider how else this limitation might be imposed.

2. A Recent Example

It may be helpful to look in some detail at a recent example of skeptical argumentation in order to see the force of the question that I am raising.

Duncan Pritchard (2016) has recently developed two skeptical arguments: a version of the Argument from Ignorance and an Underdetermination argument. He counters the first argument with a sophisticated neo-Wittgensteinian "hinge proposition" epistemology (2016, chapters 3 and 4), and he maintains that evading the second requires us to adopt a "disjunctivist" theory of the epistemology of sensory perception (chapters 5 and 6). As we will see, however, no such theories at all are needed in order to reject these skeptical arguments, if we steadfastly work from within the position Moore and Austin urge on us.

Here is Pritchard's first skeptical argument. He formulates it as an inconsistent triad of claims, the idea being that since we endorse (1) and (2), the skeptic urges us to deny (3).

(1) "One is unable to have rationally grounded knowledge of the denials of radical skeptical hypotheses" (23).
(2) ClosureRK: "If S has rationally grounded knowledge that p, and S competently deduces from p that q, thereby forming a belief that q on this basis while retaining her rationally grounded knowledge that p, then S has rationally grounded knowledge that q" (23).
(3) "One has widespread rationally grounded everyday knowledge" (23).

There is a great deal to be said about this argument, especially about Closure RK. However, I want to focus on just one key issue. Why should we accept claim (1), if we are standing in the ordinary pre-philosophical position? Why not say—since considerations about the world can constitute evidence for various sorts of things—that we have rationally grounded knowledge of the denials of the radical skeptical hypotheses?

Of course, everything here depends on what is meant by "rationally grounded knowledge." But if it is supposed to be a category that is of any significance in ordinary life, the demands that are built into it shouldn't go beyond the demands that we are committed to in our pre-philosophical position. In our ordinary position, we are committed to all of the following:

102 HOW TO TAKE SKEPTICISM SERIOUSLY

   a. There are all sorts of truths that are incompatible with the Evil Demon scenario (and thus tell quite decisively against it). For instance, that there is a table before me and I see it, and that there are no evil demons.
   b. These considerations are available right now to my conscious reflection; they are "reflectively accessible," as Pritchard puts it. At least, they are available to my conscious reflection in a straightforward sense of that phrase: I can quite readily point to these truths in my conscious reflections without engaging in any further investigation or inquiry.
   c. I recognize perfectly well that these truths tell quite decisively against the scenario in question, and I am prepared to treat them (or other considerations like them) as such.

I don't yet see any reason to think that this doesn't suffice for having "rational grounds" or "rationally grounded knowledge," especially when we note that none of my beliefs in this terrain are held as a result of wishful thinking or any other sort of non-rational process. In fact, they are all in excellent epistemic shape. So it looks to me, standing as I am in our ordinary pre-philosophical position, as though we should reject the first claim of this skeptical argument. Of course we have rationally grounded knowledge of the denials of the radical skeptical hypotheses. We possess excellent evidence that they are incorrect, evidence that we can point to in the course of conscious reflection on what is the case.

Here is Pritchard's argument to the contrary:

The contention that one cannot know that one is not a BIV ... seems entirely compelling. After all, since the BIV scenario is *ex hypothesi* subjectively indistinguishable from normal perceptual conditions, it is hard to see how one might come to know such a thing. What kind of rational ground might one have for such a belief, given that there is no subjective basis on which one can discern that one is not in a radical skeptical scenario? (11)[4]

Here Pritchard assumes without any elaboration or discussion a way of thinking on which having a rational ground for some claim requires

---

[4] That this is Pritchard's primary support for the first step of the skeptical argument is reiterated later: "As we observed, what motivated this claim was the fact that radical skeptical hypotheses are *ex hypothesi* indistinguishable from corresponding scenarios involving normal veridical experiences. It seems to follow that one cannot have a rational basis for believing that one is not the victim of a radical skeptical hypothesis, and hence that one cannot know this either" (25).

"subjective distinguishability" between the situation in which the claim is true and the situation in which it is false: one has to be able to determine which situation one is in merely on the basis of how things seem. But given the position from which we are working (following Moore and Austin), a case has to be made for this requirement—a case that shows it to be part of our ordinary commitments—and it is hard to see how that might go. For instance, consider again an earlier example. Right now I certainly have good rational grounds for believing that my spouse didn't leave the country this morning while purposefully deceiving me about her whereabouts and plans: she told me about her plans, we share calendars, she has no reason to leave the country, she wouldn't deceive me in this way, and so on. And I don't just have good rational grounds here; I have rationally grounded knowledge that she didn't do this. But if she did leave the country while purposefully deceiving me about her plans, everything would currently seem exactly the same to me. The two situations are subjectively indistinguishable. Subjective indistinguishability is consequently no bar—in our ordinary pre-philosophical position—against having rationally grounded knowledge of which situation you are in. Pritchard's argument is thus a non-starter. We don't need any particular epistemological theory to reject it. All we need are the commitments of ordinary life, given what has been said so far.

Pritchard's second skeptical argument is an underdetermination argument, built around the idea that one has no more reason to believe that one is seated at one's desk than one has to believe that one is being radically deceived by an evil demon. Again, the argument is presented as an inconsistent triad (34–35). Since it is claimed that we endorse (1) and (2), the argument urges us to reject (3):

(1) "One cannot have rational support that favors one's belief in an everyday proposition over an incompatible radical skeptical hypothesis." (35)
(2) "If S knows that p and q describe incompatible scenarios, and yet S lacks a rational basis that favors p over q, then S lacks rationally grounded knowledge that p." (34)
(3) "One has widespread rationally grounded everyday knowledge." (35)

Again, I want to focus on just one question about this argument. Why should we endorse the first claim? From the ordinary pre-philosophical position, it simply looks false. I have rational grounds that favor my belief that I am seated at my desk over the suggestion that I am a bodiless spirit being deceived by an evil demon. They include such things as that I have a body, there are no evil demons, there is a desk in front of me, I see it, and the like. Of course, it is plausible enough that my sensory experience right now, all by itself and described in a way that is noncommittal about the world, doesn't favor the one over the other. But if we are standing in our ordinary pre-philosophical position, we should say, "Wait a second! Why are you limiting my evidence like that? Why think, for instance, that the facts that I have a body and that there are no evil demons aren't relevant considerations here?" More needs to be said.

Pritchard offers a defense of (1). Here it is:

Given that the experiences had by the subject in the BIV case are subjectively indistinguishable from everyday experiences, then how is one to come by rational support for an everyday perceptual belief that epistemically favors this belief over an incompatible radical skeptical alternative? (30)

This is just the consideration that we have already addressed in relation to Pritchard's first skeptical argument: the idea that having rational grounds for or against a scenario requires being able to "subjectively distinguish" its obtaining from its non-obtaining. This amounts to an unmotivated limitation of our rational grounds to how things subjectively seem. Again, the crucial point is that if we are to be moved to a skeptical conclusion from our standpoint in our ordinary pre-philosophical position, we need to be shown that this limitation is something that we are committed to in that position. And that looks hard to do, since it looks as though everything points quite the other way.

So far, then, it looks as though we can reject Pritchard's skeptical arguments without any epistemological theory at all, just by making use of the commitments of our ordinary pre-philosophical position. So the crucial question is what might be said to preclude these sorts of responses. This is a question about the earliest stages of skeptical argumentation. What is supposed to shift our pre-philosophical commitments—commitments about what is the case in the world around us, what we know, what is evidence for or against what, and the like—off the table in such a way that the skeptical reasoning can get its grip?

3. Begging the Question, First Pass

Let's begin with a simplistic version of the charge that it is objectionably question-begging to reply to skeptical argumentation by appealing to considerations about the world. "The skeptic claims that you don't know or justifiably believe anything about the world. In making use of claims about the world in responding to the skeptic, you have to represent or take yourself to know or at least justifiably believe them. So, in responding to the skeptical argument in this way you are unacceptably begging the question against the skeptic: you are assuming or presupposing the truth of the very thing the skeptic denies."

Of course, it is true that in some sense the proposed response to the skeptical argument assumes or presupposes the truth of the very thing the skeptic denies. But from the standpoint of our ordinary practice, there's nothing wrong with that, taken all by itself. Suppose that someone contends that you don't know anything about George W. Bush's gender. And suppose that this person attempts to support this contention by inviting you to consider the hypothesis that Bush is a woman successfully engaged in a massive deception, even while granting that there is no evidence in this hypothesis' favor. The right response, given how things are, is this. "Don't be ridiculous; Bush is a man." This response might not be dialectically effective in convincing your interlocutor, and so it may not be the best thing to say if you hope to bring about conviction. But there the fault lies with your interlocutor; this is an appropriate response that you are fully entitled to make. What this reveals is that the mere assertion that you don't know something about a certain domain doesn't preclude you from making use of things that you know in that domain. The same goes for considering the possibility that you don't know anything in that domain or considering a possibility that would have the consequence that you don't know anything in that domain. Sometimes serious and sincere consideration of a suggestion amounts to little more than summarily rejecting it. So something more than the mere suggestion of the skeptic's scenarios, and even more than mere assertion or consideration of the skeptical conclusion, will be needed in order to explain why we can't appeal to considerations about the world in response to the skeptic's use of the Evil Demon Hypothesis.

4. The Adequacy of Our Evidence

Here's an argument that is sometimes offered: you don't know that you aren't being deceived by an evil demon, because if you were being deceived by an evil demon you would incorrectly believe that you aren't. This thought is codified by Nozick (1981) in his Sensitivity Condition on knowledge: to know p, it must be the case that if p were false, you wouldn't believe p. But as the burgeoning literature on this topic has shown, the Sensitivity requirement is vulnerable to straightforward counterexamples. Here's a simple one, inspired by Williamson (2000). Suppose that you are looking at a twenty-foot pole. Your perceptual experience of the pole enables you to know that it is more than ten feet tall. Now let's stipulate that the situation is such that if the pole were not more than ten feet tall, it would be nine and a half feet tall. (Suppose the pole comes in two sections, the first of which is nine and one half feet tall, and they could easily come apart). And let's stipulate that you aren't very good at estimating heights visually, so that if the pole were nine and a half feet tall you would believe that it is more than ten feet tall. So this is a case in which, looking at the twenty foot pole, you know that it is at least ten feet tall, but if the pole were not at least ten feet tall, you would still believe that it was. You would even believe it using the same "method" of belief formation, as Nozick requires (1981, 179). So your belief is not Sensitive, but you have knowledge nonetheless. It should be obvious that the same point would apply to reasonable and justified belief, as well as to the notion of having good or adequate reason to believe. We can thus have excellent evidence in favor of a belief even if that belief is not Sensitive.

Even so, we might still lack evidence that we aren't being deceived by an evil demon. Here's another proposal that we sometimes hear: we aren't entitled to believe that we are not being deceived by an evil demon because our evidence is *neutral* on the question. And here's an argument that is sometimes offered in support of that suggestion: if one were being deceived by an evil demon, one would have the very same evidence that one has now.

This argument may rely upon a principle that looks something like this: if I would have exactly the same evidence that I have now even if p were not the case, then my current evidence is neutral on the question of whether p. That principle is incorrect. For instance, suppose that I drop a bag of garbage down the trash chute from the tenth floor of my apartment building, walking away as the chute clangs shut just as I have done every week for years. Everything appears normal; there is no notice indicating that the chute is malfunctioning, no pile of trash bags in the hall or foul stench emanating from the chute. In these conditions, I have good evidence that my garbage is now somewhere in the bowels of the building. But if my garbage were not now somewhere in the bowels of the building, it would be because the trash bag somehow snagged on the way down—and if that happened, I would have no indication of it. That is, I would have exactly the same evidence that I have now even if p were not the case. My evidence in this case is not infallible, nor is it indefeasible. But it surely isn't *neutral*.[5]

There is a much more fundamental point to be made here as well. It is not true that my evidence right now is the same as the evidence I would have if I were being deceived by an evil demon.

To see this, remember first that we are standing solidly in our ordinary pre-philosophical position, in which considerations about the world often constitute excellent evidence. Here, then, is a piece of evidence that I currently possess: there are no evil demons. I might appeal to this, for instance, if someone claimed that their loved one's schizophrenic hallucinations are caused by a demon. "Don't be ridiculous," I might say. "There are no evil demons. This is a mental health issue and should be treated accordingly."

Now it is part of our best ordinary practice that if some consideration is false, then it isn't evidence for anything. Someone might reasonably *think* that it is true, *think* that it is evidence, and reasonably appeal to it as such, but they would be wrong. And I might point that out to them. "That doesn't support your claim at all," I might say, "It isn't even true!" So right now I possess a piece of evidence—that there are no evil demons—that I would not possess if I were being deceived by an evil demon, since in that case it would not be true that there are no evil demons. My evidence would consequently be different if I were being deceived by an evil demon. I thus currently have evidence that I would lack under those circumstances, and this evidence is not neutral on the question.

Some philosophers would deny my claim that if p is false, then p isn't evidence for anything. Suppose, for instance, that a reliable source tells me that p, and I thereby (reasonably) come to believe that p. Recognizing that p entails some q, I then reasonably infer q from p and thereby take p to be evidence for q in this case. Some epistemologists would say that in such

---

[5] This example is adapted from one Sosa (1999) offers as a counterexample to Nozick's Sensitivity Requirement.

circumstances, p could be evidence for q for me even if it is false; it could be *my* evidence that p.[6]

There is a slide away from ordinary ways of thinking if one takes such examples to show that p can be evidence for q even if p is false. We should grant that one could reasonably take p to be evidence in this sort of case. But note the shift in terminology—the relativization to a person—involved in the suggestion that p could "be evidence for q (for me)" in such a case. This may well just mean the same thing as "S reasonably takes p to be evidence for q" or "S would be reasonable to treat p as evidence for q"—which is compatible with p's not being evidence for q, and so not a counterexample to my claim. Perhaps what is meant is instead a relativized notion of evidence: evidence-in-relation-to-S, given what S takes to be true (including p). But saying that p is evidence-for-q-in-relation-to-S in this sense is not equivalent to saying that p is evidence for q, and so again we don't have a counterexample to my claim. You can't infer from "p is evidence-for-S-that-q," understood in the intended way, to "p is evidence for q," as is shown by the case in which you know p to be false. In that case it would be natural to judge that S (reasonably) takes p to be evidence for q, but is wrong. Evidence-for-a-person is at best a technical notion aimed at helping us explain the sense in which people can be reasonable in certain sorts of cases in which they draw conclusions from false beliefs. Confusion between this technical notion and our ordinary notion of evidence is facilitated, I think, by a commitment to the thought that if S's belief is reasonable, then it must be based on good evidence, or at least S must have good evidence for it.[7] But the judgments involved in our ordinary practice do not themselves show a commitment to that thought. Likewise, the idea that the false proposition is *my evidence* does not show that false propositions can be evidence simpliciter. Compare: you are balancing your checkbook and find a bank error. You might say, "The bank's balance is $361, but the bank is wrong. The balance is $375." Your account doesn't have two

---

[6] This has been suggested to me by Branden Fitelson and Jon Kvanvig. Something similar is explicitly claimed by Jim Joyce (2004).

[7] This is the lynchpin of Conee and Feldman's argument (2004) for the claim that our evidence is limited to our mental states. In outline, they start by saying that what one is "justified" in believing is determined by one's evidence, and then look at examples in which people's beliefs are "justified," aren't "justified," or are comparatively more or less "justified." Since the relevant factors, they claim, concern only the people's mental states, they conclude that one's evidence is limited to one's mental states. However, they do nothing to argue that "evidence"—in the ordinary sense of the term which allows that the fact that my plants are drooping is evidence that they need water—is tied in the requisite way to their technical notion of "justification." In effect, the stipulated link between "justification" and "evidence" is used to pull the term "evidence" free from its ordinary, pre-philosophical moorings.

balances. What you are calling 'the bank's balance' isn't an actual balance of your account. It is what the bank (incorrectly) takes the balance to be.[8]

In sum: in order to establish the charge that my evidence is neutral on the question of whether I'm being deceived by an evil demon, you have to somehow place limits on what counts as my evidence. You have to preclude me from including amongst my evidence such facts about the world as that there are no evil demons. But how is that limitation to be accomplished? This is just another way of putting the question with which we started. Are there any commitments or principles from our ordinary practice that put considerations about the world out of play when we encounter the skeptical argument?

Following a proposal of Ram Neta's, it might be suggested that what we count as a person's evidence that p is relative to the alternatives to p that are under consideration. So consider a hypothesis H which implies that S doesn't know that p. When one considers such a hypothesis, according to this proposal, one thereby restricts what counts as S's body of evidence to just the evidence S would have whether or not H is true.[9] This proposal has the consequence that we could not acceptably appeal to or rely upon considerations about the world in order to counter the Evil Demon Hypothesis.

This proposal is incorrect, however. Consider again the hypothesis that George W. Bush is a woman successfully engaged in a massive deception. This hypothesis implies that you do not know that Bush is a man. Does considering it limit your evidence in the suggested way? Obviously not. Bush was married to a woman, Laura Bush, in Texas (a state which did not then perform same-sex marriages). That's a piece of evidence which you would not have if the hypothesis were true, since if the hypothesis were true this consideration would be false. But this is nonetheless a piece of evidence you have that Bush is a man, and you have it even now that we are considering this hypothesis. Of course, it would not be dialectically effective to present this evidence to someone who was genuinely inclined to believe the hypothesis. But the hypothesis is patently false, and so considering it does not lead us to restrict our evidence in this way. We *would* appropriately restrict our evidence in this way if there were some good reason of the right sort in favor of this hypothesis. But the parallel point regarding the Evil Demon Hypothesis

---

[8] This paragraph and the preceding one are drawn from Leite (2013), which offers a full discussion of these issues concerning evidence and their relation to skepticism.

[9] This is the core suggestion behind Ram Neta's rule "R!" in (Neta 2002, 674). Neta's own formulation is considerably more complicated, for reasons arising from the details of his theory of evidence.

won't help the skeptical argument, because that hypothesis doesn't have any reason in its favor.

5. Epistemic Closure and Epistemic Priority

Recall the premises of the Argument from Ignorance:

1. I can't know (reasonably or justifiably believe) anything about the world around me (e.g., that there is a piece of paper here in front of me) unless I know (reasonably or justifiably believe) that I am not being deceived by an evil demon (not dreaming, not a BIV being fed misleading inputs).
2. But I don't know (reasonably or justifiably believe) that I am not being deceived by an evil demon (not dreaming, not a BIV being fed misleading inputs).

It is sometimes argued that once you accept the first premise, you are sunk: you are forced to accept the second as well. (This is a way of summarizing a key burden of Stroud's argument in chapter 1 of *The Significance of Philosophical Scepticism* [Stroud 1984]). If that's right, then something about the first premise, or about the considerations lying behind it, enforces the limitation that I have been highlighting.

On many accounts, the first premise is underwritten by a principle of *epistemic closure*: roughly, if you know that p and know that p implies not-q, then you know that not-q.[10] Similar principles might be proposed for justified belief and for having reason to believe. For the sake of argument, let's grant that some such principles are correct. Might they hold the key to the question I've been pressing?

It has always puzzled me that discussions of global skeptical arguments have placed so much weight on the idea that knowledge is closed under known implication. For one thing, as Stroud pointed out long ago the skeptical argument would seem to work just as well with skeptical possibilities

---

[10] As is familiar from the literature, a really plausible closure principle would need to be refined in various ways. Such refinements are irrelevant to my discussion, since the issue that I will focus on equally arises for any more refined principle, so long as it is simply a closure principle—not a transmission principle to the effect that the knowledge appearing on the consequent side derives from and is inferentially based upon the knowledge appearing on the antecedent side. (David and Warfield [2008] provide additional reasons why it is doubtful that the skeptical argument can be successfully underwritten by a more refined closure principle.).

that are compatible with the truth of many of one's beliefs about the world (Stroud 1984, 25). Moreover, a plausible closure principle requires that one recognizes the implication, but skepticism is meant to apply to *everyone*, even if they are ignorant of the implication.[11] Still, let's consider the closure principle, assuming one recognizes the relevant implication regarding the possibility that one is a victim of an evil demon who always deceives (so that all of one's beliefs about the world are false). Does the closure principle, in conjunction with this possibility, force us to accept the second premise of the Argument from Ignorance?

No. There is a fundamental problem for any attempt to deploy a closure principle for this purpose. The relevant instance of the closure principle yields only a necessary condition on knowing certain things: in order to know those things, you also have to know that you are not being globally deceived by an evil demon. Taken by itself, that result poses no problem. It just states a necessary condition that looks perfectly satisfiable. As discussed in Chapter 4, Stroud has argued that a premise along the lines of premise 1 becomes unsatisfiable when applied to the question of whether one knows that the skeptic's hypotheses don't obtain (Stroud 1984, 19ff.). But that's not so, if premise 1 is underwritten by a closure principle. When we apply the relevant instance of a closure principle to our knowledge that the Evil Demon scenario is not the case, we get this (ignoring the clause concerning knowledge of the relevant implication):

> I don't know that I am not being deceived by an evil demon unless I know that I am not being deceived by an evil demon.

This requirement just states the truism that you can't know something unless you know it. That's no problem.[12] And there's a more general lesson here. You can't get a vicious circle or regress out of a mere necessary condition; p is trivially and innocuously a necessary condition of itself. For this reason, no principle along these lines that merely involves a necessary condition—and that's all a closure principle can provide—will do the needed work all by itself.[13]

---

[11] See Leite (2004b).

[12] This has been stressed by Pryor (2000) as well. Jim and I discussed it in relation to an early draft of his (2000).

[13] In Stroud's version of the skeptical argument, the closure principle is replaced by this: if you know that q is incompatible with your *knowing* that p, then in order to know that p, you must know that not-q (Stroud 1984, 29–30). (This principle is designed to allow for the fact that the skeptical hypothesis apparently need not be incompatible with the truth of all of the relevant beliefs.) This

Here's a thought that might help the skeptic. It seems pretty plausible that I won't know that I'm not being deceived by an evil demon unless I also know a bunch of other things about the world, such as that there aren't any evil demons (and whatever else I need to know in order to know that). Conjoin that thought with the first premise of the Argument from Ignorance (which will be referred to as A.I.), perhaps underwritten by a closure principle. Then you get this.

   a. In order to know things about the world, I need to know that I am not being deceived by an evil demon (premise 1 of A.I.).
   b. In order to know that I am not being deceived by an evil demon, I need to know other things about the world (e.g., that there aren't any evil demons) (the additional thought).

Don't (a) and (b) create a vicious circle?

Well, no. All that they amount to is that to know some one thing I've got to know a bunch of other stuff as well, and that in order to know that other stuff I've also got to know the first thing. There's nothing problematic about that. We can perfectly well make sense of a situation in which you can't know that *p* unless you know that *q* and also can't know that *q* unless you know that *p*. (The same goes for justified belief and for having reason to believe). So no problem arises even when we conjoin a closure principle with the thought that our knowing that we are not being deceived by an evil demon *requires* our knowing other things about the world.

For example, consider the following two things I know: (1) I am on the graduate faculty of my university; (2) I have a standing entitlement to serve on PhD dissertation committees at my university. Given what I recognize about the relation between these (you can't have the one status without the other) and my ability to put two-and-two together, it's plausible enough that my knowing either requires knowing the other. There is obviously no problematic circle in this situation. For one thing, there is no reason to think that

---

principle likewise fails to yield an unsatisfiable requirement when applied to the case of one's knowledge that one is not the victim of an evil demon, and for the same reason.

   Stroud's principle may have been motivated by the thought that in order to know that *p*, one must be able to *rule out* all alternatives that one knows to be incompatible with knowing that *p*— where *ruling out* is understood to mean being able to determine that those alternatives do not obtain *only on the basis of evidence that one would have* even if *they did obtain*. This thought would do the needed work. However, it is not true that in order to know that a possibility doesn't obtain one has to be able to rule it out in this sense, as is shown by the example regarding the children of brunettes discussed in Section 6 of this chapter.

either of these beliefs is the ground on which I base the other. (Standard counterfactual tests won't establish that one of these items of knowledge is the ground on which I base the other: if I stopped believing one, I'd stop believing the other too). Moreover, there's no reason to think that there is some other sort of priority relation between these belief-contents, such that my beliefs will not be in good order unless one of these two beliefs is grounded on the other but not vice versa. Of course, this example doesn't parallel in every respect the situation with regard to the Evil Demon Hypothesis, but it makes this crucial point: there can be mutual epistemic dependence without objectionable circularity.

A skeptical conclusion would result if (a) or (b) above involved an *epistemic priority requirement*: that is, a requirement to the effect that certain things must be known antecedently to or independently of other things. What notion of "priority" is relevant here? As in the previous chapter, it needn't be a temporal requirement, but a requirement stating an epistemic *precondition* or some other relation of asymmetric epistemic dependence. Following the earlier formal characterization, the requirement will have to be formulable using an irreflexive relational predicate such that the two demands

aRb and bRa

are not co-satisfiable when a is not identical with b. For my purposes here and in what follows, we don't need to focus on a particular substantive theory of epistemic priority, but only on this formal structure (though later on I will discuss some factors that might be thought to impose epistemic priority relations).

Now, it is plausible enough that if either (a) or (b) involved a priority requirement, then the result would be that in order to know that I am not being deceived by an evil demon, I must antecedently know that I am not being deceived by an evil demon. And that *is* an unsatisfiable requirement. Given (a), skepticism would ensue.

It might seem that I have already committed myself to a priority reading of (b). I have appealed to the consideration that there are no evil demons as a ground for dismissing the proposal that one is being deceived by an evil demon. This could easily be interpreted as suggesting that the consideration that there are no evil demons is the ground for an inference through which I derived my knowledge that I am not being deceived by an evil demon. So understood, a problem regarding epistemic priority would arise. I couldn't then also grant that in order to know that there are no evil demons I would already have to know that I am not being deceived by an evil demon.

This problem does not arise, however. To appeal to a consideration as a *ground for dismissing a possible hypothesis* or as *good evidence against it*, a good reason for thinking it false, is not necessarily to say that the former consideration serves as the ground for an inference through which I have derived my knowledge that the hypothesis is incorrect. To provide a ground for dismissing a possibility is to provide a consideration that warrants treating that possibility in a certain way in the course of the deliberation. This is different from inferring from some evidence or premise that the possibility does not obtain, and it is also different from reporting a prior inference upon which one bases one's belief that the possibility does not obtain. For instance, a queer friend of mine recently had an acquaintance exclaim with surprise, "But you're straight!" "Of course I'm not," she replied. "I've been dating the same woman for five years." In so dismissing the suggestion, she was not inferring from that consideration that she is not straight, nor was she reporting an inference through which she had arrived at that knowledge. Dismissing a possibility on a particular ground is thus different from inferring or reporting an inference one has made.

Moreover, one can appropriately provide a ground for dismissing a possible hypothesis without thereby creating or tracking an epistemic priority relation amongst the beliefs in question or amongst the propositions believed. For instance, I am completely confident that my spouse loves me. I don't have any doubt, nor any reason for doubt or suspicion. Suppose now I open a fortune cookie that says, "Your spouse doesn't love you." I may quite appropriately dismiss the possibility as ridiculous: she shows me she loves me in hundreds of ways every day, including telling me, and she wouldn't deceive me about such matters. And now suppose that as I subsequently leave the restaurant, I see a man with a sign that reads, "Your spouse lies when she says she loves you!" I may quite appropriately dismiss that thought as ridiculous too: she loves me too much to deceive me about such important matters. What I just invited you to imagine is a situation in which I first dismiss the possibility that she doesn't love me by pointing out that she wouldn't deceive me about such matters, and I subsequently dismiss the possibility that she is lying to me by pointing out that she loves me too much to do that. If appropriately providing a ground for dismissing a possible hypothesis always created or tracked an epistemic priority relation, then this example would involve an objectionable circle. But it doesn't: there's obviously nothing problematic about my offering *both* of these responses. So one can appropriately provide a ground for dismissing a possible hypothesis without thereby creating or tracking an epistemic priority relation. (This thought will be unavailable if one understands every such episode on the model of performing an explicit inference. But why think in those terms? As we will see later on, there is every reason to think that this would be a mistake.)

It might be objected that I'm still not out of the woods, however, because my belief to the effect that I am not deceived by an evil demon is *based on* other beliefs about the external world, and so vicious circularity is bound to arise from my accepting both (a) and (b). But everything here depends on what is being packed into the phrase 'based on.' I can concede to this objector all of the following: (1) Beliefs about the world played a causal role in my coming to believe that I am not being deceived by an evil demon, even perhaps a causal role that a cognitive scientist might want to model for theoretical purposes as an implicit inference, (2) I believed things about the world before I believed that I was not being deceived by an evil demon, (3) I take some of the things I believe about the world to tell decisively in favor of the truth of the claim that I am not being deceived by an evil demon, (4) if I were asked to state considerations that provide good reasons for believing that I am not being deceived by an evil demon, I would appeal to considerations about the world, (5) if I stopped believing some of the things I believe about the world, then (being rational) I would stop believing that I am not being deceived by an evil demon (because I would become agnostic on the issue). Conceding all of that does not lead to vicious circularity if we add that my now knowing those other things about the world requires me to know that I am not being deceived by an evil demon.

This point will not be available if one simply assumes that there *must* be an epistemic priority relation here—that either the belief that one is not being deceived by an evil demon is inferentially based upon other beliefs about the world, or vice versa, or that at the very least one or the other of these must come before the other in the "order of justification." But I can't see anything in our ordinary commitments that forces us to accept this requirement. So far, then, no reason has emerged for thinking that the conjunction of (a) and (b) is problematic.

Pritchard's version of the argument from ignorance works with a more refined version of the closure principle. This refined principle focuses upon the derivation of rationally grounded knowledge through competent deduction. Here is the principle again:

ClosureRK: If S has rationally grounded knowledge that *p*, and S competently deduces from *p* that *q*, thereby forming a belief that *q* on this basis while retaining her rationally grounded knowledge that *p*, then S has rationally grounded knowledge that *q*. (Pritchard 2016, 23)

Pritchard helpfully specifies how this is to be understood, characterizing the principle as "describing the *acquisition* of a (knowledge-apt) belief via the *rational process* of competent deduction" (2016, 91, italics in original).

This principle would seem to generate a problem if we also accept that to know other things about the world we need to know that we are not being deceived by an evil demon. For ClosureRK would generate a priority structure, since it invites us to imagine that we *arrive at our belief* that we are not being deceived by an evil demon through competent deduction from things already known. That would not be possible, if we grant that we also can't have rationally grounded knowledge about the world unless we have rationally grounded knowledge that we are not being deceived by an evil demon, for then we couldn't know the things *from which* we are supposed to arrive through deduction at our knowledge of the falsity of the Evil Demon scenario *unless we already knew that the Evil Demon scenario is false*. If the only way to arrive at rationally grounded knowledge that *q* is via deduction from rationally grounded knowledge that *p*, and if we can't have rationally grounded knowledge that *p* unless we already have rationally grounded knowledge that *q*, then we can't have rationally grounded knowledge of either *p* or *q*.

It is a mistake, however, to think that there is any insuperable problem here. For why think that we come to believe *through competent deduction* that we are not being deceived by an evil demon? It is one thing to say that your having rationally grounded knowledge that *q* depends on your having rationally grounded knowledge that *p*, and even on your recognizing that *p* tells quite decisively in favor of *q*. It is quite another thing to say that your rationally grounded knowledge that *q* must have been arrived at via competent deduction from *p*. Here's a useful parallel. If I didn't know anything that told in favor of it, I wouldn't know that I live in the United States. And there are all sorts of considerations that I could offer that tell quite decisively in favor of the claim that I live in the United States. For instance, I live in Indiana, which is in the United States; my driver's license shows a US address; and so on. But did I arrive at my knowledge that I live in the United States via *competent deduction* from any or all of this? Surely not. There are lots of things that we know in virtue of having all sorts of evidence in favor of them even though we didn't come to know them via *competent deduction*. Competent deduction is just one way of coming to know things. It is a mistake to think that if my knowing that I am not being deceived by an evil demon depends upon my knowing other things about the world that I recognize as telling decisively in favor of this claim, then I must have arrived at this belief via a competent deduction. There is no reason to think that the antecedent of Pritchard's refined closure principle is met when it comes to our knowledge that we are not being deceived by an evil demon. So there is no reason to think that the principle applies to the case in the way the argument requires.

I've been considering the suggestion that a vicious circle arises from accepting both:

(a) In order to know things about the world, I need to know that I am not being deceived by an evil demon (premise 1 of A.I.),

and

(b) I can't know that I am not being deceived by an evil demon unless I know other things about the world.

Our focus has been on (b), and no vicious circle has been forced on us. Let's look again at (a).

Suppose that (a) involved an epistemic priority condition. Then there would be a quick path to the skeptical argument's claim that you can't know that the Evil Demon Hypothesis is false. For just apply (a), understood as involving a priority condition, to the particular case of one's putative knowledge that one is not being deceived by an evil demon. The result is that one cannot know that one is not being deceived by an evil demon unless one antecedently knows that one is not being deceived by an evil demon. That's an unsatisfiable requirement.

Is there any reason to accept (a), read as an epistemic priority requirement? There would be if a priority version of the familiar closure principle were correct.[14] For then the priority version of premise 1 of the Argument from Ignorance could be derived from that more general priority principle.

Here's what the general priority version of the closure principle would say:

If you know that p and know that p entails not-q, then you must antecedently know that not-q.

---

[14] Or a priority version of Stroud's variant (see fn. 13).

But this principle is clearly to be rejected, given our starting point in this inquiry.

For one thing, and most obviously, we do not require that it be met in ordinary life: someone might not know whether Morgan is a woman, wonder about it, and learn that he is not a woman by being told—by someone in a position to know—that Morgan is a confirmed bachelor. Here the person doesn't know that *not-q* antecedently to knowing that *p*, even while recognizing the entailment. Since this is perfectly acceptable, the principle is false.[15]

Moreover, the principle would wreak havoc with our ability to arrive at knowledge through deductive inference quite generally, for we would have to know the entailed things antecedently to knowing the premises of the inference, which makes it impossible to acquire knowledge through deductive inference.

Finally, and even more radically, the principle would straightforwardly make all knowledge impossible for anyone with minimal logical acumen. Here's a simple example that provides a template applicable to any proposition you like. Suppose that you are looking straight at a cow in normal conditions. You recognize that it's being a cow implies that it is not a chicken. So according to this principle, to know that it is a cow, you must antecedently know that it is not a chicken. Now consider your knowledge that it is not a chicken. Let "It is not a chicken" = *p*. Let *q* = "It is a chicken." You recognize that *p* entails not-*q*. That is, you recognize that its not being a chicken implies that it is not a chicken. So according to this principle, to know that it is not a chicken, you must antecedently know that it is not a chicken. But that's impossible. So you can't know it's not a chicken. And so you can't know it's a cow either, according to this principle.[16] This is no way to show that a priority version of the first premise of the Argument from Ignorance is a commitment of our ordinary practice.[17,18]

---

[15] Please forgive the use of concepts that are part of a sexist and gender-binary conceptual framework. The example makes the point—at least until we start using the concept "bachelor" in a way that is both non-sexist and gender-neutral.

[16] The implausibility of this principle has also been noted by James Pryor (2000) and Alex Byrne (2004). That it makes all knowledge impossible for anyone with minimal logical acumen was a central point of my undergraduate senior honors thesis (UC Berkeley, 1992).

[17] It should be obvious that the same points apply to a priority version of Stroud's variant of the familiar closure principle as well.

[18] Recognizing this difficulty, Jim Pryor builds a skeptical argument not around a closure principle, but around a principle that he calls SPK:

SPK: If you're to know a proposition *p* on the basis of certain experiences or grounds E, then for every [scenario] *q* which is "bad" relative to E and *p*, you have to be in a position to know *q* to be false in a non-question-begging way—i.e., you have to be in a position to know *q* to be false antecedently to knowing *p* on the basis of E. (2000, 528)

I will address this principle in Chapter 8, once we have some more materials from the pre-philosophical position clearly in view.

6. The General Reliability-Based Priority Requirement

How can we reach the claim that in order to know anything about the world, you must *antecedently know* that you are not being deceived by an evil demon?

Let's return to a key theme of the discussion in Chapter 4. It is a common thought that the skeptical hypotheses are constructed in such a way as to "neutralize" our ordinary evidence. An important strategy picks up on this thought to try to derive the claim that one can't know anything about the world unless one antecedently knows that one isn't being deceived by an evil demon. Here's how the line of thought goes. If I *were* being deceived by an evil demon, then my reliability, competence, or authority would be compromised regarding a wide range of matters, including such things as whether there are evil demons. So, the thought is, in order to be entitled to believe anything about that range of matters, I would need to have adequate grounds from outside that range for believing that I am not being deceived by an evil demon. And if that's so, then in appealing to considerations about the world in response to the Evil Demon Hypothesis, I wouldn't be showing that I have adequate grounds from outside that range. Maybe, then, that's what's wrong with my response to the skeptical argument.[19]

What's going on here can be usefully characterized in terms of the notion of *independent grounds*. Suppose that a certain hypothesis H is such that if it obtained, then one's reliability, competence, or authority would be compromised across a domain D. Say that a ground is *independent* if it is not in this domain. As discussed in Chapter 4, we can then formulate a requirement schema as follows:

General Reliability-Based Priority Requirement: If H is a hypothesis whose truth would undermine my reliability, competence, or authority regarding some domain D, then if I recognize that H is of this sort, I ought not believe anything in D unless I have adequate independent grounds for believing that not-H.

---

[19] In this paragraph and what follows, I mean the term "ground" to include anything that one might want to allow as an epistemically acceptable basis for a belief. (I do assume, however, that practical or prudential reasons won't count.) I likewise mean the phrase "reliability, competence, or authority" to be understood in a pretheoretical way.

The upshot, if some such requirement is correct, is a certain kind of epistemic priority structure between the belief that not-H and considerations in the domain D: one cannot acceptably believe anything in the domain without having adequate grounds from outside the domain for believing not-H. (I will hereafter use the term "excluded domain" to refer to this domain).[20]

Applying this schema to the Evil Demon Hypothesis, we get this:

Skeptical Reliability-Based Priority Requirement: For any proposition about which I recognize that I would be unreliable, incompetent, or lack authority if I were being deceived by an evil demon, I ought not believe it unless I have adequate independent grounds—adequate grounds from outside this domain—for believing that I am not being deceived in this way.

Could this sort of requirement, derived in this sort of way, explain why we can't reject the Evil Demon Hypothesis by appealing to considerations about the world around us?

I don't think so. As we saw in the previous chapter, Austin would reject both this skeptical requirement and the general requirement from which it is derived. He held that "any kind of statement could state evidence for any other kind, if the circumstances were appropriate" (1962, 116; cf. 111, 140). If that is right, then no such requirement holds in a fully circumstance-independent way. Austin didn't offer any considerations in support of this general claim, but I think that he was absolutely right about the commitments of our pre-philosophical position. There are straightforward counterexamples that relevantly parallel the skeptical scenarios.

To begin, note first that you can perfectly appropriately rule out a possible scenario by appealing to a consideration about which you would be radically unreliable if that scenario were the case. For instance, to make new use of an earlier example, right now I can tell from how my speech sounds that I am not drunkenly slurring my words. That's so even if when I'm drunk and slurring my words I incorrectly think that my speech sounds perfectly normal. The mere fact that I would be unreliable about a subject matter if a certain

---

[20] As formulated in the main text, the requirement is vulnerable to facile counterexamples: it has the consequence that one ought not believe that one is not dead, for instance. (I am indebted here to Kirk Ludwig.) We can avoid this specific result with a little tinkering. Perhaps surprisingly, however, as we will see in Chapters 6 and 7 such counterexamples point toward a crucial epistemic phenomenon—epistemic asymmetry—that reveals a fundamental lesson about all requirements of this sort, and indeed, about skepticism itself. But we still need to do a lot of work to get there.

hypothesis were true does not make it unacceptable for me to appeal to that subject matter as evidence that the hypothesis does not hold, *given that there is no reason to think that the hypothesis is true*.

Nothing changes when we add in considerations about generality and the lack of independent evidence. Consider the following hypothesis:

> *Children of Brunettes.* The children of brunettes are massively bad at evaluating and responding to evidence, both in conscious deliberation and in non-deliberative belief formation. They suffer from significant and pervasive perceptual and cognitive deficits compensated for by confabulation, hallucinatory perceptual infilling, and an unshakeable conviction that nothing is going wrong—with the result that they go very badly astray about all sorts of matters in ways that they cannot recognize, including everything that they would need in order to aptly evaluate this very hypothesis.[21]

This hypothesis is clearly false. We would all dismiss it out of hand. It flies in the face of ordinary experience and established science. But if (like me) you have brunette parents, you would be radically unreliable if this hypothesis were true. And if you are like me, then in dismissing it you would be relying upon considerations about which you would lack reliability, competence, or authority if the hypothesis were true. Consequently, if you are like me there is—among the things we believe—no independent evidence (in the sense I defined above) that decisively tells against this hypothesis. Do you therefore want to stand up in front of a Cognitive Science class and say you have *no idea* whether or not this hypothesis is true? Do you want to say that we have *no evidence* against it? I certainly wouldn't. Heredity of cognitive abilities has been carefully studied, and my understanding is that the evidence is quite decisive that the hair color of one's parents has no bearing on one's cognitive abilities. We have solid evidence (from psychology, genetics, and ordinary experience) that the Children of Brunettes Hypothesis is false. It's not an open question.

It may help here to notice that the hypothesis is a conjunction of a hypothesis about radical and global cognitive disability along with a *causal hypothesis*

---

[21] I use "brunette" in the now-accepted dictionary sense of "a person with brown hair." Nothing in the example is intended to indicate gender.

about the origin of that disability. Consider the hypothesis that children of brunettes suffer from very mild cognitive disabilities because of their parentage. That hypothesis is false, and one thing to say about it is that *its causal conjunct* is false. There is no causal mechanism linking cognitive disability to the hair color of one's parents. But if we say that in this case, then shouldn't we say the same thing about the radical Children of Brunettes Hypothesis? One reason why it is clearly false is that one of its conjuncts—the very same one at issue in the weaker hypothesis—is false. What could one possibly say here instead? That the causal conjunct is false in the one case but not the other? That makes no sense; if there is no such causal mechanism, then there is no such causal mechanism. Are we to say that the causal conjunct is false but not the whole conjunctive Children of Brunettes Hypothesis? That seems hard to swallow; if one of the conjuncts of a conjunctive hypothesis is false, then so is the hypothesis. I certainly wouldn't want to stand before a Cog Sci class and tell them that for one of *these* reasons it is an open question whether this hypothesis is true, that it isn't known to be false, or that we have no evidence against it.

These points apply even if the hypothesis suggests that the children of brunettes are more or less helpless, massively out of touch with reality, living largely deluded lives in the safety of institutions. The right thing to say about that hypothesis is that we know it to be false and have excellent evidence against it. It would be a non-starter to suggest otherwise to a practicing cognitive psychologist or brain scientist.

If you have brunette parents, your situation relative to this hypothesis is structurally analogous in every respect to your situation regarding the Evil Demon Hypothesis. What the Children of Brunettes Hypothesis shows is that one can perfectly properly appeal to evidence in the excluded domain in order to dismiss such a hypothesis. One can in fact have good evidence against hypotheses with this structure *even if one lacks any independent evidence against the hypothesis.* This is a key aspect of the principles and commitments of our pre-philosophical position.

I think that this should be the end of the matter: like Austin, we should reject the requirement. There's no hope of getting a compelling skeptical argument going in this way unless we can find some reason to distinguish the Evil Demon Hypothesis from the Children of Brunettes Hypothesis in some relevant respect. I do not think this can be done, for reasons that will emerge more fully in Chapters 6 and 7.

7. "Internalist" Constraints?

I now want to consider one additional strategy that is sometimes used to place a limitation on our evidence. It is sometimes suggested that we especially value "reflectively accessible evidence"—understanding that phrase as requiring evidence that one can possess and identify as such when one initially brackets all of one's convictions about the world and utilizes only the resources of introspection and a priori reflection. And the demand for such evidence is often taken to underwrite various "internalist" conceptions of knowledge, justification, or other terms of epistemic approbation, conceptions that would disallow responding to the skeptical argument by appealing to considerations about the world around us: on such views we won't have fully dealt with the Evil Demon Hypothesis unless we have provided this special sort of evidence against it. Of course, I haven't done that. Is this a problem for my approach?

In thinking about this question, it's important to keep in mind that epistemologists use the term "justification" to capture various statuses and potential features of beliefs, belief-contents, or believers that are of significance for their particular theoretical purposes. One can, of course, construct a concept for theoretical purposes that involves a demand for "reflectively accessible" evidence in the sense characterized above. However, there is no reason to think that such a demand reflects the statuses, distinctions, or requirements that are of significance in our ordinary practice.

Consider, for instance, a classic argument of Chisholm's. Chisholm's crucial premise is this:

> I am justified in believing that I can improve and correct my system of beliefs. I can eliminate the ones that are unjustified and add others that are justified, and I can replace less justified beliefs [by more justified beliefs]. (Chisholm 1989, 5)

From this we are to conclude that a particular conception of justification is in play such that a person "can know directly, just by reflecting on the state of his [sic] mind, that he is justified in believing that p" (Chisholm 1989, 7)—where this is meant to exclude knowing in a way that involves ineliminably relying on considerations about the world around us.

We can grant that Chisholm's premise is true: a key orienting principle of our epistemic practices is that it is possible for people to identify beliefs that are epistemically badly off and replace them with beliefs that are better off. But this does not commit us to thinking that we can know *just by reflecting on the state of our minds*, whether a belief is badly off or not. It's perfectly compatible with this aspect of our practice to hold that we identify and eliminate particular beliefs that are epistemically badly off by making use of other things we know about the world. So this aspect of our practices does not generate a requirement that limits our evidence in a way that would warrant dissatisfaction with my reply to the skeptical argument.

Similar problems plague every familiar attempt to show that our ordinary practice commits us to such a requirement. One commonplace is to appeal to considerations about epistemic responsibility, where responsible belief is taken to require that one have (and recognize) some reason for thinking that one's belief is true (e.g., Bonjour 1985, chapter 1). But epistemic responsibility, so understood, would not impose the limitation at issue here; for all it demands, one's reasons could perfectly well involve other claims about the world in every case. Something additional must therefore be brought into play to impose the proposed limitation. A standard argument appeals to the thought that it is constitutive of justification (or of evidence or reasons) that considerations about it can play a regulative role in deliberations about what to believe. But we can perfectly well regulate our beliefs in the light of something that is not accessible purely through introspection and a priori reflection (Goldman 1999). One would only think otherwise if one were imagining that the relevant sort of regulation must begin from a position in which one had no empirical beliefs about the world or in which all such beliefs were "off the table." But that conception does not fall out of the idea that justification, evidence, or reasons are "regulative." Rather, it is of a piece with the limitation that the argument was supposed to ground. It is a bit of Descartes' legacy to epistemology.

Another standard argument attempts to derive the limitation from the thought that our ordinary epistemic practices involve considerations about epistemic duties or obligations. Since (it is said) we cannot be held responsible for meeting or failing to meet our duties unless we are able to find out what they are, the factors determining our epistemic duties in a particular case must be something we can find out about. However, it is compatible with this requirement that in certain cases your ability to find out your duty might ineliminably depend upon considerations about matters that are not accessible through introspection and a priori reflection alone. One will think otherwise if one thinks that it must be possible to find out about one's epistemic duties even if one had no empirical beliefs about the world at all or if all such beliefs were "off the table." But, again, that conception is of a piece with what the argument was supposed to establish. It does not arise simply from the initial idea that we could not be held responsible for failing to meet our duties in any given case unless we were in a position in that case to find out what they were.

It has sometimes been suggested that epistemic rationality or justification is a kind of instrumental rationality: it is epistemically rational to believe a given proposition just if you would, after careful reflection, or after careful reflection under certain conditions, take believing that proposition to be an effective means to your overall epistemic goal.[22] However, this view would not limit our evidence or reasons—or the factors relevant to rationality—to what we can find out about through introspection and a priori reflection alone. For it is perfectly compatible with this view that our means-ends reflections in each particular case might involve considerations about the world that we could not find out about in that way. Any limitation on our evidence here will be an additional assumption arising from the idea that the relevant means-end reflection must take place from a position in which no commitments about the world are yet on the table. That is not itself a consequence of this conception of epistemic rationality.

In each of these cases we are seeing versions of the same point. The considerations that are supposed to fuel the demand for "reflectively accessible evidence" don't do that work by themselves, but only in conjunction with what amounts to the assumption of a version of the Cartesian position in which we attempt to rationally ground all of our beliefs about the world without presupposing any claims about that world. That latter position is precisely what has to be motivated.

The difficulty here isn't just that our ordinary practice doesn't involve principles of the right kind. There also aren't any examples that appropriately connect with our ordinary practice, either. Some epistemologists have suggested that examples of "chicken sexers" and the like—people able to make reliable or counterfactually secure judgments about a certain subject matter while having no reasons available to their conscious reflection and no correct beliefs about the factors that guide these judgments—show that we especially value "reflectively accessible justifications" (e.g., Pritchard 2005,

---

[22] This is roughly the view proposed in Foley (1987).

174–175 and *passim*).²³ But these examples don't show any such thing. If we ordinarily judge such people to be in a sub-optimal epistemic position, that can be explained in terms of the fact that they lack reflectively accessible reasons in the *ordinary* sense of that phrase: they can't cite any reasons in favor of their judgments.

Another example that has loomed large in arguments for "internalist" requirements is that of the "new evil demon."²⁴ Consider your twin in an "evil demon world": although this person is a disembodied spirit being globally deceived by an evil demon, everything experientially, introspectively, and intellectually seems the same to this person as it does to you, and this person has all of the beliefs that you do.²⁵ Many epistemologists claim that there is some important epistemic status (sometimes called "justification") that you and your twin share, in this sense: (a) at least some of your twin's beliefs have this status, and (b) any one of your beliefs has it if and only if your twins' corresponding belief does. I see no reason to disagree. However, from this point some epistemologists have been tempted to draw some very strong conclusions about the nature of our evidence: that (contrary to my suggestion in Section 6 above) we can't have evidence that our deceived twins lack, or that our evidence cannot include considerations about the world, or that our ordinary notion of good evidence cannot involve any requirements that aren't met by our deceived twins. None of these conclusions follow.²⁶

First, a logical point. The fact that you possess the particular good epistemic status and any evidence that your twin possesses doesn't entail that your twin possesses every good status and all the evidence that you possess. It remains perfectly possible that you have positive statuses and evidence that your deceived twin lacks, and that this evidence includes considerations about the world.

Second, we can grant that there is a sense in which your deceived, disembodied twin is justified in believing many particular things about the world. Given its sensory experiences and other beliefs, for instance, it would seem very odd, even inappropriate, for it to believe that it does not have a hand or

---

[23] It should be noted that to be relevant at all, the examples must be understood in such a way that the person can't even provide track-record considerations in favor of believing as she does.

[24] The example first appeared in Cohen and Lehrer (1983) and Cohen (1984), but it has since been widely used for a variety of purposes.

[25] To get the example exactly right, we'd have to fiddle to adjust for indexicals, any externally determined contents, and so on. I assume for the sake of argument that this can be made to work.

[26] The discussion in the next four paragraphs derives from my discussion in Leite (2013). I am grateful to Oxford University Press for permission to reuse this material.

for it to suspend judgment on the issue. It seems that the only option is to say that it is justified, in some sense, in believing that it has a hand (Silins 2005, 392–393). Does this mean that it has all the evidence that you do? No. That would only follow if this sense of "justified" exhausts the positive statuses that *your* beliefs have or if any further positive status that your beliefs have does not involve good evidence that your twin lacks. No reason has been given to think either of these things.

Third, and relatedly, the sense in which your twin's belief is justified doesn't provide any reason to privilege considerations available through introspection and a priori reflection, as distinct from considerations about the world, in what we count as our evidence. For we need not think that our twin's positive justificatory status must be accounted for via the possibility of some sort of inference-like transition from a limited evidential base that includes only the deliverances of sensory experience and introspection. Maybe if (a) all my disembodied twin had available to it were the deliverances of sensory experience and introspection, (b) it had no beliefs about the world, and (c) it started out in a situation in which it was explicitly agnostic about whether it was being deceived by an evil demon, there would be no course of explicit reasoning by which it could acceptably arrive at the belief that it has a hand. That is to say, it remains an open possibility that our twins' positive status, such as it is, depends upon their treating considerations about the world as an ineliminable part of their evidence.

Lastly, and crucially, there is a notion of good evidence that we care about in ordinary life and that outstrips anything at play in the status you and your twin share. From the standpoint of ordinary life there is an obvious way in which you are in a better epistemic position than your deceived twin, even if your twin is justified (in some sense) in believing precisely what you believe. Here's the difference: the considerations that you appeal to as evidence are true, and you are right in thinking that they make it more likely that your beliefs are true. Neither of these things are generally true of your deceived twin. This is a difference that we really do care about in ordinary life and science. Scientists *care* both whether the considerations they appeal to as evidence are actually true and whether those considerations actually make their conclusions more likely to be true. Someone who is right about these matters has a sort of positive status that is otherwise missing, and this is a way in which you are better off than your deceived twin: You have good evidence that your twin lacks. So the thought that our deceived twins are, like us, justified (in some sense) in their beliefs *does nothing* to suggest that in ordinary life we particularly care about some special conception of evidence that is limited to what we share with our deceived twins. Our good evidence includes all sorts of true considerations about the world.[27]

I turn now to one last strategy for imposing "internalist" constraints. Some philosophers have attempted to derive something like a demand for "reflectively accessible" reasons—and thus to restrict what counts as "our evidence" in relation to skepticism—by focusing upon certain kinds of questions. For instance, Bonjour (2003) proposes that a limitation to "reflectively accessible" reasons is forced on us by certain very general questions such as, "What reasons do I have for believing anything at all about the world around me?" or "What good reasons do we have for thinking that our beliefs about the world are true?" The suggestion is that when we ask such a question, we are precluded from making ineliminable use of considerations about the world in answering it, since doing so would in some sense objectionably assume or presuppose an answer to the very question under investigation. This is then taken to demonstrate that epistemic reasons must be available and identifiable as such even when one does not rely at the ground level upon considerations about the world.

In fact, however, no such requirement follows. The point can be seen by imagining that you sincerely attempt to answer the general question about reasons and find that using only the limited resources available to you, you cannot identify any good reason to believe anything about the world. Would you be entitled to conclude that you do not have any good reason to believe anything about the world? Surely not. All you would have found is that from a certain perspective you can't explain what good reasons you have for believing things about the world. The negative verdict only follows if you assume that that perspective is privileged—that is, the negative verdict only follows if you assume that the only good epistemic reasons must be available and identifiable as such when you do not rely at the ground level upon considerations about the world. That's just to assume precisely the demand that it was suggested the question would generate. The question itself does not generate that requirement. So, it still hasn't been shown that this requirement is implicit in the commitments of the ordinary, pre-philosophical position.

---

[27] For further discussion of the "New Evil Demon," see Chapter 12, Section 3. For further discussion of relevant issues relating to evidence, see Chapters 6 and 7.

I have been asking whether, from the standpoint of our ordinary practices, there is anything wrong with responding to the global skeptical argument by appealing to considerations about the world, for instance by pointing out that there are no evil demons. Since demands for "reflectively accessible" evidence for beliefs about the world do not reflect the statuses, distinctions, or requirements that figure centrally in our ordinary practices, such demands—as well as considerations about whether we possess such evidence—turn out to be irrelevant here. Admittedly, some "internalist" epistemologists have argued that we do have good "reflectively accessible" evidence for beliefs about the world, including the belief that we are not being deceived by an evil demon.[28] But from the standpoint of our ordinary practices the acceptability of my response to the skeptical argument does not depend upon their success.

8. Envoi

We have been considering whether there is anything wrong with appealing to considerations about the world as a ground for dismissing the deceiving demon and other global skeptical scenarios. As we saw, a number of moves might be made to try to show this response to be objectionable. These included the following suggestions:

- It is objectionably question-begging to dismiss the skeptic's hypotheses by appealing to considerations which the skeptic asserts you do not know or have good reason to believe.
- We can't know that the skeptical hypotheses don't obtain, because our evidence does not yield beliefs that meet the Sensitivity Requirement.
- Our evidence is neutral on the question because we would have exactly the same evidence if we were being deceived by an evil demon.
- Our evidence is generally restricted by the hypothesis under consideration, in such a way that considerations about the world become unavailable when we consider the skeptical hypotheses.
- Principles of epistemic closure somehow preclude us from knowing the falsity of the skeptical hypotheses, block us from appealing to

---

[28] Notably, Bonjour (1985, 179–188, and 2003, 92–96).

considerations about the world as a ground for dismissing them, or entangle us in vicious circularity if we do so.
- It is unacceptable to reject a hypothesis by appealing to a consideration about which we would be wrong or radically unreliable or incompetent if the hypothesis were true.
- "Internalist constraints" require us to find "reflectively accessible evidence" against the skeptical hypotheses—evidence that is available through introspection and a priori reflection alone.

The upshot in each case is that the suggestion does not properly track some key feature of our ordinary practice or pre-philosophical commitments. Considerations about the world can very often constitute good evidence, and so far no reason has emerged for thinking otherwise when it comes to the skeptical hypotheses in particular. If there is a good reason for thinking that our evidence is somehow more limited, either in general or when it comes to the skeptical hypotheses in particular, that reason has yet to be identified. It is on this key early stage of the skeptical argumentation that we must continue to focus.

You might not feel satisfied by what has been said. You might feel that some important consideration has not yet been addressed. This possibility is of a piece with the methodology. There is no single master argument to be constructed, just the patient consideration of the things that have been said or might be said to motivate the key early moves of skeptical argumentation from within our pre-philosophical position. As we go on, though, we go deeper, in this sense: we get a fuller and richer understanding of how the commitments and procedures of our pre-philosophical position actually work—and of precisely why they are so resistant to the skeptical argumentation.

Here are some particular concerns that I anticipate you might have in mind. You might be wondering about other influential presentations of skeptical argumentation, such as Crispin Wright's and Jim Pryor's—presentations that have been taken very seriously in the literature and that epistemologists (including Wright and Pryor themselves) have developed ingenious epistemological theories to overcome. These skeptical arguments will take center stage in the Methodological Interlude (Chapter 8).

You might be thinking something like this: "Of course I grant that considerations about the world can constitute evidence for various things. But there is something special about the skeptical scenarios: considerations about the world can't constitute evidence against them *in particular*, given what evidence should do." (This is a thought that is nicely expressed in Penelope Maddy's *What Do Philosophers Do?* [2017].) These issues about evidence will be the focus of Chapters 6 and 7.

You might be thinking that there is something fishy about my use of the Children of Brunettes Hypothesis. Maybe you think it isn't perfectly parallel to the skeptical hypotheses, or maybe you are happy to say that you don't know that it is false and also happy to say that you have no evidence against it. Are there really hypotheses that parallel the skeptical scenarios in every relevant respect and that (to speak from within our pre-philosophical position) we clearly know to be false? Can we really appeal to considerations in a hypothesis' domain as evidence that it is false? This is the topic of Chapter 7, which is pivotal for understanding the anti-skeptical commitments of our pre-philosophical position.

Finally, you might be concerned about the role of sensory experience in our knowledge of the world. This issue will be addressed in Chapters 9 to 12. And as we move forward, all these concerns will be progressively clarified, refined, and framed by what went before.

6
Evidence and Method

Do we really know that we are not being globally deceived by an evil demon? Do we really have evidence against this scenario?[1]

In her wonderful book *What Do Philosophers Do?* (2017), Penelope Maddy has recently argued that the answer to both questions is "No." There is, she contends, no rational support for the claim that we are not being globally deceived by an evil demon. In this regard, she agrees with the skeptic. Her arguments do not assume or entail that skepticism is true, however. On her view, we can have good evidence and even knowledge about the world, even if we have no evidence that we aren't being deceived by an evil demon. She accordingly holds that we have excellent reason to believe many things about the world, and she grants that we know them. Moreover, she does not assume that our evidence is fundamentally limited in a way that excludes considerations about the world around us. Where she agrees with the skeptic is only on this claim: we cannot have evidence against the Evil Demon Hypothesis, so insofar as we are concerned with a notion of knowledge that involves good evidence or rational grounds, we cannot know that we are not being deceived by an evil demon. If she is right about that, then it is hopeless to respond to skepticism by claiming, as I have, that we have decisive evidence and indeed know that we aren't being deceived by an evil demon.

I doubt, however, that even Maddy's limited claim is correct. More particularly, once one has taken onboard everything that Maddy's "Plain Inquirer" quite rightly accepts, this claim is very hard to sustain. Seeing why this is so will take us deep into a consideration of how evidence actually functions in our best epistemic practices. It will help us see just how hopeless it is to think that skepticism could be derived from our pre-philosophical epistemic

---

[1] This chapter is derived with permission from Adam Leite (2018), "The Plain Inquirer's Plain Evidence Against the Global Skeptical Scenarios," *International Journal for the Study of Skepticism* 8, no. 3, 208–222 (Brill Academic Publishing).

commitments. The upshot will be a deeper appreciation of the ways in which our pre-philosophical position resists skeptical argumentation.

To help frame this discussion, it should be noted that there's an important sense in which Maddy and I are on the same team. We both take our starting point in ordinary methods (including science), and we both wind up with continued confidence in them.[2] Austin, Moore, and Wittgenstein are important figures for us both, and though we interpret Moore somewhat differently, our readings are more similar than many others. This wide agreement sharpens the significance of our disagreement. It heightens the focus on the question of whether from this perspective it is right to respond to the skeptic by claiming we know and have good evidence that we aren't being deceived.

1. Maddy's Plain Inquirer and the Global Skeptical Scenarios

Maddy's Plain Inquirer—the hero of her book—works from a perspective very much like the one I have been urging. The Plain Inquirer is content to counter skeptical concerns from within our best ongoing ordinary and scientific views and methods, of which she is a voracious and wide-ranging consumer. She accepts a wide variety of claims about the world: that her perceptual faculties are generally reliable, that she is in optimal conditions right now for seeing that there is a real table here before her, that there *is* a real table there and she sees it, and so on. She likewise holds that she has good evidence for a wide variety of claims about the world and her relation to it. She allows that some considerations about the world can perfectly appropriately be appealed to as fully adequate evidence in favor of other considerations about the world. She rejects the broadly Cartesian idea that she can't be entitled to these claims, or have good evidence for them, or know them, unless she can provide a defense of them that starts from nowhere. She likewise rejects the more limited demand for a defense that makes use only of considerations that do not concern the world outside of her mind. Those sorts of demands

---

[2] I am grateful to Maddy for this way of characterizing our agreement.

simply ignore all of the good evidence and methods that we actually have (69, 74). On all of this, she is in agreement with the perspective that I have been urging.

Still, Maddy's Plain Inquirer takes a strikingly different position regarding the global skeptical scenarios. I have been urging that if you approach matters from the perspective that Maddy's Plain Inquirer and I share, the right thing to say is this: *these hypotheses are false, we know they are false, and we have all sorts of information that tells decisively against them.* For instance, I am not being deceived by an evil demon; after all, there aren't any evil demons. Maddy, by contrast, says that ruling out these hypotheses can "never be done" (2017, 230) and is a "lost cause" (230). They are, she says, "by their very nature structurally impervious to evidence" (232). We don't even have evidence that they are likely to be false (33, 73). Since the Plain Inquirer doesn't adopt views without sufficient evidence, she consequently won't even hold that she isn't being deceived by an evil demon.

This strikes me as an awkward position. The Plain Inquirer accepts our best ordinary and scientific methods, standards, and practices, as well as the results of our best science. (Of course, she embraces a healthy fallibilism about all of this.) Now, if there is anything that we learned from the scientific revolution, it is this: There are no evil demons; that's not how the world works. Consider, then, the following thought: "There are no evil demons, so I'm not being deceived by one—there aren't any to deceive me." If you are the Plain Inquirer, are you going to refuse to accept that thought? Rejecting it doesn't look like the response of someone who embraces the methods and standards that *we* accept. Either you wouldn't be accepting that there are no evil demons, in which case you are hardly embracing modern science, or you would be refusing to recognize that you can't be deceived by something that doesn't exist. Neither looks to me like a position the Plain Inquirer would be happy to hold.

Notice that I have not claimed anything about whether you could come to find out for the first time that you are not being deceived by an evil demon via an explicit, self-conscious inference from the fact that there are no evil demons. Nor have I made a claim about whether knowledge is always closed under known entailment or even about whether justification or evidential support always transmits across known entailment. The point is just that it is hard to see how the Plain Inquirer could resist the above thought, if she really accepts our methods, standards, and the results of science.[34]

For these reasons, then, I think it is awkward for the Plain Inquirer to refuse to hold that there is decisive evidence against Descartes' Evil Demon Hypothesis. Still, one might feel that even though awkward, Maddy's proposal is the best that can be made of a bad job. It therefore behooves us to look carefully at what might be said in favor of her position. Why shouldn't the Plain Inquirer reject the global skeptical hypotheses by appealing to other considerations about the world, given that the Plain Inquirer generally regards considerations about the world as fully adequate evidence? Is there any good reason for singling out *I am not being deceived by an evil demon* as requiring or deserving a different kind of treatment?

---

[3] It might be objected that natural science doesn't properly speak to the issue. Descartes' Evil Demon Hypothesis is not that there is a denizen of the spatiotemporal world affecting our beliefs and cognitive processes by intervening in the usual causal order, but instead that there is no physical world, that I have no body, and that there is a non-spatiotemporal being directly affecting my mind in some unknown way to cause me to have radically misleading experiences and a grossly incorrect belief system. How, it might be asked, does natural science even come into contact with this hypothesis? (Thanks here to Kirk Ludwig.) Leaving aside the question of whether there are any non-spatiotemporal intelligent beings, natural science is relevant here in multiple respects. Among the commitments with which we started this whole discussion—and with which Maddy's Plain Inquirer agrees—are such considerations as these: we have bodies and brains, these are part of the causal order, there are important links between brain processes and thought processes, vision works in such and such ways, we very often see objects in the world, and the like. These considerations are well-supported in various ways by various sciences; for instance, psychologists now know a great deal about the ways and circumstances in which vision is reliable and the ways and circumstances in which it isn't. Crucially, all these considerations are *incompatible with* Descartes' Evil Demon Hypothesis. And of course, if the demon hypothesis is that there is a supernatural denizen of the spatiotemporal world affecting our beliefs and cognitive processes by intervening in the usual causal order, then natural science has provided decisive reasons for rejecting it. Given all of this, I will continue to appeal to "There are no evil demons" as reason to reject Descartes' fantasy, understanding this to be convenient shorthand. It is a way of making the point that the Plain Inquirer is committed to lots of things that are incompatible with the Evil Demon Hypothesis.

[4] Here is a second relevant consideration. The Plain Inquirer has studied logic. She recognizes that *p* and *if p, then q* entail *q*, so she recognizes that the propositions *There is a desk in front of me that I am seeing right now* and *If there is a desk in front of me that I am seeing right now, then I am not being deceived by an evil demon* entail *I am not being deceived by an evil demon*. Suppose, then, that she is teaching a fledgling Plain Inquirer who is struggling to understand the notion of logical entailment. She writes "True" in front of the first proposition; she has no qualms about that. She writes "True" in front of the second, conditional proposition; after all, she recognizes that there is no way for the antecedent to be true but the consequent false. So, since she recognizes the entailment, doesn't she have to write "True" in front of "I am not being deceived by an evil demon?" And if—as Maddy would have it—she doesn't write "True" in front of it, *what on earth does she say to her student?*

Perhaps unsurprisingly, I think that the answer is "No." I will begin with some preliminary points about the skeptical scenarios and their relation to evidence. I will then turn to considerations relating to supposed limitations in our current epistemic situation and what (one might think) evidence should do for us regarding the skeptical scenarios. The question will ultimately take us into deeper methodological issues regarding epistemic asymmetry, epistemic circularity, and the stance of detached rational evaluation.

2. The Skeptical Hypotheses, Cartesian Demands, and Imperviousness to Evidence

At a number of points, Maddy proposes that the Evil Demon Hypothesis is tantamount to a demand for a Cartesian-style "from scratch" justification—a justification that does not proceed from within the Plain Inquirer's developing view or depend upon anything that she has good reason to believe about the world. As Maddy puts it, "the skeptical hypotheses ... are expressly designed to pose the 'from scratch' challenge" (232), where the "from scratch" challenge is to justify our beliefs "without appeal to anything else we think we know" (37; see also 31–32, 33, 69).

This understanding of the situation brings together two things that I think are best kept distinct. Considering the deceiving demon scenario does not *by itself* limit what might be offered as a ground for rejecting it. If the question is simply what decisively points towards the falsity of the Evil Demon Hypothesis, the Plain Inquirer can answer the question quite readily from within her developing view, as I argued in earlier chapters. The "from scratch" challenge is a distinct goal, a limitation on the grounds that one might offer. That limitation is not forced on us simply by considering the Evil Demon Hypothesis. So, to get from the Evil Demon Hypothesis to the Cartesian philosophical goal that Maddy highlights, something additional is required. To put it another way, if the Plain Inquirer rejects the "from scratch challenge" and the limitation it imposes—as she does—then she should have no qualms on that score, at least, about rejecting the skeptical scenarios by appealing to considerations about the world.

Now Maddy doesn't see things this way. She holds that the limitation is already accomplished by the hypothesis itself. She writes, "the hypothesis of extraordinary dreaming is constructed in such a way that any evidence

[we] might offer could just be part of the same all-encompassing extraordinary dream" (33, compare 232). She therefore characterizes the skeptical hypotheses as "by their very nature structurally impervious to evidence" (232). Here Maddy is not alone. It is often said that the skeptical hypotheses are constructed in such a way that their very structure undercuts, calls into question, or somehow precludes use of all the sorts of claims that I have appealed to as evidence against them.

We have already seen several reasons for thinking that this thought is incorrect.

First, recall that merely considering a hypothesis doesn't prevent you from rejecting it by appealing to something that would be false if the hypothesis were true. If I am wondering whether Morgan is a woman, learning that Morgan is a bachelor decides the question, and this is so even though if Morgan were a woman, it would be false that Morgan is a bachelor. Here I am rejecting a hypothesis by using evidence that would be false if the hypothesis were true. Merely considering the hypothesis doesn't wipe out that evidence.[5]

Of course, if I had good reasons of the right sort for thinking that Morgan is a woman, then I couldn't reject this hypothesis in this way. Those reasons would also give me reason to doubt that Morgan is a bachelor. What I would then need to do would depend upon the precise nature of the reasons in play. Whether one can reject a particular suggestion by appealing to a particular consideration depends in part upon what there is reason to believe and what there is reason to doubt in the circumstances.

There are no reasons for even suspecting that we are being deceived by an evil demon. The Plain Inquirer surely agrees with that. It is true that the Evil Demon Hypothesis proposes that our beliefs about the world are false, but it doesn't *actually* put everything into doubt, because there is no reason whatsoever in its favor. So far, then, this looks parallel to the Morgan case in a key respect: Nothing has yet happened to prevent the Plain Inquirer from appealing to the fact that there are no evil demons as a ground for rejecting the hypothesis that she is being deceived by an evil demon.

A line of thought that we have already discussed may rear its head at this juncture. One might think, "Ah—but the Evil Demon Hypothesis is different because of a crucial feature of its structure: the considerations about the world that you have appealed to as evidence against it are matters about

---

[5] Again, I apologize for making use of an example that depends upon a sexist and gender-binary conceptual framework.

which the hypothesis suggests you are deceived. Isn't there something fishy about trying to rule out a possible scenario by appealing to a consideration about which you would go wrong or be radically unreliable if that scenario were the case?"

We've seen this thought before. And as we have seen, in certain sorts of cases this isn't fishy at all. To repeat a point that was made earlier: Right now I can tell from how my speech sounds that I am not drunkenly slurring my words. That's so even if when I'm drunk and slurring my words I incorrectly think that my speech sounds perfectly normal. The mere fact that I would be unreliable about a subject matter if a certain hypothesis were true does not make it unacceptable for me to appeal to that subject matter as evidence that the hypothesis does not hold. At least, this is so when there is no reason to think that the hypothesis is true.

Moreover, as the Children of Brunettes Hypothesis revealed, nothing changes when we make the hypothesized unreliability more general.[6] If that hypothesis were true, children of brunettes (like myself) would be wrong or radically unreliable about the scientific considerations that show that the hair color of parents has no effect on the cognitive abilities of children. But I have no qualms at all about saying both that we know this hypothesis is false and that these scientific considerations provide decisive evidence against it. The important lesson to keep in mind here is this: you can have evidence E against a proposition *p* even if you would be entirely and radically unreliable about all relevant matters if *p* were true. So, merely considering the evil demon and other skeptical hypotheses does not, by itself, preclude us from offering good evidence against them. Their structure is *not* such that they are impervious to evidence.

Perhaps surprisingly, Maddy denies this lesson. This is because she draws the same conclusion about the Children of Brunettes Hypothesis that she draws about the Evil Demon scenario (2018, 236–237). She says that as the child of a brunette she does not (and cannot) get any evidence against this hypothesis—all this despite the fact that it involves commitment to the manifestly false claim that the hair color of one's parents is relevant to one's cognitive abilities. That position strikes me as incredible. My own commitments run in exactly the other direction. I would think it outrageous to tell a cognitive science class that it is an open question whether the

---

[6] That hypothesis, recall, is that the children of brunettes suffer from profound and pervasive perceptual and cognitive deficits, compensated for by hallucinatory infilling and confabulation.

Children of Brunettes Hypothesis is true. So are Maddy and I just at a standoff? To make headway here, we need to consider what might be said in favor of her view.

3. (Supposed) Limitations in Our Current Epistemic Situation and Evidence

It might be claimed that even though we know all sorts of things in ordinary life and science, including that we have bodies, that we see tables, and that the hair color of parents does not affect the cognitive abilities of children, still our current epistemic situation is nonetheless *specially limited* in some relevant way when it comes to hypotheses like the Evil Demon and the Children of Brunettes. This thought is perhaps what Maddy is getting at when she says, regarding the Dream Hypothesis, that "any evidence [we] might offer could just be part of the same all-encompassing extraordinary dream" (2017, 33). I will consider six lines of thought suggesting a limitation in our epistemic position when it comes to the global skeptical scenarios. I do not find any of them compelling.

First, let me remind you of some points that have already been made. It might be complained that everything would seem the same to us, we would believe all the same things, and we would appeal to the same considerations as evidence, if the hypothesis were true. That's right. But so what? Consider the hypothesis that my spouse left the country earlier today and purposefully deceived me about her plans and whereabouts. Everything would seem just as it does—and I would believe everything I currently do—if this hypothesis were true. I would offer all of the same considerations as reasons for thinking that nothing of the sort had gone on. But today, when there is no reason whatsoever to suspect that this hypothesis is correct, I *do* have evidence against it, including that she has other plans and doesn't have any reason to leave the country or to deceive me in this way. So I can have excellent evidence against a hypothesis even if everything would seem to me just as it does—and even if I would believe everything that I do and offer just the same considerations as evidence—if the hypothesis were true.

Second, it might be said that there is nothing in our epistemic position that differentiates it from the case in which the Children of Brunettes or Evil Demon Hypothesis is true. You might say this if you thought that your epistemic position is limited to *how things seem to you*, described in a way that involves no further commitments about what is the case. But that is not how Maddy's Plain Inquirer understands her epistemic position. She is happy to include amongst her evidence—as part of her "current epistemic position"— all sorts of facts about the world, not just about how things seem. These include, for instance, facts about psychology and genetics. She has good reason to utilize these considerations in this way: these truths have decisive evidence in their favor, were established via good methods, and so on. This means, however, that her epistemic position includes things that differentiate her situation from the case in which the Children of Brunettes Hypothesis is true. For instance, there is the fact that the hair color of parents does not genetically affect the cognitive abilities of offspring. Analogous points hold regarding the Evil Demon Hypothesis. In both cases, the Plain Inquirer is in an excellent position to point out facts that differentiate her case from those in which those hypotheses are correct.

Here is a possible objection: "But she can't tell whether she actually has that good evidence, since she would incorrectly include those things amongst her evidence if the Children of Brunettes Hypothesis were true." This is a third way in which her epistemic position might be thought to be limited in relation to these hypotheses. This thought is incorrect, however. I can tell right now that how my speech sounds is good evidence that I am not drunkenly slurring my words, even if—were I drunk—I would get this wrong. That is, the fact that if p were false, someone would incorrectly think that she had good evidence for p, doesn't mean that she can't tell now—when p is true— that she has good evidence for p.

How is this point to be applied to the Plain Inquirer's position regarding her good evidence that the Children of Brunettes Hypothesis is false? She can tell—as Maddy grants—that her methods are good ones, and that she is *right* to include certain facts on her developing list of truths. For instance, she can determine, by what she recognizes to be good methods, that the hair color of parents does not genetically affect the cognitive abilities of offspring. It is by recognizing that she is right to regard this as true, and seeing what its significance is, that she can tell that she has good evidence against the Children of Brunettes Hypothesis. And this is so even though she would incorrectly take those considerations to be good evidence against the hypothesis if the hypothesis were true.

Fourth, to return to a theme from the last section of the previous chapter, it might be said that given what is *reflectively available to us*, we have nothing to go on that would enable us to responsibly believe that the Children of

Brunettes Hypothesis is false. A lot depends here on what is meant by "reflectively available." Maddy's Plain Inquirer won't mean by this phrase what epistemologists often mean—evidence that is accessible through introspection and a priori reflection alone—since the Plain Inquirer sees no reason to limit her evidence in that way. She is content to include such things as "There is a table here" amongst her evidence even if there is no method by which she could arrive at this truth on the basis of introspection and a priori reflection alone.

By "reflectively available evidence," then, we might instead mean considerations that we are in a position to cite and that we recognize as good evidence by good methods—recognize as true, as telling in favor of the relevant claim, and so on. In this sense, the Plain Inquirer *does* have considerations reflectively available to her that tell against the Children of Brunettes and Evil Demon Hypotheses. For she sees that there are truths, reached by good methods, that tell against these hypotheses (indeed, imply their falsehood), and she is in a position to cite them. I can't see any other form of "reflectively available evidence" that she should want.

Fifth, it might be emphasized that the Plain Inquirer aims to be a responsible inquirer. She won't include a claim in her view unless she thinks she's in a good position to get the relevant matters right. And it might be claimed that she won't take this requirement to be met in the case of the Children of Brunettes Hypothesis: as the child of a brunette herself, she won't take herself to be in a good position to get right whether the hypothesis is false.

However, I don't see why this would be so. As Maddy grants, the Plain Inquirer knows a great deal about human psychology and the like. She knows a great deal about how our cognitive faculties work. This enables her to reflectively endorse her methods. That's why she feels confident going on augmenting her views by utilizing these methods. Why don't the same considerations give her an excellent reason to think that using good scientific methods puts her in a good position to get matters right when it comes to the Children of Brunettes Hypothesis? Look at it this way: if she is in a good position to get it right that the hair color of parents does not genetically affect the cognitive abilities of offspring—as she holds that she is—then she *has* to be in a good position to get matters right regarding the Children of Brunettes Hypothesis. So it seems to me that the Plain Inquirer should be quite happy to think that she is in an excellent position to assess the Children of Brunette's Hypothesis as false. The demands of responsible inquiry won't lead her to think otherwise.

Sixth, and finally, it is nearly a truism in the philosophical literature on evidence that if a prediction of a hypothesis is found to obtain, then one should raise one's confidence in that hypothesis (at least somewhat, and all else equal). But putting the point the other way around, if a hypothesis H entails some E, then E can't be evidence for not-H and against H *as distinct from for H*. And, as is commonly thought, doesn't the Evil Demon Hypothesis entail our evidence? But this is a mistake. As the Plain Inquirer is happy to grant, my evidence includes all sorts of considerations about the world, including such facts as that I have a body and am seeing a table. *Those propositions are not entailed by the Evil Demon Hypothesis.* What the Evil Demon Hypothesis entails is that *it seems to me* and *I believe* that I have a body and am seeing a table. But the Plain Inquirer doesn't see any reason to limit her evidence to how things seem and facts about what she believes; she happily includes amongst her evidence all sorts of considerations about the world and her relation to it. So if her evidence is to be somehow more narrowly circumscribed when it comes to the Evil Demon Hypothesis, some special reason has to be given for that—and we still haven't found any such reason. The truism about evidence doesn't have that effect all by itself. The same points apply *mutatis mutandis* regarding the Children of Brunettes Hypothesis.

In sum, I don't see any reason to think that the Plain Inquirer should regard our epistemic position as limited when it comes to the Children of Brunettes or the familiar skeptical hypotheses.

4. What (One Might Think) Evidence Should Do for Us

Here's another tack. It might be suggested that considerations about *what evidence should enable us to do* preclude us from having evidence against the Children of Brunettes or Evil Demon Hypotheses.

For instance, you might think that we could now have evidence for *p* only if it were possible to acquire evidence establishing not-*p* in at least some not-*p* cases. Thus, for instance, in Maddy's discussion of our ability to determine that we are not "ordinary" dreaming right now (having a dream of the familiar sort, which differs in specifiable phenomenological ways from ordinary waking experience), she appeals to the possibility of learning to determine on phenomenological grounds that you *are* dreaming when you are (2017, 25–26). The underlying idea here seems to be that if you are to have evidence for *p* (e.g., that you are not dreaming), then there must be ways for you to puzzle it out if *p* is false.

I don't see any reason to think that this requirement is correct. I can have excellent evidence for *p* now, even if I wouldn't be able to puzzle it out if *p* were false. What matters is what I can do in the case I am in: the case in which *p* is true. For instance, suppose again that when drunk I cannot tell that I am slurring my words: I incorrigibly believe that I am not. Even if that were true of me, I see no reason to think that I couldn't have excellent evidence right now that I am not drunkenly slurring my words. Right now, when I am not drunkenly slurring my words and my faculties are not impaired in this way, I can correctly register how my speech sounds. What would happen in the case in which my faculties *are* thus impaired doesn't diminish this fact.

In fact, a consideration can decisively tell in favor of *p* now, even if appealing to it would lead you astray if *p* were false. This is frequently the situation when we know something on the basis of fallible evidence. Suppose you drop your trash bag into the trash chute on the tenth floor of your apartment building—a trash chute that has operated perfectly reliably for years. There is no indication of anything out of the ordinary: no warning notices, no trash bags piled in the hall, no unusual sounds when you drop your bag. Shortly after the door clangs shut, you have excellent evidence that your trash bag is now somewhere in the bowels of the building. But if it weren't, if your bag had silently snagged on the way down, the very same considerations would lead you astray.[7] It is consequently compatible with your now having decisive evidence against the Children of Brunettes Hypothesis that the very same considerations would lead you astray if that hypothesis were true. The fact that you would incorrectly appeal to claims in psychology and genetics as reasons for rejecting the Children of Brunettes Hypothesis *in the case in which that hypothesis is true* does not undercut the fact that psychology and genetics lead you to exactly the right conclusion *in our world*, in which the Children of Brunettes Hypothesis is false.

Still, one might think that if you are to have evidence that *p*, then it must be possible to figure out in the not-*p* case that your evidence is leading you astray. But this is not so either. There are many cases in which you have evidence for *p*, but if *p* were false your evidence would lead you astray and you

---

[7] This is adapted from an example from Sosa (1999).

wouldn't then be in a position to determine that this is so. I will discuss some in Chapter 7.

It is likewise no objection that if the Children of Brunettes Hypothesis were true, you would wrongly think that the considerations you would offer against it are true. You can now have evidence E against *p* even if E would be false—and you would incorrectly think E true—if *p* were true. Considerations about my spouse's plans for the day and her love for me decisively establish that she did not purposefully deceive me by leaving the country this morning without telling me. I have that evidence now even if it is true that if I were in a world in which she had done this, I would incorrectly believe just the same things right now. It is consequently compatible with your now having decisive evidence against the Children of Brunettes Hypothesis that you'd get relevant matters badly wrong if that hypothesis were true.

It might be thought that evidence should always do something else for us: it should always enable us to resolve reasonable doubts. For instance, you might think that in order for you to have evidence that *p* in circumstances in which there is no reason to doubt *p*, that evidence should enable you to decide the question *in the circumstances in which you do have reason to doubt that p*. But this requirement is incorrect as well. I can have evidence that *p* right now even if there is a case in which I have a reason for doubting *p* of a sort that would undercut that evidence—so that in those circumstances that evidence wouldn't enable me to sort between the case in which *p* and the case in which not-*p*. For instance, right now I have good evidence that my spouse didn't leave the country this morning without telling me. But if I acquired the right sort of reason to think that perhaps she had, the evidence I now have would do nothing to resolve the question. (A similar point was made earlier regarding the Morgan example.)

Finally, you might think that evidence for *p* is always something that you should be able to utilize to resolve a question about *p* from a position of *neutrality* or *complete agnosticism*, so that if you explicitly took no stand on whether *p*—without having any particular reason for doubt, but leaving both *p* and not-*p* wide open—you could reach an answer *by deploying that evidence*. If that were so, then you obviously couldn't have evidence against the Children of Brunettes or Evil Demon Hypotheses, since these hypotheses are structured in such a way that you cannot take up an initially neutral position and then find something that will tell you which case you are in. However, I don't think that this demand is correct. As will become apparent, there is reason for the Plain Inquirer to agree with me here.

5. Epistemic Asymmetry and the Demand for Evidence That Functions Regardless of the Human and Worldly Context

To begin to make this case, I want to highlight a key structural feature of some of the examples that I have been using.

The drunken slurring example is a case of *epistemic asymmetry*. So is the hypothesis that my spouse left the country this morning without telling me, purposely deceiving me about her plans and whereabouts. Another example is my knowledge that my spouse isn't deceiving me about whether she loves me. (If she were, I would not be able to tell on the basis of my current evidence and would incorrectly believe she isn't.) As a first-pass characterization, to be refined in the next chapter, we could say: In epistemic asymmetries, one's epistemic position with regard to whether p *differs depending on whether or not p is true*. In the case in which p is true (the "good case," following Williamson 2000), one is able to tell that p is true. But in the case in which p is not true (the "bad case"), one cannot tell that p is false and often incorrectly believes that p is true. Once you recognize the phenomenon, you begin to see it all over the place.

My claim is that the Children of Brunettes and Evil Demon Hypotheses are cases of epistemic asymmetry as well. In the actual world, in which they are false, you can tell—on the basis of excellent evidence—that they are false, even though if they were true, you would incorrectly take them to be false.

I don't think that Maddy's Plain Inquirer has any reason to disagree with me about this. The Children of Brunettes and Evil Demon Hypotheses have an interesting structural feature that has been highlighted in earlier chapters. All the considerations we might offer as evidence against them are matters about whose truth or objective evidential significance we would be wrong or radically unreliable if they were true. In the next chapter I will argue that there are perfectly unexceptionable examples of epistemic asymmetry that mirror these hypotheses in this and every other relevant respect. For now, though, I want to highlight a more limited point. Maddy's Plain Inquirer has *every reason to expect* epistemic asymmetries of precisely this sort. Importantly, this isn't just a matter of "intuitions" regarding the application of certain concepts. It's a matter of how we think it best to go about conducting our lives as responsible believers. What is at issue here are our ordinary commitments regarding good methodology.

Maddy diagnoses skeptical concerns as arising from a certain demand on what evidence must be like and what it should do. She describes the objectionable demand this way:

> Proper evidence, the only truly acceptable evidence, must support the claim for which it's evidence no matter how bizarre the circumstances; it must work without depending on the contingent nature of our perceptual mechanisms, the actual makeup of the world we are perceiving, or anything else. (2017, 195)

This is a demand for evidence that we could recognize and deploy as good evidence without presupposing any contingent claims about the world.

The Plain Inquirer counters this demand with a position that Maddy very plausibly finds in Wittgenstein's *On Certainty* (1969). She puts it this way: "There's no good reason to demand a form of evidence that's independent of the human and worldly context in which it's being offered" [2017, 195–196]). That is to say, we should regard *what is evidence for what* as depending on how things are, how the world works, and what there is reason for and against. This is another way of putting the point that Austin made when he wrote:

> [I]n general, *any* kind of statement could state evidence for any other kind, if the circumstances were appropriate. (1962, 116; cf. 111, 140)

> [T]here *could* be no *general* answer to the questions what is evidence for what, what is certain, what is doubtful, what needs or does not need evidence, can or can't be verified [because these matters all depend on "the circumstances"]. (1962, 124)

As I stressed in Chapter 4, this point about evidence has an important consequence, one which Maddy's Plain Inquirer happily accepts. If we put on hold all of our commitments about the contingent nature of ourselves, our world, and our circumstances, we will not be able to determine anything at all about what tells in favor of what when it comes to conditions in the world around us (see also Leite 2005).

Given this broad methodological position regarding evidence, Maddy's Plain Inquirer should *expect* cases of epistemic asymmetry with the structure displayed by the Children of Brunettes Hypothesis. They will arise whenever our ability to tell whether *p* depends in a very particular way upon certain, quite particular aspects of the human and worldly context. Consider any case with the following two features:

1. Whether E objectively tells in favor of *p* depends upon the truth of *p*: If *p* is true, then E tells in its favor, but if *p* were false, E would either be false or would not be objectively good evidence for *p* at all.
2. One's reliability, competence, or ability to aptly evaluate the truth and evidential significance of matters pertaining to *p* varies depending upon whether *p* is true. If *p* were false, one would incorrectly believe that E is true and tells in favor of *p*.

As we have seen, there are lots of humdrum examples that display these features. In such cases, one's ability to know on good evidence that *p* depends on aspects of the human and worldly context. For instance, if *p* is false, then E won't be good evidence for *p* but one will incorrectly think that it is, whereas if *p* is true then one will be able to aptly evaluate E's truth and evidential significance with regard to *p*. That yields an instance of epistemic asymmetry with the structural feature of the Children of Brunettes and Evil Demon Hypotheses that I highlighted above. This is precisely what we should expect if we should regard *what is evidence for what* as depending upon the human and worldly context in which it is being offered.

This point has an important consequence. Let me walk up to it slowly.

We children of brunettes have no evidence that could decide the issue when we ask *from a neutral position*, "Which case am I in, the good case or the bad case?" We have no evidence of that sort, because if a child of a brunette considers the question from that neutral position, she will likewise have to put on hold all of the commitments about which she recognizes she would be wrong or radically unreliable if the hypothesis were true. About each of these considerations she should think, "I can't appeal to *that*, since I'm regarding it as a wide open possibility that the Children of Brunettes Hypothesis is true—and hence a wide open possibility that I am in no position to correctly evaluate the truth or objective evidential significance of this consideration." As a result, she will have to temporarily suspend all the ordinary and scientific considerations concerning the relationship between the hair color of parents and the cognitive abilities of their children. So, in posing the question in the way she has, she will have removed all of the resources that are needed in order to answer it.

Now here is the important implication. You might think that in order for us to have evidence on this issue, our evidence must be able to decide the question when we take up that neutral position and suspend our commitment to everything that this question, posed in this way, would call into question. But to tie *our possession of evidence now* to that demand is *to require evidence that works independently of the human and worldly context in which it is being offered*. It is to require evidence that works for us no matter how the world happens to be or what question we have taken up. Maddy's Plain Inquirer rejects this requirement both in general and in many other particular contexts. No reason has emerged against doing so here as well. It looks to me as though she should grant that here too, evidence functions against a real-world and human background. Genetics and psychology and everyday experience provide *excellent* evidence against the Children of Brunettes Hypothesis, but only given the actual worldly and human context. As a result, if you pose certain kinds of questions, you won't be able to see that good evidence for what it is. The same point applies to the familiar skeptical hypotheses.

I can't see any good methodological grounds against granting this. After all, doing so won't lead the Plain Inquirer astray!

6. Epistemic Circularity, the Reliability of Sense Perception, and What We Can Demand from Evidence

The same conclusion follows from Maddy's comments about epistemic circularity and the reliability of sense perception.

The epistemological literature has familiarized us with the important phenomenon of *epistemic circularity* (Alston 1986). In an ordinary circular argument, the conclusion appears amongst the premises. In epistemic circularity, by contrast, the issue concerns our ability to recognize the support the premises provide for the conclusion: epistemic circularity arises when we must in some sense treat the conclusion as being the case in order to recognize the evidence we have for it. Minimally: we cannot treat the conclusion as false or as something we have good reason to think to be false, nor can we genuinely wonder whether it is false or treat it as a wide open question, explicitly not holding any view whatsoever on the issue nor assigning it a probability. For instance, consider the Children of Brunettes Hypothesis. If you are the child of a brunette and think that hypothesis is likely to be true or regard it as a wide open question, then you are rationally required to call into question all of the considerations in psychology, genetics, and ordinary experience that you might appeal to as evidence against it. So in this sense, there is a kind of circularity here. Recognizing the evidence that you have against this hypothesis depends upon holding some sort of positive attitude toward the claim that the Children of Brunettes Hypothesis is false.

Epistemic circularity is importantly related to the issue about evidence that we have been discussing. If you allow that there is acceptable epistemic circularity anywhere, then you grant that it is possible to have good evidence for p even if you can't use that evidence to resolve the question of whether p from a position of complete agnosticism or reasonable doubt. This is because a case of epistemic circularity is precisely one in which you can't leave it wide open whether p is true, regard it as in doubt, or adopt a neutral position on the issue, and still recognize the good evidence that you have for p.

Consider, then, Maddy's discussion of the reliability of sense perception (2017, 223–228). The Plain Inquirer draws upon the extensive scientific discoveries about perception in order to develop a nuanced, well-supported account of the overall reliability of sensory perception, how it functions to get things right in the circumstances in which it does, and how and why it fails when it does. Sense perception is unavoidably involved in developing this account, and the dependence is one of epistemic circularity: if the Plain Inquirer thought that sensory perception was not reliable at all, or if she had good reason to suspect as much, or if she genuinely regarded it as an entirely open question, explicitly taking no stand whatsoever on the issue, then much of the evidential base for her account of the reliability of sense perception would become unavailable to her. Her ability to deploy that evidential base depends upon treating it as true that sense perception is sufficiently reliable. (This sort of dependence becomes even clearer when we consider the Plain Inquirer's theory of the reliability of human cognitive faculties in general.)

So the Plain Inquirer does not regard epistemic circularity as a failing in itself. This means that she grants that we can have good evidence for p even if we can't use that evidence to resolve the question of whether p from a position of complete agnosticism, neutrality, or reasonable doubt. So no such demand should lead her to say that we lack evidence regarding cases with the structure of the Children of Brunettes and the familiar skeptical hypotheses.

It might be urged that there is still an important difference between the question of the reliability of sense perception and the skeptical hypotheses. As Maddy notes, the Plain Inquirer's verdict regarding the reliability of sense perception "isn't a foregone conclusion" (2017, 226). Here Maddy emphasizes that it was a long, hard-won process by which we came to have the excellent evidence that we now have about the ways and respects in which sense perception is reliable. It wasn't clear at the beginning how things would turn out. But the same thing can in fact be said about the Children of Brunettes and Evil Demon Hypotheses. It was a long, hard-won process by which we acquired the excellent evidence establishing that significantly diminished cognitive abilities are not determined by such factors as the hair color of one's parents. There have been times at which many people—some claiming the mantle of science—thought otherwise. It was likewise a long, hard-won process over many centuries by which we acquired sufficient understanding of how the world works to be able to say, quite decisively, that there are no evil demons. It was not clear at the beginning—not a foregone conclusion in either case—that inquiry would go the way it did. There is no relevant difference here.

Maddy asks, regarding the reliability of sense perception, "What epistemological disadvantage *does* the Plain Inquirer's brand of circularity suffer from?" (2017, 228). She offers Alston's answer: while we can provide good evidence for each individual claim involved in the account (including the claim that sensory perception is largely reliable), "we cannot turn the trick with the whole lot all at once" (2017, 228, quoting Alston 1986, 347). That is, the only epistemic disadvantage here is that we cannot meet the "from scratch" justificatory challenge—we cannot offer the kind of evidence or justification that would meet Cartesian demands or the demands imposed by trying to answer the question from a completely neutral position. Maddy regards this as no disadvantage at all. I think that the Plain Inquirer should give the same answer regarding the Children of Brunettes and Evil Demon Hypotheses. In those cases, too, we cannot offer a form of evidence or justification that meets the "from scratch" challenge. But so what? If we reject the "from scratch" challenge elsewhere, we should reject it here too.

Maddy has recently refined her proposal, suggesting that "The Plain Inquirer isn't actually asking the global question: is sense perception (as a whole) reliable?" (2018, 238). To buttress this suggestion she emphasizes the "piecemeal" nature of the inquiry, the complexity of the scientific issues, and the empirical difficulties involved in determining what exactly it would be for a given perceptual modality to be reliable. She highlights that the relevant evidence is "actually quite nuanced" (238).

These complexities don't undercut my basic point, however. Consider what Maddy might mean when she says that "The Plain Inquirer isn't actually asking the global question: is sense perception (as a whole) reliable?" One thing she might mean is that the Plain Inquirer isn't asking a global question about the reliability of perception *from a position of initial neutrality*. That's plausible, given Maddy's comments about epistemic circularity, but it reinforces my point: if the Plain Inquirer is content not to ask that sort of question in this case, then the same should go for the Evil Demon and Children of Brunettes Hypotheses.

Another thing Maddy might mean is that the Plain Inquirer's piecemeal investigations don't even address the issue of the general reliability of sensory perception. But that looks implausible. It looks as though at the end of her difficult piecemeal investigations the Plain Inquirer could perfectly legitimately provide a summary report of what she has found, something along the lines of: "Given what counts as reliability for each modality with regard to each perceptual feature, sense perception is reliable in the following respects and circumstances, it is not reliable in the following respects and circumstances, and the following complexities and difficult cases need to be taken into account. . . ." For instance, she might provide such a statement at the beginning of a textbook. She would thereby take a stand on the general question of the reliability of sense perception as a whole, even though (as Maddy rightly says) she does not investigate the issue by raising a global question from a position of initial neutrality. So far as I can see, if the Plain Inquirer did her work well, then she and other investigators would quite rightly agree that this summary statement is well-supported by the empirical evidence. Ask yourself: if you thought that her complex, nuanced investigations were conclusive, would you (in the position of ordinary science) really want to stand before a psychology class and tell them that there was no evidence whatsoever in favor of that summary statement? I certainly wouldn't. It continues to look as though the Plain Inquirer would be content to acknowledge epistemic circularity in this case.

Moreover, it looks to me as though Maddy should agree. After all, she says that "this investigation [i.e., the "ordinary, piecemeal scientific investigation of our various senses"] does, as Alston suggests, reveal 'significant self-support'" (2018, 238), thus acknowledging epistemic circularity in those inquiries. If there is any case of epistemic circularity in any of those piecemeal inquiries, then Maddy has to grant that there can be cases in which we have good evidence for p but can't use that evidence to resolve the question of whether p from a position of initial agnosticism or neutrality. And if you acknowledge that there are any such cases, then (as I stressed above) qualms about that possibility can't be your ground for denying that we have evidence against the Evil Demon and Children of Brunettes Hypotheses.

In sum: Just as the Plain Inquirer can have excellent evidence regarding the overall reliability of the senses, we can have excellent evidence regarding the Children of Brunettes and Evil Demon Hypotheses. There is no reason to seek a form of evidence that works independently of the human and worldly context in which it is being offered. We cannot see the good evidence we have against these hypotheses unless we consider the issue from within a substantial, well-supported, and largely true view of the world.

7. Detached Rational Evaluation

A final methodological issue needs to be considered. For many beliefs, we can productively take up a certain stance of detached rational re-evaluation. We can pretend that we have no view about whether p, take up a neutral position as to whether p, and then look for evidence already in our possession which has not thereby been placed in doubt or otherwise rendered unavailable and which can be seen, from that position, to tell decisively in favor of p. When we do this successfully, we regard ourselves as having vindicated the belief by showing it to have survived one sort of test. Of course, we cannot do this regarding the claims that the Children of Brunettes and Evil Demon Hypotheses are false. Perhaps, then, that's why Maddy thinks we can't have evidence against these hypotheses: perhaps she regards detached rational re-evaluation as methodologically privileged.

For instance, in explaining why she rejects my proposals regarding epistemic asymmetry, Maddy characterizes the Plain Inquirer's epistemological concerns in this way:

> Among other things, she wants to evaluate and improve her beliefs. She's being told that what she has available to her counts as evidence if and only if the belief whose grounds she's investigating is true—but in pursuit of her project of evaluation and improvement, this kind of purported evidence isn't much help (2018, 238).

What exactly is the concern? Here Maddy obviously can't have in mind a project of evaluation and improvement that takes as its starting point the Cartesian "from scratch" challenge; the Plain Inquirer has rejected that project as methodologically misguided. But she also can't have in mind a project of evaluation and improvement that simply works from within our best current view in its entirety, for then—as I have been stressing—it looks as though the denials of the Children of Brunettes and Evil Demon Hypotheses pass with flying colors. It seems that what she has in mind is a project in which we take up a position of complete neutrality regarding the target claim, putting aside everything (no matter how well established) that is thereby rendered unavailable, and then seek evidence that can be seen, from that position of neutrality, to decide the issue. (See also what she says about the methodological significance of the "position of agnosticism" [238].) Here Maddy is highlighting the project of detached rational re-evaluation, and she is privileging it methodologically by tying the question "What evidence do we possess against the Children of Brunettes Hypothesis?" to the question "Is evidence available against this hypothesis *when we undertake this project?*"

This move looks to me like a mistake, and I think the Plain Inquirer should agree.

The Plain Inquirer recognizes that she cannot succeed in detached rational re-evaluation regarding all of her beliefs at once, nor even regarding all of her beliefs about the external world all at once. In her view, that inability does not impugn the good evidence she has for these beliefs, since she rejects Cartesian demands. As we just saw in the case of the reliability of sense perception, she likewise grants that our inability to succeed in detached rational re-evaluation *in this particular case* does not mean we lack good evidence. She *can* point to good evidence regarding the ways and situations in which sense perception is reliable. This evidence is reflectively available to her and she can cite it, so long as she hasn't taken up the stance of detached rational re-evaluation. Here she's not treating detached rational re-evaluation as methodologically privileged.

In fact, there is no good reason to regard detached rational re-evaluation as generally methodologically privileged, as we can see in perfectly ordinary cases of epistemic asymmetry. For instance, consider the possibility that my spouse is—despite the obvious difficulties—successfully deceiving me about whether she loves me. In fact, nothing like this is going on. She clearly loves me and wouldn't mistreat me in this way. I have all sorts of good evidence for this in what she says and how she treats me. But if I take up the project of detached rational re-evaluation to try to vindicate the belief that she isn't doing this, I can't do it—not because there is nothing that tells against this possibility (of course there is!), but for a purely structural reason: if I work from a position in which I really suspend any view about whether she is completely deceiving me about this in everything she says and does, a position in which I treat such deception as a wide open possibility, then I also have to suspend any view about whether the ways she acts towards me are good evidence that she loves me. The fact that she says she loves me nearly every day and regularly treats me in loving ways would then count for nothing. And the consideration that such deceptions are unusual and hard to pull off will hardly decide the issue, since the possibility that she *is* managing it (despite the difficulty) is one of the things I am explicitly regarding as wide open. Here, then, detached rational re-evaluation is like putting on a blindfold. It blinds me to the evidence that I have. For purely structural reasons, the project isn't a good tool in this case. Don't try to hang your marriage on this hook!

The same point applies to the project of detached rational re-evaluation regarding the question of the truth of the Children of Brunettes and Evil Demon Hypotheses. We can see ahead of time that the attempt will fail for purely structural reasons. This does *nothing* to show that we do not have excellent evidence against these hypotheses—evidence that is reflectively available to us and that we can cite when we ask, "What tells against this hypothesis?" We just can't deploy that evidence when we take up a certain position. Here too it looks like detached rational reflection simply blinds us to our evidence.

In fact, this point applies to other global questions the Plain Inquirer might consider as well. If you ask me to show that it is not the case that every piece of evidence I have is misleading, I can do it—so long as I am very careful about what project I am engaged in. For instance, here is a piece of evidence I have that it is 2021 as I write this: My calendar says so. This is *good* evidence. It is not misleading. So, not every piece of evidence I have is misleading. Importantly, what I just recited is a *good* line of thought; it hits a fundamental truth. I don't see why it shouldn't satisfy the Plain Inquirer. Of course, I can't show *from a position of detached rational re-evaluation* that not all of my evidence is misleading. But so what? That doesn't mean that I didn't just point to an example of non-misleading evidence that I have.

Granted, detached rational re-evaluation can sometimes be a useful form of critical reflection. For instance, on some occasions detached rational re-evaluation doesn't succeed because we discover that what we thought were good reasons actually aren't. That is a helpful discovery. But the cases that we are discussing aren't like those. In the cases we're discussing, we can't succeed in detached rational re-evaluation *for purely structural reasons that we can recognize in advance* having to do with the relation between the truth of the proposition at issue and our reliability or competence regarding the relevant evidence. In such cases, detached rational evaluation isn't a good tool. It blinds us to our evidence.

Fortunately, this isn't the only form of critical reflection available to us. We can also go over our evidence again to check whether it is true. We can consider—given what there is reason to believe and to doubt in our context—whether our evidence actually tells in favor of our beliefs. We can consider whether there is reason to believe that our methods are or are not good ones. We can seek new evidence. These are the sorts of tools Maddy's Plain Inquirer uses in the self-corrective processes of investigation that enable her to confirm the ways, contexts, and extent to which sense perception is reliable.

This, then, is the fundamental thought I want to offer: Evidence can have various uses and can do various sorts of things for us. The evidence that I have highlighted regarding the Children of Brunettes and Evil Demon Hypotheses doesn't do certain things for us. Like my evidence that my spouse is not completely deceiving me about whether she loves me, it doesn't—for purely structural reasons—enable success in a project of detached rational re-evaluation. But it can do other things for us. It is reflectively available for various purposes in reasoning and inquiry. It can play a role in detached rational re-evaluation with regard to *other* claims. It enables us to show certain things, supports various reasonable beliefs and even knowledge, and enables us to understand how our beliefs are rationally related and why some of them have the positive epistemic status that they have.

For these reasons, it looks like a methodological mistake to tie the question, "What evidence do we have?" to the question, "What evidence is available to us when we undertake a project of detached rational re-evaluation?" So far as I can see, the Plain Inquirer has every reason to agree.

In sum, then, we ought to resist privileging a certain kind of philosophical aspiration. In philosophy we sometimes seek a certain kind of reflective vindication of the credentials of our beliefs. This is something more minimal than the kind of global reflective vindication that Descartes invites, more minimal even than the demand to provide a vindicating account of our knowledge of the world without making use of any knowledge of the world. It can concern our beliefs taken *singly*. We pretend that it is an entirely open question whether p is true—even though it is obviously true. Then we set aside everything that would be made unavailable if it were genuinely an open question for us whether p is true, and we seek something that would adjudicate the question from that position. Sometimes this is a good method. In the cases I have been discussing, however, it blinds us to our evidence and to the truth.

7
Epistemic Asymmetry

1. The Project

We have been considering the prospects for what might be termed the *Moorean anti-skeptical project*: the attempt to respond to external world skepticism from within our pre-philosophical commitments—in particular by appealing to considerations about the world and our knowledge of it.[1] Speaking from within the pre-philosophical position, the Moorean anti-skeptic says that we can know things about the world outside of our minds, for instance that we have bodies and see tables. These things are incompatible with the Evil Demon scenario: if you have a body and see that there is a table right there, then you are not a disembodied spirit being fed deceptive experiences. So the Moorean anti-skeptic is committed to holding that in the actual world, in which you are not a victim of Descartes' deceiving demon, you can know that you are not, or have evidence or good reason to believe that you are not, or at least know things incompatible with this scenario—even though if you *were* a victim of Descartes' deceiving demon, you would incorrectly think you weren't. According to the Moorean anti-skeptic, then, there is an *epistemic asymmetry* between the "Good Case," the actual case in which we have bodies and see objects in the world, and the "Bad Case" in which Descartes' Evil Demon scenario is correct.[2]

Epistemic asymmetry played a central role in the last chapter's discussion of Maddy's Plain Inquirer. There I offered a number of examples of epistemic asymmetry, and I pointed out that the way of thinking about evidence shared by Wittgenstein, Austin, and the Plain Inquirer should lead us to expect asymmetries with key structural features displayed by the Children of Brunettes and Evil Demon Hypotheses. I highlighted that cases of epistemic asymmetry show that evidence needn't always enable us to decide a question

---

[1] This chapter is derived from Adam Leite (2019), "Skepticism and Epistemic Asymmetry," *Philosophical Issues* 29, Epistemology, 184–197, edited by L. Miracchi and E. Sosa (John Wiley & Sons).

[2] The useful terminology of "Good Case" and "Bad Case" comes from Williamson 2000.

from a position of agnosticism or through a process of detached rational re-evaluation. Still, someone might wonder: it's one thing to claim that we should expect instances of asymmetry like these if a certain characterization of evidence is correct; it is quite another thing to provide a clear reason for thinking that the Children of Brunettes and Evil Demon scenarios really are cases of epistemic asymmetry. Is there anything that can help decide the issue from within our pre-philosophical commitments? The burden of this chapter is to show that there is.

More than anyone else, Timothy Williamson has placed epistemic asymmetry at the center of his engagement with skepticism (2000, 168, 180–181; 2013, 8). He offers a theory of knowledge and evidence that underwrites this response (2000, chapters 9 and 10; for critical discussion see, e.g., Greenough and Pritchard 2009), and in more recent work he offers a model in epistemic logic that incorporates certain formal constraints to yield epistemic asymmetries (2013). Neither approach fits the needs of the Moorean anti-skeptic. The first depends upon a developed epistemological theory, whereas the Moorean anti-skeptic aims to work from a pretheoretical position. The second raises the question of whether those formal constraints capture the key features of the situation the Moorean claims we are in. And since this is where the real action is, perhaps the payoff might be attained more directly. It would be nice if we could show, using completely decisive examples and without assuming any contentious epistemological theory, that there really are asymmetries of precisely the sort the Moorean anti-skeptic claims.[3]

Of course, by "completely decisive examples" I do not mean examples with which the skeptic would agree, since they will concern knowledge of the world. Rather, I mean examples that would be accepted by reasonable people in ordinary life as displaying asymmetries structurally analogous in all relevant respects to those the anti-skeptic proposes. Such examples would reasonably be taken, *prima facie*, to illuminate how knowledge and related epistemic categories work, thereby providing data for downstream theorizing. If we aim to respond to the skeptic from a standpoint that does justice to our pretheoretical commitments, such examples should aid us in accepting precisely the sort of asymmetry the anti-skeptic needs.

My goal is first to identify key desiderata for an example suited to the Moorean anti-skeptic's purposes and then to provide several suitable

---

[3] Despite my different approach, without Williamson's groundbreaking work I would not have seen how to complete the work begun in Chapters 4–6.

examples. A recurrent theme of the preceding chapters has been a certain kind of reservation one might have with the Moorean approach. It can seem odd to appeal to considerations about the world as grounds for dismissing the deceiving demon-type skeptical scenarios, since such considerations are among the things about which we would be badly wrong or radically unreliable if such scenarios were the case. We saw that Austin would reject this concern on the basis of a generalization about how evidence works in our epistemic practice ("Austin's Claim"), and in Chapter 5 I offered the Children of Brunettes Hypothesis in support of Austin. As we saw, Maddy rejects this example, claiming that we cannot have good evidence against it any more than we can against Descartes' Evil Demon Hypothesis. In the last chapter I argued that this position is not well-motivated, given the rest of the Plain Inquirer's commitments. One aim of the current chapter is to pinpoint the exact structure of the relevant sort of asymmetry and to show that this sort of structure is in fact a familiar feature of ordinary epistemic life.

If this is right, then a whole way of thinking about our position vis à vis the global skeptical hypotheses can be rejected solely on the basis of the commitments of our pre-philosophical position. These hypotheses' structure will be no bar against holding that even though we would be totally off-track if they were the case, we can nonetheless have good evidence against them and even know they don't obtain. That is, there will be nothing about their structure that warrants denying that they are instances of epistemic asymmetry.

2. Refining the Target

As I propose to understand them, skeptical scenarios such as Descartes' Evil Demon have a distinctive structure arising from the combination of five key features.

> First, they are *global*, in that they purport to raise a problem about an entire domain of belief through consideration of just one scenario: if the proposed scenario obtained, we would be wrong or wildly unreliable about that entire domain.

> Second, they exhibit *perfect mimicry*. If the skeptical scenario did obtain, everything would seem precisely as it does and we would believe precisely

what we now do (*modulo* refinements for indexicals and the like, and leaving aside strong externalist claims about belief content).

Third, they are *seamless*, undetectable in principle. No matter what one does, one could never find out that one is being deceived.

Fourth, they *eliminate evidence*. If the Evil Demon scenario obtained, the world would differ in ways that would affect objective evidential relations. For instance, in the Evil Demon world an experience as of a hand does not in fact make it any more likely that there is a hand before you. Moreover, considerations about the world that now constitute good evidence would not—in that world—be good evidence of anything at all (though one would wrongly think otherwise), since they would be false (see chapter 5, Leite 2013).

Fifth, the skeptical hypotheses aim to *undercut our evidence*. If the Evil Demon scenario obtained, we would be radically misled about how things stand in the world. As a result, we would be wrong or unreliable with regard to any consideration about the world that we might offer as evidence that the scenario does not obtain. Moreover, because we would be quite wrong about the world, we would be wildly unreliable about the objective evidential significance of any consideration we might offer as evidence that we are not deceived. We would, for instance, wrongly take the experience as of a hand to be a reliable indication that there is a hand. In structural terms, the domain about which we would thereby be wrong or wildly unreliable encompasses everything that we would need in order to aptly evaluate objective evidence against the scenario's obtaining.[4] It is this feature that leads the skeptic to think that we cannot obtain evidence against the skeptical hypotheses *now*—to think, that is, that the skeptical scenarios thereby undercut our evidence here and now.

To provide a good model for the anti-skeptic's position, an ordinary example of epistemic asymmetry must parallel the skeptical scenarios in all these respects.

---

[4] Here I leave aside the possibility of a successful purely a priori argument against the Evil Demon Hypothesis. No such argument has ever been found. More importantly, to preserve the structural point made in the main text all we need to do is consider Descartes' own version of the Evil Demon Hypothesis. If that hypothesis obtained, then we would be wildly unreliable even in any a priori reasoning that we offered against it.

3. Varieties of Asymmetry

The mere existence of epistemic asymmetries should be uncontroversial. For instance, right now all of the following are true: I know that I am not unconscious, I have excellent reason to believe that I am not, and I know things incompatible with this scenario. But in many cases in which I am unconscious, I do not know this, do not have excellent evidence about what state I am in, and do not know things that are incompatible with my being conscious. Even the external world skeptic has no reason to deny that there is an asymmetry between these two cases. The external world skeptic thus has no reason to deny the very existence of epistemic asymmetries.

By the same token, however, this example does not parallel the anti-skeptic's claim in significant respects. If you are unconscious, it's not true that everything seems exactly the same to you as in the Good Case, nor do you believe all of the same things. So the anti-skeptic can't get any mileage from this sort of example. We must look much more carefully at the phenomenon of epistemic asymmetry in order to pinpoint what, exactly, the anti-skeptic needs.

Here are several different ways of characterizing epistemic asymmetries:

1. <u>Accessibility Asymmetry</u>: In the Good Case, one knows things that are inconsistent with being in the Bad Case; in the Bad Case, one does not know anything inconsistent with being in the Good Case. To put it another way, the possibility that one is in the Good Case is consistent with everything one knows in the Bad Case, but the possibility that one is in the Bad Case is not consistent with what one knows in the Good Case.
2. <u>Knowledge Asymmetry</u>: In the Good Case, one knows that one is in the Good Case and not in the Bad Case; in the Bad Case, one does not know that one is in the Bad Case and not in the Good Case (under some relevant characterizations of the cases, of course; I will leave this specification implicit in what follows).
3. <u>Position-to-Know Asymmetry</u>: In the Good Case, one is in a position to know that one is in the Good Case and not in the Bad Case; in the Bad Case, one is not in a position to know that one is in the Bad Case and not in the Good Case.
4. <u>Evidence/Reasons Asymmetry</u>: In the Good Case, one has good evidence or reasons for belief about which case one is in while having no comparable evidence/reasons in the Bad Case.

None of these are equivalent. I will discuss 1–3 now. I will leave Evidence/Reasons Asymmetry for later. As we'll see, there is good reason to focus first on Accessibility Asymmetry.[5]

The notion of Accessibility Asymmetry comes to us from epistemic logic. One world or situation is said to be "accessible" from another insofar as what one knows in the latter is true in the former.[6] That is, A is accessible from B if and only if everything one knows in B is compatible with one's being in A. (The term "accessible" is used here to capture the idea that if one is in B, it is an open alternative (given what one knows) that one is in A.) Informally, A is accessible from B just if one might be in A, for all one knows in B (Williamson 2013, 3). If A is accessible from B but B is not accessible from A, then we have an instance of Accessibility Asymmetry. If one is in A, it will not be true that for all one knows one might be in B. But if one is in B, it will be true that for all one knows one might be in A.

Here are two examples, one familiar and one new:

World A (Good Case)	World B (Bad Case)
I am conscious	I am not conscious
I know that I am conscious	I do not know anything that is relevant to whether or not I am currently conscious

World B is not accessible from world A, because in world A I know something (I am conscious) that's false in world B. But world A is accessible from world B, because what is true in world A is compatible with what I know in world B.[7]

A second form of Accessibility Asymmetry can arise from a lack of reflectiveness:

---

[5] This is Williamson's primary focus as well (2002, 165–166), though he does not always carefully distinguish Accessibility Asymmetry from Knowledge Asymmetry (e.g., 2002, 168; 2013, 8).
[6] Williamson 2000, 166.
[7] Assume here and in the following examples that everything else is held constant (so far as possible).

World A (Good Case)	World B (Bad Case)
P is true	S knows that P
S knows that P	S does not believe that she knows that P. S has not reflected at all on whether she knows P nor formed any view on the issue or any higher iteration of it. Nor has S formed a belief about whether she has reflected on whether she knows P.
S believes that she knows that P	
S knows that she believes that she knows that P	

World B is not accessible from world A, because in world A, S knows something (namely, that she believes she knows that P) which is incompatible with world B. But world A is accessible from world B, because world A is compatible with everything that S knows in world B.

Accessibility Asymmetry is not the same thing as Knowledge Asymmetry. Something true in world B might be incompatible with something one knows in A, and yet one might not have formed a belief in either case about which world one is in. One's knowledge of which world one is in would thus be on a par in both cases. This yields Accessibility Asymmetry without Knowledge Asymmetry.

Imagine, for instance, that one is judging the height of something by evaluating it perceptually. One's discriminatory capacities might vary across cases even while everything seems the same.

World A	World B
P: X is 5'11" high	Not-P: X is not 5'11" high (X is in fact 6'1" high)
S perceptually knows P	
Q: X is greater than 5'5" high	S perceptually believes P (X is 5'11" high)
S perceptually knows Q	
	Q: X is greater than 5'5" high
	S perceptually knows Q

This is a case of Accessibility Asymmetry. In world A S knows something (X is 5'11" tall) that is false in world B, so B is not accessible from A, but A is compatible with everything S knows in B, so A is accessible from B. However, suppose that in both worlds S has not reflected on whether she is in world A or B, nor has she formed any view about this. This would be an example of Knowledge Symmetry, since in neither world does S know that she is in that world and not the other.

There can likewise be Knowledge Asymmetry without Accessibility Asymmetry. For instance, consider Bernard Williams' example of high-altitude anoxia (oxygen shortage) suffered by fighter pilots (2005 [1978], 299). As Williams describes it, anoxia creates overconfidence that leads people to ignore danger signs such as blue fingernails. People suffering from anoxia consequently think they are not. However, high-altitude anoxia does not cause people to hallucinate that they are not in airplanes. So, I can tell right now that I am not suffering from high-altitude anoxia, because (among other things) I know that I am not in an airplane. And I know that I am not suffering from anoxia even though—were I in an airplane and suffering from anoxia—overconfidence would incorrectly lead me to think I'm not suffering from anoxia.

World A (Good Case)	World B (Bad Case)
Not-P: I am not suffering from anoxia	P: I am suffering from anoxia
I know not-P	I believe not-P
Not-Q: I am not in an airplane	Q: I am in an airplane
I know not-Q	I know Q

This is an example of Knowledge Asymmetry. In the Good Case, one knows one is in the Good Case, while in the Bad Case one does not know that one is in the Bad Case. That is to say: It can happen that one knows one is not suffering from high-altitude anoxia, even though if one *were* suffering from high-altitude anoxia one wouldn't know it and would incorrectly think that one wasn't.[8]

---

[8] To see this point, care has to be taken in how we characterize Knowledge Asymmetry. For in the Bad Case one knows that one is not in the Good Case, characterized as *a world in which one is both not in an airplane and not suffering from anoxia*. After all, even in the Bad Case, one knows one is not in *that* world, since one knows that one is in an airplane. What is relevant, though, is that one does not know that one is suffering from anoxia. Unlike in the Good Case, one does not know that one is in the case one is in.

However, this isn't an Accessibility Asymmetry.[9] Neither case is accessible from the other. The Bad Case is not accessible from the Good Case, because in the Good Case I know something (I'm not suffering from anoxia) that's false in the Bad Case. At the same time, the Good Case is not accessible from the Bad Case, since in the Bad Case I know something (I'm in an airplane) that's false in the Good Case. Knowledge Asymmetry does not entail Accessibility Asymmetry.

Turn now to *being in a position to know* what case one is in. One might think that an Accessibility Asymmetry should lead to an asymmetry in what one is in a position to know about which world one is in. But this isn't so. Accessibility Asymmetry does not entail Position-to-Know Asymmetry. Consider again a case resulting from lack of reflectiveness.

World A	World B
P is true	P is true
S knows that P	S knows that P
S believes that she knows that P	S has not reflected on or formed any belief about whether she knows that P, nor about whether she has reflected on the matter.
S knows that she believes that she knows that P	
S is in a position to know that she knows that P	S is in a position to know that she knows that P

Though this is an example of Accessibility Asymmetry, in both worlds S is in a perfectly good position to know which world she is in. All she has to do is: (1) Consider the minimal reflective question, "Have I, up until now, considered whether I know that P?," (2) Come to know that she knows that P (which, by stipulation, she's in a position to do), and (3) Put the pieces together. So, the two worlds are on a par regarding her ability to know which world she is in. Accessibility Asymmetry does not entail Position-to-Know Asymmetry.

As the anoxia example shows, there is likewise no entailment in the other direction. In that example the person in the Good Case is in a position to know that she is in the Good Case, but the person in the Bad Case is not in a

---

[9] This distinction is missed by Marušić 2016.

position to know that she is in the Bad Case. This is consequently an example of Position-to-Know Asymmetry. But it's not an example of Accessibility Asymmetry, for the reasons discussed above.

Finally, Position-to-Know Asymmetry and Knowledge Asymmetry are obviously distinct. Consider an example of Position-to-Know Asymmetry in which one has not yet come to know that one is in the Good Case, not the Bad. In neither case would one know which case one is in. This yields Knowledge Symmetry with Position-to-Know Asymmetry.

4. Where We Should Start

To investigate what form of asymmetry, exactly, the anti-skeptic is committed to, we should focus first on Accessibility Asymmetry. There are two reasons for this.

First, every anti-skeptic is committed to two claims. First, that we know things (such as that we have bodies and see tables) that are incompatible with the Evil Demon scenario. Second, that someone in the Evil Demon scenario would not know anything that is false in the Good Case. That is, every anti-skeptic is committed to an accessibility asymmetry.

Second, not every anti-skeptic is committed to a Knowledge Asymmetry or Position-to-Know Asymmetry. Robert Nozick (1981), for instance, claims that we know we have hands, and grants that the Evil Demon's victim knows nothing inconsistent with what's true in the Good Case. However, he denies that we know—or are in a position to know—that we are in the Good Case and not the Bad Case. This is because his "Sensitivity Requirement" says that in order to know (or be in a position to know) that one is not being deceived by an Evil Demon, it must be the case that if one *were* being deceived, one would not believe that one was not (179). That requirement is not met. Nozick is thus committed to Accessibility Asymmetry but not Knowledge or Position-to-Know Asymmetry.

Penelope Maddy (2017) agrees with that much. As we have seen, she holds that we know we have hands and know we see things in the world, facts which are obviously incompatible with the Evil Demon scenario. She grants that the Evil Demon's victim knows nothing that is false in the Good Case. So she is committed to an Accessibility Asymmetry. But, as we have seen, she also holds that in the Good Case we cannot get evidence that we are not being deceived by an Evil Demon, because the skeptical scenarios "are by

166   HOW TO TAKE SKEPTICISM SERIOUSLY

their very nature structurally impervious to evidence" (232). So insofar as we are concerned with a notion of knowledge that requires good evidence, Maddy thinks that we are on a par with an Evil Demon's victim when it comes to knowing which world we are in. She is thus committed to Accessibility Asymmetry without Knowledge or Position-to-Know Asymmetry.

I will accordingly start by asking whether there are everyday models for the Accessibility Asymmetry the anti-skeptic postulates.

5. Models for the Anti-Skeptic's Asymmetry?

Accessibility Asymmetry comes in many forms. Most do not have the relevant features of the asymmetry claimed by the anti-skeptic.

As noted, for instance, examples of Accessibility Asymmetry arising from differences in consciousness or reflectiveness are useless for the anti-skeptic's purposes. In those examples it is not the case that everything seems exactly the same to the person in both the Good and Bad Cases. A key feature of the anti-skeptic's purported asymmetry is thus lacking.

There are Accessibility Asymmetries in which everything seems exactly the same in both the Good and the Bad Case. Consider again the earlier example concerning perceptual capacities:

World A	World B
P: X is 5'11" high	Not-P: X is not 5'11" high
S perceptually knows P	(X is in fact 6'1" high)
Q: X is greater than 5'5" tall	S perceptually believes P
S perceptually knows Q	(X is 5'11" high)
	Q: X is greater than 5'5" tall
	S perceptually knows Q

Here everything seems exactly the same in the two cases. Still, this example is not a good model for the anti-skeptic. The recipe for this kind of asymmetry is this:

Consider a possible world B in which someone has less precise knowledge about something known more precisely in world A, where (a) the determinate facts in A are compatible with what is known in B, but (b) the determinate facts in B are not compatible with what is known in A.[10]

This does not capture what the anti-skeptic needs. For the skeptic's Bad Case (e.g., the Evil Demon scenario) is not aptly understood as a case in which one has less precise knowledge about something known more precisely in actuality.[11]

Another kind of example is provided by Williamson (2000, 226–227). He imagines a creature that knows all of the propositions that are recorded in its memory, but whose recall system is imperfect: there is no limit on the amount of time that might be taken to deliver propositions from its memory to working consciousness. The creature asks itself whether it knows that not-P, and no relevant proposition has yet been delivered to working consciousness (nor is it conscious of anything else relevant).

World A	World B
Not-P	P
Creature knows that not-P	Creature has no belief as to whether P
At t, it has recovered no relevant memory	At t, it has recovered no relevant memory

In world B, no relevant proposition has been delivered to consciousness. It's compatible with everything the creature knows in B that this is because it knows not-P but the delivery mechanism is slow. So, A is accessible from B. World B is not accessible from A, however, since the creature knows something in A (namely, not-P) that is false in B. Despite this asymmetry, everything seems the same to the creature in its conscious awareness.

This example does not match what the anti-skeptic needs either. In the Evil Demon scenario we have the same beliefs (modulo tinkering for indexicals and the like) as in the Good Case. This feature is lacking in this example. Moreover, the asymmetry in this case arises from "processing constraints" independently of false beliefs (226). The asymmetry relating to the Evil Demon scenario arises instead because of deception: one's beliefs are false in the Bad Case in such a way that one cannot detect that this is so.

---

[10] Thanks here to Kirk Ludwig.
[11] Williamson's example illustrating his formal model (2013) seems closely related to this recipe.

We get closer to what the anti-skeptic needs by considering examples in which one's evidence is defeated but everything seems normal. Here are two variants.

1. In the Good Case, one has ordinary perceptual knowledge that a ball taken from a bag is black. In the Bad Case everything seems the same, one believes the same things, and everything one knows is consistent with one's being in the Good Case—and yet, because of bizarre circumstances of which one is unaware, the ball is in fact red but illuminated so as to look black (Williamson 2000, 226).

World A (Good Case)	World B (Bad Case)
P: Ball is black	Not-P (Ball is in fact red)
S knows that P	S believes that P
Conditions are normal	Everything seems just as in A, but bizarre lighting conditions obtain

Everything one knows in the Bad Case is consistent with the Good Case. But in the Good Case one knows something (the ball is black) that's inconsistent with the Bad Case. So we have an Accessibility Asymmetry in which everything seems the same in the two cases, one has the same beliefs, and in the Bad Case one has a false belief without recognizing that one does.

2. One drops a bag of trash down the chute on the tenth floor of one's apartment building, as one has done every week for years. In the usual case (nothing out of the ordinary, no reasons to suspect malfunction), one now knows that one's trash bag is somewhere in the basement (Sosa 1999, 145–146). But in the Bad Case, one's trash bag snags partway down without any indication.

World A (Good Case)	World B (Bad Case)
P: Trash bag in basement	Not-P (Trash bag snagged on the way down)
S knows that P	
S has exactly the same evidence as in the Bad Case ("I dropped the bag down the chute, there is no warning notice, etc.")	S believes that P
	S has exactly the same evidence as in the Good Case

Here too we see an Accessibility Asymmetry in which one has the same beliefs, and everything seems the same, in both cases.

Still, there are three ways in which these two examples don't parallel the asymmetry claimed by the anti-skeptic.

First, in these examples nothing in the Bad Case *prevents* one from finding out one has a false belief. One could check the lighting conditions, shine a flashlight down the trash chute, and so on. In the Evil Demon deception, by contrast, one can't find out that one's belief is false.

Second, in the trash chute example one's beliefs regarding what one has done with one's trash bag, the usual functioning of the chute, and so on—that is, the considerations one would appeal to as evidence about where one's bag is now—are true in *both* the Good Case and the Bad Case. Regarding the Evil Demon deception, by contrast, many (if not all) considerations one might reasonably appeal to in the Good Case as relevant evidence would be false in the Bad Case.

Third, in both the Ball and Trash Chute examples the true considerations one might appeal to in the Bad Case in support of P are indeed evidence that P, in this sense: even in the Bad Case, there is an objective truth-related connection between those true considerations and the truth of P; those considerations do make P objectively more likely, though this objective evidential relation is defeated by the unusual circumstances obtaining in the Bad Case. By contrast, many anti-skeptics don't understand the Evil Demon scenario as a situation in which one has objectively good evidence that is defeated. They think that because objective evidential relations depend upon how things actually work in the world, in the Evil Demon world an experience as of a hand before you does not in fact make it objectively more likely that there is a hand there (even if it would be reasonable for you to believe there is). For these anti-skeptics, then, these examples would not be apt models at all.[12]

---

[12] Some anti-skeptics would regard the Evil Demon scenario as a situation in which one has objectively good evidence that's defeated. Jim Pryor 2000, for instance, could plausibly be interpreted along these lines. However, the Ball and Trash Chute examples will not be apt models for Pryor's purposes in a different respect. Pryor traces the skeptical argument to a commitment to this principle:

SPK If you're to know a proposition p on the basis of certain experiences or grounds E, then for every q which is "bad" relative to E and p, you have to be in a position to know q to be false in a non-question-begging way—i.e., you have to be in a position to know q to be false *antecedently* to knowing p on the basis of E. (2000, 528)

The Ball and Chute examples do not provide obvious counterexamples to that principle, since it's plausible enough that if one had no antecedent reason to think that the chute was likely to be functioning normally, then one wouldn't know that the trash bag is now somewhere in the basement. So these examples do not defeat SPK; they do not model everything that Pryor's anti-skeptic needs. (See Chapter 8 for discussion of SPK.)

An additional desideratum arises from the structure of the skeptical scenarios.

Consider again the example of Drunken Slurring that I have appealed to at various points in previous chapters. Right now, I can tell—on the basis of how my speech sounds—that I am not slurring my words. Suppose that if I were drunkenly slurring my speech, I would incorrectly think that I wasn't. Let the Good Case be one in which I am not drunkenly slurring my words (and there is no reason to suspect otherwise) and let the Bad Case be one in which I am. In the Good Case I know that I am not drunkenly slurring my words. In the Bad Case in which I am drunk, however, I do not competently register how my speech sounds, so I get it wrong. The key issue here is how my capacities are functioning.

World A (Good Case)	World B (Bad Case)
Not-P: I am not drunkenly slurring my words	P: I am drunkenly slurring my words
I know that not-P	Because I am drunk, I incorrectly believe that not-P

While this is a case of Accessibility Asymmetry, it is not a perfect model for the asymmetry claimed by the anti-skeptic. For one thing, it isn't clear that everything seems exactly the same to the person in both the Good and Bad Cases. (This depends on delicate issues about the relations between phenomenology, one's recognitional capacities, and one's beliefs about one's phenomenology.) More importantly, however, in the Good Case one arguably has certain sorts of information available that one lacks in the Bad Case. For instance, in the Good Case one presumably knows that one hasn't had a drink for (say) several days.[13] And the key point is that when it comes to the Evil Demon scenario there is nothing parallel that the anti-skeptic can highlight as information, available in the Good Case, that establishes that one is not in the Bad Case.

We can put the crucial point more carefully. In the Evil Demon scenario, one is radically unreliable about a certain domain: *how things are outside of one's mind*. Grant, for the sake of argument, a notion of objective evidential support that depends upon how the world works. Then a resulting key

---

[13] This point has been urged by Maddy (2018).

feature of the skeptical scenarios is this: in the Bad Case, one is radically unreliable about the truth or objective evidential significance of anything that might reasonably be appealed to *in the Good Case* as grounds for thinking one is not in the Bad Case. For instance, that one has hands and is seeing a table are things that might be appealed to in the Good Case as evidence that one is not in the Bad Case, but they are matters about which one would be wrong or completely unreliable in the Bad Case. They are in what I will call the *Bad Case's Domain*: the domain of things whose truth or objective evidential significance one would be wrong or wildly unreliable about in the Bad Case. So when it comes to the skeptical scenarios, even in the Good Case one has no evidence from outside the Bad Case's Domain that one is in the Good Case.

This highlights the further desideratum on a compelling example of asymmetry for the anti-skeptic's purposes. Everything that might plausibly be appealed to in the Good Case as grounds for thinking that one is not in the Bad Case must be something about whose truth or evidential significance one would be wrong or wildly unreliable if one were in the Bad Case. It must be in the Bad Case's Domain. In this sense, in the Good Case one must not be able to get *independent evidence* against the Bad Case.

This desideratum is closely related to a further constraint arising from the Cartesian conception of rational reflection. Descartes aspires to stand apart from everything about which he would be wrong or wildly unreliable if he were being deceived by an evil demon and to establish, utilizing only what remains available, that the Evil Demon scenario is not the case. This is what the Cartesian tradition takes rational reflection to require.

If one works under this limitation and tries to appeal to something as a reason for believing that one has a hand, it will have to be something that isn't itself a consideration about the world outside one's mind (since such considerations are off the table). To satisfyingly appeal to this further consideration, whatever it is, one must take it to be objectively good evidence. But under the proposed limitation, one cannot satisfyingly take the further consideration, whatever it might be, to be an objectively good indication that one actually has a hand: whether it is a good indication will depend upon whether one is being deceived by an evil demon, and that is precisely what is in question. After all, in the Bad Case one *thinks* that sensory experience is an objectively good indication of how things are, but one is wrong about even that—that, too, is in the Bad Case's Domain. So, to put it generally, the problem is this: if you stand apart from all of your commitments that are in the Bad Case's Domain, it looks like there is no satisfying course of explicit reasoning that will get you from your limited starting point to the conclusion that you are not being deceived by an evil demon. This is the problem that has plagued the history of epistemology: as the Cartesian conceives of rational reflection, there seems to be no satisfying course of reasoning by which one can reach the conclusion that one is not being deceived by an evil demon.

The further constraint that emerges here, then, is this:

> If one works only with materials from outside the Bad Case's Domain, there is nothing to which one can satisfactorily appeal in order to resolve the question of whether the scenario obtains.

An example satisfying this condition would provide the strongest support for the anti-skeptic, since it would meet the demands of the most stringent understanding of the skeptical scenario.

All told, then, we seek an example of Accessibility Asymmetry with the following features:

1. Everything must seem the same in the Good and Bad Cases.
2. The person must have all of the same beliefs in the Good and Bad Cases.
3. The Bad Case must be such that further inquiry would only reinforce the incorrect belief that one is in the Good Case.
4. Many considerations that one could appropriately appeal to as relevant evidence in the Good Case would be false in the Bad.
5. Relevant objective evidential relations (of the sort that depend on how the world generally works) differ in the Good and the Bad Cases.
6. In the Bad Case, one is rendered unreliable about the truth or evidential significance of an entire domain of considerations (the "Bad Case's Domain").
7. In the Good Case, one must not know something from outside the Bad Case's Domain that is incompatible with the Bad Case.
8. If one works only with materials from outside the Bad Case's Domain, there is nothing to which one can satisfactorily appeal in order to resolve the question of whether the scenario obtains.

An ordinary example of Accessibility Asymmetry with these features will give us good reason to expect precisely the sort of asymmetry that the anti-skeptic claims.

6. In Support of the Anti-Skeptic

There are perfectly ordinary examples with the requisite structure.

To bring this into view, I will begin with two examples that don't quite do what the anti-skeptic needs. Their shortcomings are instructive.

> DECEIVED IN LOVE: Right now (Good Case), I know that my spouse isn't deceiving me about whether she loves me. (She loves me and so wouldn't deceive me about matters of deep importance to me.) But there is a possible case (Bad Case) in which (a) she is deceiving me about this, (b) everything seems exactly the same to me, (c) I would appeal to exactly the same things as evidence that she isn't deceiving me, and (d) I would incorrectly believe she isn't.

This is a case of Accessibility Asymmetry:

World A (Good Case)	World B (Bad Case)
Not-P: Spouse not deceiving me about whether loves me	P: Spouse is deceiving me about whether loves me
I know that not-P	I believe that not-P
Q: Spouse wouldn't deceive me about matters of deep importance to me	Not-Q: Spouse would deceive me about matters of deep importance to me
I know that Q	I believe that Q
Spouse says and does various things	Spouse says and does exactly the same things as in Good Case
	Everything seems to me exactly as in the Good Case, and I believe all the same things

The Bad Case is not accessible from the Good Case. In the Good Case I know something—namely, that my spouse isn't deceiving me about whether she loves me—that is false in the Bad Case. But everything I know in the Bad

Case is consistent with what is true in the Good Case, so the Good Case is accessible from the Bad Case.

This example mirrors what the anti-skeptic needs in several key respects. And it is easy to construct parallel examples. Here is another:

> MY COLLEAGUE IS A SPY: Right now (Good Case) I know that my longtime colleague and former department chair is not a Russian spy. He is a completely straightforward and honest guy who never plays a part. But there is a possible case (Bad Case) in which (a) he is a Russian spy, (b) everything seems exactly the same to me, (c) I would appeal to exactly the same things as evidence that he isn't a spy, and (d) I would incorrectly believe he isn't one.

World A (Good Case)	World B (Bad Case)
Not-P: S is not a spy	P: S is a spy
I know that not-P	I believe that not-P
Q: S is honest and straightforward	Not-Q: S isn't honest and straightforward
I know that Q	I believe that Q
S says and does various things	S says and does the same things
	Everything seems the same to me as in the Good Case, and I believe all the same things

Like Deceived in Love, this example parallels what the anti-skeptic needs in several respects. Complications arise, however, in relation to three key features.

First, neither of these examples meets this requirement:

> 3. The Bad Case must be such that further inquiry would only reinforce the incorrect belief that one is in the Good Case.

Here's the problem. If my spouse were deceiving me about whether she loves me, I might very well be able to gain information that tips me off. For instance, I might read her journal, or her best friend might take pity on me. In this way, the example does not mirror the skeptic's Bad Case. However, this difference is easily removed. For instance, let the Bad Case be one in which my spouse constructs a deception that leaves no cracks in the edifice: in the Bad Case, it is impossible for me to learn anything that tips me off. Still, in the Good Case—where there is no reason whatsoever to think otherwise—I know that my spouse is not engaged in this form of deception about whether she loves me. If right now I thought that maybe I didn't know this—if I thought it a serious possibility that she might have created a seamless, undetectable deception with no cracks in the edifice—I'd be an apt subject for a psychiatric case study (much like a patient who worries that his spouse may have been replaced with a perfect duplicate).

In fact, there are many perfectly straightforward examples of Accessibility Asymmetry that exhibit this particular feature. Consider the hypothesis that my cat undetectably speaks Portuguese.[14] If that hypothesis were true (Bad Case), I could not (*ex hypothesi*) detect its truth. Still, in the actual world we know my cat does not undetectably speak Portuguese. We know this by knowing a lot about the cognitive abilities of cats. To put it crudely: Cats don't speak, whether detectably or undetectably; they lack the brain power. (Imagine telling an animal behaviorist it's an open question whether my cat undetectably speaks Portuguese!) In the Good Case, then, I know something (my cat does not undetectably speak Portuguese) that's incompatible with the Bad Case. But in the Bad Case everything I know is compatible with the Good Case. In short: it would be a mistake to think that because P would be undetectable if it did obtain, we can't know that it doesn't obtain when it doesn't. Sometimes we can detect P's non-obtaining even if we'd inevitably get it wrong if it did.

The second complication relates to the following requirement:

8. If one works only with materials from outside the Bad Case's Domain, there is nothing to which one can satisfactorily appeal in order to resolve the question of whether the scenario obtains.

Do DECEIVED IN LOVE and MY COLLEAGUE IS A SPY meet this requirement? I think this isn't clear.

Consider the Bad Case in which my spouse creates a seamless deception, so that I cannot gain any information that tips me off. It seems that in the Good Case, I have the following piece of evidence that I am not in this Bad Case: such things are extremely rare and hard to pull off (even if they are not impossible). That is a piece of information that is outside of the Bad Case's Domain; even if my spouse *is* succeeding in this sort of deception, it is still the

---

[14] Thanks to Ram Neta for this example.

case that such things are extremely difficult and very unusual. Admittedly, this isn't a very strong piece of evidence. For instance, it wouldn't be enough to resolve the question if I had some good reason to suspect that my spouse might in fact be engaged in such a deception. But it is nonetheless evidence that I possess in the Good Case (in which there is no reason to suspect that I am in the Bad Case), and it at least *bears on* the question of which case I am in. So there is some plausibility, at least, that I could argue like this in the Good Case: "Such things are extremely rare and very difficult to pull off. So, my spouse isn't engaging in such a deception." I'm not saying that such a course of reasoning *is* an acceptable way of resolving the question. I doubt that it is; that looks like pretty weak evidence to me. But I'm willing to grant that the issue is unclear. And *if* this is an acceptable way of resolving the question, then the current requirement is not met, since one can resolve the question even if one limits oneself to materials outside of the Bad Case's Domain.

The third complication is related to the second: It might be suggested that there is an asymmetry here between the Good Case and the Bad Case only because one has this weak evidence in the Good Case from outside the Bad Case's domain. By contrast, we lack any information of this sort in relation to the Evil Demon scenario. For in the latter scenario even information about how frequent such deceptions are, or how difficult they are to pull off, is in the domain about which one would be wrong or unreliable in the Bad Case. So, it might be urged that this is a key issue standing in the anti-skeptic's way: there can't be straightforward cases of Accessibility Asymmetry that perfectly parallel the skeptical scenarios in every respect.

In fact, however, evidence from outside the Bad Case's Domain—independent evidence, in this sense—is not necessary for Accessibility Asymmetry.[15] This can be seen by considering certain kinds of conspiracy theories. I don't mean conspiracy theories that are understood by their adherents to be historical or scientific hypotheses whose truth could in principle be detected or refuted. Rather, I have in mind crazed conspiracy hypotheses held in a crazed way: hypotheses that (a) claim that the deception is seamless and undetectable and (b) attempt to incorporate and defuse *anything* that might be appealed to as evidence against them by reconstruing it as a misleading appearance. If, for instance, one says to the conspiracy theorist, "That's just too unlikely; no organization is that efficient and that successful at retaining control while concealing itself," he'll reply, "That's just what they want you to think; they are masters at it—they've been doing it for years."

[15] Contra Marušić 2016.

The force of that reply is this: "It's part of my hypothesis that what you are appealing to is false, an intentionally planted misleading appearance: it's part of my hypothesis that what I am claiming is in fact not unlikely at all, but only misleadingly appears to be." This is the key element that gives us a parallel in all relevant respects to the Evil Demon scenario.

Here is an example:

THE INTERNATIONAL ANTI-GUN CONSPIRACY (IAGC): Right now (Good Case) we know that the tragic mass shootings at schools are not faked. But imagine a world (Bad Case) in which the following is true: Extremely well-financed leftist anti-gun forces have engineered a massive deception to sway public opinion in favor of repealing the US Second Amendment. They use actors to impersonate shooters and victims in staged fake shootings in schools and places of worship. The forces behind these deceptions are so wealthy, powerful, and ruthlessly unified that the deception is seamless: ordinary Americans have no way of determining that this is going on. Moreover, anything that might plausibly be appealed to as evidence against this hypothesis is just a misleading appearance designed to put the public off the scent. Real parents who are shown what are said to be their dead children's bodies are actually being shown clever fakes; supposed witnesses are coerced or paid to lie; the police and medical examiners have been deceived or massively paid off, and so on. The same forces have been engaged in multiple international conspiracies, all equally seamless, for decades. They are masters at it.

Here is the asymmetry structure:

Actual World (Good Case)	Imagined World (Bad Case)
Not-P: Anti-gun forces have not faked the last twenty years of mass school shootings in a perfectly seamless deception.	P: Anti-gun forces have faked the last twenty years of mass school shootings in a perfectly seamless deception.
Know that not-P	Believe that not-P
	Everything seems exactly as it does, and one believes all of the same things as in the Good Case

In our dark times some people take this scenario (or something very like it) seriously. Some even believe it. They are all quite rightly regarded as nuts by reasonable people. It's part of how our epistemic practice works, when we are doing it right, that this hypothesis is correctly dismissed as false. And we don't just know it is false; we also know various things that are incompatible with it. For instance, we know that some fifty children and teachers died at Columbine, Parkland, and Sandy Hook.

This example meets all of the requirements necessary for a parallel in all relevant respects with the Evil Demon scenario. It is obvious that it meets desiderata (1), (2), (3), and (6). Moreover:

(4) Considerations one might appropriately appeal to as relevant evidence in the Good Case would be false in the Bad Case. For instance, in the Bad Case it's not true that no organization is that effective at retaining control while concealing itself.

(5) The effects of the conspiracy are so wide-ranging and far-reaching that relevant objective evidential relations differ between the Good and the Bad Case. For instance, imagine that the conspiracy has so thoroughly infiltrated the media that news reports are no longer reliable sources of information.

(7) In the Good Case, one does not know anything from outside the Bad Case's Domain that is incompatible with the Bad Case.

(8) If one works only with materials from outside the Bad Case's Domain, there is nothing to which one can satisfactorily appeal in order to resolve the question of whether the scenario obtains. One can't even appeal to likelihood considerations, because it's part of the hypothesized scenario that the conspiracy is not in fact unlikely, but only misleadingly seems to be.

The key point is this. While the example parallels the Evil Demon scenario in all relevant respects, it's also an example of Accessibility Asymmetry. We consequently have reason to expect precisely the sort of Accessibility Asymmetry claimed by the anti-skeptic.

It might be objected that there is a crucial difference between the Evil Demon scenario and this case: the Evil Demon scenario is sweeping, while this conspiracy theory relates only to a limited domain. However, skeptical arguments are always global relative to some domain. The domain is sometimes more restricted, sometimes wider, but the structure is the same. Skepticism about other minds attempts to raise a problem about knowledge of other minds by appealing to the possibility that all of the human bodies around me are mere mindless automata. Skepticism about the past attempts to raise a problem by appealing to the possibility that everything was created but a moment ago, replete with apparent memories, fake fossils, and seemingly historical manuscripts. These domains are more limited than the domain of external world skepticism, but these skeptical scenarios are structurally parallel in the relevant respects to the Evil Demon scenario. They all share the key features exemplified by the nutty anti-gun conspiracy theory. So the fact that the Evil Demon hypothesis is wider in its reach is no reason to deny that the anti-gun conspiracy is an entirely unproblematic asymmetry paralleling the Evil Demon scenario in all relevant respects.

The argument can be extended. The IAGC is not just an example of Accessibility Asymmetry. It is also an instance of Knowledge Asymmetry. We (in the Good Case) know that anti-gun forces have not faked the last twenty years of mass school shootings as part of a seamless deception designed to sway public opinion against guns. We know we are not in the Bad Case. But someone who is in the Bad Case does not know whether she is in the Bad Case or the Good Case. The example is also a Position-to-Know Asymmetry. We (in the Good Case) are in a position to know that anti-gun forces have not faked the mass school shootings. This is something that people come to know. But someone in the Bad Case is in no position to know whether she is in the Good or Bad Case.

Since there is no relevant difference between this example and the Evil Demon scenario, it looks as though we should accept that in the latter case, too, there is a Knowledge Asymmetry and a Position-to-Know Asymmetry. We (in the Good Case) know, and are in a position to know, that we are not being deceived by an evil demon. But someone in the Bad Case does not know, and is in no position to know, whether she is in the Bad Case.

Nozick would object to this extension of the argument on the ground that here we fail to meet the Sensitivity Requirement. But that requirement is false. It is shown false by the example we've just been considering. We know that anti-gun forces have not faked the last twenty years of mass school shootings as part of a seamless deception designed to sway public opinion against guns. But if anti-gun forces had faked all recent mass school shootings as part of a seamless deception, we would believe exactly what we do.[16]

---

[16] For other counterexamples to Nozick's Sensitivity Requirement, see, e.g., Sosa 1999, 145–146, Williamson 2000, and Leite 2004b, as well as several of the other examples discussed earlier.

Penelope Maddy would reject this extension of the argument for a different reason. She holds that the Evil Demon and other skeptical scenarios are constructed precisely so as to be "by their very nature structurally impervious to evidence" (2017, 232). However, this characterization of the skeptical scenario now looks incorrect. The skeptical scenario is structurally identical to the crazed anti-gun conspiracy. We have excellent evidence that anti-gun forces have not faked the recent mass school shootings as part of a seamless deception designed to sway public opinion against guns. (Fifty dead at Columbine, Parkland, and Sandy Hook is evidence enough.) All of the relevant evidence is in the Bad Case's Domain. In this regard there is no relevant difference between this example and the Evil Demon scenario. There is consequently no reason to think that the Evil Demon scenario is "structurally impervious to evidence." The mere fact that the evidence comes from within the Bad Case's Domain does not show that in the Good Case we cannot have evidence against the Bad Case.

It would be a mistake to argue in the other direction, holding that because (a) we can't know that the Evil Demon scenario is false, and (b) it parallels the IAGC in every relevant respect, we can't know that the IAGC is false either. For one thing, we do know that the anti-gun conspiracy theory is false. Moreover, there are possible conspiracy theories with exactly the same structure that are not just false, but *utterly insane*. Consider:

DUCKS RULE THE WORLD: Ducks have been the guiding force behind human history, shaping it seamlessly to serve their own ends. We can't determine how they do it, nor how the events they have engineered serve them; it's part of their diabolical brilliance that they have fully obscured all such matters from us. They have deceived us about their abilities, causing scientists and casual observers to think them vastly less intelligent and powerful than they are. To hide their influence, they have manipulated matters so that we are massively deceived about key aspects of how the world works, and so we not only believe all sorts of false things about ducks, but also go badly wrong in our evaluations of the relevant evidence and of the likelihood of just such a deception. Anything we could do to get further information would only reinforce the convictions that no such deception is taking place and that ducks are incapable of such things.

Here is the Asymmetry Structure:

World A (Good Case)	World B (Bad Case)
Not-P: Ducks have not engineered world history for their own purposes in a perfectly seamless deception of both scientists and ordinary observers	P: Ducks have engineered world history for their own purposes in a perfectly seamless deception of both scientists and ordinary observers.
Know that not-P	Believe that not-P
	Everything seems exactly as it does, and we believe all of the same things as in the Good Case

This scenario is manifestly false, utterly preposterous. (I dare you to try to tell a wildlife biologist that we don't know it's false.) In the Good Case, we know something that's incompatible with the Bad Case: we know that ducks have not engineered world history. And we know this on the basis of ordinary observation, scientific knowledge of animals, the natural history of ducks, and the like (matters that are all in the Bad Case's Domain). In the Bad Case, by contrast, all of that is mere misleading appearance, and everything we know is compatible with the Good Case. And yet this scenario has exactly the structure of the Evil Demon scenario and the anti-gun conspiracy. It too regards all evidence that might be offered against it as mere misleading appearance, and it parallels the Evil Demon Hypothesis in every other respect. Since it would be utterly ridiculous to claim that we do not know that the Ducks Hypothesis is false, so with the others.

Lest one think that all we have here is a possible "clash of intuitions" regarding an example, let's play things out a bit. Suppose that someone really did quite seriously hold, in our ordinary pre-philosophical position, that we don't know that the Ducks Hypothesis is false. There are two main options for what this might look like. First, someone might deny that there is an Accessibility Asymmetry here at all. To do that it would have to be claimed that we, in the Good Case, don't know anything incompatible with the Ducks Hypothesis. This person has to claim, for instance, that we don't know that ducks lack the intelligence and social organization needed for very significant and highly organized collective action over many generations. Try telling *that* to a wildlife biologist. This won't fly from within our ordinary position.

Second, it might be claimed that while we do know things that are incompatible with the Ducks Hypothesis, we have no evidence against it and don't know that ducks haven't engineered world history for their own purposes. What would that look like in detail? We might imagine an article being written:

Scientific Crisis: Annals of Ornithology
Did ducks engineer the fall of the Roman Empire? Were they the power behind the Hapsburgs? Did they purposefully create the conditions that led to the devastation of the American Civil War? And did they do it all so cleverly that we can't even detect their influence? These are serious questions, reflecting a fundamental gap in scientific knowledge that has recently become a subject of intense scrutiny by ornithologists and animal behaviorists. "We know a great deal about ducks," said Cameron Dabble, president of the American Ornithological Society, "and it is quite clear that their intelligence is limited. They lack sophisticated social structures and have no significant capacity for social coordination. On standard intelligence and problem-solving measures, they come out above shrimp, but below rats. There are no means by which they could steer the ship of human affairs. Still, it is an open question whether they have—with diabolical brilliance and coordination over many, many generations—shaped the course of human history for their own benefit, all in a way that we can't detect. Despite all the above considerations, we simply don't know whether or not that is true." Dabble went on to point out that this isn't just an intriguing hypothesis; it may be a fundamental limit-point of our scientific knowledge. "When you think about it, that we really can't know whether this is going on right now," Dabble said, "It's quite terrifying." Entomologists have recently begun to express the same concern about dung beetles.

This is what it would look like if, standing in our ordinary, non-philosophical position, we held that this is something we couldn't know or have any evidence about, despite all we know about ducks. And the crucial point is this: *This reads as a joke, a second-rate article on a comedy website*. It is entirely out of line with our ordinary epistemic practices and commitments. There are limits on scientific knowledge, but this is not one of them.

One further point needs to be stressed here. If you say we can't know or have evidence that the Ducks Hypothesis is false, you really do have to say the same thing about dung beetles. *In fact, you have to say the same thing about rocks!* I can't see any way to make that fly from within the commitments of our ordinary position.

I have said that we have evidence against both the Anti-Gun and the Ducks Conspiracies, both of which are structurally analogous to the Evil Demon scenario. And I noted that in cases alike in all relevant respects, we should draw the same conclusions. What, then, might my evidence be against the Evil Demon Hypothesis in the Good Case, where there is no reason whatsoever to think it's correct? Here is some relevant evidence that I possess: I have hands, I am seeing a table before me right now, and, what's more, there are no evil demons. In light of such facts it looks as though in the sense of knowledge that involves having good evidence, we are in a position to know—and have no reason to deny that we know—that we are not in the Bad Case. We are not being deceived by an evil demon. And it looks as though the only way in which we can explain *how* we know this will involve appealing to information in the Bad Case's domain—information about which we would be wrong or wildly unreliable if the hypothesis were true. This might seem strange. But it's a feature of this kind of asymmetry more generally. We cannot explain how we know the Ducks Conspiracy is false except by appealing to considerations that would be false, or about whose truth and evidential significance we would be wildly unreliable, if the hypothesis were true. This doesn't prevent us from knowing that it's false.

7. Evidence Asymmetry

The claim of Evidence Asymmetry is that even though everything seems the same in the two cases, one can have evidence in the Good Case that one is not in the Bad Case—even if in the Bad Case one has no comparable evidence about which case one is in. For instance, in the Good Case regarding My Colleague Is a Spy, one has the following evidence that one's colleague is not a spy: one's colleague is an honest and straightforward guy. This is evidence that one lacks in the Bad Case, though one thinks one has it.

I have claimed that there is an evidential asymmetry between the Good and Bad Case when it comes to skeptical scenarios. It is accordingly worth considering what we need to be committed to in order to secure that result, given what we have seen so far.

Williamson secures such an asymmetry by equating one's evidence with what one knows (2000, chapter 9). This equation has an odd result in certain cases of Accessibility Asymmetry. Consider again the Trash Chute example of Accessibility Asymmetry.

World A (Good Case)	World B (Bad Case)
P: Trash bag in basement	Not-P (Trash bag in fact snagged on the way down)
S knows that P	
S knows: She dropped the bag down the chute, there was no warning sign and no indication of failure, the chute has functioned properly for years, etc.	S believes that P
	S knows: She dropped the bag down the chute, there was no warning sign and no indication of failure, the chute has functioned properly for years, etc.

On a view like Williamson's, this comes out as a case of Evidence Asymmetry. One has evidence in the Good Case that one is not in the Bad Case, even though in the Bad Case one has no comparable evidence about which case one is in. In particular, since one's evidence is what one knows, one has the following evidence in the Good Case that one's trash bag did not snag on the way down: one's trash bag is in the basement. But that doesn't sound right. Suppose someone asks me in the Good Case, while I am standing there in the hallway on the tenth floor just after putting my trash down the chute, "What is your evidence that your bag didn't snag on the way down?" It would at best be a (rather poor) joke to reply, "Well, my bag is currently in the basement." In fact, one has *exactly the same evidence in both cases about whether the chute has malfunctioned.* That evidence comes from considerations about how the chute has worked in the past, the absence of warning signs and trash piled up in the hall, and so on. The difference is that in the Bad Case, unlike the Good Case, this evidence is defeated. That is to say, Accessibility Asymmetry doesn't entail Evidential Asymmetry regarding which case one is in, as this example shows.[17]

This point is compatible with allowing that there can be Evidential Asymmetries regarding which case one is in. The key source of Evidential Asymmetry is this: A consideration can't be evidence for anything if it is false. As I argued earlier, this seems to be part of our pretheoretical thinking about evidence; it's quite natural to object to someone who offers something false as evidence, "But that's no evidence at all—it's not even true!" Of course, if you incorrectly and reasonably think that something is true, you will be quite reasonable in using it as evidence in support of certain further conclusions, at least until its falsehood is pointed out to you. It doesn't follow, however, that it really is good evidence (Chapter 5; Leite 2013).

Here, then, is how this point generates Evidential Asymmetries. Consider *any* theory of what it is to have or possess evidence—any theory, that is, that (a) accepts the pretheoretical judgment that in the Good Case we do have excellent evidence that the Ducks Conspiracy Hypothesis is false, including such facts as that ducks lack capacities for sophisticated social coordination, and (b) is compatible with the point just stressed, namely that a consideration isn't evidence for anything if it is false. Supplement the theory with the latter claim, that a consideration isn't evidence for anything if it is false. Bingo: Evidential Asymmetry results. In the Good Case we have evidence that this hypothesis is false and that we are in the Good Case, evidence that includes the fact that ducks lack capacities for social coordination. In the Bad

---

[17] It is important, when thinking about this case, to remember that our pre-philosophical position is *fallibilist*: it allows that one can know something on the basis of defeasible evidence. Here is how you know that the bag didn't snag in the ordinary case: you've used the chute successfully every week for years, nothing is out of the ordinary, nothing weird happened when you used it this time, plus all of your background knowledge of how trash chutes work, what it would take for something to happen to a chute such that your trash bag would silently snag, and how unusual that would be. Now imagine someone saying, "Yes, but all of that is consistent with the possibility that the bag snagged, so how do you know it didn't snag?" The correct reply is the fallibilist one. "I just told you how I know it didn't snag. You can know something on the basis of evidence that is consistent with the alternative. That's how we know that smoking causes lung cancer and that climate change is real: on the basis of evidence that is logically compatible with the falsity of what we know. Just as it is mistaken in those cases to demand entailing evidence (a mistake that is sometimes encouraged by those with an economic or political interest in getting us to think we don't know these things), it is likewise a mistake to demand entailing evidence when it comes to my knowledge that my trash bag didn't snag."

Case, however, that and other similar considerations about ducks are false. So, in the Bad Case we don't have comparable evidence about which case we are in, though we incorrectly think that we do.

In fact, we can secure Evidential Asymmetries even more minimally. Consider *any* theory that allows:

(i) A consideration isn't evidence for anything if it is false,
(ii) It is possible to be mistaken in other cases about the truth of some of the propositions that are part of your evidence in the Good Case.

Any such theory will yield Evidential Asymmetries, no matter how it characterizes what evidence is or what it is to have evidence. For if (i) and (ii) are both granted, then there will be a possible Good Case in which some consideration is good evidence about which case you are in and a possible Bad Case in which that consideration is false (and so not evidence you have) but you incorrectly think it is true and regard it as good evidence. That's all that's needed for Evidential Asymmetry.

What, then, do we need in order to secure the Moorean anti-skeptic's Evidential Asymmetry? Just this:

(a) In the Good Cases of Accessibility Asymmetries with the structure we see in the Ducks Hypothesis, one can have evidence from within the Bad Case's domain that one is not in the Bad Case, and
(b) If a consideration is false, then it isn't evidence for anything.

And to allow for the hoped-for result regarding the Evil Demon scenario, we have to make clear what (a) entails for this case (which is surely a commitment of our ordinary epistemic practice):

(c) Considerations about the world sometimes constitute good evidence about how things are in the world.

Whatever theory one adopts regarding when one counts as having some evidence in favor of some claim, so long as it allows these three commitments to have their natural results it will generate Evidential Asymmetries regarding the Evil Demon scenario. These look to me like the three minimal pretheoretical commitments that are sufficient to do the trick. They suffice, without developing any particular theory of what it is to have evidence, to secure the pretheoretically plausible result that in the Good Case we have evidence that we are not in the skeptic's Bad Case.

An additional source of Evidential Asymmetry appears if one also allows that evidential support relations often depend on contingent facts about what is a good indication of what—as determined by what is the case in the world, how things tend to go, causal regularities, and the like. But that is mere icing on the asymmetry cake.

8. The Upshot

Epistemic asymmetry is indeed central in coming to terms with external world skepticism, as Williamson has urged. But we don't need any epistemological theory—Williamson's or any other—to convince us that there is nothing inherently objectionable about the asymmetry that the Moorean anti-skeptic claims. Perfectly ordinary examples show that we are pretheoretically committed to asymmetries with exactly the necessary structure. There is thus no objection in principle to this aspect of the Moorean anti-skeptical position. *Nothing about the structure of the skeptical hypotheses warrants saying that we lack evidence, good reasons, or knowledge that they don't obtain.* Moorean anti-skeptics interested in finding pretheoretically compelling reasons to dismiss external world skepticism can now confidently add a significant additional resource to their arsenal.

Epistemologists interested in developing a theory of knowledge face an intriguing new question as well. We *do* know that the Anti-Gun and Ducks Conspiracy Hypotheses are false; we *do* have good evidence against them. What must a theory of evidence and knowledge be like in order to do justice to this datum and our other key pretheoretical commitments? This is an important question for anyone interested in theorizing about our knowledge of the world. It is part of the downstream project that Moore calls 'analysis,' and what we have seen are some of the data that such a project would aim to accommodate. But that is not our project here. Our aim is to explore the anti-skeptical resources of our ordinary, pre-philosophical position. Our question is whether there is anything to be said against the Moorean anti-skeptic from within that position. The prospects of that are looking increasingly dim.

This is not to say that we have here a complete anti-skeptical position. For even if the asymmetry the anti-skeptic postulates is not objectionable in itself, there might nonetheless be independent reasons in favor of external world skepticism arising from the role of perceptual experience in our knowledge of the world. To provide a fully satisfying response to external world skepticism, we still need to follow out those lines of thought and identify where they go wrong. That will be our focus shortly (Chapters 9–12). First, though, I want to examine four prominent discussions in contemporary epistemology that challenge what I have been saying up to this point.

8
Methodological Interlude

Four Moments in Contemporary Epistemology

> Don't think, but look!
> —Wittgenstein, *Philosophical Investigations*, par. 66

I have been arguing for two main claims. First, that we have good evidence against the global skeptical scenarios and good reason for rejecting the suggestion that they might obtain; indeed, we know that they do not. As we have seen, this claim can play a significant role in heading off attempts to get a skeptical argument going from within our pre-philosophical position. My second main claim, then, has been this: no principles or requirements of our pre-philosophical position generate the skeptical conclusion.

I now want to pause to consider four contemporary discussions that challenge these claims. I will begin with some lines of argument from Duncan Pritchard aimed at showing that we cannot have rationally grounded knowledge that we are not globally deceived. I will then examine two prominent versions of skeptical argumentation due to Jim Pryor and Crispin Wright. Finally, I will discuss Krista Lawlor's recent objections to my approach.

In opposing these lines of thought there is—for reasons I've already stressed—no single, overarching argument to be had, no Archimedean fulcrum, just the patient Moorean work of carefully scrutinizing the arguments that have been offered. Indeed, the thought that we need a master argument here is a temptation toward philosophical theory; it is to lose track of the nature of the inquiry. Similarly, each of the four writers I will discuss succumbs in one way or another to the temptation to privilege epistemological theory even as they may aim to resist it. In various ways they lose sight of the details of our pre-philosophical commitments or import philosophical assumptions. And they are sometimes unclear about where they are standing while considering skeptical arguments: Are they articulating pre-philosophical commitments, imposing philosophical assumptions, developing or assuming an epistemological theory, or what? In engaging with these writers, however, I will insist on remaining squarely in the pre-philosophical position. As we will see, considerations already on the table are enough to head off these challenges without the development of any epistemological theory. The commitments of our pre-philosophical position will suffice.

1. Pritchard on Rational Support

A persistent strand of anti-skeptical thought holds that while the skeptic's overall claim should be rejected, the skeptic is right that we don't know (or have good evidence, good reason, or justification to believe) that the global skeptical scenarios don't obtain (Dretske 1970, Nozick 1981, Maddy 2017). Duncan Pritchard (2016) has recently enlisted Wittgenstein into this tradition, taking *On Certainty* (1969) as inspiration for a "hinge epistemology" that holds that we cannot have rationally grounded knowledge or any good epistemic reason for believing such things as that we aren't being deceived by an evil demon. As I will argue, however, a careful look at our ordinary epistemic practice and commitments shows that Pritchard's arguments for this view depend on the imposition of substantial and unsupported demands regarding what rational grounding must be.

Wittgenstein writes:

> My having two hands is, in normal circumstances, as certain as anything that I could produce in evidence for it.
> That is why I am not in a position to take the sight of my hand as evidence for it. (1969, §250)

Pritchard interprets these passages as follows.

> Wittgenstein contends ... that it is in the very nature of these Moorean certainties, in virtue of the fact that they are optimally certain, that they cannot coherently be thought of as rationally grounded. (2016, 64)

> Wittgenstein is suggesting that to conceive of this proposition as rationally grounded is to suppose that the rational grounds are more certain than the proposition itself. (2016, 65)

To apply this to the Evil Demon scenario in particular, the suggestion is that if I am to offer the fact that there are no evil demons as support—as a rational ground—in favor of the claim that I am not being deceived by one, then I have to regard the former as *more certain* than the latter. But since the falsity of the Evil Demon scenario is as certain as the non-existence of evil demons, this requirement cannot be met. So we cannot have rationally grounded knowledge of the falsity of the Evil Demon scenario.

Now, I doubt that it is right to read Wittgenstein as endorsing this view. I am strongly inclined to follow Penelope Maddy's interpretation, which holds that these passages are rather an interlocutory voice to which Wittgenstein responds (Maddy 2022). However, I want to leave aside issues of Wittgenstein interpretation and focus on the thought that Pritchard is putting forward. Is it true that to offer one consideration as rational support for another, I must regard the former as *more* certain than the latter?

I don't think that it is. Pritchard does not tell us how to understand the word "certain" in this context. The epistemological tradition presents a number of possibilities: highest degree of confidence, immunity to error, incorrigibility, maximal warrant, and so on. In whatever way we understand the term, though, this claim does not seem to be a commitment of our ordinary, pre-philosophical position. If two considerations are *equally* certain, one may be offered as rational support for the other. For instance, on any notion of certainty, I regard it as equally certain that I live in the United States and that I live in Indiana, a state in the United States. I could perfectly well point out that I live in Indiana as a ground for dismissing the suggestion that I don't live in the US. If asked what tells in favor of the claim that I live in the US, I could likewise point out, among other things, that I live in Indiana. Here I offer one consideration as evidence or rational support for another, though the two are equally certain. A consideration can thus be adduced as telling decisively in favor of the truth of another even if it is not more certain than the latter.

It might be objected that the key point Pritchard draws from Wittgenstein concerns the structure of the relation between the claim that I'm not being deceived by an evil demon and claims about the world: if I had strong reasons of the right sort for suspecting that the Evil Demon Hypothesis were true, then I couldn't acceptably appeal to considerations about the world in order to defeat these reasons; those considerations would, in those circumstances, have been placed in doubt. This, it might be said, is why considerations about the world can't *now* be appealed to as rational support or evidence that I'm not being deceived by an evil demon. But notice that it is equally true that if I had reasons of the right sort for suspecting that I don't live in the US, those reasons would also preclude me from acceptably appealing to the consideration that I live in Indiana. That latter consideration, too, would then be placed out of play. So in this regard there is no fundamental structural difference between the claim that the Evil Demon Hypothesis is false and the claim that I live in the US.

What we are seeing here is an illustration of a point that Austin made (1962). What may be appealed to as evidence for what depends upon the circumstances. And *now*, in our actual circumstances, when there is no reason whatsoever to suspect that the Evil Demon Hypothesis is true, or that one doesn't live in the US, nothing blocks appealing to the consideration that there are no evil demons, or that one lives in Indiana, if one wants to point out something that is certainly true and that tells decisively in favor of one's claim.

Pritchard offers another reason for thinking that we cannot have either evidence against the skeptical scenarios or rational support for their denial. On Pritchard's view, denials of the particular skeptical scenarios are "codifications" of the "über hinge commitment," the general conviction that one's beliefs are not radically and fundamentally mistaken (2016, 95-6). As such, our commitment to the claim that we are not being deceived by an evil demon is, he says, "an immediate consequence of our commitment to the über hinge commitment" (97). But, he claims, there is no rational support for the über hinge commitment.

> ... what possible reason could we have for holding the über hinge commitment? Whatever grounds we cited would already presuppose the truth of this commitment after all (97).

> There is simply no rational process through which we could have gained rational support for belief in the über hinge proposition (98).

For this reason, he says, we cannot have a rationally supported belief that we are not being deceived by an evil demon.

> Since we are unable to have a rationally supported belief in the über hinge proposition, it follows that we are unable to have rationally supported beliefs in the ... anti-skeptical hinge propositions that codify our über hinge commitment (98).

And this, he thinks, has an important Wittgensteinian upshot.

> Once we see that the other hinge commitments we have . . . are simply a consequence of our über hinge commitment, then it becomes clear that the extent to which our system of rational support presupposes essentially groundless commitments is quite considerable. (98)

This is a heady consequence. But it depends essentially on the claim that nothing tells in favor of the über hinge proposition. Is that really something we are committed to in our ordinary, pre-philosophical position?

Speaking from within our pre-philosophical position, here's one reason for thinking that the über hinge proposition is true (that is, that my beliefs are not radically and fundamentally mistaken): There is a great deal that I know about the world around me. It follows from this that my beliefs are not radically and fundamentally mistaken. Of course, if I genuinely wondered whether my beliefs are radically and fundamentally mistaken and thought they very well might be, or if I had a strong reason of the right sort to suspect that they are, then I could not acceptably appeal to the consideration that I know things about the world in order to resolve the question. Whether I really know those things would—in those circumstances—be part of what is in question or in doubt. But *now*, when there is no reason to suspect that my beliefs are radically and fundamentally mistaken, I can see no bar against pointing to the consideration about what I know as one absolutely decisive consideration in favor of the claim that my beliefs are not radically and fundamentally mistaken.

Prichard considers a response along these lines. He imagines someone who puts forward a general closure principle in support of the suggestion I just made:

The Closure$_{KK}$ Principle:

> If S has rationally grounded knowledge that p, and S competently deduces from the fact that she knows that p that q, thereby forming a belief that q on this basis while retaining her rationally grounded knowledge that p, then S has rationally grounded knowledge that q. (99)

This principle suggests that quite generally, competent deduction *from the fact that you know something* yields knowledge of the proposition deduced. And the application here is supposed to be an imagined deduction from *the fact that you know various things about the world* to the conclusion that your beliefs are not radically and fundamentally mistaken.

Pritchard objects that this principle has the result that rationally-grounded knowledge is *iterative*, in the sense that if one knows that *p*, then one is in a position to know that one knows it, and so on for infinitely higher levels (99). But even if that charge is both true and a good ground for objection, it is beside the point, because this closure principle is not at issue in my argument. For one thing, I have not made any claim that you could arrive at your belief that you are not radically and fundamentally mistaken *through competent deduction*. I was just offering one sort of consideration that decisively tells in favor of the claim. So a *competent deduction* principle is not what is at issue.

A more fundamental point is relevant here, too. So far I have been considering Pritchard's claim that we can't have rational support for the über hinge proposition. We have been considering this because of how Pritchard argues. He claims that since we can't have such rational support, we can't have rational support for "I am not being deceived by an evil demon" either, because the latter is "simply a consequence of our über hinge commitment" (98). I have been scrutinizing one key premise of this argument. But notice that this argument also depends on an assumption: that since the claim that one is not being deceived by an evil demon is a "codification," instantiation, or consequence of the über hinge proposition, any rational support one has for the former must derive from rational support one has for the latter. But that is hardly obvious, either. The claim that I live in the US is an instantiation of the true claim that everyone in my immediate family lives in the US, but the fact that I live in Indiana is an excellent reason in favor of the claim that I live in the US, and I can offer it as such without running by way of a deduction from that general proposition. Why couldn't something analogous hold for the claim that I am not being deceived by an evil demon? To offer evidence for it, or show that it is rationally grounded, one needn't first offer evidence in favor of something more general from which it follows.

This last point highlights a feature of our practice directly relevant to Pritchard's claim that we have no rational support for the über hinge commitment. Something much simpler could be said in support of the claim that my beliefs are not radically and fundamentally mistaken. My belief that my name is Adam Leite is true, as is my belief that I live in Indiana. So is my belief that I am sitting at a table and typing on a computer. Those are several excellent considerations in favor of the claim that my beliefs are not radically and fundamentally mistaken. Since I have just listed three perfectly representative beliefs of mine that are true, it is not true that my beliefs are radically and fundamentally mistaken. I have thus offered rational support for the über hinge proposition.

Perhaps anticipating this sort of response, Pritchard offers a second strand of argument in some of the passages quoted above. This second argument is pitched as support for the claim that we can't have rational grounds for the über hinge proposition, but it would equally apply to our commitment to the claim that we are not being deceived by an evil demon. It is this: we cannot have good reasons or rational grounds for the commitment at issue, because "whatever grounds we cited would already presuppose [its] truth" (97).

This charge has something to be said for it, but to see exactly what it is—and what its significance is—we have to be very careful with the word 'presuppose.' For instance, the claim that Morgan is a bachelor presupposes *in one sense* that Morgan is male: the former obviously requires the truth of the latter. Nonetheless, someone in the know can point out that Morgan is a bachelor as way of resolving the question of whether Morgan is male. The other participants in the discussion—the ones who were wondering whether or not Morgan is male—will take the speaker to have provided an absolutely decisive consideration. If a consideration presupposes another proposition in *this* sense, that is no objection at all to offering the consideration as a reason in favor of the proposition thus presupposed.

Here's a second sense in which any attempt to cite reasons will "presuppose" the claim that one is not radically and fundamentally mistaken: the truth of that latter claim is required for success in the activity of citing reasons. This is gestured at by Pritchard when he writes, "The über hinge proposition seems to be such that it must be true for one to even be in the market for knowledge of specific empirical propositions" (99). However, the same is true of the fact that I am alive: I must be alive, if I am to be in the market for knowledge of specific empirical propositions. Clearly, that is no bar whatsoever to my having good empirical reasons for believing that I am alive!

What, then, could Pritchard have in mind here? It seems that what he is really after is brought out by his comment, "There is simply no rational process through which we could have gained rational support for belief in the über hinge proposition" (98). What Pritchard means by 'rational process' seems to be a process of explicit reasoning by which one could acceptably arrive *for the first time* at a view about the truth of the über hinge proposition, that is, a process of "competent deduction," or at least competent reasoning, from a starting position of neutrality on the issue. He is imagining someone who starts out by thinking something like this: "Are my beliefs radically and fundamentally mistaken? I currently have *no view about that*. Now, to what can I appeal in order to answer this question?" And his point is that someone *who is in this position* cannot acceptably reason like this: "I have no view about whether my beliefs are radically and fundamentally mistaken. I'm neutral on that issue; it might very well be true that my beliefs are radically and fundamentally mistaken. Still, I know all sorts of things about the world. So my beliefs are not radically and fundamentally mistaken."

Pritchard is right: this sort of reasoning wouldn't be acceptable. If the person genuinely had no view about whether their beliefs are radically and fundamentally mistaken, then they cannot just assert their premise; the claim appealed to as a premise is, in those circumstances, one of the things that they should be regarding as wide open. To put it the other way around: to acceptably assert their premise, they can't take it to be an open question whether the über hinge proposition is true. In this sense, whatever grounds we cite in defense of the über hinge proposition presuppose its truth. Still, I don't think that it follows that "there is no rational process through which we could have gained rational support" for the belief that our beliefs are not radically and fundamentally mistaken. That wouldn't follow unless the only sort of rational process by which we can gain rational support for a belief is a process that can be modeled as an acceptable course of linear reasoning from an initial position in which we explicitly start out with no view on the question. And why think that? Isn't that just one way in which we can gain rational support for a proposition?

Suppose that you have a belief that you did not acquire through any sort of objectionably irrational process such as wishful thinking, though you also did not arrive at it through a process of explicit linear reasoning. Suppose too that you know other things that (a) are available to your conscious reflection, (b) you can cite in its favor, and (c) you recognize to decisively support (indeed, entail) its truth. I don't see any reason why there couldn't be a case of this sort in which you have rationally gained rational support for the belief in question, even if you couldn't arrive at the belief for the first time via an acceptable course of explicit reasoning from an initial position of agnosticism or neutrality in which you explicitly held no view on the issue.

In fact, we have already seen several examples of this sort.

Return, for instance, to the Children of Brunettes Hypothesis. Suppose someone recognizes that they are the child of a brunette. They explicitly hold no view whatsoever on whether this hypothesis is true or even whether it is likely. They are wide open on the issue, and in particular are entirely open to the possibility that the hypothesis might very well be correct. They now want to resolve the question. They reflect as follows:

> I have no view on whether the Children of Brunettes Hypothesis is true, and I see that it would apply to me if it were. So I have no view as to whether I am competent at all to evaluate the truth or significance of anything that might be offered as evidence for or against it. Now, as genetics, cognitive psychology, and the like reveal, the hair color of parents does not affect the cognitive abilities of their children. So, the Children of Brunettes Hypothesis is false.

That is clearly objectionable: in citing those grounds the person is already presupposing the falsehood of the very thing that they claimed to have no view on, or—to put it the other way round—the person can't acceptably view themselves as in any position to engage in that very course of reasoning, given where they started.

For this reason, the complaint Pritchard makes regarding the über hinge proposition would apply here as well. If, as Pritchard maintains, there is no rational process through which we can gain rational support for the über hinge proposition because "whatever grounds we cited would already presuppose the truth of this commitment" (97), exactly the same thing should be said regarding the Children of Brunettes.

And yet, we do have rational grounds for dismissing the Children of Brunettes Hypothesis. For instance, they include the fact that the hair color of parents does not affect the cognitive abilities of their children. And we arrived at those grounds via rational processes. The processes of scientific investigation and information-sharing through which we gained the relevant data in genetics, cognitive psychology, and the like are surely "rational processes" if anything is. Pritchard's complaint thus looks wrong.

In fact, this is not an isolated example. Over the past two chapters we have seen repeated instances with the same structure: my knowledge that my spouse isn't deceiving me about whether she loves me, our knowledge that ducks don't rule the world and that the International Anti-Gun Conspiracy scenario is false, psychologists' knowledge of the ways and extent to which perception is reliable, and so on. Each of these cases has the very structure that concerns Pritchard. For the reasons we have seen earlier, none of these cases can be mirrored by a course of acceptable reasoning from a neutral starting position in which one explicitly suspends any view on the relevant issue, regarding both p and not-p as equally wide open. But (to speak from our Moorean position amidst our pre-philosophical commitments and practices) in all these cases we have attained rational support for our beliefs through rational processes.

The upshot, then, is this. Pritchard's argument that we have no rational support for the über hinge proposition crucially depends upon the assumption that any instance of rational or evidential support must be mirrored by a possible course of competent deduction/acceptable reasoning from a very particular sort of starting position: a starting position of self-conscious, complete agnosticism or neutrality. But this demand is not a commitment of our ordinary, pre-philosophical position. In fact, ordinary examples point in exactly the other direction. To speak from within the commitments of our pre-philosophical position: It is a mistake to understand rational support quite generally on the model of arriving at a view on an issue for the first time via a process of linear reasoning from an initial position of neutrality. And it is a mistake to impose this demand here, in the particular case that concerns Pritchard. For as we have seen, it is out of place in cases (such as the Ducks Conspiracy) that are structurally identical in all relevant respects.

2. Pryor's Skeptical Principle

In his influential paper "The Skeptic and the Dogmatist," Jim Pryor (2000) carefully develops a skeptical argument which he then counters with a distinctive and sophisticated theory of perceptual justification. A great deal has been written about this theory, but his skeptical argument has received much less attention. Is it at all compelling when considered in the way Moore urges, from a position squarely within the commitments of our pre-philosophical position? As I will argue, the answer is, "No." We can reject it without developing any particular epistemological theory at all.

Pryor rightfully attempts to structure his skeptical argument in such a way that considerations about the world are taken off the table. The crucial move in his argument is a principle that he terms SPK (Skeptical Principle about Knowledge):

SPK: If you are to know a proposition p on the basis of certain experiences or grounds E, then for every q which is "bad" relative to E and p, you have to be in a position to know *q* to be false in a non-question-begging way—i.e., you have to be in a position to know *q* to be false *antecedently to* knowing *p* on the basis of E. (2000, 528, italics in original)

To say that you have to be in a position to know *q* to be false antecedently to knowing *p* on the basis of E is to say that you have to be in a position to know *q* to be false in a way that does not draw upon your knowing *p* on the basis of E. Since Pryor is happy to think of knowledge of the world around us as a class, and since the Evil Demon Hypothesis is "bad" relative to all such knowledge and whatever evidence we might have for it, SPK has the consequence that we must have some independent basis upon which we can know that the Evil Demon is false. But, his skeptic then argues, we have no such basis. So we can't have any knowledge of the world after all.

Pryor rejects SPK by developing a distinctive theory of perceptual justification. According to this theory, an experience as of a hand in front of you provides *all by itself* a prima facie justification for believing that there is a hand in front of you. This theory has the consequence that we do not need antecedent justification or knowledge that we are not being deceived by an evil demon in order to have perceptual justification or knowledge about the world. The theory thus denies SPK. But we do not need this theory, or any particular epistemological theory at all, in order to have good reason to deny SPK. Perfectly straightforward examples show that our pretheoretical position already commits us to denying SPK without yet saying anything one way or the other about Pryor's theory of perceptual justification.

Here's one sort of example that makes the point. Suppose that you are wondering whether Morgan is a woman. You acquire the following evidence (E): S (who you take to be reliable) tells you that Morgan is a bachelor. On the basis of this you believe (P): Morgan is a bachelor. And from this you conclude (not-Q): Morgan is not a woman. In the ordinary sort of case, this might be a perfectly good way of coming to know not-Q. Notice, however, how E, P, and Q are related. If you learned that (Q) Morgan *is* a woman, then you would have good reason not to take S's testimony as a trustworthy source of information about Morgan's gender. That is a clear way in which Q is "bad" relative to E and P; learning Q would undercut your ability to come to know P on the strength of E.[1] But still, contrary to SPK, you don't need to know that

---

[1] This feature of the example corresponds to one of the characterizations of "badness" that Pryor offers: "If you were to learn that you are dreaming, then you would have reason to doubt that your experiences were a trustworthy basis for beliefs about the external world. So we might want to count

Q is false *antecedently* to learning P via E. You can come to know that Q is false precisely by way of E and P. So, this is a counterexample to SPK.

SPK likewise gets things wrong when it comes to examples with the structure of the skeptical hypotheses. Recall, for instance, the International Anti-Gun Conspiracy and Ducks examples from the previous chapter. More than fifty people died at Columbine, Parkland, and Sandy Hook (call that P). And I know this thanks to various documentary evidence and the like (call it E). On any plausible characterization of "badness", the International Anti-Gun Conspiracy scenario is "bad" relative to these considerations. For instance, if the IAGC is the case, then all that supposed evidence is staged and does not objectively increase the likelihood of P at all—but I would nonetheless believe exactly what I do, and the hypothesis would explain why I believe as I do in that situation.[2] Likewise, if I learned that the IAGC is the case, then I couldn't take E as good evidence for P.[3] So SPK has the result that in order for us to know this P on the strength of this E, we must have independent, antecedent knowledge of the falsehood of the IAGC. But we can have no independent evidence against the IAGC. Given how the hypothesis is constructed, there can be no evidence that would enable us to know its falsity while satisfying SPK. But we do know that the anti-gun conspiracy theory is false. So SPK must go.

An exactly analogous argument against SPK could be run using the Ducks and Children of Brunettes examples. For instance, consider the Ducks Conspiracy Hypothesis. Ducks have not engineered world history for their own purposes in a perfectly seamless deception of both scientists and ordinary observers. This is something that we know. And we know it courtesy of considerations such as the following: Ducks lack the cognitive capacities and social organization needed for such a deception, as is revealed by scientific investigations of animal capacities and ordinary observation. We can structure this in precisely the way Pryor understands SPK in relation to the skeptical scenarios:

---

a hypothesis as 'bad' for the purposes of a skeptical argument if it could undermine your experiences, in this sense" (2000, 527).

[2] This feature of the example corresponds to another characterization of "badness" that Pryor offers: A hypothesis *h* is bad relative to some proposition *p* if, if *h* obtained, "we'd still believe *p* but our beliefs would be false, and *h* gives an explanation of why we'd still believe *p* in that situation" (2000, 544 fn. 18, quoting DeRose [1995]).

[3] This corresponds to the characterization of badness highlighted in fn. 1 of this chapter.

E: Observational data (observations of ducks doing this or that, observations of animal behavior in labs and in the wild, neurological observations, and so on.) which constitute the good grounds ordinary people and scientists have for believing that ducks lack the cognitive capacities needed for such a deception.
P: Ducks lack the cognitive capacities needed for such a deception.
Q: The Duck Conspiracy Hypothesis.

Q is incompatible with P. But if Q were true, we would have the same E.[4] If we learned that Q were true, that would undermine our ability to know P on the strength of E.[5] And if Q were true, P would be false, we would believe it nonetheless, and Q would explain why this is so.[6] So, Q is "bad" relative to E and P. But we do not have to be able to know Q to be false on the basis of independent grounds in order to be able to know P on the strength of E. *There are no* independent grounds that suffice to enable us to know not-Q. Still, we do know P on the strength of E. Moreover, we know Q to be false on the strength of considerations such as P. So, SPK is false.[7] (Again, notice that if you aren't

---

[4] This corresponds to another characterization of "badness" that Pryor offers:
Say that some grounds E you have "allow" a possibility *q* iff the following counterfactual is true: if *q* obtained, you would still possess the same grounds E. Many skeptical scenarios are incompatible with what we purport to know on the basis of our experiences, but are "allowed" by those experiences, in this sense. For instance, your experiences at the zoo seem to justify you in believing that there is a zebra in the pen. This belief is incompatible with the hypothesis that the animal in the pen is a mule painted to look like a zebra. But that is a hypothesis which is "allowed" by your experiences: if it *were* a painted mule in the pen, you would most likely be having *the same experiences*, and hence, the same grounds for believing that there is a zebra in the pen. Likewise, the belief that there is a zebra in the pen is incompatible with the hypothesis that your experiences are false appearances presented to you by an evil demon; but this Demon Hypothesis is also "allowed" by your experiences. If it were to obtain, you'd be having exactly the same experiences. This is what tempts so many people to believe that they *can't tell* whether or not the Demon Hypothesis obtains. So we might want to count a hypothesis as "bad" for the purpose of a skeptical argument just in case it is—and is recognized to be—incompatible with what you purport to know, but it is nonetheless "allowed" by your grounds E, in the sense I described. (2000, 527)

[5] This corresponds to the characterization of "badness" highlighted in fn. 1 of this chapter.

[6] This corresponds to the characterization of "badness" highlighted in fn. 2 of this chapter.

[7] Pryor offers a fourth characterization of "badness": Those hypotheses are bad "which entail that we have all the evidence for *p* that we actually have" (2000, 544). It looks likely that SPK comes out false when we understand it in terms of this characterization of "badness" as well. Let Q = the Ducks Conspiracy Hypothesis is correct, and let P = Ducks lack the cognitive capacity to do any such thing. It is plausible that Q entails that we have all the evidence for P that we actually have. Still, we know not-Q, and we know P, and we do not satisfy SPK. However, nothing much depends on this for our purposes here, because if we understand SPK in terms of this notion of "badness," it *does not* apply in the case of the skeptical hypotheses. This is because, as I stressed in earlier chapters, the skeptical hypotheses do not entail that we have all of the evidence for P that we actually have. For instance, my evidence right now includes that there is a table in front of me, and the Evil Demon Hypothesis does not entail that I have this evidence. If the Evil Demon scenario were the case, we would lack evidence

convinced by this appeal to the Ducks Conspiracy Hypothesis, we can make all the same points about *rocks*.)

Crucially, what we are seeing here is that SPK comes out false for pretheoretical reasons. It imposes a demand that is no part of our pre-philosophical position when it comes to instances of knowledge regarding hypotheses with the structure displayed by the Ducks Conspiracy. Since the Evil Demon scenario has exactly the same structure, we should draw the same conclusion: SPK does not hold there either. SPK does not do the work the skeptic needs, if the aspiration is to get a skeptical argument going from within our pre-philosophical position. That is to say: Even if Pryor's theory of perceptual justification is true, it is not needed—any more than any other particular theory—to refute Pryor's skeptic.

A point of detail is relevant here as well. Pryor (2004) closely connects denying SPK with the idea that under conditions of agnosticism we could acceptably reason from E to p and then to not-q (where q is "bad" relative to E and p), thereby arriving at knowledge that not-q for the first time. For instance, he claims that someone could explicitly begin with no view whatsoever on whether they are being deceived by an evil demon, explicitly regarding it as a wide open possibility, then acceptably transition from their experience as of a hand to the conclusion that they have a hand, and then finally move from there to the conclusion that they are not being deceived by an evil demon. I think that is wrong; such a course of reasoning looks objectionable to me, for reasons that I will discuss below. The point that I want to highlight here is that it is perfectly consistent to deny SPK while also holding that we cannot acceptably reason in the way Pryor suggests. So the denial of SPK does not commit me to Pryor's account of how I know that I am not being deceived by an evil demon.

3. Wright's "Information-Dependence" Skeptical Argument

I have been asking why we shouldn't respond to skepticism by appealing to considerations about the world. None of the argumentation we have looked at so far has convincingly ruled this out. Crispin Wright, however, has offered

---

that we currently have. (The Evil Demon scenario entails that we would believe the propositions that state the evidence that we actually have, but that is a different matter.)

a different sort of skeptical argument than we have examined so far, one that focuses on the structure of the justification or warrant of our beliefs about the world (Wright 1985, 2002, 2004a, 2004b, 2004c). This argument has been treated as particularly challenging in the literature (e.g., Lawlor 2013, 2015). It behooves us to examine it carefully.

3.1 Wright's Argument

On Wright's view, Moore's "Proof" fails for reasons that highlight a powerful argument for skepticism (1985, 2002, 2004a, 2004b, 2004c). Moore held up his hands, noted "Here is one hand, and here is another," and pointed out that this establishes that there are external things. Taken at face value, then, Moore's Proof starts with claims about the existence of his hands. On Wright's reading, however, it must in fact begin with a suppressed premise about Moore's current subjective informational state:

(e) My current state of awareness seems in all respects like being aware of a hand held up in front of my face. (2004a, 26)

From this, according to Wright, Moore derives:

(P) Here is a hand.

And from that:

(I) There is a material world.

So understood, Moore attempts to arrive at the conclusion that there is a material world via a course of reasoning that begins with his subjective experience.

This attempt fails, Wright charges:

> The status of Moore's experience as a warrant for his original premise, "Here is a hand," is not unconditional but depends upon needed ancillary information, and . . . paramount among the hypotheses that need to be in place in order for the putative warrant for the premise—Moore's state of consciousness—to have the evidential force that Moore assumes is the

hypothesis that there is indeed a material world whose characteristics are mostly, at least in the large, disclosed in what we take to be routine sense experience. (2004a, 26)

That is, the transition from (e) to (P) is only acceptable—only yields "warrant" for believing (P)—if one *already* has the information that (I), that is, both believes (I) and has some independent "warrant" for doing so. Wright thus charges that this argument is an example of failure of "warrant transmission": one cannot *get* "warrant" to believe (I) for the first time through a course of reasoning from (e) to (P) and then on to (I), because "(P) is warranted only if Moore is independently entitled to [the inference's] conclusion" (2004a, 26).

Wright urges that this objection points toward an argument for external world skepticism. In brief: One needs "warrant" to believe (I), that there is a material world, in order to make the transition—which, it is claimed, must be made if we are to have any knowledge or reasonable beliefs about the world—from subjective information such as (e) to beliefs about the world such as (P). But the only way to have "warrant" to believe (I) would be through an inference from premises such as (P)—which can't in fact provide such "warrant" after all, for the reason just discussed.[8] An analogous argument could obviously be made regarding the claim that one is not being globally deceived by an evil demon.

3.2 A Moorean Rejoinder

Wright responds to this argument by developing a theory of the structure of empirical warrant for beliefs about the world. According to Wright's theory, we have an "unearned warrant" for accepting that there is a material world, and this warrant puts in place the information that is needed in order for us to make the transition from our subjective experiences (such as (e)) to beliefs about the world such as (P). No final transition to (I) is needed, because an unearned warrant for (I) was in place at the beginning.

In this response to the skeptical argument, all of the weight falls upon the development and defense of a theory of the nature and basis of this "unearned warrant" (see, e.g., Wright 2004b). However, there is a simpler and

---

[8] See, for instance, Wright 2004a, 26–27.

more direct response if one is working—like Moore—from within our ordinary, pre-philosophical position. This is a response that, unlike Wright's, does not require developing a theory of the structure of empirical warrant.

Wright's skeptical argument requires two key ideas. The first is that any particular piece of knowledge or reasonable belief about the external world must be based on subjective information of the sort typified by (e). The second is that in order to gain any knowledge or reasonable belief about the external world on the basis of this sort of subjective informational state, some background information about the existence of material things (and that one is not merely dreaming or deceived by an evil demon, etc.) must already be in play. Wright puts these claims as follows:

1. That there is no way of justifying particular beliefs about the material world save on the basis of the (inconclusive) evidence provided by our states of consciousness [described in a way that is noncommittal about the external world] (2004a, 27).
2. Such evidence for any particular proposition about the material world depends for its force on collateral information that the material world so much as exists—it would not be warranted to treat how things seem to us as evidence for claims about our immediate physical environment if we were antecedently agnostic about the existence of a material world (2004a, 27).

The crucial question is this: Are both of these claims among the commitments of the position within and from which Moore invites us to work?

Wright's second claim surely captures something in our pre-philosophical position. If one is going to consciously move in an epistemically acceptable way from sensory experience—described in the manner in which Wright describes it—to 'here is a hand,' one does at least need to assume that there is an external world, that one is not merely engaged in a life-long dream, and the like. It would be epistemically objectionable in ordinary life for a mature adult to reason explicitly from her sensory experience, described in subjective terms, to a conclusion about the world while consciously and explicitly being *entirely noncommittal* about whether there are external things and whether she is at that moment dreaming or being deceived by an evil demon.

For instance, consider what you would think if some mature adult said, "I am having an experience precisely as if there is a hand before me. I have no view about whether I am being deceived by an evil demon or even whether there are external things, so I don't have any view about whether such experiences are positively correlated with particular circumstances in an external world. Still, I conclude nonetheless that there is a hand before me." That would be an outrageous conclusion to draw, even if it were true. This would be no better than a mature adult saying, "My lawn is riddled with hillocks and collapsed tunnels. I don't have a view about whether these things are a sign of moles. Still, I conclude from this that my lawn has moles." All else equal, if you don't have any view about whether moles cause such damage it is straightforwardly nutty from your own point of view to conclude on that basis that your lawn has moles. As Judith Jarvis Thomson puts it, "Surely he must believe that p is a reason for q or he can't mean his 'so'" (1965, 296; cf. Stroud 1977, 60–61; Leite 2008, 2011b). And if one has no view at all about whether moles do such things, how can one regard the one as a reason for the other?

There has been significant debate between Pryor and Wright about the correctness of Wright's claim. As highlighted above, Pryor claims that explicitly reasoning in the described way would be perfectly unobjectionable. Wright, of course, disagrees. This debate has been couched in highly theoretical terms. Here I am siding with Wright, but at the end of the day my reason is simple: for reasons highlighted by the moles example, *I wouldn't reason in the way Pryor suggests*, or if I did, I'd think I was behaving wrongly. If I were in a position in which I explicitly had no view about whether I was being deceived by an evil demon and thought it genuinely a completely open question, then I would not think myself entitled to move from how things perceptually seem to me to the conviction that I have a hand. I should think, "Well, maybe I have good reason to draw this conclusion, maybe I don't; I can't reach a verdict here, because it is an entirely open question for me whether my sensory experience is a good guide to how things are *at all*." So I would not endorse any such course of reasoning in ordinary life. I would not think it any better than the above example about moles.

A methodological point is relevant here. It is quite unclear how to assess this issue when it is pitched as a question about the structure of justification or warrant. But what counts as acceptable reasoning in our ordinary practice is quite a bit clearer. And since both Wright and Pryor take their claims to track considerations about acceptable reasoning, this is the place to look. Here, at the end of the day, we come to rest on our actual considered commitments. Of course, no one ever really has to reason about the Evil Demon Hypothesis from a position in which they have no knowledge of the world and no view as of yet on the matter. This is why we have to look at parallel cases. And here I regard the moles example and others like it as conclusive. I would be embarrassed to reason in the way Pryor suggests.

Elsewhere I have attempted to provide an account of *why* these sorts of moves would be objectionable; the fundamental problem, I have urged, centers on requirements pertaining to responsible reasoning and deliberation on the part of a mature adult (Leite, 2008, 2011b). Wright offers a very different account, one that depends upon ideas of "information-dependent warrant" and "warrant transmission". But that dispute is not what matters here. What matters right now is the surface of our practice when we are doing it right. And here I think that the verdict of our ordinary commitments and procedures of epistemic assessment is clear. In this regard, Wright is making use of the very materials Moore wants us to be working from and within.

By contrast, however, the first key claim underlying Wright's skeptical argument does not appear to be part of our ordinary commitments. That claim, recall, is that any particular piece of knowledge or reasonable belief about the external world must be based on one's subjective conscious states, described in a way that is noncommittal about the world. In ordinary life, however, we do not require people to derive their beliefs about the world from that sort of evidential basis. Still, we hold that people do know things about the world.

For instance, I can perfectly satisfactorily justify a particular belief about the world around me by appealing to other things I know about the world around me. I am not required to make use only of information about my subjective states of consciousness described in a way that is noncommittal about the external world. I can satisfactorily justify my belief that I am going to turn 54 this year by pointing out that it is 2023 and that I was born in 1969, thus appealing to other things I know about the world around me. To take another example, I can support the claim that I live in the US by pointing out that I live in Indiana, a state in the US. Here information about my current subjective state of consciousness isn't playing any particular role. Moreover, I might satisfactorily justify a perceptual belief that there is a pencil before me by noting that I see it. Here I presuppose a host of knowledge about the world and do not merely make use of "evidence provided by [my] states of consciousness". For instance, I depend upon all sorts of knowledge about my current circumstances, the conditions in which my vision is reliable, what pencils look like in conditions such as mine, and the like. (Take all that away, and I would no longer think myself in any position to offer this sort of support for the claim that there is a pencil before me.)

Wright's skeptic, however, imports a distinctive and familiar philosophical conception of what is going on in all such cases. According to this conception, the epistemic acceptability of all our beliefs about the world depends upon the rational propriety of an imagined transition from an informational state that does not yet involve any knowledge of the world. That this is the crucial thought can be seen in the following way. Grant Wright's skeptic that if you *were* in a situation in which your evidential basis regarding the world around you was limited to the sort of information in (e), you would need to attain an epistemically acceptable belief in (I) before you could move to beliefs such as (P)—and grant that under those circumstances you could not meet that requirement. Does a negative conclusion about the epistemic standing of our beliefs about the world follow straight from these concessions, all by themselves? No. To reach a negative conclusion, you need to accept a further thought: *that our beliefs about the world could not be in good epistemic shape unless we could acceptably arrive at them through some such reasoning from some such limited evidential base.*

Wright's skeptical argument, and his objection to Moore, thus presuppose precisely what is most in need of motivation: first, the limitation of our evidential base to exclude information about the world, and, second, the assumption that this limitation reflects something important about the epistemic status of our beliefs about the world. That is, Wright simply presumes, rather than motivates, a conception—not manifest in our ordinary, prephilosophical position—according to which our possession of knowledge or reasonable belief about the world is held hostage to our ability to acceptably make such a transition or to show how such a transition could acceptably be made. If we are working in the way Moore and Austin urge, we are not yet operating with that conception. Crucially, Wright has given us no reason to shift to it.

Wright attempts to respond to this sort of objection. Regarding his claim about the justificatory basis for our beliefs about the world, he comments,

> The thought is so far unchallenged that it is on information so conceived that the ultimate justification for our perceptual beliefs must rest.... [O]ne

kind of material world scepticism certainly so conceives the justificational architecture of perceptual claims. So Moore is begging the question against that adversary at least. (2004a, 27)

This charge misunderstands the dialectical situation. Remember the understanding of Moore urged in Chapter 2. As I argued, Moore does not invite us to adjudicate the merits of various theories of "the justificational architecture of perceptual claims" from a position external to our ordinary commitments; rather, he invites us to stand in our ordinary, pre-philosophical position and ask what reason, if any, we can find to change our view in the way the skeptic suggests. If Wright's skeptic's theory of "the justificational architecture of perceptual claims" turns out to impose unsatisfiable demands and thus to be in tension with our ordinary commitment to the truth of a great many claims to knowledge or reasonable belief, then so much the worse for that theory—*particularly if no considerations whatsoever have been offered to support it or the demands it would impose.* To charge this response with objectionably begging the question is already to have taken a step outside our ordinary, pre-philosophical position—to have imagined that the task is one of evaluating rival epistemological theories from a position outside our pre-philosophical starting point—without giving any reason for moving to this position. If we keep our heads about where we are standing, the response is no more objectionable than it would be to point out something I know about English history in order to rebut the suggestion that being an American, I could not possibly know any such thing.

This reply to Wright's skeptic has the form of Moore's characteristic response to skeptical arguments. Speaking now from within our ordinary, pre-philosophical position, we do know and reasonably believe all kinds of things about the world. So *one* of Wright's skeptic's premises should, prima facie, be denied. Which one? We concede (to put it roughly) that we could not acceptably move in conscious, explicit reasoning from our subjective experience as of a hand to the conclusion "So, there is a hand here," if we are agnostic about whether there is a material world, whether we are dreaming or being deceived by an evil demon, and so on. We likewise concede that our knowledge of these latter matters depends in part upon things that we know about the world. That latter thought is certainly Moore's view; as noted earlier, he thought that he had no better reason in favor of the existence of external things than is provided by such considerations as that here is one hand and here is another.[9] What has not yet been conceded to the skeptic is the crucial thought that our beliefs about the world, as a class, could not be in good epistemic shape unless we could acceptably arrive at them by reasoning from a limited evidential base of sensory experiences described in a way that involves no commitments about the world. Wright gives us no reason to accept that further thought and no reason to see it as being among the commitments of our pre-philosophical position. And if we are working from within the everyday, pre-philosophical position, there is good reason to reject it. For in that position we do not require people to derive or justify their beliefs about the world in that way, but we do hold that people know things about the world. Since we concede Wright's skeptic's other premises while denying the skeptical conclusion, we consequently deny this crucial thought. We thus reject this skeptical argument.

At this point you may be thinking, "But it remains possible, despite surface indications to the contrary, that our pre-philosophical position *does* involve a commitment to that thought as well." Be patient. We will get there (see Chapters 9–12). The key point for now is that Wright hasn't done the work that is needed here in order to get a skeptical argument going from within our pre-philosophical position. To do that, it would be necessary to make the relevant demands explicit and, crucially, to *motivate them* from within the terms of our pre-philosophical position. Until that is done, we have been given no reason whatsoever to change our view.

It is arguable that Moore implicitly offered precisely the response I just sketched. Wright demands what Moore described as "a general statement as to how *any* propositions of this sort [propositions such as "Here's a hand"] may be proved" (1993d, 169), that is, a general account of how we may acceptably make the transition from our subjective experience to claims about the world. And here is Moore's response:

> This, of course, I haven't given, and I do not believe it can be given: if this is what is meant by proof of the existence of external things, I do not believe that any proof of the existence of external things is possible (1993d, 169).

Moore thought this impossibility to be irrelevant to our ability to know things about the world. Moore thus rejects Wright's demand when standing squarely in our pre-philosophical position.

---

[9] See Moore 1993d, 166, and 1953, 126.

3.3 The Demands of Cogent Reasoning: Wright's I-II-III Template

It might be urged that Wright's skeptical argument is closer to our ordinary, pre-philosophical commitments than I have made out. The core of the argument is the idea that for our beliefs about the world to be in good epistemic shape, we need a prior and independent warrant—one not dependent upon the rest of our knowledge of the world—for believing such things as that there is an external world and that we are not being deceived by an evil demon. And it might be maintained that Wright shows that this idea *does* arise from our ordinary, pre-philosophical position, because it arises out of "common sense judgments about what constitutes cogent reasoning" (Lawlor 2015, 242).

> Wright takes pains to show that ordinary patterns of reasoning are at work in the skeptical argument. He . . . begins with a homely case: You see a soccer ball kicked into the net. A goal! Do you thereby know a soccer game is being played? No—that's something you needed warrant for believing before your seeing the ball go into the net can count as evidence that a goal has been scored (as opposed, say, to a re-enactment of a famous goal having been executed). (Lawlor 2015, 241)

Given this point, Wright invites us to compare the following two lines of reasoning:

SOCCER	EXTERNAL WORLD
I. A ball has been kicked between the white posts.	I. My experience is in all respects as of a hand before me.
II. So, a goal has been scored.	II. So, there is a hand before me.
III. So, a game of soccer is being played.	III. So, there is a material world.

In both cases, Wright urges, the propriety of the move from (I) to (II) depends upon your already possessing the information in (III). You consequently can't arrive for the first time at an epistemically acceptable belief in (III) via this line of reasoning. This much I have granted to Wright. But the charge is that this much already suffices to show that in order for any of our beliefs about the world to be in good epistemic shape, we must possess an independent warrant for believing that there is an external world and that we are not being globally deceived. The key requirement of the skeptic's argument thus might be thought to arise out of perfectly ordinary considerations about acceptable reasoning.

In fact, however, these considerations don't show any such thing. What they show, at most, is that *if* we had to reach all of our beliefs about the external world by explicitly reasoning from an evidential base limited to how things seem in our sensory experience, *then* we would need to have an independent warrant for believing that we are not dreaming or being deceived by an evil demon, that there is an external world, and the like. *It does not follow from this that our beliefs about the world cannot be in good epistemic shape unless we have an independent warrant for believing these things.* For why think the antecedent of the above conditional is true when it comes to the body of our beliefs about the world quite generally? No reason has been given. Moreover, the key examples of epistemic asymmetry from the last chapter suggest that as things are we can perfectly appropriately draw upon considerations about the world to provide good evidence that we are not dreaming or deceived by an evil demon, that there is an external world, and the like. Such considerations are fully sufficient grounds for rejecting the skeptical hypotheses, given that there are no reasons in those hypotheses' favor; independent grounds are not required. By *modus tollens*, then, it looks as though the antecedent of the above conditional is incorrect.

To get the demand for independent warrant out of the comparison with the Soccer reasoning, you have to assume that steps I and II provide an appropriate model for the totality of our beliefs about the world. You have to think that just as the soccer fan comes to believe that a goal has been scored on the basis of a reasoning-like transition from seeing the ball go through the white posts, so our beliefs about the world must ultimately be derivable through a good reasoning-like transition from the limited evidence provided by our subjective conscious experience. This is to assume a very particular epistemological conception regarding our beliefs about the world: *that our beliefs about the world could not be in good epistemic shape unless we could acceptably arrive at them through some such reasoning from some such limited evidential base.* But we have already rejected that thought; it is precisely what—working from within our ordinary, pretheoretical position—we rejected in the previous section. Wright's "homely" examples consequently do nothing to prevent Moore or us from using considerations about the world and our knowledge of it as part of a reply to the skeptical argument. Instead, we can simply point out that the soccer case, understood as Wright understands it, doesn't provide an apt model for our beliefs about the world taken on the whole or for our knowledge that we aren't being dreaming or being deceived by an evil demon. From our ordinary, pre-philosophical position, then, Wright's skeptical argument hasn't gotten off the ground—not even when we have granted his point about cogent reasoning in relation to the soccer case.

One further point should be stressed. Underlying Wright's discussion is a key assumption about evidence. Here is what Wright says in support of the thought that we have no evidence that there is a material world and no evidence against the Evil Demon scenario:

> In doubting a type III proposition, one would not be setting oneself against any overwhelming body of evidence. We don't have any evidence for them, for it is a peculiarity of their situation that they are beyond supportive evidence too. As the skeptical argument shows, if confidence in them were once suspended, no evidence could make it rational to reinstate them again. (2004a, 41)

I agree with Wright regarding the point made in the last sentence. If one is explicitly in or adopts a position in which one has no information or view regarding whether one is being deceived by an evil demon, there is no course of explicit reasoning by which one could acceptably arrive at the conclusion that one is not thus deceived. But notice what Wright takes this to show. He argues from the fact that one could not rationally re-establish a claim "if confidence in [it] were once suspended," to the conclusion that one *now* lacks evidence for it. That is, Wright takes it that if E is evidence for *p*, then it **must be possible** for a rational being to explicitly begin with *no information or view about whether p*, from that position acceptably acquire E, and from there acceptably move in reasoning to the conclusion that *p*. That is to say, here Wright argues from the fact that one could not rationally argue from E to *p* in circumstances of agnosticism or doubt, to the conclusion that one *now* lacks evidence for *p*.

As we have seen over the course of the last two chapters, however, this is incorrect. It can be true *both* that one has overwhelming, decisive evidence in favor of some proposition, and *also* that if one rationally lost or never had rational confidence in that proposition one could not rationally attain such confidence by appealing to that evidence. This is precisely the position that we are in with regard to the Ducks Conspiracy and other hypotheses with that structure. Wright thus has done nothing to show that things we know about the world do not constitute excellent evidence that there is a material world, that we are not being deceived by an evil demon, and the like.

The fundamental point that Wright has missed is this: It is part of our ordinary, pre-philosophical position that we can sometimes have decisive evidence against a hypothesis even if we couldn't acceptably utilize that evidence to reason our way to the falsehood of the hypothesis in conditions of explicit agnosticism, neutrality, lack of background information, or reasonable suspicion that the hypothesis is true. We may therefore vindicate a claim to know something, such as the falsity of the skeptical hypotheses, by citing evidence that decisively supports the truth of what we claim to know, even though we could not arrive at that knowledge for the first time through an inference from that evidence in conditions in which we are antecedently neutral, agnostic, or in doubt.

4. Lawlor's Objections: Information-Dependence and Closure

Krista Lawlor (2015) has expressed dissatisfaction with my anti-skeptical appeal to considerations about the world and our knowledge of it. "Skeptical arguments from closure and information-dependence are challenging arguments," she writes, "and not so easily dismissed. Crucially, they represent themselves as growing out of common epistemic judgments and practice" (235). Indeed, that is how they represent themselves, but self-presentations can be misleading. Consideration of her criticisms can clarify what I am proposing—and what I am not.

4.1 Wright's "Information-Dependence" Skeptical Argument

Lawlor holds that it isn't so easy to reject Wright's skeptical argument. As she puts it:

> Leite seems to think we can know the anti-skeptical proposition III on the basis of II. But Wright's Soccer case makes it clear that this is a difficult position to uphold in general. Perhaps Leite thinks that Moore's argument is free of the flaw that Soccer exhibits? If that is the case, Leite has not told us why it is. (2015, 243)

And again:

> Leite doesn't make clear what he means when he says that skeptical hypotheses do not "neutralize our evidence." . . . It seems he must mean that if one just lets oneself start with proposition II, *I have hands*, instead of with proposition I, *I have the experience as of hands*, then one can know that one is not the victim of global deception. But it is not clear how this is supposed to work. A parallel move in the Soccer argument would have us starting with seeing a goal scored and reasoning to the claim that a soccer game is being played. That bit of reasoning would leave your average soccer fan cold, rightly enough. (2015, 243)

These passages fundamentally misunderstand several of my key methodological and substantive claims. Before we get into the details, however, it will be helpful to have on the table what strikes me as a core misunderstanding. Lawlor seems to think that I am trying to answer the same *kind* of question that Wright thinks Moore is trying to answer. I'm not.

To put this in a little more detail: By reconstructing Moore's argument in terms of the I-II-III reasoning, Wright understands Moore to be arguing with a very particular aim; he takes Moore to be trying to present an acceptable argument through which a rational being could come to arrive at knowledge of the existence of the world for the very first time from a position of initial neutrality. As we've seen, that is indeed Pryor's aim. Lawlor seems to think it is my aim as well. But it isn't, and as I've argued, it wasn't Moore's. In fact, I think (with Moore) that that aim is unsatisfiable, and I think this fact is of no skeptical significance, as I've argued in the preceding chapters.

Here's one way in which this misunderstanding shows up. Lawlor thinks that (like her) I would agree "that we could not get positive warrant for III without collecting evidence for it, of the kind provided by discrete encounters with the world provided by I and the inference to II" (242). Here Lawlor is imposing a very particular understanding of the epistemology of our knowledge of the world, according to which if we do have knowledge of III, we should be able to provide a specific sort of line of explicit reasoning by which a rational being could arrive for the very first time at that knowledge via steps like I and II from a starting point of initial neutrality or agnosticism. That's already framing things in terms of the aim I reject. Or, to put the point more guardedly: this is to frame things in terms of an aim which has yet to be articulated as such and defended from within our pre-philosophical position. As we've seen, it in fact looks as though our pre-philosophical commitments militate against any such demand. (See Chapters 9–12 for more on this.)

A further point will help orient the discussion. Steps I and II of Wright's I-II-III reasoning exhibit an important ambiguity. This concerns the difference between an account of particular instances of perceptual knowledge, on the one hand, and, on the other hand, an account of knowledge of the world as such—that is, of how we come to know anything about the world at all, of how our beliefs about the world *as a class* can constitute knowledge.

I begin with the first side of this distinction. We do know particular things about the world via perception. I look and thereby come to know, for instance, that there is a red book on the table. *One* way of understanding steps I-II of Wright's argument is as concerned with *particular instances of knowledge of this sort*. We want to know how we know that there is a red book there. We reconstruct this as something like a bit of reasoning, an argument. If we are Wright's skeptic, we start with our subjective conscious experience, characterized in a way that does not imply anything about the world. We think, "That is our fundamental evidence, what fundamentally justifies or warrants our particular perceptual beliefs about the world." If we are Jim Pryor, we start in pretty much the same place.

Notice that if you understand Wright's version of Moore's argument in this way, as being concerned in its early stages with providing an epistemological reconstruction of particular cases of perceptual knowledge, no global skeptical argument gets going *without a whole lot of additional assumptions*—all of which would have to be motivated from within our pre-philosophical position. Here's why. If the reasoning or argument is supposed to capture the underlying epistemological structure of particular instances of perceptual knowledge about the world, then it is just silent—all by itself, at least—on how we know the vast majority of what we know about the world. After all, the vast majority of our knowledge of the world does not rest in this way on any particular sensory evidence. Consider, for instance, my knowledge that my name is Adam Leite, that I live in Indiana, that Indiana is in the United

States, and that ducks lack the cognitive abilities needed to pull off a global conspiracy. None of this rests directly on any particular sensory evidence. Admittedly, one might think "But even if it doesn't rest *directly* on such evidence, it *has to* rest on it *indirectly*, in something like the way the later stages of an argument rest upon the initial premises." One might then begin to imagine, at least schematically, how this must go, with all of our knowledge of the world somehow deriving from a restricted base of perceptual evidence. But to understand the epistemology of these cases in that way is already to bring into play a very substantial philosophical interpretation of our prephilosophical position.

Once you see this, then you see that to get a global skeptical argument going, Wright has to regard stages I-II of his reasoning as somehow capturing something fundamental about our knowledge of the world merely *qua* knowledge of the world. And this brings us to the second way of understanding Wright's I-II-III argument: on this understanding steps I and II are not, in the first instance, an account of how I know any particular thing about the world via perception. Rather, they are supposed to be a schema that captures our situation regarding all knowledge of the world merely as such, our fundamental position when it comes to knowing anything about the world at all. This is already to import a distinctive understanding of our knowledge of the world. The thought that drives Wright's skeptical argument, then, is that unless we can provide an acceptable schematic argument or line of reasoning of this sort that would provide an account of our knowledge of the world merely as such, we should conclude that we lack knowledge of the world. This is the demand that I rejected in the previous section, following Moore's lead.

I turn now to the details of Lawlor's objections. As we will see, the general points just highlighted weave their way through the specifics of Lawlor's arguments.

4.1.a The parallel with the soccer reasoning

In the above passages, Lawlor suggests that I think that Wright's version of Moore's argument is free from the flaw exhibited by the Soccer reasoning. I don't. That argument, intended as Wright intends it, would not be acceptable, as I argued in this chapter's earlier discussion of Pryor and Wright. One cannot acceptably reason from I to II as the initial steps of an explicit attempt to find out such things as whether there is an external world and whether one is globally deceived, because one must not be neutral on those matters if one is to acceptably make the step from I to II. Wright's version of Moore's argument thus shares the flaw that the Soccer reasoning displays.

Still, I think that one can appeal to considerations about the world to reject the global skeptical hypotheses nonetheless, for reasons that have been highlighted in the preceding chapters' discussions of epistemic asymmetry. To reject the Evil Demon Hypothesis by appealing to considerations about the world and our knowledge of it is *not* ipso facto to endorse reasoning along the lines of Wright's version of Moore's Argument.

4.1.b "Leite seems to think we can know the anti-skeptical proposition III on the basis of II."

Here we have to be very careful. What is meant by "know on the basis of"? I have said something quite minimal: certain considerations about the world are entirely decisive with regard to whether the Evil Demon scenario is true (since they imply that it isn't), and we can quite properly offer such considerations both as a ground for dismissing the suggestion and as a decisive reason for thinking that the scenario is false. The same goes for the other global skeptical scenarios. In one sense, this might be enough to warrant saying that we can know that the global skeptical scenarios are false on the basis of considerations about the world.

However, this shouldn't be taken to pack in more than it does. It does not commit me to saying that we could arrive for the first time at knowledge of the falsity of the skeptical scenarios via an inference from II. It does not involve trying to fulfill the aim that Wright and Lawlor think Moore is trying to fulfill. So if *that* is what is meant by "know III on the basis of II," I have not made any such claim.

What I have claimed is simply that considering the skeptical scenarios does not preclude you from rejecting them by appealing to considerations about the world.

4.1.c A clash with our pre-philosophical commitments?

Lawlor claims that my position actually *clashes* with our response to the Soccer case:

> A parallel move in the Soccer argument would have us starting with seeing a goal scored and reasoning to the claim that a soccer game is being played. That bit of reasoning would leave your average soccer fan cold, rightly enough. (2015, 243)

Here Lawlor is construing the Soccer situation in a very particular way. She has in mind circumstances in which we are trying to figure out, from a position of initial neutrality, whether a soccer game is being played. As she quite rightly brings out, in those conditions we cannot *simply* start from the thought that a goal was just scored and thereby come to learn that a game is being played. That is no way to resolve that question asked from that position. It would be a mistake, however, to think that anything I have said commits me to thinking that such a move would be acceptable. This is because my response to external world skepticism does not have the aim that parallels the aim Lawlor has in mind here.

The move that I am making with regard to external world skepticism parallels a perfectly acceptable ordinary move that we could make in a different version of the Soccer case. If someone asks me whether the game has begun, I can quite correctly answer their question by pointing out that a goal has just been scored. This *is* a decisive consideration when it comes to whether a game is being played. When I appeal to considerations about the world as a ground for dismissing the Evil Demon Hypothesis, I am doing something similar. I am not trying to figure out, from a position of initial neutrality, whether there is an external world or whether I am being deceived by an evil demon. I am just considering what is the case that bears on the truth or falsity of these propositions. And given that that is the issue, of course there are considerations I can point to that are true and entirely decisive.

4.1.d Do I "just start" with type-II propositions? Methodological and substantive reasons for understanding our evidence as I do

To speak from within our pre-philosophical position, we have all sorts of evidence right now, including various considerations about the world. As I argued at length in earlier chapters, the skeptical hypotheses do not preclude us from appealing to that evidence as a reason for rejecting those hypotheses. This point was supported by the parallel with the Ducks Conspiracy and the Children of Brunettes. Merely considering these latter scenarios doesn't eliminate our evidence against them. Ducks lack the cognitive abilities needed for such a conspiracy, and the hair color of parents doesn't impact the cognitive abilities of their children. I can point to such facts as decisive reason for rejecting these hypotheses. This is what I mean when I say that the skeptical hypotheses do not "neutralize" our evidence.

In claiming that considerations about the world are evidence for all sorts of things, I am simply stating a commitment of our pre-philosophical position.

It is part of my methodology that such commitments can be taken as starting points for anti-skeptical argumentation, since the question is whether a skeptical argument can be made to fly from within those commitments.

Lawlor finds this unsatisfactory, as is displayed by her phrase "if one **just lets oneself start** with proposition II, *I have hands*..." (2015, 243, bold emphasis added). Here Lawlor is imagining that I am trying to engage in a certain kind of reasoning with the same sort of aim as Wright's I-II-III argument: that is, trying to provide a course of reasoning by which one could figure out that the anti-skeptical propositions are true from a position of initial neutrality. She just takes me to be starting at the second step. As I emphasized above, however, that isn't even the *kind* of enterprise in which I am engaged.

Lawlor's framing of the issue here is bound up with very specific epistemological presuppositions, presuppositions that have not been motivated from within our pre-philosophical position and that we have seen reason to reject. She takes the task to be one of explaining how we could arrive via acceptable reasoning at the type-III propositions from a very particular sort of experiential starting point. If that's how we understand the task, then of course my reply looks inadequate. But that understanding of the task involves a version of the same demand that we dismissed above when discussing Wright.

If we step back from this conception, there is a straightforward sense in which I don't "just start" with considerations such as that I have a body and hands, that there are no evil demons, that human beings don't have dreams of certain kinds, and the like. If asked how I know these things, I can offer good reasons in their favor. I would think my epistemic position deficient if I couldn't do this. So what I have said only counts as objectionably "letting myself just start with proposition II, *I have hands*" if one has a very restricted conception of the options—if one thinks that either one has to offer a very specific sort of account here (along the lines of steps I and II of Wright's I-II-III reasoning) or one has nothing. We won't think anything of that sort if we keep an eye on the full range of relevant cases, including the Ducks Conspiracy and other key examples that I have discussed.

At bottom, Lawlor has missed a central point stressed in Chapters 6 and 7. We can correctly and successfully appeal to reasons for rejecting the global skeptical scenarios *even if* we couldn't appeal to those very same considerations to figure out from a position of initial neutrality whether we are in the Good Case or the Bad Case. To think otherwise is to make a mistake that both Wright and Pritchard made. It is to fail to see the range of things that we can do with epistemic reasons/evidence. Not everything that goes on when we make good use of reasons in epistemic life is to be understood on the model of trying to figure something out via explicit linear reasoning from a position of initial neutrality. And sometimes our good epistemic standing does not require that there be any way to reconstruct our good position in terms of that model.

4.1.e Am I offering an alternative theory?
At one point Lawlor suggests that I "suppose that direct realism constitutes an ambitious response to the skeptic—one that would give us knowledge of anti-skeptical propositions" (2015, 243). This would be to argue from a particular epistemological theory to the conclusion that we know that we are not being deceived by an evil demon. As I hope has been made clear, in responding to skeptical arguments by appealing to considerations about the world, I am not doing anything of the sort. That is precisely not the project, if we are responding to skepticism in the way that Moore and Austin urge. Rather, I am responding to skeptical arguments by appealing to the commitments of the pre-philosophical position. Insofar as one has epistemological theory-building in view here at all, we are simply assembling some of the materials to which any such theorizing should aim to do justice. And a commitment to direct realism has played no role at all in the responses I have offered to skeptical arguments.

4.2 Closure-Based Skeptical Arguments

Lawlor expresses a second concern regarding my claim that we have excellent evidence, indeed knowledge, that we are not the victims of the global skeptical scenarios. She worries that this claim clashes with what we are inclined to say about certain ordinary examples.

To make this case, she invites us to imagine looking out across a lake and identifying a Gadwall duck based on its coloration, bill, and markings. Since circumstances are perfectly normal, you feel perfectly comfortable claiming to know that it is a Gadwall duck. But, she asks, "Do you also know it is not a very convincing decoy? Its not being a decoy follows from its being a Gadwall. (The first proposition implies the second.) Yet it would be natural for you to feel you need more evidence to know that it's not a decoy" (2015, 236). Here she sees "a natural pattern of epistemic judgment and related linguistic behavior" that militates against the thought that you know that it is not a decoy (236). In conjunction with the thought that you should know the things that you recognize are implied by things you know (the principle that knowledge is closed under known implication), this pattern threatens us with the conclusion that you don't know that it is a Gadwall duck after all. This is the closure-based skeptical argument.

Given this concern, Lawlor writes:

> Leite's question is why not say that one knows that one is not the victim of global deception? My answer is that whatever we say here we should say about the more homely Gadwall case as well—the structure of the skeptical problems is the same. So would Leite have me hold that on looking across the lake your basic birding identification also enables you to *know* that it isn't a very convincing decoy? That doesn't square with common sense. (2015, 236)

Lawlor's charge, then, is that my approach to the Evil Demon and other global skeptical scenarios yields the wrong response in the humdrum Gadwall case, which she regards as structurally identical.

In fact, however, the cases are not structurally identical—at least not in the way that Lawlor thinks they are. But before I get to that, I want to stress that the Gadwall example is significantly under-described. In any ordinary case, you would have a wealth of relevant background information. What time of year is it? Is it hunting season or not? Are you in a sanctuary area where no hunting is allowed? Is there any reasonable way for a decoy to have gotten there? Are Gadwalls likely to be around, or are they in their winter grounds? For how long have you observed the thing? Has it moved? Was there nothing at that spot just a few moments before? Is it reasonable to think that a duck just landed while you were messing with your binoculars? All of this and more would come into play and would be essential to the actual judgment you would make in the case. Different details would yield different verdicts, both on whether (and how) you know it isn't a decoy and on whether (and how) you know it is a Gadwall duck.

I emphasize such features of the particular case because they are relevant, at a much more basic level, to Lawlor's claim that "the structure of the skeptical problems is the same." Recall Chapter 4's discussion of a key point of Austin's: How an alternative possibility needs to be treated depends upon the circumstances, especially upon the reasons that bear on it in the particular case. In this regard, we can crudely demarcate a spectrum or range of cases. For instance, to take Austin's example of identifying a goldfinch in the garden, consider the following possible alternatives:

- It is an extragalactic spying device
- It is stuffed (in circumstances in which no one in the vicinity is inclined toward that sort of practical joke)
- It is stuffed (in circumstances in which a neighbor goes in for that sort of thing—several stuffed birds have been found in local trees in the past few months)
- It is some other sort of similar-looking, common bird

What you have to do in order to eliminate these alternatives differs. The last requires you to acquire some specific evidence relevant to distinguishing goldfinches from the particular sort of bird in question. By contrast, the first doesn't require you to acquire any special evidence but can instead be dismissed out of hand—given everything we know, there is no reason whatsoever to think *that* is going on. Everything depends on whether there are reasons in favor of the specific possibility and what those reasons are.

Return now to Lawlor's example. Where on this spectrum should we place the possibility that one is seeing a decoy? Given the world as it is (and depending on further details), this possibility will fall somewhere in the territory of the last three possibilities. More precisely, there may be some significant reason to think that it might well be a decoy, especially if one hasn't seen it move. For instance, even if you don't have much relevant background information, you know this much: decoys show up with some non-negligible frequency, especially around hunting season. It's more likely to be a decoy, for instance, than to be a remote-controlled animatronic simulation of a duck. It's also more likely to be a decoy than a Canadian goose genetically engineered to look just like a Gadwall. On the other hand, it is more likely to be a female American wigeon or mallard than a decoy, all else equal. (Local circumstances might warrant modifying this latter judgment of comparative likelihood.)

All of this background information comes into play in your determination of how to handle the possibility. If it is hunting season here in the Midwest, then in order to know that it is a Gadwall duck you need to take a second look to see if it moves. On the other hand, you don't need to do anything at all to acquire special evidence that it isn't a genetically modified Canadian goose; that possibility is already eliminated by your knowledge of just how very unlikely it is, given that there is no special reason in its favor here and now. What is required of you differs depending on the nature of the reasons that bear on the case.

Now compare this with the Evil Demon and other global skeptical possibilities. There is no reason whatsoever to suspect that one is being deceived by an evil demon. There are no evil demons. As things stand, there is likewise no reason to suspect that one is a brain in a vat. (This could change.) There is no reason to think that one is having a dream that is indistinguishable in all respects from a waking experience; human beings don't have dreams like that. These skeptical scenarios are thus like the suggestion that the bird might be an intergalactic spying device. They fall at a different point on the range of cases than the decoy Gadwall possibility.

As we have seen over the course of several chapters, for this very reason they are appropriately handled in a different way. Since there is no reason whatsoever in their favor, each of these possibilities is properly dismissed on the basis of background knowledge that we would lack if the possibility were actual. This is exactly parallel to what we see in the Ducks Conspiracy and other cases of epistemic asymmetry that structurally parallel the skeptical hypotheses.

For this reason, Lawlor is wrong when she says that "whatever we say [regarding the Evil Demon and other global skeptical scenarios] we should say about the more homely Gadwall case as well" (2015, 236). Different sorts of responses are called for in the two cases. If the decoy possibility does raise a problem about your knowing that the bird is a Gadwall, it is a different problem, with a different structure, than anything raised by the Evil Demon and other global skeptical scenarios that have nothing in their favor.

Notice that none of what I have said depends on whether closure holds universally. Whether or not it does, it still remains the case that the global skeptical scenarios are properly rejected out of hand given that one recognizes that there is nothing in their favor. And I am precisely *not* saying what Lawlor suggests when she asks, "So would Leite have me hold that on looking across the lake your basic birding identification also enables you to *know* that it isn't a very convincing decoy?" (2015, 236). Of course not. Your basic birding identification is just a matter of color, markings, and other morphological features—something that could be accomplished on the basis of examination of a photo. Such information is not sufficient to enable you to know that it is not a realistic-looking decoy of the sort hunters use; rather, given that there is some substantial likelihood that it is such a decoy, what enables you to know that it isn't one will be some special evidence pertinent to the case: you saw it move, for instance. By contrast, what enables you to know it isn't a genetically modified Canadian goose is your background information that such things are vanishingly unlikely. In neither case does your basic birding identification do the relevant epistemic work.

In sum: There is indeed a certain sort of structural similarity between the possibility that one is seeing a decoy and the possibility that one is being deceived by an evil demon. However, the similarity is not at all what Lawlor thinks it is. The structural similarity is simply the point that Austin stressed: what has to be done depends on the reasons that bear on the case. And the key dissimilarities between the two are a product of the same point. They correspond to an important methodological stricture also stressed by Austin: Pay attention to the details of the particular case.

5. Methodological Closing

I will not reprise all of the methodological points highlighted in the above discussion of Pritchard, Wright, Pryor, and Lawlor. What I do want to emphasize in closing are some key lessons that must be kept in mind when engaging in the kind of project that I have undertaken in this book.

- Keep your eye squarely on the question at hand: do our pre-philosophical commitments generate any requirements or principles that could fuel a skeptical argument? Don't get distracted by the temptation to build an epistemological theory. Be extremely sensitive to whether and how we might be bringing into play assumptions that are not part of our pre-philosophical position.
- Pay attention to the full range of cases, and make sure to characterize them at the right level of detail for the purpose at hand.
- Look very closely at the initial steps that are supposed to motivate various ways of conceptualizing what is going on when reasons are offered for or against a claim. Are you assimilating one sort of use of evidence to another, importing a gratuitous assumption about what rational grounding must be like, importing a philosophical conception or assumption that is not clearly supported by careful scrutiny of our pre-philosophical practice and commitments?

- Be especially careful about the difference between: (1) speaking from within our pre-philosophical commitments and summarizing the commitments thereby manifested, and, (2) developing a theory that attempts to systematize, explain, vindicate, or regiment those commitments.
- Do not let preconceptions about what an adequate or satisfying theory "must be like" constrain your sense of the range of the possible or get in the way of seeing what is actually the case.

With these methodological considerations in view, we now turn to a new question. Can skepticism be successfully motivated by considerations about the role of perceptual experience in our knowledge of the world?

PART III

ON "THE SENSORY BASIS OF OUR KNOWLEDGE OF THE WORLD"

9
Skepticism and Perception

1. Skepticism and the Epistemology of Perception

Innumerable renditions of skeptical argumentation begin by assuming a limitation on what counts as our evidence. They start with the thought that our evidence is limited to our sensory experiences and other mental states, all described in a way that is neutral about the world around us. They assume that the crucial epistemological task is to show how we could possibly make a rational transition from that limited evidential base to conclusions about the world. And the fear is that if this cannot be done, then skepticism follows.

It is rarely noted that this way of presenting matters presupposes a great deal that must be going on behind the scenes. Given the commitments of ordinary life, how are we supposed to arrive at this way of thinking about our epistemological situation? After all, in ordinary life we are perfectly happy to treat considerations about the world as part of our evidence.

One common suggestion is that a certain conception of the epistemology of sensory perception is what accomplishes this task. According to this conception, sensory experience on any given occasion doesn't, all by itself, *inform us* that things are a certain way in the world: it doesn't, all by itself, suffice for knowledge of the world. At most, it provides knowledge of how things seem or appear to us, where such characterizations do not entail anything about the world around us.

This conception has taken many different forms over the centuries and has been developed in many different ways. For my purposes here, what matters is just the basic conception. This is the conception that appears when people characterize sensory experience as being "as of" a hand before me. It appears in Wright's thought that Moore's evidence really amounts to no more than this: "My current state of awareness seems in all respects like being aware of a hand held up in front of my face" (2004a, 26). As Stroud puts the core idea, the proposal is that "in one way or another . . . the most we can know by perception alone is something that in itself implies nothing about the way things are in the world around us" (2011, 92).

This conception is epistemological, not metaphysical. It is compatible with various accounts of the metaphysics of perception. For instance, it would not prevent you from saying that sensory perception of the world around you— seeing a table for instance—is object-involving and so a metaphysically different kind of state from hallucinating that there is a table before you. That form of metaphysical disjunctivism about perception is compatible with holding that either way, all that is ever given to you epistemologically by the experience itself is what would be captured by saying, "It seems to me as if there is a table before me." The conception is likewise compatible with many versions of the view that the content of a perceptual experience is (at least in part) propositional, something like "There's a brown table." Even if your sensory experience (whether perceptual or hallucinatory) has a content like "There's a brown table," it might still be the case that that sensory experience doesn't, all by itself, suffice to inform you that there is a table there. Maybe you are only thereby informed that it experientially seems to you as if there's a brown table there.

My question in this chapter is not whether this conception is true, nor even what might be said for or against it. I want to remain neutral on those questions. In fact, I'm inclined to think that the pre-philosophical position doesn't involve any commitment about this issue either way. It isn't even clear to me what is really meant by talk of "perception alone" or "the experience all by itself." But I want to play along, supposing that I have a good enough handle on what is being talked about, and ask this question: What would follow from the commitments of the pre-philosophical position if this conception were accepted? I think that the answer is, "Nothing like what many people fear."

Stroud suggests that this conception is what fuels skepticism. "What carries the sceptical implications of Descartes' reasoning in the first *Meditation*," he writes, "is his conception of the restricted scope of sense-perception at its best" (2018, 228). He argues that if each sensory experience could—for all I can tell from that sensory experience alone—just be a dream, then I can never know through sensory experience whether I am dreaming or awake, and so can never know anything about the world around me (2009, 561).

Jason Bridges puts the underlying concern another way:

> If our aim is to explain how "sensory experience" yields knowledge of objects located outside us, and if "sensory experience" itself is to be understood as provisioning knowledge of a certain [more limited] domain,

then our question seems to assume the following shape: how do we derive knowledge of the former domain from knowledge of the latter? How are we to secure a ground for our knowledge of the outside world in the knowledge we are given in "sensory experience"? Since the domain of "sensory experience" is to be construed so that nothing we can know within that domain has any implications of any kind for how things stand in the domain of objects located outside us, this question seems to have an immediate and obvious answer: we can't. If our "sensory experiences" never tell us anything about what is going on in the world outside, how could the knowledge they provision possibly ground our knowledge of that world? (2016, 81–82)

Bridges' underlying thought here is this: if what sensory experience yields on each occasion is, all by itself, not yet knowledge of the world, then sensory experience cannot give us knowledge of the world.

A number of different philosophical theories have been developed to avert this threat. Stroud, for instance, maintains that our only hope is to deny the conception entirely. On his view, we are sometimes simply able to *see that* p *is so*, without thereby depending on any further background knowledge. "I think it is possible to get knowledge [of what is so in the world] that is not based on anything else that we know that we somehow combine with what we get from sense perception alone to give us knowledge that *p*. We simply see, and in seeing know, that *p*" (2011, 93). Pritchard (2012, 2016), too, denies this conception, though in a somewhat different way inspired in part by work of John McDowell (McDowell 1982, 1995, and 2011). According to Pritchard's "epistemological disjunctivism," sensory perception alone is a source of knowledge, because seeing that *p* gives you a reflectively available factive ground for believing that *p* is true.

Pryor (2000) is more concessive, even while he also rejects key aspects of this conception. He grants that what perceptual experience provides in each case is most accurately characterized in a way that does not imply anything about how the world is. But he claims that having an experience as of a hand gives you prima facie immediate justification for believing that there is a hand there, and he seems to take it that this prima facie justification can underwrite knowledge.[1]

Other philosophical theories accept the conception but supplement it, maintaining that in one way or another what sensory experience gives you

---

[1] Similar suggestions were explored earlier by Chisholm, Firth, Pollock, and others.

can justify or warrant belief about the world, or give you knowledge about the world, when in some sense combined with certain considerations that go beyond anything that sensory experience gives you all by itself. Coliva, for instance, holds that if you assume such things as that there is a world of objects outside of our minds, then the experience "as of" a hand can justify the belief that there is a hand before you, and she argues that this assumption is central to epistemic rationality (2015). Wright proposes that in addition to what is given by sensory perception alone, we need an independent warrant for believing such things as that there is a world of objects outside of our minds, and he has explored various attempts to explain how such an independent warrant might arise (see, for instance, Wright, 2004b).

These are all *epistemological theories*, designed to head off the threat of skepticism that appears to arise from this conception of sensory perception. How do matters look if we instead consider the issue from our Moorean standpoint within our ordinary, pre-philosophical position, without any epistemological theorizing that attempts to go beyond descriptions and summaries of our ordinary practice and commitments? Perhaps surprisingly, I think that when we clearheadedly stand in our ordinary, pre-philosophical position we can see that this conception presents no skeptical threat at all. And seeing why this is so will have an additional pay-off. It will enable us to better appreciate key aspects of ordinary epistemic life.

2. Why This Conception Doesn't Yield What the Skeptic Needs

To begin, I want to highlight several relevant commitments of the pre-philosophical position which particularly pertain to the issue at hand. We've seen the first one before, but the others are new.

First, as I've already stressed, it's part of the ordinary position that we know all sorts of things about the world, and also that it can be entirely correct to appeal to particular considerations about the world as evidence in support of other claims about the world.

Second, it's part of the ordinary position that there are many occasions on which we are aware that there's some reason for concern about whether our senses are functioning properly and whether they can be trusted to reveal what is going on in the world. We recognize these occasions by relying on background knowledge about the world: for instance, about how our senses work, about how things tend to go in the world, about particular and general matters-of-fact relevant to the case, and knowledge regarding our circumstances.

Third, we sometimes use background information to resolve such situations. Sometimes this information serves as an additional premise for an inference to a conclusion as to how things are. Other times it functions more like a confirmation or disconfirmation of the appropriateness of relying on the senses in the particular circumstances. Either way, our acquisition of new knowledge of the world in these cases depends on what our senses tell us then and there *and* on a lot of background knowledge.

Finally, consider now my knowledge that there is a pen here in front of me. Again, background knowledge is in play. To speak from within our ordinary position: I have a great deal of information upon which I could draw, if necessary, to vindicate this claim. I can point out that I see the pen. My knowledge that I see the pen brings into play all sorts of further background knowledge about the conditions in which my vision is reliable and about the particular conditions I'm in. And I know I put the pen here a little while ago, haven't moved it, no one has been near enough to surreptitiously replace it with a papier-mâché facsimile (nor has any reason to do so), and so on. These things are all relevant to my judgment that I am currently seeing a pen. As in cases in which background knowledge enables us to overcome a reason to suspect our senses are misleading on a particular occasion, here too a wide variety of background knowledge of the world can be brought to bear on the particular case.

In light of these considerations, suppose now that a theorist of the epistemology of perception declares that what my visual experience *all by itself* gives me right now, epistemologically speaking, is merely a visual appearance "as of" a pen: right now visual experience doesn't, all by itself, suffice to *inform me* that there is a pen here now. Just taken on its own, this declaration—even if true—does nothing whatsoever to remove all my background knowledge of the world. The situation is still as before. I can perfectly well think: "Maybe my visual experience right now *by itself* only gives me something that could be put by saying that it *appears* or *seems* to me that there is a pen here. But fortunately I don't just have that visual experience. I also have a wealth of other information that gives me excellent reason for thinking that I can rely on my visual experience here and now: things are as they seem—there is a pen here."

This point generalizes. Suppose that *in each case*, taken one by one, sensory experience by itself gives us no more than it is said to give us in the case of the pen. Instead of concluding we can't know anything about the world, we should think: "Well, maybe each case is like that of the pen. Maybe in each case in which we gain knowledge from a particular experience, it works like that: the experience by itself only gives us that things seem a certain way, but we also have other relevant information that enables us to determine whether things are as they seem."

Thus, we began by thinking:

1. Considerations about the world can constitute good evidence that can be brought to bear on particular cases, and
2. In many particular cases we have a great deal of background knowledge concerning the world.

Those two claims are perfectly compatible with:

3. In each particular case, what sensory experience gives us all by itself is nothing more than what could be captured by saying that things seem a certain way.

The first two claims are compatible with the third claim, because that latter claim does not by itself force us to think that our evidence in each case is *limited to* sensory appearances described in a way that is not yet committal about the world. In the context of (1) and (2), (3) entails merely that in each case our evidence will include whatever sensory appearances our experience gives us in that case, *along with* whatever background information we have about the world. That is to say, (3) does not force on us what the skeptical argument crucially needs: first, a division between "sensory evidence" (described in a way that is neutral about the world) and our beliefs about the world taken as a class, and second, a demand that none of the latter can be justified or count as knowledge unless it is possible to somehow reason acceptably from the former to the latter.

A second point is crucially important here. Many discussions of skepticism assume a *Global Epistemic Priority Thesis*, according to which all our knowledge of the world—taken as a whole—must in some sense be grounded upon what sensory experience gives us. The underlying picture is one of epistemic priority relations between domains: we imagine drawing a circle around all of our knowledge of the world, and then we require that whole circle to be somehow grounded upon or justified by what sensory experience itself gives us (perhaps along with our other non-factive mental states)—where all of that is understood as being, in the first place, characterizable in ways that imply nothing about the external world. This is the picture at play in innumerable presentations of the skeptical problem in twentieth- and twenty-first-century epistemology. It is the picture at play, for instance, in under-determination arguments when it is claimed that the "totality of our evidence about the world" is neutral between the Real World Hypothesis and the Evil Demon Hypothesis.[2]

But the Global Priority Thesis is not entailed by the conception of sensory perception we've been discussing. The Global Priority Thesis says:

A. All our knowledge of the world, as a whole, must rest upon and be justified by something else that is not yet knowledge of the world.
B. That "something else" consists of what is given by sensory experience (perhaps along with our other non-factive mental states).
C. What is given by sensory experience in each case is captured by a description of how things seem, formulated in such a way as to be non-committal about anything about the world.

What we have seen is that the conception of perception captured by C is distinct from the Global Priority Thesis, most significantly because that conception of perception does not, all by itself, force us to accept A. This is because that conception is perfectly compatible with holding that in each case in which you acquire knowledge of the world through sensory perception, other knowledge of the world is involved as well. C might be true (that is, in each case sensory experience all by itself might give us something less than knowledge of the world), and we could have knowledge of the world, and yet it could be false that all of our knowledge of the world, as a whole, rests entirely upon a body of evidence that is not yet knowledge of the world.

Bridges misses this point in the earlier passage. He asks, rhetorically, "If our 'sensory experiences' never tell us anything about what is going on in the world outside, how could the knowledge they provision possibly ground our knowledge of that world?" (82). He thinks the answer is obviously, "It can't; the antecedent of the conditional makes knowledge of the world impossible." But he's assuming the Global Priority Thesis: he's requiring that all of our knowledge of the world must be grounded as a totality on "sensory

---

[2] Ayer (1956) offers an early expression of this way of understanding the skeptical problem.

experience." There is an alternative. Perhaps in each particular case in which we acquire knowledge of the world via the senses, that knowledge of the world is grounded upon what that sensory experience gives us, along with—or in the context of—some other knowledge of the world.

The state of play, then, is this. We were asking what could motivate restricting our evidence in the way the skeptic needs. In particular, we were considering the widespread view that the restriction is imposed by a certain conception of sensory experience. We have seen that this isn't so. The proposed view of sensory experience does not by itself impose the crucial restriction. It does not prevent us from continuing to treat considerations about the world as amongst our evidence. This is because no particular view of what Wright calls "the justificational architecture" of our knowledge of the world—whether foundationalist or otherwise—necessarily follows in its wake. A further step is thus needed to move us from our ordinary position, in which we are content to treat considerations about the world as amongst our evidence, to a conception on which our evidence in each case is *limited* to sensory appearances. A further step is likewise needed to move us to a conception on which all of our knowledge of the world must be grounded, as such, on a body of sensory evidence of this sort. Those steps are not motivated by the conception of sensory experience itself.

Skepticism results from the conception of sensory experience, in other words, only if we *also* make a presumption for which no reason has been offered. We can avoid the problem by seeing the optionality of the framing assumptions that make it look as though there is a problem. We do that by recognizing that it is perfectly compatible with the commitments and practices of ordinary epistemic life to say that on each occasion on which we acquire knowledge of the world via sensory experience, some background knowledge of the world is involved as well. In the end, all we are really using here is the following undisputed commitment of our ordinary position: it's appropriate to appeal to considerations about the world as reasons, evidence, or otherwise relevant considerations when considering whether and how you know any given thing or determining what to believe on particular occasions. Importantly, nothing is being put forward as an epistemological *thesis* or *theory* here. All we are doing is elaborating the implications of the practices and commitments of the pre-philosophical position.

In fact, the point that I have made is perfectly compatible with very different sorts of epistemological theories. For instance, here is one way of elaborating it. We could develop an epistemological theory on which perceptual knowledge is based, on each occasion, upon both what sensory experience provides *and* our relevant background knowledge. The two, taken together, would constitute the reasons which ground our knowledge on that occasion.

Here is a very different way of elaborating the point I have been making. We could develop a theory according to which possessing relevant background knowledge is a necessary condition for *seeing that* p *is so*. Here's how this might go. First, its seeming to you that *p* is plausibly a necessary condition for seeing that *p*. We could accept that this seeming or appearance would be all that is given epistemologically by your state characterized merely as sensory experience—that is, that this talk of "appearance" is the proper way to characterize what is given when there is no further specification of whether *p*, whether you are properly visually related to the fact that *p*, or whether you possess the relevant background knowledge. But it could then be held that when *p is* the case, and you are properly visually related to the fact that *p*, and you possess the relevant background knowledge and recognize its significance, and . . . [fill in some more requirements of the theory], then you see and thereby know that *p*. On this view, the background knowledge isn't part of an argument upon which your knowledge that *p* is based, even though you must recognize its rational pertinence; rather, it is a necessary condition for your counting as seeing (and thereby knowing) that *p* is so. In fact, there could even be a version of this latter view which holds (to put it roughly) that *seeing that p* is a non-analyzable factive epistemic state which entails knowing that *p* and has, as a necessary condition, possessing and recognizing the pertinence of relevant background knowledge about the world.

None of these particular theories, nor anything else developed at this theoretical level, is needed for the point that I have been making. In fact, I am not even sure that our ordinary position is committed to the conception of sensory experience that these theories would presuppose. All that is really needed here is the recognition that given the clear commitments of the pre-philosophical position, the proposed conception of sensory experience, by itself, does not force us to divide things up in the way the skeptic needs. That's enough to block the claim that the framing required by the skeptical argument is generated by this conception of the epistemological upshot of sensory experience.

It might be suggested that the requisite division between our "sensory evidence" and our beliefs about the world, with its concomitant demands, follows straightaway from the addition of one simple thought. Near the beginning of the *Meditations* Descartes writes that "Whatever I have up till now accepted as most true I have acquired either from the senses or through the senses" (1984 [1640/1], 12; AT 18). Let's suppose that this is true. Combine it with the conception of sensory experience at issue, according to which sensory experience all by itself on any particular occasion never yields more, epistemologically, than knowledge of how things seem or appear (something less than knowledge of the world). Doesn't that force us to think that to evade the threat of skepticism we need to explain how there could be a good, rational transition from what sensory experience yields all by itself to any beliefs about the world at all?

I don't think that it does. For Descartes' claim does not say that everything I have accepted as most true has been derived through such a transition. It is more neutral than that. Taken in the most minimal way, it just notes that the causal origin of these convictions lies in the senses. For this reason Descartes' claim is perfectly compatible with the suggestion that I have been making, even when his claim is combined with the conception of sensory experience that we've been discussing. It might be true that sensory experience all by itself on each occurrence does not deliver more, epistemologically, than knowledge of how things seem, and yet it might also be true (as a causal matter) that I have acquired a wide range of beliefs about the world through sensory encounters with it. And it might also be true that while those beliefs constitute knowledge of the world, they only do so in the context of other knowledge of the world. This combination is only ruled out if one is already smuggling in a very particular way of reading Descartes' claim, namely in terms of the Global Epistemic Priority Thesis highlighted earlier. And that is to bring in an additional assumption that has yet to be motivated.

3. Can This Really Work?

Three important worries might be raised in response to what I have been saying.

3.1 This Looks Impossible! How Could It All Start?

Here's an argument that what I have proposed is actually incompatible with seeing ourselves as having knowledge of the world.

1. Everything we know about the world comes (directly or mediately) from what is given in sensory experience.
2. So, it has to be the case that we can know something about the world on some occasion *via sensory perception alone*, in a way that depends on no other knowledge of the world. Otherwise, our knowledge of the world could never get started.

The worry could be put like this. "Consider the *first* item of knowledge of the world that we acquire through sensory perception. It can't have arisen in a way that involves other knowledge of the world; after all, it's the first. But there must have been a first piece of knowledge of the world, since we manifestly do have knowledge of the world. So it must be possible to get knowledge of the world through perception in a way that involves no other knowledge of the world."

I think this argument fails. To put it curtly, why think that there must be a *single* first piece of knowledge of the world?

To elaborate the point, consider the following propositions:

1. Sensory experience all by itself on any given occasion does something less, epistemologically speaking, than give you knowledge about the world.
2. Sensory experience yields knowledge on any given occasion only in the context of other knowledge of the world.
3. Absent sensory experience, we could know nothing of the world around us; sensory experience is the ultimate source of all of our beliefs about the world around us.

Notice that if you are not assuming a general priority thesis, these propositions taken together amount to no more than:

A. On each particular occasion on which you gain knowledge about the world around you by having a sensory experience, some other knowledge about the world comes into play.
B. You couldn't have had that other knowledge if you hadn't had some appropriate/relevant sensory experience.

Why think that these two requirements can't both be met? It seems to me that a difficulty only appears here if a general priority thesis is in play. Otherwise, all that is dictated is this:

> *Mutual Dependence*: There is no occasion on which we acquire knowledge of the world on the basis of sensory experience alone; knowledge of the world always requires other knowledge of the world.

If you haven't yet taken on a general priority thesis, this isn't a problem. It just says that no particular belief counts as knowledge of the world except if it is appropriately related to some other knowledge of the world. There is no reason in principle why that would be unsatisfiable.

An objector might retort, "Well, but then how does the first piece of knowledge of the world arise? It looks impossible." But why think that knowledge of the world must come into being atomistically? I don't see anything in the ordinary, pre-philosophical position that supports this demand. Knowledge of the world could sometimes come into being in clumps or clusters—clumps or clusters of true beliefs appropriately related to each other and to sensory experiences (and other requirements). It might even be that some beliefs only acquire the status of knowledge retroactively (or are called "knowledge" prospectively). Perhaps, that is, what happens is something like this. First, there are some experiences and some true beliefs formed in some good way in response to them, and some further true beliefs formed in some good way in response to those beliefs and to further experiences. After this goes on for a while the result is a network of largely true beliefs standing in certain sorts of good relations to each other—relations that the person adequately recognizes and that are appropriately related to the person's dispositions to form and revise beliefs. Somewhere in the later stages, all the beliefs in the cluster come to have a good status, which we call "knowledge." This is a picture on which it would be true that all our knowledge of the world comes from sensory experience, and also true that on each occasion on which we acquire knowledge of the world through sensory experience, other knowledge of the world is involved. It's a picture on which there is no single "first" item of knowledge of the world acquired through sensory perception.[3]

---

[3] It should be obvious that it would just be repeating the same mistake to ask, "What about the first clump—how did it get to be knowledge?," as though my suggestion was that this would have to be a matter of an inference-like transition from some sense experiences, via some background knowledge already independently in place, to a clump of new knowledge about the world. That is precisely *not* what I just suggested.

The possibility that knowledge can arise in this non-atomistic way is entirely compatible with the thought that particular instances of perceptual knowledge of the world (e.g., my knowledge that there is a table here in front of me) are often based upon particular experiences in the context of some other very particular beliefs about the world. It's also compatible with the facts that we sometimes arrive at knowledge through linear processes of inference and that when we give reasons for our beliefs we offer linear arguments.

It might be objected that there is difficulty in seeing the results of this non-atomistic process *as knowledge*. In particular, it might be said that the resulting beliefs are just a hypothesis, a theory, relative to one's real data, which consists of the totality of how things have appeared in one's sensory experience. And since the data are thus understood as neutral regarding the world, it is hard to see how they could do anything to turn that hypothesis into knowledge.[4]

This worry again smuggles in the Global Priority Thesis. For without that thesis, standing in our pre-philosophical position we are content to allow that our "evidence," our "data," can include things that we know about the world. So the non-atomistic story includes the thought that for each piece of knowledge, part of what makes it knowledge might include the fact that we recognize evidence that tells decisively in its favor—where that evidence includes or is made available by other things that we know about the world. What is thereby rejected is the thought that this good epistemic status must be capable of being reconstructed, as the Global Priority Thesis imagines, in terms of a single linear inference or transition from a set of data that includes no considerations at all about the world to a set of beliefs about the world. The Global Priority Thesis is distinct from the conception of sensory experience that is our focus, and without that thesis the present worry dissolves.

Another, related worry might arise here. Consider the situation that we are in as very young children, before we have any empirical knowledge or even beliefs about the world at all. How, starting from that position, do we arrive at our first empirical knowledge of the world? To make any sense of this, we have to see the child as making a transition from its experiences—understood in the way the view currently under consideration understands them—to some beliefs about the world, and we have to see this transition as knowledge-producing. One might think that even if we leave aside any

---

[4] This worry was urged on me by Barry Stroud.

commitment to the Global Priority Thesis, this imposes a significant requirement: we must be able to reconstruct this transition in terms of, or as conforming to, a good argument that could be used to rationally get from a position involving no beliefs about the world to some conclusions about the world. That is, one might think that none of our beliefs about the world can count as knowledge unless it is possible to explain how a rational creature could get—*via an unobjectionable course of reasoning*—from the child's initial position in which it has no beliefs about the world to a position in which it does have knowledge about the world. The non-atomistic story that I have sketched does no such thing, and so one might be inclined to reject it on that basis.

However, I think that this line of thought depends on a mistaken assumption. The assumption is this: we can't know something unless it is possible to explain how a rational creature could arrive at that conclusion through an acceptable course of reasoning from a position of initial neutrality. As we have seen, Moore rejects this. He points out that we do know things about the world and that we can't do what this assumption requires when it comes to the situation of the child imagined above (as he writes, "I don't believe it can be done," (1939, 169)). So, he holds that knowing things can't require this. And as we have seen at length over the last three chapters, it looks as though Moore was right to reject this assumption. There are many examples—our knowledge of the falsity of the Children of Brunettes Hypothesis, of the Ducks Hypothesis, and so on—which show that it is not the case that every piece of knowledge must be such that we could arrive at it via the transmission of warrant through an acceptable course of reasoning from a position of initial neutrality. Inability to show how we could arrive at an item of knowledge via an acceptable course of reasoning from an antecedent position of neutrality, ignorance, agnosticism, or doubt *does not show that we do not have that knowledge.*

3.2 But What about Regresses?

Consider my knowledge that there is a pen here (call it **KW1**, short for Knowledge of the World 1). The proposal so far is that this knowledge depends upon both my sensory experience "as of a pen" and some background knowledge of the world (call it **KW2**). It has also been granted that all our knowledge of the world depends in some sense upon sense experience.

So consider the background knowledge of the world KW2 that is crucially involved in my knowing that there is a pen here. Suppose that KW2 is ultimately grounded somehow in what is provided by some sense experiences. Whatever those sense experiences give us will only do its job—on the proposed view—given some background knowledge of the world, call it K3. And so on. The worry, of course, is that given our starting assumptions, there are only two possibilities, neither satisfactory. Either this chain must go on infinitely, or it must be circular. And so, one might conclude—as, for instance, Stroud does (2015, 391)—that this conception of what is given to us in sensory experience must be incorrect: there must be cases in which we simply *perceive that* p *is so*, where our knowledge that *p* does not depend upon any further knowledge of the world.

It looks to me as though this worry arises from two failures: a failure of epistemological imagination and a failure to look seriously at our ordinary epistemic practice.

First, the failure of epistemological imagination.

Notice, to begin with, that a specific item of knowledge might depend upon other items of knowledge in many different ways. Not all of them are the kinds of dependencies that can give rise to problematic regresses. For instance, it might be that in order to have the concepts involved in a particular belief, you have to know certain other things. This sort of dependence obviously generates no problematic regress or circularity. There is nothing problematic about mutual dependence of this sort. A similar point holds regarding any necessary condition for knowledge that simply relates two items of knowledge in such a way that you can't know the one without knowing the other and also cannot know the latter without knowing the first. That yields mutual dependence, not vicious circularity. To get objectionable circularity or any other form of vicious regress, you need more structure than is provided by a mere necessary condition.

A similar point applies at the level of evidential relations between propositions. For instance, it could perfectly well happen *both* that *p*'s truth is an excellent indicator of *q*, *and* that *q*'s truth is an excellent indicator of *p*. The fact that I am on the graduate faculty of my university is an excellent indication that I'm entitled to supervise PhD dissertations there; the former tells quite strongly in favor of the truth of the latter. And the opposite holds as well. The fact that I am entitled to supervise PhD dissertations is an excellent indication that I'm on the graduate faculty. This is not problematic; these relations go in both directions without difficulty. Nor is it unusual. In any reasonably comprehensive body of knowledge there will be a dense network of crisscrossing and reciprocal evidential relations amongst the believed propositions.

Once we see this point about evidential relations, we can also see a further way in which mutual dependence amongst items knowledge is not problematic. Suppose that in order to know *p*, you must know things that tell in its favor. In order to know those latter things, you must know things that tell in their favor as well. And so on. This doesn't generate a problematic regress. The worst we'll get is a requirement that generates mutual dependence amongst items of knowledge, that is, a requirement to the effect that to know any given thing, you must know other things that tell in favor of its truth. That sort of requirement can be satisfied by relations of evidential support that are reciprocal. There is no structural bar to the thought that part of what enables you to count as knowing *p* is that you know some *q* which tells in favor of *p*, *and* that part of what enables you to count as knowing *q* is that you know some *p* which tells in favor of it.

Of course, if you have offered *q* as your reason for believing *p*, then you cannot turn right around and offer *p* as your reason for believing *q*. That is unacceptably circular. But it is also beside the point. For the requirement at issue does not state that each item of knowledge has to be *based upon* some other item of knowledge, nor anything like that, but only that you must know other things that tell in favor of its truth. The *epistemic basing relation*, by contrast—that is, the relation involved when one item of knowledge is your ground for another, or when a consideration is the reason upon which you base another—does have the kind of structure that turns mutual dependence into vicious circularity. That is the sort of relation that the worry about a regress depends upon.

To put it another way: the worry about a regress imagines that a very particular sort of dependence relation must be in play at each step. It must be one that, like the epistemic basing relation, can't (acceptably) hold reciprocally between two items of knowledge. More particularly, it must be *transitive, asymmetric, and irreflexive*—or it must involve normative requirements to that effect[5]—so that (a) pairwise dependence relations can be linked together into bigger chains of the relevant sort and (b) those chains will be unacceptable if they are circular. Crucially, the worry about a regress requires

---

[5] Is it impossible to base *p* on *q* and also to base *q* on *p*, or is it just normatively unacceptable? We needn't try to decide this question here.

the assumption that *every* relevant instance of dependence upon background knowledge *must* be like this. If this isn't assumed, then the regress could terminate quite unproblematically in items of knowledge whose status as knowledge depends upon the person knowing other things. This is why I said earlier that it looks to me like the worry about a regress arises from a failure of epistemological imagination. After all, there are readily imaginable, perfectly coherent forms of epistemic dependence that capture everything that is in play and yet do not involve the kind of structure that is involved in basing relations.

For instance, consider what it takes to avoid a vicious regress of basing relations. Suppose that part of how I know p is this: q (something which I know) is my reason for believing p, and r (something which I know) is my reason for believing q. If we want to avoid vicious circularity or infinite regress, do we have to suppose that this chain ends in something that doesn't depend, for its status as knowledge, on any other knowledge at all? No. All we have to say is that some items of knowledge can count as knowledge without being *based on* any other beliefs or items of knowledge. That is a special status that certain items of knowledge might have in certain circumstances. Chains of basing relations could then acceptably terminate with items of knowledge that have that special status relative to the knowledge downstream in the chain. *That is enough to break the threat of a vicious regress or circular chain of basing relations.* Importantly, however, we could then go on to hold that those terminating items of knowledge have the status that they do only because the person has certain other items of knowledge, *where this requirement does not itself create a basing relation.*

There are many different ways in which such a structure could be instantiated. Here's a rough sketch of just one example. Perhaps some items of knowledge count as such—and are able to provide a proper basis for other items of knowledge—even though they aren't themselves held on the basis of anything in particular. And perhaps they can do so because requirements such as the following are met: the believed proposition is true, you know other things that tell decisively in favor of its truth, you recognize that these other things tell decisively in favor of its truth, you recognize that nothing tells against it, you don't hold any of these beliefs as a result of wishful thinking or in some other bad way (and one could add—if one thinks it is required for a good theory—you hold the belief in a reliable or counterfactually good way, as the result of the exercise of a competence, or whatever). This is just the briefest sketch of a possibility. But if anything along these lines were right, the result would plausibly be items of knowledge that (a) can terminate chains of basing relations, (b) depend on other items of knowledge, but (c) are not based on those other items of knowledge.

As soon as you see such possibilities, you lose the feeling that a vicious regress *must* arise from the idea that sense experience provides knowledge of the world only in the context of other knowledge of the world. That threat arose from gratuitously assuming that things *must* be a certain way. So, the burden has now shifted. To show from within our Moorean starting point that what I've been suggesting about the epistemological role of perception can't be right because it generates an unacceptable regress, you would now have to show that the kinds of epistemic dependence structures I've just sketched—structures that would break the threat of vicious regress—are *precluded by some aspect of our pre-philosophical position*. That seems pretty implausible.

In fact, something stronger can be said. Our ordinary epistemic practices and commitments are quite in line with the idea of knowledge that is not based on anything in particular but that nonetheless depends on other knowledge. The worry about a regress thus arises not only from a failure of epistemological imagination, but also from a failure to look seriously at our ordinary epistemic practice.

For instance, consider again an example that I elsewhere used for other purposes: my knowledge that I live in the United States. I recognize all kinds of things that (as I recognize) tell in favor of the truth of this proposition, and if I didn't, my belief surely wouldn't have the excellent epistemic status that it has. But suppose someone asks me, "What are your reasons for believing you live in the US? On what do you base this belief?" This isn't a request merely for me to point out some true considerations that tell in favor of the truth of this belief. Instead, the question asks for the reasons on which I base this belief, and that request draws a blank. I simply wouldn't know what to say. What, precisely, *are* the reasons for which I believe that I live in the US? Do they include the fact that my driver's license shows an Indiana address? That all my junk mail does? That Google Maps shows my house's location as being in the US? That the vast majority of people in my town speak English with an American accent? That at the conclusion of my last international flight a voice on the loudspeaker said, "Welcome to the United States"? These are weird questions, from the vantage point of ordinary life. They leave us flummoxed. How would we even go about trying to answer them? We don't have any idea how to proceed, if we are standing in the pre-philosophical position.

(I hope it is clear that this is just one example of a readily recognizable sort. Having pointed it out, I expect you will begin to see such cases all over the place.)

One response to this situation is to think that there must be some hidden fact of the matter here, one that will require ferreting out via proper investigation. Perhaps—one might think—the question will only be answered once we have the correct philosophical theory of what it is to hold a belief for a reason, or maybe an answer awaits some sort of psychological inquiry or a theory of "the structure of empirical justification." Such responses all assume that the question is in good order and so urge us to set to work to find the answer. But why make that assumption? After all, there is another option: to stick with the surface level of our practice. Why not take our befuddlement, which is itself a manifestation of our ordinary practice, as an indication that something is wrong with the question? Perhaps it has a false presupposition. Maybe there *are no particular reasons* upon which I currently base my belief that I live in the US. Is there, after all, any reason to think that there *must be* some reasons in particular upon which this knowledge is based? I don't see that there is. Nothing in the practice suggests any such thing.

Here is what we actually see:

1. I do not hold the belief about where I live (nor any of the other relevant beliefs) as a result of wishful thinking or in some other bad, criticizable way.
2. I can easily mention all kinds of things that tell quite decisively in favor of my living in the US: things I've been told, my driver's license, my tax forms, the address that appears on my mail, my voter's registration and history, my travel experiences, etc.
3. I recognize that there is no reason for doubt about any of these matters, nor about where I live.
4. I also recognize that there is a tangled web of criss-crossing evidential support relations in this territory. For instance, I recognize that the fact that my driver's license says I live in the United States is a good indication that I do, but I likewise recognize that the fact that I live in the United States is a good indication that my driver's license says that I do. I also recognize that as things are, what my mail says about where I live is a good indication of what my driver's license says, and vice versa.
5. Moreover, as I recognize, argument about these matters doesn't have to follow a single linear structure; I can quite acceptably argue in one

direction on some occasions and in exactly the opposing direction on others. For instance, I can prove (say, to an inquiring official) that I live in the United States by presenting my driver's license. But at the same time, when I was sent my driver's license I was instructed to check that it is correct, and when I did that I took it for granted that I live in the United States.
6. Importantly, there is *no* situation in which we think it important—circumstances being as they are—to identify a single linear structure in which some of these considerations in particular are picked out as "the reasons" upon which my belief that I live in the United States is based. We don't even hold that there must be a fixed ordering of directionality amongst my beliefs in this terrain, with some prior to others in some sort of argument-like structure.

Our actual epistemic practice thus does nothing to support the idea that there must be a determinate structure of basing relations here. To the contrary, if our concern is to capture the commitments that manifest themselves in the practice, we will impose no such demand. Taking the actual practice at face value, we will instead think something like this:

> What matters here are not basing relations, but rather factors such as these: that there is a wide-ranging network of relevant truths that I know and that (as I recognize) stand in a tangled web of evidential support relations, that there is (as I recognize) no reason to doubt any of this, that I am able make use of the truths in this territory on particular occasions to resolve questions and doubts as they arise, that I don't hold any of these beliefs as a result of wishful thinking or in some other bad or criticizable way, and the like.

So understood, we will not think that my knowledge that I live in the United States requires a determinate structure of basing relations supporting this belief. But we will nonetheless think that this belief's excellent epistemic status depends upon a whole host of other things that I know. If we take our epistemic practice at face value, then, it looks for all the world as though there are relevant epistemological dependence relations that do not have the structural features of basing relations and so do not generate threat of vicious regress.

In fact, I would go one step further. Questions about the commitments of our epistemic practice are equally questions about how we are willing to live. So let me declare my commitments: I make no demands for determinate basing relations here, nor for any other dependence relations with that structure. I am perfectly content to say that I know that I live in the United States, to treat that as something I know, and indeed to accord this belief an extremely positive epistemic status—all while eschewing anything like a demand that there be any particular reasons upon which I base it. I likewise extend the same courtesy to many of your beliefs as well. So far as I can see, any demand in such cases for determinate basing relations is pointless, an idle wheel. The same goes for any demand in such cases for a dependence relation with all of the structural properties of the basing relation (a standing priority or ordering relation, transitivity, asymmetry, and the others.) But without the demand for a dependence relation of that kind for every item of knowledge, worries about a vicious epistemic regress simply won't get off the ground.

It is a further question what form all of this actually takes in our epistemic lives. One might wish to develop a detailed reflective account of this, but that is not needed for my purposes here. To develop such an account one would consider questions such as these: "What exactly are all of the relevant dependence relations that *do* have the abstract structure of basing relations? What exactly is involved in the special status that enables some items of knowledge to be terminating points in certain circumstances or on certain occasions relative to other items of knowledge in a single chain of such relations? Under what conditions is an item of knowledge a terminating point? In what ways does it nonetheless depend upon other items of knowledge for its status as knowledge or as a terminating point? How is all of this instantiated or exhibited in our ordinary epistemic practice?" However, all of these questions, as well as the development of a satisfactory account answering them, are downstream from my purposes right now. The point right now is simply that there is no reason to think that the sort of view of perceptual knowledge under discussion *must* or even *does* force a vicious regress. But seeing the possibilities and features of our epistemic practice that underwrite that point is one of the pay-offs of the approach that I am urging. We can thereby break up ossified assumptions and free ourselves to really look at how things work in our epistemic lives. That is one of the ways in which this investigation is profitable.

A common assumption both shapes and restricts philosophical imagination in a way that obscures the possibilities I am highlighting. It makes worries about a regress seem inevitable in this context. The assumption could be put this way: "All the good arguments I give or could give, when I am asked to explain how I know particular things or to justify particular beliefs, are part of one big argument, one big evidential structure that must be somehow instantiated in my psychology or at least must exist and be available if I am really to have knowledge. If we could put it all together, we'd have the one big argument that covers all of my beliefs. The basic outline of this underlying structure is a key part of the theory of our knowledge of the world." This assumption leads one to think that any local structure of basing relations that shows up when we defend particular beliefs must be part of a single large structure. And this assumption thereby leads to the sorts of failures highlighted a moment ago: it leads one to fail to see the wide range of dependence relations that could be in play, and it blocks a clear-eyed look at our epistemic practice.

Roderick Firth—a mid-twentieth-century epistemologist who is no longer read as much as he should be—encapsulated this assumption nicely. He wrote that what we seek in epistemology is a "reconstruction" of our empirical knowledge, which he summarized as: "a schematic ordering of our beliefs in the form of an argument that will exhibit the justifying relations that hold amongst them" (1998, 296). Look seriously at what Firth is seeking here. *An* argument? A *single argument* that exhibits *the* justifying relations that hold amongst *all* of our beliefs? Why think that there is any such thing? Why think that there *must* be such a thing, if we are to have any knowledge of the world at all? These are extraordinary assumptions. I don't see anything that forces them upon us.

Now it might be objected that there are features of certain questions ("How do you know? What is your reason for that?") that might seem both to suggest the picture of a larger underlying structure and to warrant the iterated question "What is your reason?" even in the cases I have been discussing.

The first such feature has to do with the *aim* of these questions. While they are sometimes asked in a pointed way when we suspect that someone does not know (a way that challenges the person to defend and establish a certain positive epistemic status then and there), they do not have to be asked in this spirit. Sometimes they are asked out of mere curiosity. Sometimes we just want to find out something about a person's knowledge or reasons.

The second feature concerns the *subject matter* of these questions. Very often it seems that such questions concern something that is already the case.

They invite articulation of an ordered structure amongst our beliefs that we very often take to pre-exist its articulation.

Taken together, these two features can easily seem to suggest that there is a larger underlying structure of which we only glimpse small parts in ordinary life but that we could pursue in much greater depth if we wished. This is, for instance, how epistemologists such as Chisholm (1982, 131, 145) understood the matter, when they used the repeated iteration of such questions as part of a "Socratic" exercise of attempting to determine what it is to have empirical knowledge or empirically justified beliefs. And thinking in these terms would lead one to think that any view on which each case of experientially supported knowledge also depends upon some other knowledge of the world is ultimately fated to unacceptable circularity, since iterations of the question "How do you know?" or "What is your evidence/reason?" would ultimately *have* to be answered circularly, given the assumption that the chain of reasons can't go on forever.

However, the two features I just identified do not in fact require us to adopt any such interpretation of the practice. For what is being urged is to take what we find in certain cases in which the question *does* have clear application and *doesn't* leave us flummoxed about how to proceed, and then to assume that the same sort of thing must be present in the cases in which the question *doesn't* have clear application and *does* leave us flummoxed. And this extension is then proposed as a reason for *discounting* the fact that the question doesn't have a clear application and leaves us flummoxed in those latter cases. But this is to proceed in the wrong direction. It is to neglect the fact that the two features of the practice pointed to above might very well be circumstantially constrained and limited to cases of the sort in which the question has clear application. No reason has been given to think otherwise or to assimilate cases in this way.

Admittedly, there are perfectly ordinary cases in which we think that the question applies but we don't yet know the answer. For instance, I might discover that I have reached a mistaken conclusion and ask myself, "What was I basing my conclusion on, what was I wrongly assuming, that led me down this incorrect path?" In cases like this we take it that there is something determinate that was our reason for believing as we did, and we attempt to determine what it was. However, the existence of such cases does not undermine the point I just made. For in these cases, the question has clear application and we are not flummoxed about how to proceed, even though we might not yet know the answer. That is to say, these cases are treated entirely differently in our actual practice from cases such as my belief that I live in the United States. Given this fact, the existence of such cases does not provide any reason to think that there must be a structure of basing relations hidden in every case. To think it does is to assimilate cases in a way that ignores perfectly ordinary distinctions without any reason for doing so. This would be a mistake, given that our overarching concern is precisely with the commitments of our ordinary epistemic position.

In sum, I think that when we look carefully at our actual epistemic practice, it does not support the picture of "the one big underlying structure of argument that exhibits the justifying relations between our beliefs." Quite the opposite, as we see once we think seriously about examples such as my knowledge that I live in the United States. Importantly, the points that I have made about this example apply just as well to my knowledge that there is an external world and that my senses are reliable in circumstances like the present ones—that is, knowledge of the sort that would plausibly figure in the account of perceptual knowledge that we have been exploring. We don't have to fear vicious regress here, because this knowledge isn't held on the basis of any particular reasons—though it plausibly depends on our recognizing all sorts of things that tell quite decisively in these propositions' favor.

So much, then, for worries about a regress generated by the suggestions that:

a. In each case in which we acquire knowledge of the world by sensory experience, other knowledge of the world is crucially involved, and
b. All of our knowledge of the world depends upon sensory experience.

The threat of regress is blocked by general features of our epistemic practice that are quite independent from the specific question of what is given to us, epistemologically speaking, in sensory experience. That threat only arises given additional assumptions that are not forced on us by the prephilosophical position and are in fact quite out of line with our actual epistemic practice.

3.3 But Isn't This Really Circular Nonetheless?

Recall Wright's attempt to extract a skeptical worry from Moore's "Proof of an External World" (see Chapter 8, Section 3). This worry might seem to highlight a problem for the proposal that we've been discussing. According to that proposal, in each case in which you acquire knowledge of the world through sense perception, some experience is involved *along with some further knowledge of the world*. That additional knowledge will quite plausibly include *that there is a world of external things* and *that sensory experiences in circumstances like these are a good indication of how things are*. Now, these latter items of knowledge ultimately depend upon sense experience, and so also depend upon some knowledge of the world—including ultimately the knowledge that there is an external world. So isn't the account committed to an unacceptable circularity after all?

I don't think it is. First, it's unclear that there is a circle here of the sort the objector imagines. The worry is that the justifying structure reduces to this:

Experience + There is an external world

There is an external world.

(Where the arrow represents something like a basing relation, an inferential transition in the course of explicit reasoning, or some other dependence relation with the relevant structural properties.) That would indeed be unacceptably circular.

However, there is no reason to think that the proposal I've been considering is committed to seeing the justificatory structure in this way. What the view says is twofold: (1) that in each case in which you acquire knowledge through sensory perception, background knowledge—plausibly including knowledge that the external world exists—is in play, and (2) that your knowledge that there is an external world depends upon a lot of knowledge of the world and a lot of sensory experience. Why assume that all of this can be put together into a single structure of basing relations or inferential transitions? Maybe that isn't the form of dependence involved. As we saw in the discussion of regresses, we can't just assume that the dependence relations involved in any given item of knowledge can be combined with the dependence relations involved in another item of knowledge to generate a single larger justificatory structure of the sort required for vicious circularity. That is, maybe the structure here is more holistic, such that some of this knowledge isn't acquired or underwritten by anything capturable in the form of an acceptable linear inference. Maybe this is all part of a network of mutually dependent knowledge that gets put in place over the course of an individual's development, but not through anything like a linear process of inference or reasoning of the sort that generates basing relations. Perhaps we can chart some of that network now by stating various truths that decisively tell in favor of—indeed entail—that there are external things. But in doing that, perhaps we are not sketching out anything like an argument by which we acquired or could acquire this knowledge for the first time.

You won't find this suggestion satisfactory if you think you can't know a given thing unless it is possible to construct something like an acceptable line of argument or reasoning by which a rational creature could come to know that thing, starting from an initial position of neutrality in which they are completely agnostic about the issue. But as I asked before, why impose that requirement? Nothing in our ordinary, pre-philosophical position commits us to such a thing. Moreover, as we have seen there are aspects of ordinary epistemic practice that tell decisively against it (see Chapters 6–8). For a case in point, consider again our knowledge that ducks aren't successfully engaged in an undetectable conspiracy to shape world history for their own hidden ends.

If the account we've been considering does generate a form of circularity regarding our knowledge of the world, it will be epistemic circularity: if we thought that there isn't an external world, or suspected as much, or thought we had reason to believe that there isn't one, or were just agnostic about it (with no view at all), then we couldn't recognize the evidence that there is one. But this kind of situation is something we are content with in ordinary epistemic life, as we have already seen (Chapters 6 and 7). This sort of structure shows up in my knowledge that my wife isn't deceiving me about whether she loves me, in psychologists' knowledge about the ways and extent to which our perceptual faculties are reliable, and in our knowledge that neither ducks nor dung beetles are successfully engaged in an undetectable conspiracy to shape world history for their own ends. In all of these cases we are content in ordinary life to regard ourselves as having excellent evidence on these matters, though we cannot recognize this excellent evidence if we take up a position of complete agnosticism or neutrality on these issues.

4. Conclusion

I have been concerned with the epistemological consequences of the thesis that sensory experience all by itself never gives you more on any particular occasion than would be captured by characterizations of how things "seem" or by talk of your experience being "as of" such and such, where such characterizations do not to entail anything about how the world is. It's often asserted that this view leads straight to skepticism. I've argued, to the contrary, that this thesis about sensory experience can be integrated into the commitments and practices of ordinary epistemic life without raising any threat of skepticism whatsoever. We just have to allow that in each case in which we acquire knowledge of the world through sensory experience, other knowledge of the world is involved. To be clear, my point here is *not* to claim that this is the correct theory of perceptual knowledge. I make no such claim. Rather, my point is that so far, at least, nothing in the pre-philosophical position precludes us from allowing this, and consequently that the limited conception of what is given to us epistemologically in sensory experience does not—given the commitments of our pre-philosophical position—force us into skepticism. It doesn't even force us into framing things in the way that sets the scene for the skeptical argument as it is presented in many canonical formulations.

If that's right, then the *Global Priority Thesis* takes center stage as the fundamental issue that we must now consider in order to see whether there is any threat of a global skeptical argument from within our ordinary position. Is there anything in our pre-philosophical position that can reasonably motivate the thought that all of our knowledge of the world, as a whole, must rest on something else that is not yet knowledge of the world, in particular on a body of sensory evidence characterized in a way that implies nothing about the world? That is the question to which we now must turn.

10
What Is the Global Priority Thesis?

1. The Global Epistemic Priority Thesis

It may seem to some readers that the preceding chapters have ignored an elephant in the room. I have repeatedly asked what, if anything, in our ordinary, pre-philosophical position could motivate excluding our background knowledge of the world when we evaluate skeptical argumentation. You may have thought the answer is just obvious. To put it roughly: our evidence for the totality of our beliefs about the world is limited to what is given to us by our experiential states. Or, to put the thought a little more carefully: in order for us to know or reasonably believe anything about the external world, our beliefs about the world—taken as a whole—must be supported by, based upon, or inferable from something that is not yet knowledge of the world, in particular a body of "internal" evidence comprising or provided by our experiential and other mental states (or facts about those states) characterized in a way that does not entail the truth of their contents when they have contents about the world. If something along those lines is correct, then that gives us a straightforward reason to restrict what is available when we confront the skeptical argumentation.

This answer is a version of what I have called the "Global Epistemic Priority Thesis." This thesis has a long history in epistemology, and it is presupposed by many discussions of skepticism. For instance, ideas along these lines are in play whenever someone begins a skeptical argument by simply declaring that "our evidence" for our beliefs about the world is limited to experiential states that are equally compatible with Descartes' Evil Demon scenario.[1]

In preceding chapters I have highlighted aspects of our ordinary, pre-philosophical position that don't fit well with the Global Priority Thesis.

---

[1] At the same time, however, some philosophers have argued that the Global Priority Thesis is a consequence, not a starting point, of the skeptical argument. On Stroud's view (1984, chapter 1), for instance, we begin with some other sort of aspiration, question, or line of thought that gets the skeptical argument going. It is only at the conclusion of that argument, when we assert that we can have knowledge only of how things experientially seem, that we then face the task of showing how our knowledge of the world could rest, as a whole, on such a thin body of experiential evidence.

But I have not considered whether there is anything in its favor. Is there any reason to think that the Global Priority Thesis is true? As throughout this book, I raise this question from our Moorean standpoint squarely within the ordinary, pre-philosophical position. The suggestion that I want to explore in this and the next two chapters is that the thesis is itself among the commitments of this position, or at least is motivated by certain aspects of those commitments. If that is so, then there is no great mystery about how the crucial framing for the skeptical argument gets put into place. It is lurking in wait all along.

In order to successfully set the scene for the skeptical argumentation, the Global Priority Thesis must involve several key components.

- It must suppose that each of us can sensibly treat all our beliefs about the world as a group for justificatory purposes.
- It must characterize some limited justificatory base that does not include any considerations about the world.
- It must identify that limited base with our sensory experiences and other non-factive mental states, or facts about those mental states, or propositions or judgments concerning such states.
- It must treat that limited base as comprising the totality of our evidence for any beliefs about the world: it must take that limited base to be all we have to go on in arriving at or justifying those beliefs.
- It must hold that if we are to know or have reasonable beliefs about the world, then that limited base must provide adequate support or evidence for conclusions about the world in this specific sense: it must be possible for a rational being to acceptably transition in explicit conscious reasoning from the limited base (a position that does not yet involve any views about the world) to conclusions about the world.

This last requirement is needed for a version of the Global Priority Thesis that could do the work required by the skeptic. Without it, our inability to see how anyone could acceptably move in explicit reasoning from the limited evidential base to beliefs about the world would carry no skeptical implications, because the acceptability of such a move would not be a necessary condition for knowledge or reasonable belief about the world.

Anti-skeptical proponents of the Global Priority Thesis have tended to supplement it with the idea that there are a priori principles of inference or justificatory support that satisfactorily link the body of our beliefs about the world with the restricted evidential base. I think it is safe to say that no one has conclusively shown that this is so, but that issue is beside the point here. Our concern is with a form of the Global Priority Thesis that meets *the skeptic's* needs, and for that purpose what we need to focus on is the very idea that our beliefs about the world as a whole must rest on an evidential base limited to our non-factive mental states (or to considerations about them).

The crucial question for our purposes, then, is whether anything in the ordinary, pre-philosophical position commits us to or can reasonably motivate the Global Priority Thesis. My approach to this question will be straightforward. In this and the next two chapters I will examine the main arguments in support of the Global Priority Thesis, and I will argue that none of them carries conviction from the standpoint of our ordinary position. I will consequently conclude that nothing in our ordinary position commits us to or gives us reason to accept a Global Priority Thesis that could do the work the skeptical argument requires. Given the Moorean perspective within which we are working, that's all that's needed. Admittedly, it's possible that someone could come along and show us a compelling line of thought that we have missed. Until they do so, however, there is no reason not to be content.

2. Evidence from Ordinary Practice?

One initial suggestion can be dispensed with quickly. It is plausible enough, as Descartes said, that everything we know about the world comes to us "by or through the senses." In fact, however, the sensory provenance of this knowledge does not force the Global Priority Thesis upon us. As noted in the preceding chapter, the pretheoretically plausible point about the provenance of our knowledge is a causal one, not a claim about an evidential basis. For this reason our knowledge could perfectly well depend upon and be gained through the senses, even if it can't be understood on the model of an inference from a limited body of sensory evidence to a total body of beliefs about the world. Even at the level of philosophical theorizing, there are many alternatives. Several of them have been the focus of epistemological interest in recent decades.[2]

---

[2] Theoretical alternatives explored in recent decades range from coherentism to reliabilism to various virtue epistemologies to epistemological disjunctivism and more. I am not asking which theoretical approach is superior, nor am I defending any theoretical alternative in particular, since my question instead concerns the relation between the Global Priority Thesis and our practice.

It might be thought, however, that our ordinary practice manifests a straightforward commitment to the Global Priority Thesis in another way. We very often appeal to *how things look* in order to support claims about the world or to provide vindicating explanations of why we believed as we did. For instance, suppose that I thought I saw a male scarlet tanager, but it later turned out to be a genetically modified cardinal. If you ask me why I thought I saw a male scarlet tanager, I might reasonably reply, "Well, it looked just like one." Here, I try to show the reasonableness of my false belief by providing an explanation that appeals to *how things looked*. I can do something similar regarding beliefs that arise as the result of a hallucination. And we can likewise appeal to how things look even when we think our beliefs are correct. In ordinary circumstances it would be intelligible, though not very informative, to answer the question, "Why do you think it's a male scarlet tanager?" by saying, "Because it looks just like one."

Of course, such responses include words like "it," which in these contexts appear to refer to external objects. However, having come this far it can easily seem that this reference to the external world can be dropped; we might replace this reference—albeit a little awkwardly—with something less committal, such as "It looks just like there's a male scarlet tanager before me." And this might seem to point toward the Global Priority Thesis showing up in our ordinary practice.

These considerations don't get us all the way there, however. If I didn't have any view at all about what male scarlet tanagers tend to look like, I would think it utterly bizarre for me to reply to such questions by appealing to how things looked. All else equal, someone with no views at all about what scarlet tanagers characteristically look like has no business making claims about their presence based on how things look. That is to say: in our actual practice these sorts of appeals to how things look function against an implicit background of information about the world. For this reason, these sorts of examples do nothing whatsoever to indicate an ordinary commitment to the Global Priority Thesis. They are equally compatible with the possibility that background considerations about the world are inextricably involved every time we successfully defend a belief about the world by appealing to how things look to us.[3]

---

[3] Some epistemologists have offered theories of justification according to which an experience as of p is sufficient to make it reasonable for one to form the belief that p, in a way that does not depend upon any justified background beliefs about the world. These theories are offered as a solution to skepticism, but by assuming the Global Priority Thesis without any motivation they concede too much (in addition to the failing I highlighted in Chapter 8, Section 3.2).

A third initial thought can be dispensed with quickly as well. It is sometimes vaguely thought that if things could seem just the same to you regardless of whether p is true or false, then p cannot be part of your evidence for q: your evidence in such a case must really be only that it *seems to you as if* p. And this thought can then lead quickly to the Global Priority Thesis: since things could seem exactly the same to us even if everything we believe about the world were false, nothing we believe about the world can really be part of our evidence—or so one might think. In this way, considerations about subjective indistinguishability from a certain limited vantage point can be taken to show that our evidence for our beliefs about the world in fact contains no considerations about the world: it is limited to how things (experientially) seem.

The trouble with this line of thought is that nothing in our practice suggests a commitment to the claim that if things would seem just the same to you regardless of whether p is true or false, then p cannot be part of your evidence for q. Quite the contrary: our practice goes against this claim. For instance, I would be perfectly happy to offer the following argument:

1. Alex Jones claims that the Sandy Hook school shooting was just a highly successful hoax.
2. The Sandy Hook school shooting was not a hoax.
3. So, Alex Jones has claimed at least one false thing.

And I might quite reasonably follow up by commenting:

4. So, there is decisive evidence that Alex Jones has claimed at least one false thing.

That is to say, I am perfectly prepared to count amongst my evidence the fact that Sandy Hook was not a hoax. But if the Sandy Hook shooting *were* a hoax of the sort Alex Jones has in mind, then given my current circumstances everything would seem to me exactly as it does. Our ordinary practice thus runs counter to the proposed claim about evidence.

It is sometimes inchoately thought that the "New Evil Demon" thought experiment (Cohen and Lehrer 1983, Cohen 1984) shows that our evidence is limited to how things experientially seem, since if we had twins who were being deceived by an Evil Demon, *their* evidence would be limited to their sensory experiences. But no such conclusion follows straight away from the thought experiment. We can have evidence that our deceived twins lack. That is the lesson of evidential asymmetry, a phenomenon straightforwardly exemplified in the Alex Jones/Sandy Hook example above. (For further discussion, see Chapter 7, Chapter 5's discussion of the "New Evil Demon" thought experiment, and Chapter 12.)

If we hope to find motivation for the Global Priority Thesis in our ordinary position we will have to dig deeper.

3. The Shadow of the Past

While the Global Priority Thesis is often implicitly assumed in many contemporary discussions, it is rarely argued for. We have to look to the past in order to understand and evaluate the way in which it lives on.

The Global Priority Thesis or something very like it was endorsed or explored by many of the great epistemologists of the early-to-mid twentieth century, including C.I. Lewis, Bertrand Russell, A.J. Ayer, Roderick Chisholm, and Roderick Firth. Lewis and Russell tended to leave the thesis somewhat implicit, taking for granted the structure that it imposed on epistemological theorizing. However, later epistemologists such as Firth and Chisholm attempted to bring this structure into clear view.

Firth, for instance, articulated the core features of what he called a "Cartesian reconstruction of empirical knowledge" (1998, 278). A "reconstruction," Firth wrote, would

> order the propositions that we know in the form of an argument that exhibits the structure of the justifying relations that hold among them.... A reconstruction will thus show, in a schematic way, the extent to which certain parts of our empirical knowledge are dependent for their justification or warrant on other parts, and it will formulate the principles of non-deductive inference—including, for example, a principle of inductive generalization—in virtue of which these justifying relations obtain. (277)

A "Cartesian reconstruction," Firth wrote, would meet three requirements:

> *The Requirement of Self-Warrant*: A Cartesian reconstruction divides the total body of a man's empirical beliefs into two distinct classes—a class of beliefs that are epistemically basic and a class of beliefs that are epistemically

derivative. A derivative belief is one that derives all its warrant (not just part of it) from its non-deductive inferential relationships to basic beliefs. A basic belief, on the other hand, is one that is warranted, at least in part, non-inferentially: it is, we might say, at least partially self-warranted. Basic beliefs must appear as premises in the reconstruction. Derivative beliefs must appear only as conclusions. (278)

The Immediacy Requirement: The basic propositions that serve as premises for a Cartesian reconstruction can be distinguished from derivative propositions by the nature of their subject-matter. Specifically, according to the Cartesian, all of the basic propositions for a particular person at a particular time t are propositions about the intrinsic character of his own immediate experience at t. (280)

The Sensory Requirement: Perceptual judgments are always accompanied by the occurrence of sense-experience. All the warrant possessed by a perceptual judgment in virtue of its being perceptual, is derivative from the warrant possessed by propositions about the character of the accompanying sense-experience. (281)

So understood, a "Cartesian reconstruction" has specific features that are not required by the Global Priority Thesis as such. However, the project requires that the totality of things we take ourselves to know about the world can be divided from an evidential base that does not contain any considerations about the world, and it supposes that if we do indeed know anything about the world, the warrant possessed by our beliefs about the world must derive from that limited base. The demand for a "Cartesian reconstruction" thus both presumes the Global Priority Thesis and offers a detailed way of spelling it out.

In "The Myth of the Given," Chisholm (1982) likewise attempted to thematize the Global Priority Thesis. He offered the following metaphorical characterization of the thesis:

A) The knowledge that a person has at any time is a structure or edifice, many parts and stages of which help to support each other, but which as a whole is supported by its own foundation. (126)

B) The foundation of one's knowledge consists (at least in part) of the apprehension of what have been called, variously, "sensations," "sense-impressions," "appearances," "sensa," "sense-qualia," and "phenomena." (127)

> C) The *only* apprehension that is thus basic to the structure of knowledge is our apprehension of "appearances" (etc.)—our apprehension of the given. (127)

Chisholm went on to elaborate (A) and (B) in terms of the idea of statements that justify themselves, and he rejected (C). But he rejected (C) because he thought that it needed to be broadened somewhat: he thought that the "foundations" specified by requirement (B) include not just apprehensions of "appearances," but also apprehensions of one's own psychological states (characterized in a way that does not entail anything about the external world). So elaborated, Chisholm offers a fairly minimal version of the Global Priority Thesis.

Both Chisholm and Firth tend to characterize the "foundations" (Chisholm) or "premises" (Firth) as propositions concerning one's own psychological states or as states with propositional content concerning one's own psychological states. However, the Global Priority Thesis does not have to take this form. It could be claimed instead that our experiential and other relevant psychological states themselves provide the evidential/justificatory/warranting base for the totality of our knowledge of the world. Later epistemologists such as Jim Pryor have thought in these latter terms even while retaining the core of the Global Priority Thesis (2000).

In *Sense and Sensibilia* J.L. Austin offered a rare dissent to this whole way of thinking.

> [I]t is not the case that the formulation of evidence is the function of any special sort of sentence. The evidence, if there is any, for a "material-object" statement will usually be formulated in statements of just the same kind; but in general, *any* kind of statement could state evidence for *any* other kind, if the circumstances were appropriate. (1962, 116 [italics in original])

> [E]ven if we were to make the very risky and gratuitous assumption that what some particular person knows at some particular place and time could be systematically sorted out into an arrangement of foundations and super-structure, it would be a mistake in principle to suppose that the same thing could be done for knowledge *in general*. And this is because there *could* be no *general* answer to the questions what is evidence for what, what is certain, what is doubtful, what needs or does not need evidence, can or can't be verified. If the Theory of Knowledge consists in finding grounds for such an answer, there is no such thing. (1962, 124 [italics in original])

Here Austin challenges not just the Global Priority Thesis, but also the very demand for a "reconstruction" of our knowledge of the world. What is evidence for what, Austin thought, depends upon the particulars of the circumstances in such a way that the idea of a general, abstract "structure of our empirical knowledge" is hopeless. We cannot stand apart from all of our commitments about the world and the particularities of our circumstances and hope to sort our beliefs into the kind of general structure that Firth and Chisholm imagine.[4]

In light of Austin's criticisms, it is retrospectively striking that epistemologists such as Russell, Ayer, and C.I. Lewis offered little by way of argument in favor of the Global Priority Thesis and did even less to connect it with our ordinary epistemic practices and commitments. Rather, they tended simply to assume it as part of an overall "empiricist" framework. In fact, with the exception of Chisholm, no prominent epistemologist has argued carefully and at length in its defense, despite the fundamental way in which it has shaped much epistemological thinking right up to the present day.

4. Sorting Out Orthogonal Issues

To some extent, the lack of argumentation was the result of confusion. In early-twentieth-century epistemology the Global Priority Thesis wasn't clearly distinguished from the conception of perception discussed in Chapter 9 or from various theses about the certainty, indubitability, or incorrigibility of judgments about experiences. As a result, the focus of debate often strayed to one side or another of the Global Priority Thesis itself.

To take just one instance, a 1952 symposium in the *Philosophical Review* titled "The Experiential Element in Knowledge," involving C.I. Lewis, Hans Reichenbach, and Nelson Goodman, appeared to be about the Global Priority Thesis. That was certainly how Reichenbach saw it. He framed his contribution with the following question, which is squarely about the Global Priority Thesis:

> there arises the problem of whether there is a certain experiential basis of the elaborate structure of knowledge, a substratum which is composed of

---

[4] For one way of elaborating a criticism in the spirit of Austin's, see Michael Williams, *Unnatural Doubts* (1996) and *Problems of Knowledge* (2001).

the experiential data alone and which carries the total edifice that includes so many results of highest abstraction. (Reichenbach 1952, 148)

In fact, however, the debate focused on a different issue: whether judgments about experience—described in a way that entails nothing about the external world—are ever or always *certain*, in the particular sense of being absolutely immune from error.

It might not seem that this is a distinct issue. But notice two simple points. First, as later foundationalist epistemologists recognized, the Global Priority Thesis does not entail that any judgments about experience are absolutely immune from error; someone could perfectly well hold *both* that sensory experience (or, more generally, sensory experience along with our non-factive mental states) is the sole evidential base for the totality of our beliefs about the world *and also* that in principle we can make mistakes regarding the characterization of our current sensory experience. If you find it difficult to prize these apart in this way, just recall that our ordinary way of thinking about evidence allows that something can be part of your evidence even if it is something about which you could make a mistake. To speak from within our ordinary position: You can make a mistake about whether your plants are wilting, but it is nonetheless true that if they are wilting, that can be evidence that they need water.

Second, suppose that some judgments about experience *are* absolutely immune from error. It doesn't follow that in order to be knowledge (or justified, or rationally based) all of our beliefs about the world must, as a class, rest upon nothing but such judgments or upon the mental states they are about. For instance, suppose that each instance of perceptual knowledge rests in part upon a sensory experience that by itself gives us something less than knowledge of the world, and suppose that we cannot make an error about what that sensory experience gives us. It might still be true that each instance of perceptual knowledge *also* depends crucially upon other knowledge of the world in a way that violates the requirements of the Global Epistemic Priority Thesis. This point is a direct implication of the lesson of Chapter 9. It gives us a straightforward way in which it could be true that judgments about experience are immune to error and yet the Global Priority Thesis could still be false.

So, we need to focus squarely on the Global Epistemic Priority Thesis itself, and not get distracted by the issues about "certainty" that saw so much debate in the middle of the twentieth century. Differences in the extent or ways in which error is possible with regard to two classes of judgments do not dictate relations of epistemic priority between those two classes.

Similarly, we should not get sidetracked by considerations about "dubitability" and "corrigibility" that also came in for a great deal of debate in the early-to-mid twentieth century. For instance, in an influential passage, H.H. Price focused on what could possibly be doubted:

> When I see a tomato there is much that I can doubt. I can doubt whether it is a tomato that I am seeing, and not a cleverly painted piece of wax. I can doubt whether there is any material thing there at all. Perhaps what I took for a tomato was really a reflection; perhaps I am even the victim of some hallucination. One thing however I cannot doubt: that there exists a red patch of a round and somewhat bulgy shape, standing out from a background of other colour-patches, and having a certain visual depth. (1932, 3)

Chisholm offered an important rejoinder. He noted that what it is possible to doubt (for instance, given the right sort of circumstances) is distinct from what is dubitable or in doubt here and now. Even if there are some possible circumstances in which we would have reason to doubt whether there is a material thing there at all, it may not be dubitable in the *actual* circumstances. There is sometimes no reason to doubt (for instance) that there is a clock on the mantelpiece, and likewise no reason to correct this judgment. So, considerations of dubitability or corrigibility *in situ* don't divide things up in the way that the Global Epistemic Priority Thesis supposes (1982, 130).

Appeals to "certainty," "dubitability," and "incorrigibility" look like they lead to a Global Priority Thesis only when we have *already* taken up a position in which we stand apart from all of our commitments about the world and ask, "What could provide evidence for all of this?" If we have done that, then it may seem irresistible—especially for Descartes' heirs—to think that the evidential base should be provided by something that is more certain, less dubitable, or less corrigible. But in posing the question in this way, we are already assuming key aspects of the conception at issue. This is no way to find an argument for the Global Epistemic Priority Thesis, because it still won't have been shown that anything in our ordinary position commits us to thinking that all of our knowledge of the world, as a totality, must rest upon or be supported by something else that is not yet knowledge of the world.

Ayer (1956) tried a different tack. He understood the Global Priority Thesis to make a claim about *inference*, in particular a claim about an evidential base from which our beliefs about the world are inferred. Taking the thesis in this way, he attempted to establish it by introducing a class of statements which do not entail any statements about the world, but some member of which is true whenever a perceptual judgment or claim is made about the world. For instance, if I perceptually judge that there is a tree in front of me, then even if there is no tree and I am just the victim of an evil demon's deceptions, it will still be true that it looks to me as if there is something with a certain color and shape before me. However, *contra* Ayer, this point does nothing to establish an *inferential* relationship between the two. As Strawson put it,

> From the bare fact that such a class of statements can be introduced it in no way follows that the introduced statements function as the premises of inferences of which statements asserting or entailing the existence of material objects are the conclusions. (1957, 306)

Here's an example that helps make Strawson's point. Whenever someone sincerely claims (whether truly or falsely) to have a certain feeling, it is true that they are thinking. So, there is a class of statements that are true whenever someone sincerely makes a claim about what they are feeling, a class of statements which do not entail any claims about what they are feeling. It does not follow from this that the fact that the person is thinking is even part of a premise from which they have inferred that they have that feeling. Nor does it follow that this is the evidential base, or even part of the evidential base, for their knowledge that they have that feeling. The relation highlighted by Ayer is orthogonal to the question of epistemic priority between classes of judgments.

5. Chisholm's Contrast

Chisholm invites us to focus on the question, "What reason do I have to think (or, what justifies me in thinking) that I know that *p*?" Taking it for granted that we do know that *p*, he intends this question not as a challenge to our knowledge but as a way of articulating "what the criteria are ... in terms of which we believe ourselves justified in counting one thing as an instance of knowing and another not" (1982, 131). The goal is thus to unearth our implicit conception of what it takes to know something.

When we ask this question, Chisholm says, we frequently find that we can reasonably raise the very same question about the answer. For instance, I might say that what justifies me in thinking I know that there is a clock on the mantlepiece is that "I saw it there this morning and no one would have taken it away" (130), but then I can equally ask, "What reason do I have to think that I know that I saw it there this morning and that no one would have taken it away?" Chisholm claims, however, that there are certain cases in which it is reasonable to answer the question, "What reason do I have to think I know that p?," by repeating p itself. For instance, in answer to the question, "What reason do I have to think that I know that I believe that Socrates is mortal?," there is "nothing to say" (137) other than, "Well, I *do* believe that Socrates is mortal." Similarly, in response to the question "What reason do I have to think that I know that it appears to me as if there is a white rectangle before me?," Chisholm takes it that the only reasonable answer is, "Well, it *does* appear to me as if there is a white rectangle before me."[5] Chisholm describes these latter sorts of claims as "justifying themselves" (136), in the following sense: "A statement, belief, claim, proposition, or hypothesis may be said to be self-justifying for a person, if the person's justification for thinking he knows it to be true is simply the fact that it is true" (137).

Chisholm's key contention, then, is that these "self-justifying" beliefs, judgments, or claims form the foundation of all of our empirical knowledge. As he puts it, spelling out the metaphor of foundations:

[A'] Every statement which we are justified in thinking that we know, is justified in part by some statement that justifies itself (129).

[B'] There are statements about appearances that thus justify themselves (129).

---

[5] It should be noted that here Chisholm has in mind what he calls the "non-comparative" sense of "appears," where what is at issue is the characterization of the intrinsic quality of my sensory experience, not a characterization of how it compares to how standard white and rectangular things look.

He rejects the claim that *only* statements about appearances justify themselves, claiming that statements about certain other psychological states can do so as well (137–139), but he also asserts that "the only empirical 'basic statements'... are certain psychological statements about oneself" (82). He thus proposes a conception on which all of our knowledge of the world rests on a base of "self-justifying" judgments about our own psychological states, thereby offering a version of the Global Priority Thesis.

Chisholm sometimes presents his argument as if it concerned the need to avert the threat of a regress of justification.[6] However, we can isolate a central contention of Chisholm's argument from any such considerations. What Chisholm offers, most fundamentally, is a *contrast* and a *claim*.

Contrast:

(a) There are some beliefs which are such that if you are asked, "What reason do you have to think you know that *p*?," you can come up with other considerations that look like a plausible response, other things that you could plausibly say.

(b) There are other beliefs which are such that when asked, "What reason do you have to think you know that *p*?," it seems that there is nothing plausible to be done but to repeat the very thing that you believe, and doing so seems to provide an adequate answer to the question.

Claim:

(c) For each belief of type (a), there is a chain of possible, plausible answers leading to a belief of type (b). That is, for each belief of type (a) that does not immediately lead to a belief of type (b), repeatedly asking the question about each plausible response will yield a structure depicted in the following diagram, ultimately leading to a point where a belief of type (b) can plausibly be appealed to as at least part of an answer.

---

[6] He writes, for instance:
  When we reach a statement having the property just referred to—an experiential statement such that to describe its evidence "would simply mean to repeat the experiential statement itself"—we have reached a proper stopping place in the process of justification (136).

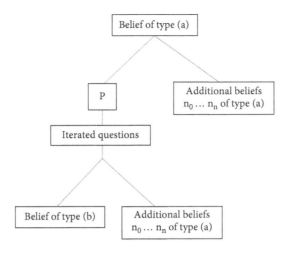

Let us grant for the sake of argument that Chisholm is right about both the contrast and the claim.[7] Would this support the Global Epistemic Priority Thesis?

I think not, for two main reasons.

First, in order to support the Global Priority Thesis, Chisholm's claim would have to reveal something about what is evidentially fundamental in relation to the belief of type (a) with which we started. But in fact the answers to Chisholm's question do not dictate any claims about "evidential fundamentality" at all. When asked what reason I have to think I know "there lies a key," I might quite reasonably reply, "I see the key" (Chisholm 1982, 135). That doesn't mean that "I see the key" is more evidentially ultimate than "there lies a key;" for instance, it is hardly obvious that we now must reconstruct my knowledge as a structure in which "there lies a key" is derived as conclusion from "I see the key," which appears as an earlier premise, or even as a structure in which "there lies a key" "gets its warrant" from an antecedent warrant that I have for "I see the key." In any ordinary sense of relations of evidential fundamentality, we can't read such relations directly off of the relations provided by acceptable answers to Chisholm's question.

Second, suppose that we waive that point and concede for the sake of argument that for each belief of type (a), there is at least one belief of type (b) that is

---

[7] Whether he is in fact right could be (and has been) challenged on the ground that you could in principle appeal to considerations about the world as part of an explanation of what justifies you in thinking you know that you believe that Socrates is mortal, that it appears to you as if there is a white rectangle in front of you, etc. For instance, you might appeal to considerations about how you behave or are disposed to behave. I want to leave such objections to one side, however, and focus on what Chisholm's contrast would show.

more evidentially fundamental in the following sense: part of our evidential base for that particular belief of type (a) is pointed at by some "self-justifying" belief of type (b). Even if that is granted, it doesn't provide a motivation for the Global Priority Thesis. This is because the Global Priority Thesis must make a *global* claim about a justifying or evidential relation holding between all beliefs of type (a) as a group and beliefs of type (b) as a group. The concession we just considered doesn't establish any such thing. To think otherwise is to slide too quickly from a point about *each* belief of type (a) and its relation to some belief of type (b), to the conclusion that *all* beliefs of type (a) *as a group* stand in precisely that same relation to a group of beliefs comprising only beliefs of type (b). This simply does not follow.

It might initially seem otherwise when we first look at a diagram like the one above. It might seem that we should be able to do the following: First, repeat that diagram for each of the beliefs $n_0 \ldots n_n$ of type (a) that appear on it, and so on for all the further beliefs of type (a) that appear; then, connect all the diagrams together, thereby creating a single giant diagram in which all beliefs of type (a) ultimately lead to only beliefs of type (b) at the bottom of the diagram. But there is nothing in the above diagram that guarantees that this can be done. We could accept that the above diagram captures a truth and yet perfectly compatibly hold that the diagram cannot be repeated and combined into one big diagram in the imagined way. To think otherwise is to make a logical mistake.

Here is a way to make this point more concrete. The claim we conceded above (for the sake of argument) is perfectly compatible with the following possibility: in *each particular case* in which the claim of type (a) is appropriately inferable from or based upon some claim of type (b), *there is some other claim of type (a) that plays a crucial role as well and upon which the target item of knowledge depends for its status as knowledge*. If that were so, then the Global Priority Thesis would be false. So, denial of the Global Priority Thesis is perfectly compatible with any reasonable claim about evidential fundamentality that could arise from Chisholm's contrast.

This isn't merely a hypothetical possibility. For instance, consider the relation between "It looks to me like there is a key here in front of me" and "There is a key here." To speak from within the commitments of ordinary life: If on a particular occasion I had no view at all about whether how things appear here and now is a good guide to how things are, I wouldn't base a belief about the latter on the former. Instead, I'd say something like, "Well, I don't know if it can be relied upon, but it sure looks like there is a key here." So when I claim that there is a key here on the basis of how things look, I rely upon other considerations about the world: I rely on background considerations about the reliability of how things look here and now. But if considerations about the world are involved in this way in every case—and Chisholm's contrast does nothing to show they aren't—then even if it is true that for each item of knowledge in Chisholm's first class some item of knowledge in Chisholm's second class is evidentially more fundamental, the Global Priority Thesis still will not be true.

The logical/structural point that I have been making is evident when we think carefully about the structure captured by Chisholm's Claim (again, see the diagram above). And a close reading suggests that Chisholm may in fact have recognized this. For when Chisholm restates the key theses of his foundationalism, he writes:

[A'] Every statement, which we are justified in thinking that we know, is justified *in part* by some statement that justifies itself (1982, 129, italics added).

That crucial phrase "in part" indicates that Chisholm recognizes that he has in fact done *nothing* to motivate the thought that the totality of all of our beliefs about the world must rest entirely upon some other basis, such that we could start from nothing but that more limited basis and still acceptably reason our way to our view of the world. It's possible that here he wasn't aiming to defend the full-blown Global Priority Thesis after all.

6. Can We Be Wrong About Our Evidence?

Hobbes reportedly quipped that "the inn of evidence has no signboard" (cited by Chisholm 1957, 34).[8] Here we see denial of a thought that is often

---

[8] It is very unlikely that Hobbes is the actual source of this delightful saying. Chisholm quotes it several times over many years, admitting in later publications that he has been unable to locate the source in Hobbes. He takes the quote from Coffey, who writes only, "Hobbes has said somewhere that 'the inn of evidence has no signboard,'" without giving any reference (Coffey, 2009, p. 146 fn. 1; reprinted from Coffey, 1917). In fact, the source appears to be Helvetius, who wrote critically of Descartes "not having placed a sign ... at the inn of evidence" (*De l'esprit: or, Essays on the mind, and its several faculties, Tr. from the edition printed under the author's inspection* [London, 1759], p. 3, note e). Multiple online French sources attribute a similar quip to Leibniz without citation: for instance, "Leibniz qui reprochait à Descartes d'avoir logé la vérité à l'auberge de l'évidence, mais d'avoir négligé de nous en donner l'adresse" (Tenaillon, 2013; see also Spire, 2012). A related attribution to Leibniz appears in Jean-Luc Nancy. However, Nancy gives no references, and to my knowledge there is no

closely allied with the Global Priority Thesis: that we are always in a position to tell what our evidence is or whether we have adequate evidence. Chisholm articulated this thought particularly clearly. He asserted that "whenever a man [sic] has adequate evidence for some proposition or hypothesis, he is in a state which constitutes a *mark of evidence* for that proposition or hypothesis" (1957, 34), by which he meant a state or condition of the person which:

(1) "could be described . . . without using any other epistemic term" (34),
(2) is "such that S could not make any mistake at any time about his [sic] *being* in that state or condition at that time" (35), and
(3) is "such that, whenever S is in that state or condition, S has adequate evidence for *h*" (35).

The result is the view that when a person has adequate evidence for a proposition at a given time, that fact "is capable of being directly evident to that [person] at that time" (1982, 75).

Requirements of this sort have indeed featured prominently in epistemology at least since Descartes. Noticeably, however, this conception does not seem to be a commitment of our ordinary position. To speak from within the ordinary position, the unfortunate color of my plants provides excellent evidence that they need water. However, their sorry state is not something about which I cannot make a mistake, nor is it a fact about me. Moreover, there is *no* state or condition of myself which (a) I cannot be mistaken about and (b) guarantees that I have this evidence. Of course, this fact about my plants can't provide me with evidence that my plants need water unless I am in some sort of appropriate relation to it. Maybe I need to know about it, for instance. But again, that I know that my plants are turning brown isn't something about which I can't make a mistake. It is something that I could get

---

evidence that Leibniz ever said this. There are other references of various sorts to Descartes and "the inn of evidence" in publications from the eighteenth century. For instance, a text on venereal diseases titled *Observations pratiques, rares et curieuses, sur divers accidents vénériens [et] autres qui leur sont relatifs: pour servir de supplément au Mémoire clinique sur les maladies vénériennes* (1783) contains the comment "A certain person named Descartes doesn't—as is often said—locate his opinions in the Hotel of Evidence" ("Quoique personne, a dit Descartes, n'ait encore loge son opinion à l'Hôtel d l'evidence . . ."). It is unclear whether such phrases were "in the air" and picked up by Helvetius, or whether Helvetius is the originator of the phrase. I am grateful to Kate Abramson, Victor Caston, and Tito Magri for historical guidance on this matter, and especially to Victor Caston for finding the Helvetius quotation, to Kate Abramson for checking the Hobbes corpus, and to Tito Magri and Kate Abramson for checking the attribution to Leibniz.

wrong: people often wrongly think that they know things. So there is nothing here that indicates any commitment to Chisholm's demands.

What (it might be asked) about my *belief* that my plants have turned an unfortunate color? Suppose we grant for the sake of argument that I can't make a mistake about whether I have this belief. Even so, my belief doesn't guarantee that I actually have this evidence. For whether the color of my plants is in fact adequate evidence that they need water depends on *the actual state of my plants*, and that is not something that is guaranteed by the fact that I have this belief.[9] Again, there is nothing here that indicates a commitment to Chisholm's demands.

In fact, our ordinary epistemic position involves commitment to the possibility that I can have adequate evidence for the truth of p even if there are certain cases in which I would inevitably get wrong whether I have this evidence. To take an example from Chapter 7: As things stand, I have excellent evidence that neither ducks nor dung beetles are engaged in an undetectable conspiracy to shape the course of human history to their own ends. (My evidence includes such things as this: dung beetles lack the cognitive and cooperative capacities required for anything of the sort.) But if such a deception *were* going on, I could have no way to detect it; as a result, I'd unavoidably go wrong about what my evidence is: I would think I have excellent evidence against this scenario, but I would be wrong. This is the lesson of evidential asymmetry (Chapter 7, Section 7). It conflicts with Chisholm's demand that to have adequate evidence, you must be in a corresponding state or condition that guarantees that you have this evidence and is such that you "could not make any mistake at any time about . . . *being* in that state or condition at that time." There is no such state or condition in this case.

Chisholm offers one argument in favor of his conception. He claims that requirement (2), that the state or condition in question must be one about which one could make no mistake, is required, "If we are to formulate our second requirement in 'epistemically neutral' language [as demanded by requirement 1]" (1957, 35). However, this is simply not so. If we allow that someone can be wrong about whether they have adequate evidence, then we allow that the relevant states or conditions are things one can get wrong. It doesn't follow that we have to appeal to "knowing," "discovering," "finding

---

[9] The argument here depends on the thought that p cannot provide evidence for anything unless it is true. I argue that this is a commitment of our ordinary position in Chapter 5. For further discussion, see my 2013.

out about," or anything else epistemic in order to characterize those states or conditions.

For instance, we could state something with the form of Chisholm's principles of evidence by saying that having an experience in which something looks blue in the "comparative sense"—that is, looks to you the way blue things characteristically look—is a mark that you have adequate evidence that the thing is blue. Importantly, this is a state or condition about which you could be mistaken. But whatever the defects of this proposal as part of a theory of evidence, it cannot be charged with relying on epistemic terms in order to characterize the relevant state or condition, since on Chisholm's own account "appears" in the "comparative sense" is non-epistemic (1957, 45). So, Chisholm's argument fails; the restriction to states or conditions characterized in "epistemically neutral" terms doesn't force anything like Chisholm's requirement that the state or condition must be one that the person could not make a mistake about. Chisholm has thus done nothing to show that requirement (2) is part of our ordinary epistemic commitments.

Here some readers might be inclined to point out that evidence is supposed to be something that we can use to *guide* our beliefs, and it might be inchoately felt that such a thing must be something about which we can't go wrong. But no such requirement in fact follows. I can be wrong about what my income is, but considerations about my income can still guide my decisions about how much to pay in taxes. The same goes for forming or revising beliefs: considerations about the world can perfectly well guide me in forming beliefs about the world, if we consider each on a case-by-case basis. Things might seem otherwise, I suspect, only because one has in mind the thought that evidence must be available to guide us in forming beliefs about the world from a position in which we have put all of our commitments about the world on hold. But that is to assume precisely the perspective that needs to be motivated.

The idea that we can't be wrong about our evidence is not merely a historical curiosity. It is a focus of prominent contemporary discussion. Timothy Williamson, for instance, has also argued against conceptions of evidence like Chisholm's. He traces a purely phenomenal conception of evidence to the thought that rational thinkers are always in a position to know what their evidence is, which he formalizes as:

For any appropriate property π, in any case in which one's evidence has π, one knows that one's evidence has π. (2000, 171)

This latter principle, he argues, is incorrect, because we can argue from it to a clearly false conclusion using a sorites-like argument that parallels his well-known "anti-luminosity" argument (which aims to establish that one is not always in a position to know that one is in a mental state such as feeling cold [95])). The result, as he puts it, is that "*Whatever* evidence is, one is not always in a position to know what one has of it" (179).

I am in agreement with where Williamson ends up, since I hold that we can have adequate evidence that *p* even if there are possible cases in which we would incorrectly think—unavoidably so—that we have this evidence even though we don't. My argument does not depend on Williamson's, however, and it is of a fundamentally different sort. My argument, in summary, is this: The examples appealed to in Chapters 6 and 7 reveal that a central consequence of the commitments of the ordinary position is that we cannot always know what evidence we have or what it supports. If it were true that ducks rule the world through an undetectable conspiracy and deception, we would be perfectly reasonable in incorrectly thinking that the evidence shows that ducks can do no such thing. We would have no way to find out that we are wrong about this. These are not cases of *irrationality* in any ordinary sense. So rational thinkers are not always in a position to know what their evidence is or what it supports. Since nothing has been done to show that the ordinary position also commits us to the idea that evidence must be something about which we cannot make a mistake, and since that idea runs contrary to how we think about evidence in our ordinary practice, that idea is no way to motivate the Global Epistemic Priority Thesis from within our ordinary epistemic position.

To sum up the discussion so far: The Global Epistemic Priority Thesis frequently figures in epistemological discussions as though it is a piece of pretheoretical common sense. In fact, however, even those historical epistemologists who have been most concerned to defend it have failed to root it in the commitments of our ordinary, pre-philosophical position. Why, then, does it appear so persistently as an unquestioned backdrop in debates about skepticism? Perhaps it is simply a dogma that has acquired a truistic air through constant repetition, an unmotivated framing assumption that has taken on a life of its own.

11
Seeking an Argument I
Regress Arguments and the Global Priority Thesis

I have suggested that it is merely an accident of history that the Global Priority Thesis routinely figures in the epistemological literature as an unarticulated presupposition in discussions of skepticism. We've seen what our predecessors had to say in its support, and it was not convincing. However, the literature contains one important line of thought that we need to consider. Contemporary foundationalists, prominently Fumerton (1995) and Bonjour (2003), have appealed to justificatory regresses to support key aspects of the Global Priority Thesis. Chisholm did so as well. However, few epistemologists have thought carefully about the relation between regress arguments and our ordinary epistemic commitments and practice. That is where we have to focus for the purposes of this inquiry, insofar as our goal is to determine whether the Global Priority Thesis arises from the commitments of our ordinary, pre-philosophical position.

To approach this question it is useful to distinguish two forms of justificatory regress: dialectical and structural (Audi, 1993). The dialectical regress is generated by imagining someone who persistently requests reasons in support of an initial claim, further reasons in support of those reasons, and so on. The structural regress, by contrast, focuses upon structural requirements pertaining to knowledge or justified belief. Since the dialectical regress purports to arise from features of justificatory practice, I will begin with it.

1. The Dialectical Regress as an Argument for the Global Priority Thesis

The suggestion here is that when we imagine conversation with a persistent interlocutor, we see that in order to avoid both objectionable circularity and an infinite regress, we must find a stopping point in beliefs where the only reasonable answer is to repeat what we have just said. When we do that, we point to the very state or condition the belief is about in order to identify a reason for the belief. The argument for the Global Epistemic Priority Thesis is complete if it can then be shown that when it comes to our beliefs about the world, these justificatory stopping points always concern some other subject matter, particularly certain psychological states.

This argument faces a fundamental difficulty, given the goal of motivating the Global Priority Thesis from within our ordinary standpoint: the persistent, reiterated demand for justifying reasons is not motivated by our actual justificatory practice.

A request for justifying reasons sometimes functions as a challenge to the speaker's knowledge or reasonableness. When issued under appropriate circumstances (as when there is reason to doubt the truth of what has been said or to think the speaker lacks knowledge or good reasons for their belief), such a challenge requires a response: the speaker is required to offer reasons in support of their belief or to address the doubts or (putative) reasons for doubt that have been raised. It isn't acceptable—from within the terms of a sincere justificatory conversation—simply to repudiate the demand for reasons in such cases. Suppose for, instance, that I tell you my mother is very sick, and you—who saw her quite recently and thought she was fine—ask me why I say this. It wouldn't be acceptable for me to respond, "Don't be ridiculous." I might instead say something like, "I talked with her on the phone last night, and she said her doctor informed her she has cancer." In such cases the doubts or putative reasons for doubt provide shape and direction for the justificatory conversation. They determine what sorts of considerations the speaker can acceptably appeal to and what sorts of concerns must be allayed.

Importantly, however, not every belief about the world is—here and now—appropriately challenged in such a way. For instance, imagine that the above conversation continues as follows. You, with no reason whatsoever for doubt, try to issue a justificatory challenge by asking, "But what reason did you have to think it was your mother?" This is at best a lame joke offered at a bad time. There might be things that I could say about my reasons for thinking it was my mother, but I am not required by the very structure of justificatory conversations to provide them. It would be perfectly appropriate for me to repudiate the challenge, for instance by saying, "Don't be ridiculous. There's no reason to think it wasn't my mother." The attempted dialectical regress thus fizzles out.

Such examples show that the kinds of cases in which justificatory challenges appropriately arise and require justificatory responses are special.

These cases consequently do not reveal justificatory requirements applying to our beliefs in general. Chisholm notes this limitation and consequently clarifies that we are to understand the persistent request for reasons differently. Rather than offering a challenge, the question is "Socratic" in nature, as he puts it; it "presupposes that we *are* justified . . . and what it seeks to elicit is the nature of this justification" (1982, 131).

Sometimes Chisholm's form of the question is perfectly intelligible in ordinary life. If I tell you that hostas can be divided so long as there is one stem-bud on each root-division, you can reasonably ask for my evidence even if you have no doubts or reasons for doubt and you just want to learn something. It would be inappropriate—and wouldn't even make clear sense—if I were to respond by saying, "Don't be ridiculous. There is no reason to think hostas can't be divided in this way." I can reasonably be expected to answer your question: I learned it last night from Monty Don on the BBC's *Gardener's World*. Here, my belief is buttressed by something like a linear argument from evidence to conclusion (even if it may not be exactly that), and I can reasonably be expected to be able to provide my reasons to a curious interlocutor upon request.

Not every case requires this sort of answer, however. For instance, to return to a key example from Chapter 9, suppose that someone asks, purporting just to be curious, "What is your reason for believing that you live in the United States? On what evidence or ground do you base this belief?" What would you really say if someone asked you this question in ordinary life? I would feel completely befuddled. I would think, "*My* reason? Do I have any consideration in particular singled out as 'my reason'?" It seems not, and there doesn't seem to be any reason why I should. In fact, the question seems bizarre. The correct thing to say in response, insofar as I take the request at all seriously, would be something like this:

> Well, there are lots of things that prove that I live in the US. But is there some reason to think that I am wrong and that I don't live in the US? If not, then I don't know what to say in response to your question. There is no reason to single out any of the myriad things that prove that I live in the US, nor to think that they all—taken together—somehow constitute my reason. If you are just inviting me to list some things that tell in favor of the claim that I live in the US, then I am happy to point to my driver's license, my passport, my experiences of leaving the country and returning, and so on. But I wouldn't want to point to any of those in particular as "my reason."

And if you are trying to get me to set up something like an argument from premises to conclusion, then it is quite unclear what its relevance or significance would be (or even what considerations would constrain such an attempt or render it anything other than arbitrary), since I didn't arrive at this belief via anything like an argument from premises to conclusion. All told, then, unless you give me some reason for doubt, the right way for me to respond is to refuse to play along. There are tons of things that tell decisively in favor of my living in the US and there is no reason to doubt it—and that's all there is to say at this point in our conversation. Of course, if you could point to some reason to think I might be going wrong, I'd be happy to address it.

This is a case in which the persistent request for "your reasons," understood as Chisholm proposes to understand it, is weird and out of place, and we recognize it as such. To offer anything in particular as "my reason"—or even to say, "All of that"—is to take a further step than our practice calls for. It is part of our ordinary practice that *this* request, in these circumstances, is appropriately repudiated.

In short, then, our practice involves a distinction between two kinds of cases: those in which the request is in order, and those in which it is properly repudiated. It is very implausible to say that *it is part of the practice* to assume that there is nonetheless a similar sort of structure underlying them. Nothing in the practice pushes toward assimilating them in this way. I say: let's take all of this at face value.

Since the 1960s it has been fashionable to reject this sort of argument on the ground that relevant aspects of the practice are shaped by extraneous matters of practicality, convenience, and the like (Grice 1989, Stroud 1984). One might be inclined to make a similar move here, suggesting that though in both cases you are required to meet the request, in the latter case we ignore this requirement for reasons of mere convenience or utility. But if that were so, we shouldn't be baffled by the question and feel that it is entirely unclear what we should say even when we have lifted any practical constraints that might be operative; rather, we should feel that it is clear what should be said, but that it isn't worth asking or bothering about. You might think, "Well, maybe the very difficulty of the question in the second case, and the unclarity of how to answer it, are the reasons why we ignore it as a matter of practical utility. It isn't worth bothering about, and so we ignore it." But this is to let the tail wag the dog. The question was whether anything in the practice warrants or even encourages assimilating the two cases. The current proposal assumes that they should be assimilated and then tries to explain away the surface features of the practice on the basis of that assumption.

As a matter of fact, such suggestions don't fit the practice in another way as well. We can point to something clearly relevant—epistemically relevant— that distinguishes the two cases. Given how I arrived at the belief about hostas, there *is* something in particular that is my reason for the belief, something that can be pointed to as something like the premise for an argument to a conclusion. We all recognize that this is the sort of case about which something like this is properly expected. Matters are very different when it comes to my belief that I live in the United States. I didn't arrive at this belief in anything like that sort of way (though I recognize all sorts of things that tell in favor of it), and everyone recognizes perfectly well that this is so. In the absence of doubt or reasons for doubt, it is out of place to request "my reasons" in a case of this sort. And in a conversation with a child who doesn't yet understand that I didn't arrive at this belief through anything like a linear argument, the right thing to do would be to explain to the child more about how the world and our justificatory practice actually work. This would be part of teaching the child that repeatedly asking a question to the effect of "And what's your reason for believing that?" isn't always the correct way to proceed.

Here, then, is a rough and ready characterization of how the practice actually works.

> The request for justification—when offered in the spirit of a challenge—is in order in certain circumstances and not in others. In some circumstances it is properly repudiated. Likewise, the request for "your reasons," for the reasons on which you base your belief—when motivated simply by "Socratic" curiosity—is in order in certain circumstances but not in others. With regard to both, the requests are sometimes out of order, and are properly repudiated, because of certain aspects of the epistemic situation. In those cases, the request for justification hits context-specific stopping points. On some occasions, these include considerations about the world.

If that characterization is correct so far as it goes, then we can't get a justificatory regress started from within our ordinary epistemic practice by imagining a reiterated, persistent request for justification. Far from motivating this route to the Global Priority Thesis, our ordinary epistemic practice cuts it off at the knees.

So far I have focused on justificatory challenges and on the request for "your reasons" or "your evidence," but the same lesson applies even regarding the repeated request, "What reason is there to believe that?" Here too there are points at which the request for further reasons is properly repudiated. For instance, imagine that you are a detective trying to solve a particularly puzzling murder with your team. You recount the available evidence, listing everyone who was in a position to fire the deadly shot. At this point, an intern—someone with all the usual background knowledge that we all share—says, "Wait—you're assuming that the dog didn't pull the trigger." You resist the temptation to blurt out, "Don't be ridiculous!" and instead ask, "Is there any reason to think that the dog pulled the trigger? Is there any reason to think the dog would even have been *able* to fire the gun?" The intern replies, "No. But it's possible. I just want to play devil's advocate. What reason is there to think the dog didn't pull the trigger?" Of course there are reasons you could offer in response, but at this point there is no requirement that you do so. The request is quite properly dismissed. In fact, the intern's response is bizarre; if anyone is failing to engage properly in rational discourse and inquiry, it seems to be the intern. "Okay, I think we can move on. The dog didn't pull the trigger. Again, here is who was in a position to shoot the victim . . ." Notably, this response is perfectly appropriate even if you have all the time in the world and no other practical exigencies bear on the case.

Michael Rescorla (2009) has argued that I reach the wrong verdict regarding cases of this sort. He maintains that even in such cases "the norms of reasoned discourse" require the speaker to provide reasons in support of their claim when asked. He thus denies that the structure of rational discourse blocks the regressive request for reasons in the way I have suggested.

To make this case, Rescorla has to walk a fine line. He acknowledges that something seems to be going wrong in a case like the intern's. If an interlocutor hasn't offered (and doesn't have) any reasons in support of the request, the interlocutor is behaving deviantly in asking the speaker to provide reasons in defense of a claim when all parties recognize that there is every reason to believe the claim and no reason to doubt it. Moreover, a speaker behaves perfectly reasonably in not defending the claim in response to this sort of unmotivated request. Rescorla claims, however, that this "interlocutor-deviance" and "speaker-immunity" can be explained away: these features of the practice don't show that the speaker isn't required to provide reasons in support of their claim when asked.

Rescorla's proposed explanation makes use of a key background idea. He claims that rational discourse aims at what he calls "rapprochement": the identification of "mutually acceptable premises relevant to the truth of disputed propositions" (96). This is a "constitutive goal" of the activity, he claims, in the same sense that winning is a constitutive goal of tennis. You can play tennis without aiming to win, but insofar as you do so you are playing deviantly. Similarly, "someone who fails to pursue *rapprochement* engages deviantly in reasoned discourse" (98).

Here, then, is Rescorla's explanatory strategy. Suppose that all parties recognize that there is every reason to believe the asserted proposition and no reason to doubt. If, in such a case, the interlocutor challenges the speaker to defend the claim and gives no reasons in support of the challenge, then the speaker is left with "no idea which premises [the interlocutor] will leave unchallenged" (100). In this way, the interlocutor subverts the goal of *rapprochement*, because the speaker is prevented from determining what premises might be mutually acceptable. The interlocutor thus behaves deviantly, but the deviance does not lie in the request for further reasons. Rescorla puts it this way:

> The challenger must elucidate his position, thereby helping the original speaker isolate the relevant mutually acceptable premises which *rapprochement* requires. . . . The challenger assumes an obligation to help the original speaker fulfil *his* obligation. The former obligation is parasitic upon the latter. Speaker and challenger must jointly pursue argumentative common ground, the speaker by isolating premises that support his position, the challenger by elucidating which premises he might accept or reject. The speaker's obligation persists even if the challenger does not provide the requisite assistance. (2009, 100–101)

"Interlocutor-deviance" is thus explained in a way that preserves the claim that the speaker is required to provide reasons in defense of their claim when asked. On this proposal the interlocutor's behavior is indeed deviant in these cases, but the failing arises not because the interlocutor demands reasons when the speaker is not required to provide them, but rather because the interlocutor leaves the speaker unable to determine what premises might be mutually acceptable.

What then of "speaker immunity"? Here Rescorla proposes that the key issue is the speaker's vulnerability: "to answer an interlocutor's challenge is to risk further challenges" (101). Faced with an interlocutor who requests reasons for my claim that the dog didn't pull the trigger, a claim that is extremely well confirmed for both of us, I will "naturally worry" (102) that any premises I appeal to will be equally met with requests for reasons. I will see little hope of finding *rapprochement* and will be concerned to avoid "digging myself deeper into the dialectical hole" by accumulating a larger stock of undefended claims (102). Rescorla urges that these concerns make it reasonable for me to leave my claim undefended. Moreover, he maintains that even though this move violates rational discourse's structuring norms, "it flows from my desire to avoid accumulating undischarged dialectical commitments, a desire which reflects internal features of dialectical interaction" (101). As he sums up, "in suitable circumstances, an interlocutor should promote *rapprochement* by indicating which premises he might accept. When the interlocutor provides no such indication, then the speaker's most reasonable choice may be dogmatic illicit insistence" (102).

This attempt to explain away the surface features of the practice fails on several points.

First, Rescorla's explanation of "speaker immunity" builds on the idea that "A speaker's refusal to defend a premise seems more reasonable the more likely his interlocutor seems to challenge any additional assertions" (103). This is not true. Consider a speaker who is flying in the face of the evidence and basing their argument on a manifestly false claim (e.g., that the 2020 US election was stolen through massive electoral fraud). If I were in conversation with such a person, I would think it wholly unreasonable for them to refuse to provide reasons in support of this claim merely on the ground that I would challenge any further assertions they might make to attempt to support it. Such behavior might be *prudentially* reasonable in a certain sense. However, the person is behaving quite unreasonably as a participant in rational discourse, and the problem stems from the fact that they are radically failing to take proper stock of the relevant evidence.

Second, the "reasonableness" of the refusal to provide reasons in response to the intern's request in my earlier example seems to be something quite different. It does not appear to be merely a form of *prudential* reasonableness when a speaker moves on rather than accede to an unmotivated request for reasons in support of a claim that everyone acknowledges there's every reason to believe and no reason to doubt.

Third, Rescorla's attempted explanation of speaker immunity appeals to a claim about *why* speakers behave as they do in such cases. But just to speak for myself, this explanation gets my motives quite wrong. When I dismiss the request for reasons for thinking that the dog didn't pull the trigger, I don't do so out of "desire to avoid accumulating undischarged dialectical commitments." I do so because the interlocutor is behaving like an idiot.

Finally, Rescorla's attempted explanation of "interlocutor deviance" fails as well. The problem with the intern's behavior is not that the intern failed to make clear what premises they might accept. For instance, suppose that the intern clarified: "I want you to provide reasons that would be acceptable to a member of the Dog Doubters Society of America"—a group that (let's imagine) holds that dogs strategically hide their abilities and kill over 25,000 Americans every year in concealed acts of gun violence. This clarification doesn't help matters at all, given that the Dog Doubters hold manifestly false views and the intern agrees that there is no evidence whatsoever in support of the suggestion that the dog pulled the trigger. Contra Rescorla, therefore, the problem in the initial version of the example isn't that the interlocutor has demanded reasons without specifying what premises might be acceptable: the interlocutor's request continues to be deviant even when such specification is provided. The problem is rather that the interlocutor is demanding reasons in an epistemic context in which none need to be provided.

Given these considerations, I conclude that Rescorla has given us no good reason not to take the surface of our practice at face value. Even when participating in rational discourse and inquiry, and even if we bracket considerations of practicality, politeness, and the like, we are not always required to provide reasons for our beliefs when asked.

Objection can arise from another direction, however. We do, after all, have reasons that support the claim that the dog didn't pull the trigger. We can point to considerations that quite decisively tell in its favor. So imagine a situation in which we just want to make everything explicit. In this situation, nothing precludes us from stating those reasons. This isn't *forbidden* by our ordinary position. But then it looks as though nothing prevents us from doing the same thing again, and so on. Regress initiated—or so it might seem.

Notice, however, that if *all* we want to do is make explicit what tells in favor of the truth of a given claim, then the range of acceptable answers is no longer structured in the way that the envisioned regress requires. Suppose that all I am doing is stating what reasons there are to believe various things, what considerations tell in favor of their truth. Then—to return to an earlier example—I can point out that the fact that I am on my university's graduate faculty is a reason to believe that I am entitled to supervise PhD dissertations, and I can also point out that the fact that I am entitled to supervise PhD dissertations is a reason to believe that I am on my university's graduate faculty. I am not thereby guilty of some sort of objectionable circularity, for what I have said is quite simply *true*. Each of these considerations does tell decisively in favor of the other; each is a reason to believe the other. That is to say: The simple desire to state the reasons that there are in favor of believing various claims does not force a demand for a linear ordering of the kind that is needed if one hopes to generate a regress argument for the Global Priority Thesis from within our ordinary position.

Here's the upshot. As we have seen earlier, it is part of the ordinary practice that the requisite ordering relation does get imposed in certain epistemic contexts. However, it is also part of the practice that in those contexts the demand for supporting reasons terminates. One can't appropriately just go on repeatedly asking "And what reason is there to believe that?", using the question in a way that requires a non-circular ordering. To get a dialectical regress argument going from within the ordinary position, then, what would be needed is a perfectly ordinary sort of request for reasons that both generates a demand for a non-circular ordering *and* is not properly repudiated at certain points. But that's not how the practice works. To get both, one has to take a kind of request that is in order in certain epistemic contexts precisely because of particular features of those contexts, and then one has to apply it beyond those contexts even while also trying to retain exactly the significance that it has in them. One has to stand with one foot inside the ordinary practice and one foot outside it. That won't yield an argument for the Global Priority Thesis from within the ordinary position.

One last move needs to be considered. Someone might say, "Look, this is what I want: I want a vindication of my beliefs that provides an adequate, non-circular argument in defense of a target belief, of each belief appealed to in that defense, and so on. That desire is enough to get the regress started." Of course, this desire sets up a project that might well lead one to think that the only satisfactory overall vindication will have to take the form envisioned by the Global Priority Thesis. But in order for this project actually to yield the Global Priority Thesis, one also needs to answer this question: why think that what happens when you engage in this project shows anything of importance about the structure of reasons/evidence-relations relevant to our knowledge of the world? Crucially, our ordinary position doesn't involve a commitment to any such thought. From the vantage point of our ordinary position, the restrictions involved in this project are no less arbitrary epistemically than a demand to vindicate our other beliefs only on the basis of things learned on Tuesdays.

So much, then, for the attempt to use a "dialectical" regress to generate an argument for the Global Priority Thesis from within our ordinary position.

2. Structural Regresses as an Argument for the Global Priority Thesis

Let us turn now to the possibility of a "structural" justificatory regress generated by necessary conditions of knowledge or justified belief. One might, for instance, begin by noting that many instances of knowledge or justified belief are based on an adequate reason, ground, or evidence, where the basing relation at issue involves certain structural features that render circularity unacceptable. One might then generalize and think that for any given belief to count as knowledge or as justified, it must be based on an adequate reason, ground, or evidence. To avoid the seeming improbability of an infinite justificatory sequence, one might then seek non-belief states upon which one's beliefs about the world might ultimately be based—such as, for instance, experiential states. And in this way one might find oneself led to the Global Epistemic Priority Thesis.

Here we can be brief. For reasons highlighted in Chapter 9, our ordinary epistemic position provides no motivation for this line of thought. In particular, nothing in our ordinary position supports the demand that to be justified or to count as knowledge, each of my beliefs must stand in a particular position in a total system of dependency relations with the structural/relational features required by a regress argument.

To take just one example, consider again my belief that I live in the United States. There is no reason to think that I couldn't know this, or that this belief couldn't be justified, unless there is some set of considerations upon which I currently base it. Of course, I recognize all sorts of true considerations that tell decisively in favor of the truth of the claim that I live in the United States, and I couldn't know that I live in the US unless I knew those other things. There are truths that are—as I recognize—excellent reason to believe that I live in the US. But that doesn't require this belief to be currently based on any or all of those considerations. Our practice is perfectly compatible with the thought that (to put it roughly) it is enough that I know those other things, recognize that they tell decisively in favor of the claim that I live in the United States, recognize that there is no reason to doubt that this belief is correct, and don't hold this belief out of wishful thinking or in some other bad way. Moreover, as we saw in the previous chapter, it is very implausible that there is any one single, overarching argument-like structure amongst my beliefs here. Without that idea of a single, overarching, argument-like structure in which this belief has its place, however, there is no hope of generating a structural regress argument for the Global Epistemic Priority Thesis.

Careless usage of the term "inferential justification" can foster confusion on this point. Richard Fumerton, for instance, offers a regress argument for a form of experiential foundationalism. As he characterizes the view, if there are to be any justified beliefs at all, there must be "noninferentially justified beliefs," defined as follows: "A belief is noninferentially justified if its justification does not consist in the having of any other beliefs" (1995, 56). The core of his argument is this:

> If all justification were inferential, then to be justified in believing some proposition P I would need to infer it from some other proposition E1. According to the first clause of the principle of inferential justification [a principle which Fumerton endorses], I would be justified in believing P on the basis of E1 only if I were justified in believing E1. But if all justification were inferential, I would be justified in believing E1 only if I believed it on the basis of something else, E2, which I justifiably believe on the basis of something else, E3, ... and so on..." (56)

Taking it that we cannot complete an infinitely long chain of reasoning and that circular reasoning cannot yield justified beliefs, Fumerton concludes there must be some noninferentially justified beliefs, in the sense of beliefs whose justification "does not consist in the having of any other beliefs." This then pushes him toward a version of the Global Priority Thesis.

However, Fumerton's conclusion (that there must be some beliefs whose justification "does not consist in the having of any other beliefs") does not follow from the considerations in the passage quoted above. Fumerton's argument makes use of the notion of "inferring" in the *ordinary* sense of that term: reasoning from a premise to a conclusion in such a way that one comes to believe the conclusion on the basis of the premise. This is what is relevant when it is said that as finite beings, we cannot complete infinitely long chains of reasoning and that circular reasoning cannot yield justified beliefs. So, the conclusion of the argument should only be that there must be some beliefs whose positive epistemic status does not depend on their having been *inferred from* or *based upon* any particular beliefs. That is not at all the same thing as Fumerton's foundationalist claim that there must be some beliefs whose justification "does not consist in the having of any other beliefs." For all Fumerton's argument shows, the belief that I live in the United States might stop the threat of the structural justificatory regress, even though its positive epistemic status constitutively depends upon my having a wide variety of other beliefs with positive epistemic status.[1]

It might be suggested that I am wrong to relate the idea of a structural regress to considerations about inference, reasoning, and what one actually bases one's belief upon. According to a familiar philosophical conception, there is a justificatory order amongst the propositions we believe, an order that holds quite independently of whether we have arrived at those beliefs through inference or reasoning. The thought is that if *we* are justified in believing as we do, it is because we hold our beliefs in a way that mirrors that order. The question then becomes pressing: what is the structure of this justificatory order? When one attempts to construct a theory to answer this question, it might seem that considerations about a regress can reveal something about its structure: since justificatory circles are unacceptable and an infinite series of reasons looks implausible, the structure must be foundationalist if we are to have any justification at all. That is, we seem driven to the thought that no justification is possible for beliefs about the world unless chains of justification can somehow terminate with experiential and other non-factive psychological states. In this way, then, one might find oneself led toward a version of the Global Priority Thesis.

But what is supposed to motivate the claim that there *is* such a justificatory order? I cannot see anything in the commitments of our ordinary practice that does so. I grant that we are committed to the thought that some things tell in favor of the truth of others quite independently of what we believe or how we have arrived at our beliefs. We are also committed to the idea that such relations constrain what count as good and bad ways of arriving at or defending beliefs through inference or argumentation in particular circumstances. But these relations, in themselves, do not have the structural

---

[1] For further discussion of regresses and Fumerton's Principle of Inferential Justification, see Leite 2008.

features that a regress argument requires. Our ordinary practice allows that *p*'s truth might tell decisively in favor of *q*, even as *q*'s truth might also tell quite decisively in favor of *p*. There is no "objectionable circularity" here. The relevant relations can run every which way amongst the propositions we believe, and there is nothing problematic about that.

Of course, when we engage in inference or offer an argument in support of a belief, we must proceed in linear fashion. That's part of how the practice works. And which proposition can properly be used as a premise for a particular inference, or offered as a reason in defense of believing another, will depend upon the broader epistemic situation and the particular circumstances at hand. These context-dependent constraints often depend upon considerations about the world. There is nothing here that indicates a commitment to the idea of an independent justificatory order in which all chains of justification for propositions about the world as a whole must bottom out only in sensory experiences and other mental states.

It might be suggested, to the contrary, that Jim Pryor has called attention to a notion of "having justification" that points in the needed direction. As he characterizes this notion, "You have justification to believe P iff you're in a position where it would be epistemically appropriate for you to believe P, a position where P is epistemically likely for you to be true" (2014, 203). So understood, you can "have justification" for believing P even if you don't in fact believe P. If we can identify priority relations that obtain with regard to "having justification," then this might seem to tell in favor of the conception of a justificatory order that could be used to support the Global Priority Thesis.

Pryor offers an example that might seem to support the idea of such priority relations.

> For some propositions, you have justification to believe them because other propositions you have justification to believe epistemically support them. For instance, suppose you look at the gas gauge of your car, and it appears to read "E." So you have justification to believe: (Gauge) The gas gauge reads "E." That, together with other things you justifiedly believe about your car, gives you justification to believe: (Gas) Your car is out of gas. (It's not important for our purposes whether you actually do believe (Gauge) or (Gas)....) In this example, your justification to believe (Gas) comes in part from the fact that you have justification to believe (Gauge). That is, having justification to believe the latter is part of what makes you have justification

to believe the former. The justification you have in this example to believe (Gauge) does not in the same way come from your having justification to believe (Gas). (One mark of this is that evidence that undercut your justification to believe (Gauge) would ipso facto undercut your justification to believe (Gas); but not vice versa.) When your justification to believe P comes in part from your having justification to believe other, supporting propositions, I'll say that those latter propositions mediate your justification to believe P. . . . When your justification to believe P does not come from your justification to believe other propositions, I'll call it immediate. (2014, 204)

The example is aimed at illustrating the idea of *mediate* justification by showing what is meant by saying, "your justification to believe P comes in part from your having justification to believe other, supporting propositions." The example thus exemplifies the sense in which certain propositions are to be understood as "supporting" others even with regard to "having justification." In this way the example might seem to suggest a justificatory order that obtains quite apart from how we arrive at our beliefs in reasoning or inference—in particular, to suggest that we can sort propositions into "supporting" and "supported," and into more complicated chains of mediated support, all independently of considerations about what the person believes and how they arrived at those beliefs in their particular circumstances.

In fact, however, the example shows no such thing. We can see this by varying the example and noting how the "support" structures shift.

Consider, for instance, the case in which you know on independent grounds that your car is out of gas, and also know that your gas gauge functions properly. In that case too you have justification to believe that the gas gauge reads "E," a "mediate" justification that "comes in part from justification you have to believe other, supporting propositions"—in particular, from justification you have to believe that your car is out of gas and that your gas gauge functions properly. This is a *different* justification than the one Pryor has in mind in his example. You have it only because you know certain things in this example that you didn't know in Pryor's example.

Suppose, then, that while knowing your car is out of gas and that your gas gauge is reliable, you happen to glance at the gas gauge and it appears to read "E." Now the situation is complex. In these circumstances your new visual experience gives you justification to believe that your gas gauge reads "E." Given that you know your gauge is functioning reliably, this in turn gives you mediate justification to believe that your car is out of gas. At the same time, your pre-existing knowledge that your car is out of gas and that your gas gauge functions reliably gives you mediate justification to believe that your gas gauge reads "E." So, in these circumstances you have *two sequences of mediate justifications which run in opposite directions*: you have mediate justification to believe that your car is out of gas, which comes by way of the justification you have to believe the "supporting" proposition that your gas gauge reads "E," and you *also* have mediate justification to believe that your gas gauge reads "E," which comes by way of the justification you have to believe the "supporting" proposition that your car is out of gas.

There are two important lessons to be drawn from this. First, in different circumstances there will be variation regarding which propositions support believing what. In particular, this will depend on what you already know and how you arrived at that knowledge. The examples thus do nothing to support the existence of the sort of circumstance-independent priority relations needed by the Global Priority Thesis.

Second, notice that in the case involving two sequences of justifications running in opposite directions *there is no objectionable circularity*. All of the relevant beliefs are in terrific epistemic shape. This means that the sort of directionality involved in Pryor's "support" relation *doesn't result in priority relations with the structure that are needed by a regress argument for the Global Priority Thesis*. The directionality involved in "having justification" allows for the possibility both that justification you have to believe P is part of the justification you have to believe Q *and* that justification you have to believe Q is part of the justification you have to believe P. In one of these justifications, the justification you have to believe Q comes via justification you have to believe the "supporting" proposition P; in the other, the justification you have to believe P comes via justification you have to believe the "supporting" proposition Q. So *this* notion of "support" doesn't generate a relation with the structure needed for a regress argument for the Global Priority Thesis. When you put the two "support" relations together, you don't get an objectionable circularity. The regress argument, however, requires a notion of "priority" or "support" on which it *is* objectionable if *p* supports *q* while *q* also supports *p*.

This feature of the situation shouldn't be surprising. As Pryor tells us, by "having justification" to believe P he just means that conditions obtain that make it appropriate for the person to believe that P. Conditions involving knowledge that Q can make it appropriate for you to believe that P, even as conditions involving knowledge that P also simultaneously make it appropriate for you to believe that Q. Any one of these justifying structures may be linear, but they don't *combine* in the sort of way that would be needed by a regress argument.

The upshot, then, is this: Pryor's example gives no support to the idea of an independent order of priority relations amongst propositions, the structure of which might be explored by consideration of a regress argument. Again, the clear commitments of the practice give no support to a regress-style argument for the Global Priority Thesis.[2]

Here's one last tack that might be tried. We might think of a structural regress as mirroring the reiterated question "How do I know?," a question that is repeated at each stage with regard to each consideration offered in reply. What one would have in mind here is not (as in the dialectical regress) a request for an argument for the truth of the relevant proposition, so much as an explanation of what it is in virtue of which one knows. The thought then would be that the answers to this question must stand in a certain sort of structural relation to each other that yields something like the Global Priority Thesis.

In fact, however, this approach will only lead to the Global Priority Thesis if one starts out thinking that only *a certain sort* of explanatory account will do—a theory that imposes the right sort of structure—and in thinking *this* one is asking for something that goes beyond the commitments of the ordinary position. After all, one can ordinarily explain how one knows things about the world by appealing to other things one knows about the world. That familiar sort of explanation must be ruled out as *not the sort of thing that was sought*, since an explanation of that sort does nothing to support the Global Epistemic Priority Thesis. But how is this constraint to be motivated by the commitments of our ordinary epistemic position?

It might seem that it would be viciously circular to use things we take ourselves to know about the world in order to explain our knowledge of the world quite generally. (This thought is suggested by some passages in Stroud, 2000). But if one is simply out for an *explanation*, say a scientific one, there

---

[2] Pryor himself does not utilize a regress argument to argue for his thesis that there is immediate experiential justification. Though to my knowledge he never says so, I suspect this is because he recognizes that since his characterization of mediate justification is compatible with cases of reciprocal support, his notion of mediate justification is perfectly compatible with the possibility that in *each case* in which we have justification to believe something about the world, that justification might be mediate and ultimately depend both on how things experientially seem *and* on justification one has to believe other "supporting" propositions about the world. That is to say, one cannot take Pryor's notion of mediate justification, ask how that justification arises, and follow out a regressive chain to the conclusion that if there is to be any justification at all, there must be immediate justification.

is nothing viciously circular here at all (Sosa 1994; Leite 2005). For instance, to provide a fully general explanation of how people know things about the world, we can perfectly well talk about the eyes and how they work. Something else has to be brought into play in order to motivate the thought that the only acceptable explanation would be one that divides things up in the way the Global Priority Thesis demands.[3]

All told, then, I conclude that considerations about regresses do not provide a route from our ordinary epistemic commitments to the Global Priority Thesis. We will need to look elsewhere.

---

[3] That division would plausibly be generated if we asked, "How do I know anything about the world?" in a way that tries to vindicate or justify all of our beliefs about the world at once. But as we have seen (see especially Chapter 3), from our Moorean standpoint in our ordinary epistemic position, failure in that global vindicatory or justificatory project carries no negative implications for our ability to know things about the world. (See also Chapter 13.)

12

Seeking an Argument II

The Global Priority Thesis and the Explanation of Belief

1. Recapitulation

We have been considering whether anything supports the suggestion that the Global Priority Thesis arises from the commitments of our ordinary, prephilosophical position. The Global Priority Thesis, recall, is a multifaceted conception of our epistemological position vis-à-vis the world. It asserts that our evidence is limited in just the way the skeptic needs.

- It supposes that each of us can sensibly treat all our beliefs about the world as a group for justificatory purposes.
- It characterizes a limited justificatory base that does not include any considerations about the world.
- It identifies that limited base with sensory experiences and other non-factive mental states, or facts about those mental states, or propositions or judgments concerning such states.
- It treats that limited base as comprising the totality of our evidence for any beliefs about the world: it takes that limited base to be all we have to go on in arriving at or justifying those beliefs.
- It holds that if we are to know or have reasonable beliefs about the world, then that limited base must provide adequate support or evidence for conclusions about the world in this specific sense: it must be possible for a rational being to acceptably transition in explicit conscious reasoning from the limited base (a position which does not yet involve any views about the world) to conclusions about the world.

The question before us, then, is whether we can find any reason to think that this bundle of claims is something that we are committed to in the ordinary, pre-philosophical position. If we can't, then—standing as we are in the ordinary, pre-philosophical position—we have no reason not to continue to utilize considerations about the world when confronting skeptical argumentation.

We have seen that none of the mid-twentieth-century proponents of the Global Priority Thesis provided a convincing argument for it. Attempts to establish it through considerations about justificatory regresses fare no better, as we saw in the previous chapter. Surprisingly enough, however, the contemporary literature contains very few explicit arguments of any other sort. In the spirit of due diligence, then, we need to consider what *might* lead one in this direction. Here considerations about the explanation of belief and reasonable error loom large. As we will see, however, none of these lines of thought are compelling.

2. Rational Belief Formation and Folk-Psychological Explanation

In Chapter 10, Section 6, we considered the thought that the Global Priority Thesis is supported by the role of evidence in guiding processes of belief formation. There the question was whether this guiding role requires our evidence to lie in something about which we cannot be mistaken, and I argued that it does not. However, the guiding role of evidence might seem to support the Global Priority Thesis in another way. After all—it might be said— whenever I rationally revise my beliefs in light of some consideration about the world, there must be some mental state (for example, a belief state, or an experiential state) which represents that consideration to me or in some sense makes it available to me. And this thought might seem to lead to the conclusion that what I am actually being guided by in the process of rational belief revision are *other mental states*. So, it might be concluded, those are what really constitute the evidence I am going on in rationally forming and revising my beliefs. And this looks awfully close to a version of the Global Priority Thesis.

This rough line of thought can be made more precise by considering an argument offered by Ralph Wedgwood (2002) for the "internalist" view that the rationality of a belief supervenes purely on facts about the thinker's non-factive mental states and the explanatory relations between them (340, 358).[1]

---

[1] This presentation of Wedgwood's argument will be somewhat imprecise; I will leave aside various aspects of his subtle discussion that are irrelevant to the points I want to make.

Wedgwood himself does not offer this line of argument as a defense of the Global Priority Thesis, but—as will become evident—it can easily seem appropriate to extend it in that direction.

Wedgwood begins with the thought that rational belief revision is a matter of modifying or reaffirming one's beliefs in a way that is guided by rules. These rules will have the form, "In conditions C, you may (or must) believe . . . ." Insofar as one is following such a rule, one will respond to the obtaining or non-obtaining of the relevant conditions in revising one's beliefs as one does. The crucial question, then, is what sort of conditions these are.

Wedgwood suggests that there is a particular sort of relation between this sort of guidance by a rule, on the one hand, and folk-psychological causal explanation, on the other: what one is directly responsive to when one revises a belief in this way is whatever figures in an adequate folk-psychological explanation as (part of) the proximate cause of the belief revision. Wedgwood then argues that in such explanations, the proximate causes of belief revisions are always other mental states, not external facts. In particular, they are non-factive mental states (states whose obtaining does not depend upon the truth of their propositional contents) such as belief states and experiential states. For instance, when I form the perceptual belief that there is a pink flower before me, my belief formation isn't directly caused by the fact itself (2002, 359–360). There is an intervening experiential state which plays a role as a proximate cause of my belief.

From these considerations Wedgwood concludes that the conditions by which we are guided and to which we respond in rational belief revision are always non-factive mental states. As he puts it:

> In general, then, it seems that an explanation of a belief revision that appeals to an external fact can be a correct folk-psychological explanation only if there is also a "fully-articulated" explanation in which the link between the external fact and that belief revision is mediated by intervening internal facts about the believer's mental states. So, in any "fully-articulated" explanation, the proximate explanation of the belief revision is not an external fact, but some internal fact about the believer's mental states (361). . . . In general, following . . . basic rules always involves revising one's beliefs in response to such internal facts. (364)

From here it can seem a short step to the Global Priority Thesis. Here's why. What has been argued is that in rational belief formation, we arrive at our views about the world by a process of responding to internal mental states. But when we rationally revise our beliefs in light of evidence, it might be said, the evidence is what we are going on—it is what we are responding to in modifying our beliefs as we do. So it seems that our evidence must comprise internal mental factors. And if that's so, then it seems that it should be possible to perform the global division postulated by the Global Priority Thesis, in which we put everything we take ourselves to know about the world on one side and then locate our evidence for all of that in our non-factive mental states.

For the sake of argument, I want to grant to Wedgwood that there is an "internalist" notion of rationality that supervenes upon facts about our non-factive mental states. I also want to grant—again for the sake of argument—that he has called attention to perfectly ordinary considerations about folk-psychological explanations of people's beliefs.[2] What I want to bring out is this: none of this shows that the ordinary epistemic position involves commitment to the claim that our evidence comprises (or supervenes upon) only non-factive mental states.[3]

The key point concerns the relation between folk-psychological explanations of people's belief revisions and claims about what the evidence is. The relata in a folk-psychological causal explanation are not the same as those involved when we evaluate a belief in light of the evidence upon which it is based. In fact, if we assume that the mental states that provide the proximate folk-psychological explanation of a person's belief are the evidence upon which the person bases their belief, then we lose important distinctions that appear in our ordinary practices of inquiry and epistemic assessment.

To see this, note first that there are forms of epistemic evaluation that go beyond assessing a person's "internal" rationality. In particular, and very importantly, there is a form of evaluation that centrally concerns the truth or falsity of the considerations that the person offers as evidence for their belief. Suppose, for instance, that we ask, taking the detective to be a bit of a blunderer, "Why do you believe Smith is the murderer?" The detective might reply, for instance, "Because Smith's fingerprints were on the murder weapon,

---

[2] One important objection to this overall line of thought targets the claim that the relevant mental states must be *non-factive*. For instance, it might be suggested that I rationally form the belief that q because I *see that* q, or because I *know* both that p and that if p, then q. Wedgwood argues that in all such explanations, the factive element plays no essential role in the proximate causal explanation of the belief state (362–363). I will not challenge this claim for the purposes of the present discussion. My interest right now lies elsewhere.

[3] It should be noted that nothing here will turn on how one interprets the notion of "supervenience."

the victim's blood was identified on Smith's clothing, and Smith blurted out a confession when he was arrested. That's why." We might retort that he's gotten things badly wrong: Jones' fingerprints—not Smith's—were on the gun, the blood was on Jones' clothes, and it was Jones who confessed. And we might quite properly conclude, "So, you don't know it was Smith after all!" It *matters* that the considerations the detective offered were false, even if they would have established the truth of the detective's belief if they had been true and even if it turns out that the detective does happen (bizarrely) to be right that it was Smith who did it.

This form of evaluation is directly concerned with questions of evidence. What the detective offered in response to the "why?" question is what the detective would have offered if we had asked, "What is the evidence that Smith is the murderer?" That is, the detective would have pointed to various considerations about the world. By contrast, it would be very strange if the detective responded to our request for evidence by saying, "Well, I believe Smith's fingerprints were on the murder weapon, I believe the victim's blood was identified on Smith's clothing, and I believe Smith blurted out a confession when he was arrested." In ordinary circumstances, our response would be something like this: "I'm not asking what you believe. What I want to know is what the facts are and whether they actually tell in favor of the conclusion that Smith did it." That is to say: in the usual sort of case, our interest is in the world, not the person's mind. And if—very unusually—it really was the detective's beliefs that were being offered as evidence, then considerations about such matters as the detective's track record would become directly relevant to the evaluation of the force of the evidence in a way that they otherwise wouldn't be. We might say, for instance, "That you *believe* these things about Smith isn't any evidence that he did it, given your rotten track record—and that's so even if your belief that Smith did it fits very well with your other beliefs about Smith." So, it is part of our ordinary practice that offering p as evidence for q is a very different thing from offering *I believe p* as evidence for q. The two get treated in entirely different ways, raise very different sorts of issues, and are not equally good in most circumstances. It is not always or even often true that the evidence on which a person bases a belief is to be identified with any of their mental states.

There is a closely related point about explanation. If what someone says about Smith's fingerprints, and so forth, is all true and something they know, then we can explain why they believe that Smith is the murderer by pointing to those facts about Smith. We say, "They believe that Smith is the murderer because X, Y, and Z [external facts about Smith]." This is a form of explanation that cannot be correct unless the propositions about the world that appear in the explanans are true. The explanation is informative as a matter of epistemic assessment because it tells us something about a respect in which the person is in good epistemic shape. Their belief that Smith is the murderer is a response to the facts, and those facts strongly indicate that (as they believe) Smith is the murderer.

Of course, to respond to the facts in this good way, the person has to have mental states that represent them. Those mental states are or constitutively involve beliefs. They are—as we are conceding to Wedgwood—the proximate cause of the belief that Smith is the murderer. At the level of folk-psychological proximate causal explanation, then, what explains the person's belief that Smith is the murderer are plausibly their other beliefs about Smith. But that doesn't turn those other belief-states into the evidence that they are responding to. The evidence that they are responding to is given by those other considerations about *Smith*.

What if the considerations they offer about Smith are all false? What, then, is the evidence to which they are responding? The question has a false presupposition. There doesn't have to be any evidence to which they are responding. Suppose, for instance, that they believe those things about Smith as a result of error or out of wishful thinking. Then we will say, "You actually don't have any evidence that Smith did it." They wrongly take those considerations to be true, and they accordingly draw further conclusions from them. They are treating them as evidence that Smith did it. In that sense we will refer to them as "their evidence": those considerations are what the person is going on in forming the belief that Smith is the murderer. But that doesn't turn those considerations into evidence that Smith did it. Here's a simple parallel. Suppose you are attempting to reconcile your checkbook and the balance you reach differs from the bank's balance. We will then talk about "your balance" and "the bank's balance." That doesn't mean that your account suddenly has two different balances. If you've gotten things wrong, then the term "your balance" refers to what you incorrectly take your account's balance to be.[4]

The folk-psychological causal explanation coexists peacefully with the forms of assessment that focus on the truth or falsity of the considerations appealed to as evidence, and also with explanations of the sort that treat the facts about Smith as explanatory of the person's belief. There is no tension

[4] For further discussion of these points, see Leite (2013).

here. The upshot is thus that our practice involves no commitment to treating the mental states that are the proximate cause of a person's belief as being the evidence to which the person is responding in believing as they do. The temptation to think otherwise only arises when we think that whenever we properly use the phrase "his evidence" it picks out something that actually is evidence, or when we get confused by the word "respond" and assume that the form of response involved in a proximate folk-psychological causal explanation is exactly the same thing as what goes on when a thinker responds to evidence.

3. The Explanation of Error

So far I have been examining the folk-psychological explanation of belief revision. However, there is another way in which considerations about explanation might seem to lead us to the Global Priority Thesis. It can be set out as follows. In effect, it amounts to a novel use of the "New Evil Demon" scenario to defend the Global Priority Thesis.

> Suppose that as a result of a visual hallucination someone incorrectly believes that there is a dagger before them. Here it is natural to explain the false belief by appealing to the person's experience. In doing so, we are not primarily focused on their experience as the proximate cause of their belief. Rather, we are identifying what the person, *qua* thinker, was going on in forming the belief: they were going on their experience. The relation that is involved in this case seems to be just the one that is involved when we are going on evidence in forming our beliefs. So, it seems that the person is treating the experience as if it were good evidence, and this is what explains their erroneous belief.

> Consider, then, your twin who is being globally deceived by an evil demon. Suppose that because of their visual experiences they form the belief that there is a computer before them. Again, it seems that what they are going on in forming the belief is their visual experience: they are treating the experience as if it were good evidence. It is plausible, moreover, that this point doesn't apply just to this single belief, but rather generalizes to all of their beliefs about what is going on around them: in forming all of their beliefs about the world, they are ultimately going on their sensory experience,

treating it as if it were good evidence. Importantly, they have *nothing else to go on*. So, it seems that we can consider a demon's victim's beliefs about the world as a group and ask what evidence the demon's victim has for all of those beliefs. When we do so, we see that the evidence can comprise only mental factors, particularly sensory experiences or how things seem in sensory experience. That is to say, generalizing from certain cases of ordinary perceptual error suggests that *the Global Priority Thesis is true of the evil demon's victim*.

Having come this far, however, it is hard to see how we can avoid drawing the same conclusion about ourselves. After all, the evil demon's victims can't tell the difference between global deception and veridical perception, and we likewise can't tell the difference between global deception and veridical perception from *our* first-person subjective perspective; everything would seem exactly the same to us either way. We have no additional cognitive capacity that the evil demon's victim lacks, no other special way of accessing the world. So, it looks as though our position is precisely analogous to that of the evil demon's victim: *our* evidence can comprise only our non-factive mental states, sensory experiences, or how things seem. That is to say, it looks as though the Global Priority Thesis is true of us as well.[5]

The first step of this line of thought is questionable: it is hardly obvious that someone who is misled by a hallucination is going on their visual experience (understood as the Global Priority Thesis understands that notion) in exactly the way that we go on evidence in ordinary life. True, the person's visual experience causes them to believe that there is a dagger in front of them. If asked to justify their belief, however, they might very well say that they *see a dagger*. That is, they think that they are seeing a dagger, and they are wrong. It is already a philosophical interpretation of this situation to say that they are "treating the experience as if it were good evidence that there is a dagger there." However, for present purposes I propose to grant this interpretation and to focus on two crucial moves that the line of thought goes on to make. The first is to claim that the Global Priority Thesis is true of the evil demon's victim. The second is to generalize that claim to us. Neither is actually motivated by the commitments of our ordinary practice. In fact, both run afoul of several points that have already been made.

[5] A version of this line of thought is offered by Kirk Ludwig in his unpublished paper, "Skepticism, Logical Independence, and Epistemic Priority." I am grateful to him for urging me to take it seriously.

Let's begin with the generalization from the evil demon's victim to us. The basic thought here could be put like this: if the demon's victim's evidence is limited to its experiential states or how things experientially seem to it, then the same is true of us—even if we are not a demon's victims. That is, the argument proposes to compare a Bad Case—the evil demon case, in which one is undetectably globally deceived about the world—with a Good Case in which no such deception is taking place. The claim, then, is that our evidence in the Good Case can be no better than—can include nothing more than—what we share with the person in the Bad Case. But if we are working from amidst our ordinary, pre-philosophical commitments, we should regard the *form* of this argument as invalid for reasons that were explored at length in Chapter 7. It is subject to straightforward counterexamples.

For instance, consider the hypothesis Ducks Rule the World. In the Bad Case ducks are engaged in an undetectable conspiracy to shape the course of human events for their own nefarious ends. In the Good Case, they aren't. We, in the Good Case, have excellent evidence that no such thing is going on. This evidence includes facts such as these: ducks lack the intelligence and other capacities necessary for such an undertaking. Such facts tell quite decisively against the hypothesis. But such considerations would not be amongst our evidence in the Bad Case, since they would all be false. So, it would be a mistake to conclude that our evidence in the Good Case is no better than, includes no more than, the evidence possessed by someone in the Bad Case. We cannot conclude that since the evidence is limited in the Bad Case, it is similarly limited in the Good Case.

Such examples show that (to speak from within our ordinary, pre-philosophical commitments) the form of the argument is invalid. But something more can be said. If we are standing in the ordinary position, we should also regard the argument as failing in the particular case at hand. This is because—as I argued in Chapter 7—in the ordinary position we are committed to precisely this sort of evidential asymmetry regarding the Evil Demon scenario itself. The asymmetry is generated by two commitments of our ordinary epistemic practice:

1. Considerations about the world often constitute evidence for other claims about the world.
2. P isn't evidence for Q if P is false.

The first commitment means that in the Good Case, where we are not being deceived by an evil demon, our evidence for various claims about the world can include other considerations about the world. The second means that in the Bad Case, where we are being deceived by an evil demon, we would lack all of this evidence, since all of these considerations would be false; in that case our evidence would be restricted in just the way the argument assumes. So, the commitments of our ordinary, pre-philosophical position clash with the key move in the argument. Even if the evil demon's victim's evidence is limited, it does not follow that *our* evidence is limited in a similar way.

A savvy defender of the Global Priority Thesis could grant this last point. They could reply that it is perfectly compatible with the Global Priority Thesis to hold that while considerations about the world are indeed part of our evidence, our "basic" or "ultimate" evidence is more limited. That is quite right, and some non-skeptical foundationalists could happily endorse such a view. However, this rejoinder is useless in this dialectical context, where the aim is to put in place a form of the Global Priority Thesis that will do the work needed for a skeptical argument. The skeptic, after all, has to *deny* that considerations about the world are part of our evidence: to do otherwise is to give away the game, since (as we have seen in the preceding chapters) allowing that considerations about the world are part of our evidence leaves us free to reject the skeptical hypotheses precisely by appealing to considerations about the world.

So far, then, I have urged that the generalization from the evil demon's victim to ourselves *clashes* with commitments of our ordinary position. However, there were also reasons offered in support of this generalization, and so we have to consider whether those actually reflect commitments of our ordinary position. After all, it is possible that the ordinary position contains countervailing elements in tension with each other.

The first thought was that like the evil demon's victim, we can't tell the difference from our subjective perspective between veridical perception of the world and undetectable global deception: everything would seem exactly the same to us either way. I concede that this much is true: everything would seem exactly the same to us either way. Speaking from amidst our ordinary commitments, however, it does not follow that our evidence cannot comprise more than what we share with the evil demon's victim. For in general, the fact that everything would seem the same to you in both scenarios A and B *does not* entail that you have the same evidence in scenarios A and B. The hypothesis Ducks Rule the World is a straightforward illustration of the point, as are many of the other examples discussed in Chapters 6 and 7.

The second thought was that we do not have some special cognitive faculty that our deceived twins in the demon world lack. There is an obvious sense in which this is true. If we limit our attention to faculties described in a way that does not take account of the real-world circumstances, then both we and our deceived twins have no relevant faculties beyond our faculties for reasoning, memory, and experience. However, it does not follow from this similarity that our *epistemic positions* are the same. Our epistemic position can depend upon contingent facts about how we are situated. Again, this is the lesson of epistemic and evidential asymmetry (Chapter 7), as exemplified by hypotheses such as Ducks Rule the World. Two beings with identical cognitive faculties may be situated in such a way that one of them can have good evidence of a sort which the other cannot.

Given these points, I conclude that from within our ordinary position there is no good motivation for the thought that if the Global Priority Thesis (understood as the skeptic must understand it) is true of the demon's victim, then it must be true of us.

However, should we even concede that the Global Priority Thesis is true of the evil demon's victim? I don't think so. I do think that we should concede that the demon's victim's evidence is limited and does not include any considerations about the world. But the Global Priority Thesis says much more than that. It claims that a very particular justificatory structure must obtain between the limited evidential base and the demon's victim's beliefs about the world as a class, if any of those beliefs are to be in good epistemic shape. It is one thing to grant that the demon's victim's actual evidence is limited. It is quite another thing to impose this requirement.

In brief, the argument for imposing this requirement ran as follows:

> When the demon's victims form the belief that there is a computer in front of them, they are going on their sensory experience, treating it as if it were good evidence. This case generalizes: in forming all of their beliefs about the world, they are ultimately going on their sensory experience, treating it as if it were good evidence. Importantly, they have *nothing else to go on*. So, if their beliefs are to have any positive epistemic status, it must be because of some appropriate general justificatory relationship that holds between that limited evidential base and the totality of their beliefs about the world.

None of the key moments in this argument stands up to scrutiny.

First, we have to ask: what is actually going on when the demon's victim explicitly treats sensory experience as good evidence in any particular case? Importantly, considerations about the world will be in play as well. For instance, when justifying a belief that there is a computer right there, my deceived twin would not simply appeal to their current visual experience (if they do so at all), since *I* would not do so; like me, my twin would be prepared to appeal to considerations about what computers characteristically look like, the state of their perceptual organs, the conduciveness of their circumstances, and so on. They would thus rely upon a wide range of considerations about the world. Being a reasonable, well-functioning inquirer, if they lacked any view at all about such matters, they wouldn't treat their sensory experience as good evidence for their belief; rather, they would say, "I don't know what to think."

These considerations highlight a crucial point. From the demon's victim's own viewpoint, commitments about the world are inextricably intertwined with the supposed experiential evidential base in any particular case. *The demon's victim* doesn't proceed in a way that divides things up as the Global Priority Thesis demands, taking the propriety of beliefs about the world to depend upon the possibility of an acceptable inference from a limited experiential evidential base in a way that involves no considerations about the world. So, the example does not support the generalization to the Global Priority Thesis. That generalization depends upon an antecedent distortion of what goes on in the particular case.

This distortion is facilitated by the thought, "they have nothing else to go on." However, this thought is slippery and must be handled with care.

We may have two things in mind when we think, "They have nothing else to go on." First, we may be acknowledging the fact that our deceived twins' total evidence cannot actually include the considerations about the world that they are prepared to treat as evidence, since those considerations are all false. This fact is important, but it doesn't quite show what is wanted, since one can perfectly well "go on" what one *incorrectly thinks* is good evidence. A detective might form the belief that Smith is the murderer on the grounds that Smith's fingerprints were on the weapon. Here he treats that latter consideration as evidence that Smith did it and is guided by that consideration, but he might be quite wrong about it: Smith's fingerprints might not be on the weapon at all.

Second, we might be thinking something stronger, something more like this: "You can't go on something that is nonexistent or not the case. Whatever you are going on must be something real or something true. So, the demon's victim *can't* be going on false considerations about the world." But in fact, this thought isn't right, for the reason I just highlighted. One can perfectly well go on false considerations in forming a belief, if one incorrectly thinks that the considerations are true.

To the extent, then, that the thought "They have nothing else to go on" reflects a truth about the demon's victims' situation, it doesn't support the idea that the Global Priority Thesis is true of them. This much, at least, is true: the evidence that the demon's victims *actually have available* is more limited than what they are prepared to appeal to as part of their evidence; the actual evidence available to them is limited and includes no considerations about the external world. But this point does *nothing* to motivate a crucial aspect of the Global Priority Thesis: it does not show that in order for their beliefs about the world to have any sort of positive epistemic status at all, it must be possible for them to arrive via acceptable explicit reasoning at their total view of the world from a starting position that includes only a limited experiential base and without making use of any considerations about the world in the process. It remains the case that the propriety of what they do whenever they explicitly appeal to their experience in support of particular beliefs about the world ineliminably depends on making use of other things they believe about the world.

To put the key point another way, the fact that the demon's victims have "nothing else to go on"—in the sense in which that is true—doesn't show that in order for any of their beliefs about the world to count as knowledge or even as reasonable, those beliefs must stand, as a group, in the requisite sort of relation to some limited justificatory base that does not include any considerations about the world.

I conclude that considerations about the explanation of error do nothing to show that our ordinary epistemic practice commits us to or motivates the Global Epistemic Priority Thesis.

4. "Ultimate Evidence"

A final sort of example might seem to suggest that you and an evil demon's victim can't differ in the way I've been suggesting. Imagine two cases in a world very much like our own. In both cases someone explicitly performs an acceptable ampliative inference from A to B and from there to C. In one case B happens to be true, while in the other it is false. (The person's relevant background information is identical in content and truth value in both cases.) It seems plausible that both people have the same evidence for C. After all, in both cases the reasoning began with A, and neither person had any further evidence for B. So it seems that they have the same evidence: in both cases, their evidence is A, and B is a mere lemma. But then shouldn't we say the same thing about you and your deceived twin in an evil demon world? You both have the same evidence—namely, whatever experiential evidence you have for all your beliefs about the world.[6]

I do not think that the example supports the conclusion. It is crucial to the example that both people arrived at the belief C through an acceptable, explicit, ampliative inference starting from A: this is what leads us to trace the person's evidence back to A in both cases. But neither you nor your deceived twin has arrived at a total set of beliefs about the world through an explicit ampliative inference from sensory experience or considerations about sensory experience, so there is no parallel here. It only looks otherwise if you have already assumed the Global Priority Thesis. The example thus doesn't provide reason to say that *your* evidence can include nothing more than your deceived twin's evidence. Nothing has been done to show that in arriving at your beliefs about the world in the way you have—not via explicit ampliative inference from a limited experiential evidential base—the evidence you currently have for particular beliefs about the world can't include other considerations about the world.

It might be said that the relevant parallel holds, because even though you didn't arrive at your beliefs about the world through an acceptable explicit ampliative inference from the total course of your experience, it must be possible to do so. But why think this is true? What we have here is mere insistence: "It must be possible to do so, if our beliefs about the world are to be in good epistemic shape." But this insistence is born of the thought that what our evidence now amounts to is provided by facts about our sensory experience and other non-factive mental states. Here again the Global Priority Thesis is already appearing as a presupposition of the argument. But it is

---

[6] I am grateful to Richard Fumerton for both the example and the question. As before, I grant for the sake of argument that both you and your deceived twin can have the same experiences and the same or counterpart beliefs in some relevant sense.

precisely what needed to be motivated using the commitments of our ordinary position.

5. Where We Are Now

We have been looking for reason to think that the Global Priority Thesis can be successfully motivated from within the commitments of the ordinary, pre-philosophical position. Despite having carefully considered all of the most important arguments that have been or might be offered, we have not found any such thing.

Where does this leave us? Standing as we are in the ordinary, pre-philosophical position, we can say this: there is no reason to accept the Global Priority Thesis. We have no reason to accept the framing it would put in place, no reason to grant the limitation on our evidence that it would impose. If—as seems overwhelmingly plausible—we can't do what it requires, that doesn't matter: those are requirements that we have found no reason to accept.

Here is why this result is important. Recall that the skeptic's task was to show us, standing in our ordinary, pre-philosophical position, that there is a route that leads *us* to the skeptical conclusion. That has not happened. So, in a crucial sense, we are still where we have been all along. We know and reasonably believe all sorts of things about the world. Considerations about the world are among our evidence. We still have no reason not to appeal to such considerations as part of our response to skeptical argumentation.

Of course, there are epistemologists who have developed sophisticated theories aimed at showing that we can do what the Global Priority Thesis requires. (These epistemologists are not skeptics, obviously.) Fortunately, we do not need to enter into that debate for our purposes here. Since we have carefully considered all of the relevant arguments and no good motivation has emerged for the Global Priority Thesis, we have no reason to accept that knowledge or reasonable belief about the world requires the ability to do what it demands. So even if some epistemologists think that we can meet its requirements, the acceptability of my response to the skeptical argument does not depend upon either their success or their failure.

There has been a tendency in recent epistemology to think that the Global Priority Thesis captures something fundamental about our epistemic relation to the world. As Stroud nicely describes it, we can think that we are in the position of someone waking up to find himself locked in a room full of television sets and trying to find out what is going on in the world outside. For all he can know whatever is producing the patterns he can see on the screens in front of him might be something other than well-functioning cameras directed on to the passing show outside the room. The victim might switch on more of the sets in the room to try to get more information, and he might find that some of the sets show events exactly similar or coherently related to those already available on the screens he can see. But all those pictures will be no help to him without some independent information, some knowledge which does not come to him from the pictures themselves, about how the pictures he does see before him are connected with what is going on outside the room. The problem of the external world is the problem of finding out, or knowing how we could find out, about the world around us if we were in that sort of predicament. It is perhaps enough simply to put the problem this way to convince us that it can never be given a satisfactory solution. (1984, 33)

I agree with Stroud that once the problem is put that way, it is very difficult to see how there could possibly be a satisfactory solution. From our ordinary, pre-philosophical standpoint, however, that predicament is only one that some unfortunate person might find themselves in *if they came to have adequate reason in favor of one of the global skeptical hypotheses.* As things stand, that is not our predicament. We have no such reasons. And I have argued that our pretheoretical stance does not involve or motivate any such conception of our epistemic relation to the world in general. The problem, so conceived, thus does not arise from our ordinary epistemic commitments and practices.

What is the alternative to this conception? Minimally, we could say this:

In order to know or reasonably believe things about the world, it does not have to be possible for a rational being to acceptably transition in explicit conscious reasoning from some limited experiential basis to conclusions about the world in a way that does not ineliminably depend upon any considerations about the world.

Importantly, this fits with what we see elsewhere in the ordinary, pre-philosophical position. It simply puts the body of our knowledge of the world on the same footing as our knowledge that neither ducks nor dung beetles undetectably control human history for their own nefarious purposes.

To put this point more fully: In the absence of any good motivation for the Global Priority Thesis, that thesis just amounts to a version of the requirement that in order to have a certain body of knowledge or reasonable beliefs, it must be possible to reconstruct a line of rationally acceptable, explicit, reasoning-like transitions by which we could acceptably arrive at those beliefs from an initial starting position of complete neutrality or agnosticism. (In this case, the relevant body of knowledge or beliefs concerns the world around us, and the restriction to experiential evidence and the like captures what's left over after we've removed all our beliefs about the world in line with the demand for initial neutrality or agnosticism.) As we have seen over many chapters, there are lots of examples that tell against any such demand. These include my knowledge that my spouse isn't deceiving me about whether she loves me, my knowledge that the Children of Brunettes Hypothesis is false, and our knowledge that ducks are not engaged in an undetectable conspiracy to rule the world. In all of these cases we have knowledge, reasonable beliefs, and good evidential support for our beliefs, but none of this can be reconstructed in terms of a path by which we could acceptably arrive at the relevant beliefs through explicit, conscious reasoning from an initial position of neutrality or agnosticism. So, the case of our beliefs about the world fits with what we see elsewhere in our practice. In the absence of any reason to think the Global Priority Thesis is correct when it comes to our beliefs about the world in particular, we can say about these beliefs just what we say about these other cases. In all of these cases we have knowledge and reasonable beliefs, and we have good evidence in support of these beliefs, but we won't be able to make use of our good evidence or see it for what it is if we try to take up a stance of initial agnosticism or neutrality regarding the relevant beliefs. In the case of our beliefs about the world, this evidence includes other beliefs about the world.

The upshot is that although the senses obviously play various roles in our attainment of knowledge of the world, those roles are distorted if we think that what is going on must be modeled as a good reasoning-like transition from experiential evidence starting in a position of initial neutrality about the world. We can thus stand with Moore in the midst of our ordinary prephilosophical position, accept that we can't do what the Global Epistemic Priority Thesis requires of us, and quite reasonably respond with a shrug.

None of this adds up to an alternative epistemological theory or even a schema for a theory. At most, what I have highlighted are constraints on a theory that would do justice to our ordinary epistemic commitments and practices. This leaves all sorts of questions wide open. For instance, it would be compatible with what we have seen to maintain, with some reliabilists and other paradigmatic forms of epistemological externalism, that we can know some things even if we can't provide any evidence at all for them. However, it would be equally compatible to maintain that a mature adult can't know or reasonably believe something unless they are able to point to considerations that tell in its favor. To take another example, it would be open to hold that seeing that *p* gives you a reason that is sufficient for knowledge but that cannot be reconstructed in terms of experiential evidence (understood in a way that implies nothing about the world), and it would equally be open to hold that in each case of perceptual knowledge a reason involving something usefully termed "experiential evidence" is in play. These are just a few examples of questions left wide open. All such debates, if we are working from a Moorean position, are ultimately about our ordinary commitments (including our best scientific commitments and theories), what they involve, and what happens when we attempt to systematize or regiment our ordinary practice. Insofar as the questions concern our actual commitments and practices, they are equally questions of how we are willing to live.

Those are the sorts of issues that will be at the forefront of our minds if we are thinking about epistemological theory. But that is precisely what I have been urging us *not* to focus on. My project has been to see just how far we can get without engaging in any epistemological theorizing beyond articulation and general description of the commitments involved in our ordinary position. What we have found, taking up a Moorean stance within that position, is this: There is nothing that tells in the Global Priority Thesis's favor, no reason to accept its demands. The reasonable response—standing within the ordinary, pre-philosophical position—is consequently to reject it. There is nothing here that sets the scene for a successful skeptical argument.

PART IV
TAKING STOCK

13
Enough Is Enough

Satisfactory: (of evidence or a verdict) sufficient for the needs of the case.
—Oxford Languages

One might say: the axis of reference of our examination must be rotated, but about the fixed point of our real need.
—Wittgenstein, *Philosophical Investigations*, §108

1. The Path We've Traveled

Throughout this book I have been focusing on the earliest stages of skeptical reflection, the initiating moves that are supposed to get the whole thing started. In particular, I have been asking about the relation between those initiating moves and ordinary life. How are we supposed to get skeptical reflection going from within what I have called our pre-philosophical position—our ordinary practices, procedures, and commitments regarding inquiry and epistemic assessment?

To approach this question, I have urged us to follow Moore's lead. We begin by standing squarely within the pre-philosophical position and asking whether we can somehow be moved in a reasonable way to accept the skeptical conclusion. When we do so, we find that the would-be skeptic faces a fundamental problem: it looks for all the world as though we can acceptably appeal to our knowledge of the world to reject key steps of the familiar skeptical arguments. The crucial question therefore becomes this: what, if anything, might block us from responding to skeptical argumentation in this way?

Over the course of this book I have addressed many suggestions about what might do this work.

1. You might have thought that the very structure of the global skeptical scenarios themselves has this effect: that they somehow neutralize all of our ordinary evidence, rendering it useless for rebutting the suggestion that one of these hypotheses might actually be the case. This is not so, as we saw in Chapters 4–7.
2. It might be suggested that what does this work is the project of understanding or vindicating our knowledge of the world with complete generality. However, as we saw in Chapter 3, Chapter 4 Section 5, and Chapter 5 Section 7, such a project does not generate a compelling route to a skeptical conclusion from within our ordinary position.
3. You might have thought that our positive epistemic evaluation of the beliefs of someone globally deceived by an evil demon—that is, our evaluation of such a person as being in some sense "justified" in believing as they do—shows that our evidence is limited to considerations about our mental states (and particularly to how things seem to us in our perceptual experience). This is not so, for reasons we saw in Chapter 5 Section 7, Chapter 7, and Chapter 12 Section 3.
4. You might have thought that "internalist" demands for "reflectively accessible" evidence—understood as evidence available through introspection and a priori reflection alone—have the necessary effect. However, as I argued in Chapter 5 Section 7, the demand for "reflectively accessible evidence" *understood in this way* plays no particular role in our ordinary, pre-philosophical position, while the demand for reflectively accessible evidence understood in ordinary terms—as evidence that you could, under appropriate conditions, offer in defense of your belief—allows for evidence that includes facts about the world around us. Likewise, if we are standing in the ordinary position, none of the familiar considerations about the methodological or regulative role of reasons or evidence forces a restriction here, as we saw in Chapters 5 and 6.
5. It might seem that skeptical arguments in the contemporary literature offered by Crispin Wright, Jim Pryor, or Duncan Pritchard do the trick. However, this is not so, as we saw in Chapter 5 and Chapter 8 Sections 1–3.
6. It might be suggested that considerations about sensory experience are sufficient to generate the relevant restriction—in particular, that if on any given occasion sensory perception all by itself yields (at most)

knowledge about how things seem or appear to us, then this must be the evidential base upon which all of our knowledge of the world must rest. As we saw in Chapter 9, however, this is not so. Unless we assume what I there called the "Global Priority Thesis," this conception of sensory perception does nothing to help get skeptical argumentation started.
7. Schematically, the Global Priority Thesis amounts to the claim that our beliefs about the world won't be in good shape unless they stand in a certain sort of epistemic relation to a body of evidence comprising or provided by only our experiential and other non-factive mental states. It amounts to the claim that the skeptic's restriction on our evidence tracks something fundamental about the nature of our reasons for belief. However, we have found that the Global Priority Thesis does not arise out of the commitments of our ordinary position. The arguments offered by twentieth-century epistemologists such as Chisholm fail to motivate the Global Priority Thesis, and arguments appealing to regresses and the explanation of belief fare no better (Chapters 10–12).

Putting this all together, we have not found a way for external world skepticism to get going when we stand squarely in our pre-philosophical position. We started out affirming that we know and have good reason to believe all sorts of things about the world. We then gave every serious line of thought a run for its money, and we ended up where we began.

Suppose, then, that this is how things turn out: Every skeptical argument suffers from the sorts of flaws we have been discussing, and from within the ordinary, pre-philosophical position there is no good way of motivating the insistence that our response to skeptical argumentation must not make use of considerations about the world and our knowledge of it. We find no reason, from this vantage point, to think that our ordinary, pre-philosophical position is leading us astray: no reason to think that the principles and procedures of ordinary epistemic assessment somehow mislead us even when we are doing it right, and no reason to think that the claims about the world we have appealed to are wrong. If we are standing within the ordinary epistemic position, this will look like a fully adequate basis for rejecting external world skepticism.

For one thing, it will have been shown that it isn't true that the commitments of our pre-philosophical position lead to skeptical disaster. Skepticism's self-understanding is thereby revealed to be incorrect. Moreover, we will have found (to speak from within our pre-philosophical position) that there is no reason to think external world skepticism true and every reason to think it false. We will consequently affirm—just as we did at the beginning of our inquiry—that we know and have good reason to believe all sorts of things about the world. For reasons articulated in Chapters 2 and 3, I think that this is a result with which we can rest content. Moore is right.

Some readers might be concerned that, despite all, our ordinary, pre-philosophical standpoint could be radically mistaken: it is possible that we are just *duped*, since everything could seem just as it does and yet we could be wildly wrong. However, as we saw in Chapter 3 our ordinary, pre-philosophical position swallows this possibility without a hiccup, given that there are no reasons in its favor. I know that my spouse isn't a foreign spy engaged in a seamless deception, even though everything could seem just as it does if she were. So the mere fear that we could be wildly and radically duped isn't a ground for serious intellectual concern that we have no knowledge or good reasons for beliefs about the world, given the position we are working within. Standing in the ordinary position, the mere possibility that everything could seem just as it does and yet we could be badly mistaken is epistemically inert. The same goes for the possibility that the epistemic principles and procedures of our ordinary position are wildly mistaken. One might still feel these sorts of worries nonetheless, but (as highlighted in Chapter 3) they are thus revealed to be existential at their core. Their resolution requires neither epistemological theory nor a philosophical vindication, but rather reconciliation and acceptance of our situation.

A related anxiety may arise. I have rejected skeptical arguments by appealing to contingent considerations about the world that we happen to know now, at this point in history. One might have a vague sense that this isn't good enough; one might wish for a response that is not historically and contingently located, a response that could be deployed by any rational being under any possible conditions. One might feel that in the absence of such a thing, we lack a satisfactory response to external world skepticism.

This is a version of the yearning for a form of evidence that functions independently of any particular real-world and human context. As we saw in Chapter 6, Maddy rejects the demand for this form of evidence, and I think she is quite right to do so. For one thing, no such demand appears in the commitments of our ordinary, pre-philosophical position. It is part of our best methodological commitments in ordinary life and science that we are content with contingent evidence, and we work from within what is already known at a particular juncture in history. To speak from our position within the commitments of ordinary epistemic life: nothing more is needed.

Moreover, it is quite unclear what this is really a yearning for or whether we can fully coherently specify in detail what is being sought. I'm inclined to think not. If that's right, then what is driving dissatisfaction here is not really that there is some other form of evidence, recognizable as such, that I have failed to provide, but rather a wish for a form of security that is somehow more solid than the contingent and historically located. If anything like this is what is going on, then (again) it is an existential concern more than an epistemic one.

2. Cavell's Concern

Some philosophers most concerned about the relation between skeptical reflections and ordinary life might object from another direction. They might urge that in arguing that skepticism isn't generated by the principles and procedures of ordinary epistemic life, I have inappropriately ignored the way in which skeptical imaginings can intrude into the life of any thoughtful person. This would certainly have been the view of Stanley Cavell (1979). Cavell thought that the skeptic's "original—and originating—question" (138) arises from a certain kind of experience that is available to all of us. Once this question is on the table, he claims, the procedures of ordinary inquiry and epistemic assessment lead us to the skeptical conclusion. As he puts it, "[O]nce it seems a real problem, the [skeptical] answers to it may not seem so clearly, or wrongly, forced" (138). On Cavell's view, no response to skepticism can be satisfactory unless it does justice to these considerations.

What is that originating question? It is something like, "How can we know anything about the world?," where that question is posed in a way that prevents us from appealing to anything we believe about the world as part of our answer. Cavell grants that the skeptic must arrive at this question in a way that seems "natural" and draws on perfectly ordinary epistemic procedures. In order for the skeptical conclusion to have the proper level of generality, the question and subsequent inquiry must apply completely generally, so that nothing about the procedures utilized or the conclusions reached are tied to the specifics or peculiarities of a particular case. And the question must arise from a starting point that acknowledges everything Austin and Moore would insist upon regarding the proper conduct of inquiry and epistemic assessment. Cavell's claim, then, is that this question can arise in a way that meets these constraints. "[W]hen the ordinary language philosopher says, 'You have no reason to raise the question of existence or reality in your context,' he must seem to the [skeptic] to beg his question, because for him the context is one in which the question has, and reasonably, already arisen. It has been forced upon us" (139).

What forces this question upon us, Cavell claims, is a "sense of something amiss" regarding our knowledge of the world (139–140). This sense is grounded in a distinctive kind of experience:

> My major claim about the [skeptical] philosopher's originating question . . . is that it (in one or another of its variations) is a response to, or expression of, a real experience which takes hold of human beings. . . . It is not a response to questions raised in ordinary practical contexts, framed in language which any master of a language will accept as ordinary. But it is, as I might put it, a response which expresses a natural experience of a creature complicated or burdened enough to possess language at all. (140)

Putting all of this together, then, Cavell's key claim is that when we are reflecting under the aegis of this experience, led by it to wonder how we can know anything about the world at all, our *ordinary procedures of inquiry and epistemic assessment* inevitably lead us to a skeptical conclusion.

What is this distinctive experience? Cavell describes it as one of feeling "sealed off from the world, enclosed within my own endless succession of experiences" (144). He writes:

> I can here only attest to my having had such experiences and, though struggling against them intellectually, have had to wait for them to dissipate in their own time. It seems to me that I relive such experiences when I ask my students, as habitually at the beginning of a course in which epistemology is discussed, whether they have ever had such thoughts as, for example, that they might, when for all the world awake, be dreaming; . . . or that the things of the world would seem just as they now do to us if there were nothing in it but some power large enough either to keep us in a sort of hypnotic spell, or to arrange the world for our actions as a kind of endless stage-set, whose workings we can never get behind. . . . I know well enough, intellectually as it were, that these suppositions may be nonsense, seem absurd, when raised as scruples about particular claims to knowledge.

But if these experiences have worked in the initial motivation of particular claims, then the attempt to prove intellectually that they have no sense is apt to weaken one's faith in intellectuality. (143)

Here Cavell appeals to a certain feeling that one can have when considering the skeptical hypotheses, and his claim is that once one has had this distinctive, uncanny experience, it is bound to seem unsatisfactory to reply, as I have suggested, by appealing to considerations about the world.

I agree that when one is in the grip of such an experience, this form of reply will feel unsatisfactory. The crucial question, however, is whether this is really a path into skeptical reflection that fully conforms with the principles and procedures of our pre-philosophical position. I don't think that it is.

It is undoubtedly true that people sometimes have such experiences. It is also undoubtedly true that when one is in the grip of such an experience, it will seem both inappropriate and useless to appeal to considerations about the world. But the fundamental issue concerns our ordinary principles and procedures of inquiry and epistemic assessment. What significance do those principles and procedures accord to such experiences and responses? If our ordinary position would have us discount them, then this is no way to show that skepticism grows out of the commitments and procedures of ordinary epistemic life.

It can be helpful here to think about certain parallels from the position of everyday life. When we do, we are reminded that while strange, uncanny feelings or anxious worries can be psychologically and emotionally informative, it is a mistake to take them to have the same significance as reasonable doubts if they have no root in reality. The point is familiar to those of us who occasionally suffer from neurotic worries about whether we have turned off the stove or locked the door even when we clearly remember having done so. But it also applies to cases that more closely parallel the experience that Cavell attests to. For instance, years ago I had an uncanny experience while riding the subway with my spouse of twenty years. I looked at her and had a feeling that would best be captured by saying, "Who is this woman? This isn't my spouse, even though this person looks just like her; this is a complete stranger." To be clear, this wasn't simply a vivid realization of the extent to which we inevitably remain a mystery to one another no matter how deeply interwoven our lives. Rather, the feeling was, "This is really somebody else; this isn't my spouse; this is a person I have never met." In point of fact, there was no reason whatsoever to think it was somebody else, and so the right thing to do—the right thing to do in epistemic terms—was simply to discount this feeling until it passed. I mean: to discount it insofar as the question, "Who is this person in front of me?," was concerned. I didn't discount the *emotional experience*, insofar as it revealed something important about the movements of my mind and feelings in our relationship, something that needed to be thought about and discussed with my spouse. In proceeding in this way, I was in accord with the principles and procedures of ordinary epistemic life. I was doing it right.

Consider now a case that more closely parallels the question of external world skepticism as Cavell describes it. Imagine that someone has been in an excellent marriage for many decades. They consider the possibility that perhaps their spouse has never loved them but has instead been engaged in a seamless deception. Nothing whatsoever actually suggests any such thing; everything in fact points in exactly the opposite direction. Still, they become gripped by the thought, and as they are imagining this possibility they have a distinctive, uncanny experience, a feeling of being sealed off from the truth about their spouse's love, of being entrapped within the web of their spouse's actions and words. They have a sense of something amiss, and they wonder—really, seriously wonder, taking it as an important, open question: "Do I know the truth about this? How can I know it?" They become seriously concerned that perhaps their spouse has never loved them. They see that to resolve this concern they can't appeal to anything their spouse has said or done over these many years, nor to anything about how they feel when with their spouse; all of that could, they take it, just be a part or result of the deception. They likewise see that it is not probative that such a deception would be hard to pull off; after all, their concern is precisely that their spouse may have managed it despite the difficulty. Now they are really in desperate straits: they are concerned that their spouse has never loved them, and they see that there is nothing available to help resolve the concern. They are quite distressed. Their spouse reassures them that of course they love them, aren't deceiving them, and so on. But everything their spouse says and does immediately becomes worthless: with despair, they recognize that all this might just be further moves in a web of deception. The more strident the attempted reassurance, the greater their suspicion and anguish. They become hopeless, terrified that it is impossible to find out the truth about their spouse.

The point that I want to make about this example is simple: what we see here does not perfectly accord with the commitments and procedures of ordinary epistemic life. Rather, what I have just described looks like some sort of paranoid psychosis. This is a person who needs the assistance of a mental health professional. Everything this person thinks, does, and feels would be in accord with the commitments and procedures of ordinary epistemic life, *if there was some reason of the right sort to suspect that their spouse was engaged in some such deception.* But in the absence of any such reason, this person took a wrong turn right at the beginning. In terms of the relevant epistemic considerations, they should not have taken their uncanny feeling to have the kind of significance that they took it to have. (This is not to say that they necessarily had any control over how they responded to this experience.)

It is important to see that I am not denying that such things are a part of what I have been calling our "ordinary, pre-philosophical position." They are, and that itself is something that we recognize perfectly well in ordinary life. The crucial point is rather this: In terms of the commitments and procedures of ordinary epistemic life, this person makes a mistake when they take their uncanny feeling to open up a genuine, serious question about whether they can really know anything about the truth of their spouse's feelings—a question raised in such a way that it cannot be answered by considering anything about what their spouse says and does. In fact, they had no good reason to raise this question in this way.

The same points apply to Cavell's suggestion regarding external world skepticism. Of course it is part of human life that we can have an uncanny feeling of the sort that he describes. That is a truth that is recognized in the ordinary, pre-philosophical position. But it is no part of ordinary epistemic life that the right response is to follow up on that feeling in the way Cavell suggests. To do so—that is, to take that feeling as an indication that something might really be amiss with your knowledge of the world, and then seriously to attempt to inquire into the issue from that vantage point, taking the question of whether you really know anything about the world to genuinely be at stake—is not to follow out the principles and procedures of ordinary epistemic life. We have departed from those principles and procedures at the first step if we treat an uncanny feeling, itself not grounded in any good reasons for doubt, as if it were an actual indication that things might be amiss even though everything points in exactly the other direction.

I conclude that if we are standing squarely within the principles and procedures of our ordinary position, Cavell has given us no reason to be dissatisfied with where we have ended up. We still have found no reason to think anything other than that we know and have good reason to believe all sorts of things about the world.

3. The Demand for a Global Account

Trouble might seem to emerge here nonetheless. At various points in this book we have seen an insistent suspicion that certain global questions or requirements are a way of deriving skeptical results from within the ordinary, pre-philosophical position. For instance, in Chapter 3 we considered Stroud's attempt to utilize our familiar practice of reflective critical reappraisal to generate a general evaluative question about the totality of our knowledge of the world—a question that would, he claimed, require an answer that makes use of none of our knowledge of the world. We just saw Cavell's attempt to locate the source of a similar global question in a distinctive kind of experience. And at the tail end of Chapter 4 we addressed Stroud's and Bonjour's attempts to bracket all of our knowledge of the world by asking fully general explanatory questions about our knowledge or reasons for beliefs about the world. In all such cases, there is an attempt to generate a demand for a certain kind of global explanatory or justificatory account of our knowledge or reasons for beliefs about the world—an account that proceeds without making use of any of our knowledge of the world. This is then followed by the claim that we cannot satisfy the demand, and finally by the conclusion that because we cannot satisfy the demand, we lack knowledge or good reasons regarding the world.

Once we see this pattern, we might wonder about a skeptical argument of roughly this form:

1. I can't defend my individual beliefs about the world without making use of other things I think I know about the world.
2. If I can't defend my individual beliefs about the world without making use of other things I think I know about the world, then I have no good reason to believe anything at all about the world around me.
3. So, I have no good reason to believe anything at all about the world around me.

What is to be said about this sort of argument, if we resolutely take the Moorean approach that I have been exploring in this book?[1]

In Chapter 4 I offered a response on behalf of Austin. In effect, this response highlighted that Austin's central points explain why premise 1 is true

---

[1] I am grateful to a referee for the press for stressing the importance of this question.

in a way that shows premise 2 to be incorrect: if we keep Austin's central points in mind, then we can see that our inability to provide such a defense simply doesn't speak to the question of whether we have good reasons for beliefs about the world. However, an even simpler, more direct rejection of premise 2 is available from our Moorean standpoint. Here's why. (Keep in mind that as always, here we are speaking from within our ordinary, pre-philosophical position.) First, we do know things about the world, and we do have good reasons to believe things about the world. Second, it is perfectly acceptable to defend individual beliefs about the world by appealing to other considerations about the world. So, granting that premise 1 is correct, premise 2 imposes a demand that conflicts with manifest truths and that does not comport with correct epistemic assessments and procedures. Moreover, no reason has been located in its favor or for thinking that it is something that we are committed to in the ordinary position. So, taking all of these considerations together, we should reject the second premise. It is incorrect.

The situation would be very different if the demand imposed by premise 2 *did* arise from the principles and procedures of the ordinary position. Then we would be in real trouble. That is why arguments like Stroud's and Cavell's are so important. They try to generate a question from within the ordinary position that (it is hoped) will place all of our knowledge of the world out of bounds and generate a requirement with the force of something like premise 2. Likewise, if there had been a convincing route from our ordinary position to the Global Priority Thesis, then again we would have reason to think that something like premise 2 is true. As we have seen, however, none of these lines of thought has succeeded, and no other reason in favor of something like premise 2 has emerged. So, standing as we are in the ordinary position, we have excellent reason to reject premise 2. It has consequences that conflict with manifest truths, and no good reason has appeared in its favor despite a careful search.

4. But Is This Really a Satisfactory Refutation of Skepticism?

The argument I just made is an instance of the method that was elaborated in Chapter 2 and then put into practice over the course of this book. In Chapter 1 I invited you to try out the method yourself—to read this book in its spirit—and I urged that the result provides a fully satisfactory refutation of external world skepticism even without the development or use of a general explanatory epistemological theory. By "fully satisfactory," I do not mean that the result provides everything someone might want from a refutation of skepticism. It doesn't, for instance, come accompanied by a check for $1 million. Rather, what I mean is that it is fully adequate as a refutation. It fully meets the need.

Here, again, is what I invited you to do:

Stand squarely within the ordinary position. Start out with all of our ordinary commitments about what is the case, about what evidence we have for what, about what we know or have reason to believe, about when someone knows, is justified, or has good reason to believe something, and about how we should proceed when assessing people's knowledge, defending our beliefs and deciding what to believe. Working from within that position, ask: can we somehow be moved in a reasonable way to accept the conclusion that we know far less about the world around us than we initially thought, or that we don't even have any reason to believe anything about the world? Address this question by freely making use of the commitments of our ordinary position to respond to the key assumptions, principles, and early moves of skeptical argumentation—unless and until you find some aspect of our ordinary commitments that blocks you from doing so.

In this spirit, we considered all of the most important lines of skeptical thought. We found that none of them provided a good reason for thinking that skepticism is true, and that both skepticism and key premises in central skeptical arguments conflict with manifest truths. We consequently concluded that skepticism is false. And we found no reason to think that we were going astray in our assessment.

Is this a fully satisfactory refutation? As always, we approach this question from within the position of ordinary epistemic life. To speak from within that position: Here is one sort of refutation that is entirely satisfactory. We consider all of the most important arguments that might be offered for a view, and we determine that there is no good reason in its favor. We find that it conflicts with manifest truths. We carefully consider whether there is any reason to think we are going astray in our assessment, and we find that there isn't. We consequently reject the view as false. That's exactly what we've done regarding external world skepticism, and it's a fully satisfactory refutation in terms of the principles, requirements, and procedures of ordinary epistemic life. Those standards frame the position within which we are conducting this inquiry, and we have seen no reason arising from within that starting point to demand something else. It's internal to the method that our result is fully satisfactory on its own terms.

5. The Question of Theory

The work involved in this refutation went considerably beyond the ordinary person's blunt denial of skepticism in the course of everyday life. It involved, for instance, offering clear examples that refute attempts to support various premises of skeptical arguments (e.g., Chapters 5 and 6), considering parallel cases (such as our knowledge that neither ducks, dung beetles, nor rocks rule the world through an undetectable deception) to remove concern as to how we could know that we aren't being deceived by an evil demon (Chapter 7), and carefully describing how our justificatory practices actually work in order to head off certain regress arguments (Chapters 9 and 11). Importantly, however, none of this involved the provision of an epistemological theory, that is, a general, systematic account of knowledge, evidence, justification, and the like aimed at explaining the truth of the epistemic assessments of ordinary life. Nor was an epistemological theory needed for our purpose.

Of course, it's plausible that some value would be added to any refutation of anything if it is supplemented by a fully general epistemological theory to explain how we count as knowing the things appealed to as evidence in the refutation, why they constitute good evidence, how we thereby count as knowing the falsity of what has been refuted, and so on. However, in ordinary life and science we don't hold that to be fully satisfactory, a refutation has to be accompanied by any such thing. For instance, phrenology has been fully satisfactorily refuted. No serious scientist working today denies this. But the refutation of phrenology was not accompanied by a general theory of knowledge, justification, or evidence. Nobody thinks the refutation of phrenology was less than fully adequate for that reason.

No special demand for a general epistemological theory arises in the particular case of skepticism, either. A hypothesis can be fully satisfactorily refuted without the development or provision of a completely general theory that explains why the hypothesis is false. For instance, what would it take to fully satisfactorily refute phrenology? It would be fully adequate if it were shown, first, that there is no good evidence in support of the phrenologists' hypotheses and, second, that there are no significant correlations between surface contours of the skull and the traits phrenologists focused upon. That's enough to show fully satisfactorily that phrenology is to be rejected. If we wanted to refute phrenology's underlying ideas as well, we would show in addition that there are not simple neuro-anatomical correlates for most of the relevant personality traits and that increased neurological activity in localized regions of the cortex does not cause changes to the contours of the skull. However, a fully adequate refutation of phrenology *does not* require supplementation by a full theory of neuro-cranial anatomical functioning that enables a complete explanation of why the phrenologists' claims are false. That would perhaps be nice to have for some purposes. But it isn't needed for a fully satisfactory case that phrenology belongs in the dustbins of science.

I can't see any reason to think any differently regarding external world skepticism. To speak from our Moorean position: We have not provided an explanation from first principles of why skepticism is false, but we have done what is needed to show without a doubt that it is.

From this perspective, then, the aspiration to develop a completely general explanatory epistemological theory looks optional—optional, that is, as opposed to a matter of intellectual necessity so far as the refutation of skepticism is concerned. It becomes a matter of simple curiosity: can a certain, very particular kind of explanatory theory be developed or not? This is an interesting question, at least to many of us. But nothing hangs in the balance when we are considering the truth of skepticism from our Moorean standpoint within the commitments of ordinary epistemic life. Our refutation will be none the weaker even if it turns out that no satisfactory general epistemological theory can be developed.

It might be replied to all of this that without an epistemological theory, our rejection of skepticism is not *philosophically* satisfactory—where a special stress is placed on the word "philosophically." Such a response is suggested by a passage from Jim Pryor quoted in Chapter 1. In discussing the role of epistemological theory in providing a "supporting argument" for Moore's approach, Pryor writes, "If we're to have a satisfying *philosophical* response to skepticism, it will consist in that supporting argument, not in the reasoning that Moore's argument articulates" (2004, 370, italics added). Here Pryor suggests that without an epistemological theory to buttress it, a Moorean response to skepticism cannot be philosophically satisfying.

Should we accept that assessment? One way to reach it comes cheap. If we simply use the word "philosophical" as a way of packing in the demand for an epistemological theory, then of course nothing can be philosophically satisfying that eschews such a demand. To Pryor's credit, however, he doesn't go cheap. He tries to provide support for his demand by specifying what he takes the task of philosophical engagement with skepticism to involve.

> Nowadays, it's commonly agreed that an adequate philosophical response to the skeptic need not be capable of rationally persuading the skeptic that the external world exists, or that we have justification to believe it exists. Nor need it be capable of persuading someone who's seized by skeptical doubts. What it does have to do is diagnose and explain the flaws in the skeptic's reasoning.... These are ... responsibilities we have when we're doing philosophy. That's the business of philosophy: to diagnose and criticize arguments like the skeptic's. (2004, 370)

I agree with everything Pryor says here. But isn't Pryor describing exactly what we have done over the course of this book? We have diagnosed and criticized the skeptic's arguments. And of course, we've done it without developing or appealing to an epistemological theory.

Some readers might feel that at the very least an encounter with skepticism ought to provide us with epistemological theory by way of pay-off. What else—it might be asked—would be the point? To return to another passage cited in Chapter 1,

> Skeptical arguments are useful and important because they drive progress in philosophy. They do this by highlighting plausible but mistaken assumptions about knowledge and evidence, and by showing us that those assumptions have consequences that are unacceptable. As a result we are forced to develop substantive and controversial positions in their place. (Greco 2000, 2–3)

On this line of thought, it is precisely a pay-off in epistemological theory that makes it worthwhile to engage with external world skepticism.

But why, I want to reply, should we think that any such pay-off is the mark of philosophical importance?

If the argument of this book has been right, we can properly respond to the questions and arguments that fuel external world skepticism simply by appealing to truisms of ordinary life. These truisms do not add up to an epistemological theory. The attempt to develop an adequate theory is consequently optional downstream work. But this encounter with skepticism is philosophically significant nonetheless: we come to see the falsehood of an important position in philosophy that has intrigued serious thinkers for hundreds of years. That is nothing to take lightly!

Moreover, our encounter with skepticism yields a form of illumination that is aptly termed "philosophical" even if it doesn't involve development of an epistemological theory (though of course here we do not mean "philosophical" in the sense at issue in my characterization of the ordinary, pre-philosophical position [Chapters 1 and 2]). Wittgenstein wrote that "A philosophical problem has the form 'I don't know my way around' " (2009, §123) and that "the problems are solved by arranging what we have always known" (§109). When we wonder, for instance, "How *could* we know that we aren't being deceived by an evil demon?," we are in the midst of the feeling that we don't know our way around. And when we consider parallel cases in which epistemic asymmetry shows up in our ordinary epistemic lives (as we did in Chapter 7), we are arranging what we have always known about how ordinary epistemic life actually works. This enables a form of reflective understanding that is quite different from what would be provided by an explanatory theory. We come to "know our way about." This sort of reflective self-understanding is a central part of what is most valuable in the humanistic intellectual tradition. And it is precisely this sort of understanding that enables us to rest content despite the fear that, even given all that has been said, we might just be being duped—for we come to see how the possibility of being duped actually functions (again, see Chapters 3 and 7). For those of us who have found ourselves alive to this fear, the work Moore shows us how to do is thus philosophically important even if it doesn't have any immediate pay-off in epistemological theory. This is a form of philosophical importance that is largely occluded in contemporary analytic philosophy, though it was of central importance to our near-ancestors such as Moore, Wittgenstein, and Austin.

6. A Closing Question

Epistemologists sometimes voice another form of dissatisfaction with the sort of approach we find in Moore: it fails to identify why skeptical argumentation might be tempting. As Richard Feldman puts it, "Moore's remarks may not be satisfying because they fail to make clear why the skeptical argument is both appealing and wrong" (1986, 306). But we haven't merely argued that skepticism is false; we have carefully scrutinized the lines of thought that might prompt one in that direction. Moreover, if our concern is whether some skeptical argument is correct, why must a satisfactory refutation explain why it is appealing in addition to showing it to be wrong? Consider this parallel: Once you see that the Gambler's Fallacy is indeed a fallacy, there is no pressing question—so far as the truth of the matter is concerned—about why someone might have thought otherwise; that is at best a topic of psychological curiosity. The same goes for the case at hand. Once we have found that there is no good reason in favor of a particular skeptical premise, principle, or argument, then the question of why we might have found it appealing is no longer relevant to the question of what we should believe.

The crucial question, then, is this—and here I would ask you to speak for yourself and not for some hypothetical interlocutor: Is there any skeptical premise, principle, or argument that you really think is intellectually well-motivated *now*, any skeptical premise, principle, or argument that you really think has some reason in its favor despite all we've said? If so, then let's talk. If not, then we are done.

Bibliography

Alston, William. 1986. "Epistemic Circularity." In his *Epistemic Justification: Essays in the Theory of Knowledge*, 319–349. Ithaca, NY: Cornell University Press, 1989.

Alston, William. 1980. "Level Confusions in Epistemology." *Midwest Studies in Philosophy* 5, no. 1, 135–150.

Audi, Robert. 1993. *The Structure of Justification*. Cambridge, UK: Cambridge University Press.

Austin, J.L. 1979. *Philosophical Papers*. 3rd ed. Edited by J.O. Urmson and G.J. Warnock. Oxford: Oxford University Press.

Austin, J.L. 1962. *Sense and Sensibilia*. Edited by G.J. Warnock. Oxford: Oxford University Press.

Austin, J.L. 1958. *Lectures at the University of California, Berkeley*. Unpublished lectures, with notes by R. Lawrence and W. Hayes, supplemented by Wallace Matson.

Ayer, A.J. 1956. *The Problem of Knowledge*. London: Macmillan.

Ayer, A.J. 1940. *The Foundations of Empirical Knowledge*. London: Macmillan.

Baldwin, Thomas. 1990. *G.E. Moore*. London: Routledge.

Bergmann, M. 2006. *Justification Without Awareness: A Defense of Epistemic Externalism*. Oxford: Clarendon Press.

Blumenfeld, D., and J.B. Blumenfeld. 1978. "Can I Know That I Am Not Dreaming?" In *Descartes: Critical and Interpretive Essays*. Edited by Michael Hooker, 234–255. Baltimore, MD: Johns Hopkins University Press.

Bonjour, Laurence. 2003. "A Version of Internalist Foundationalism." In *Epistemic Justification: Internalism vs. Externalism, Foundationalism vs. Virtues*. Edited by Laurence Bonjour and Ernest Sosa, 3–77. Malden, MA: Blackwell Publishing.

Bonjour, Laurence. 1985. *The Structure of Empirical Knowledge*. Cambridge, MA: Harvard University Press.

Bridges, J. 2016. "Skepticism and Beyond." *Sképsis: A Journal for Philosophy and Interdisciplinary Research* 14, 76–99.

Byrne, A. 2004. "How Hard Are the Sceptical Paradoxes?" *Noûs* 38, 299–325.

Cavell, Stanley. 1979. *The Claim of Reason*. New York: Oxford University Press.

Chisholm, Roderick. 1989. *Theory of Knowledge*. 3rd ed. Englewood Cliffs, NJ: Prentice-Hall.

Chisholm, Roderick. 1982. *The Foundations of Knowing*. Minneapolis, MN: University of Minnesota Press.

Chisholm, Roderick. 1982. "The Myth of the Given." In *Philosophy*, 261–286. Englewood Cliffs, NJ: Prentice-Hall, 1964. Reprinted in *The Foundations of Knowing*, 126–147. Minneapolis, MN: University of Minnesota Press, 1982. Page references are to the 1982 edition.

Chisholm, Roderick. 1957. *Perceiving: A Philosophical Study*. Ithaca, NY: Cornell University Press.

Clarke, Thomson. 1972. "The Legacy of Skepticism." *Journal of Philosophy* 69, no. 20, 754–769.
Coffey, P. 2009. *Epistemology or the Theory of Knowledge*. Volume I. Longmans, Green & Co., London: 1917. Reprinted in *Epistemology or the Theory of Knowledge: An Introduction to General Metaphysics*, Volume I. Eugene, OR: Wifp & Stock, 2009. Page references are to the 2009 edition.
Cohen, Stewart. 2005. "Why Basic Knowledge Is Easy Knowledge." *Philosophy and Phenomenological Research* 70, no. 2, 417–430.
Cohen, Stewart. 2002. "Basic Knowledge and the Problem of Easy Knowledge." *Philosophy and Phenomenological Research* 65, no. 2, 309–329.
Cohen, Stewart. 1984. "Justification and Truth." *Philosophical Studies* 46, 279–296.
Cohen, Stewart, and Keith Lehrer. 1983. "Justification, Truth, and Coherence." *Synthese* 55, 191–207.
Coliva, Annalisa. 2015. *Extended Rationality: A Hinge Epistemology*. New York: Palgrave Macmillan.
Coliva, Annalisa. 2010. *Moore and Wittgenstein: Skepticism, Certainty, and Common Sense*. New York: Palgrave Macmillan.
Conant, James. 1998. "Wittgenstein on Meaning and Use." *Philosophical Investigations* 21, no. 3, 222–250.
Conee, Earl. 2001. "Comments on Bill Lycan's Moore Against the New Skeptics." *Philosophical Studies* 103, 55–59.
Conee, Earl, and Richard Feldman. 2004. *Evidentialism*. Oxford: Clarendon Press.
David, Marian, and Ted A. Warfield. 2008. "Knowledge-Closure and Skepticism." In *Epistemology: New Essays*. Edited by Quentin Smith, 137–188. New York: Oxford University Press.
DeRose, K. 1995. "Solving the Skeptical Problem." *Philosophical Review* 104, 1–49.
Descartes, René. 1984. "Meditations on First Philosophy." Paris, 1647. Reprinted in *The Philosophical Writings of Descartes*. Volume II. Edited by John Cottingham, Robert Stoothoff, and Dugald Murdoch, 1–62. Cambridge: Cambridge University Press, 1984. Page references are to the 1984 edition.
Dretske, Fred. 1981. "The Pragmatic Dimension of Knowledge." *Philosophical Studies* 40, 363–378.
Dretske, Fred. 1970. "Epistemic Operators." *Journal of Philosophy* 67, 1007–1023.
Feldman, Richard. 1986. "Review: The Significance of Philosophical Scepticism." *Philosophical Review* 95, no. 2, 305–308.
Firth, Roderick. 1998. "The 1969 Notre Dame Lectures." In *In Defense of Radical Empiricism: Essays and Lectures by Roderick Firth*. Edited by John Troyer, 275–303. Lanham, MD: Rowman & Littlefield Publishers.
Flanagan, Owen. 2001. *Dreaming Souls: Sleep, Dreams, and the Evolution of the Conscious Mind*. Oxford: Oxford University Press.
Foley, Richard. 1987. *The Theory of Epistemic Rationality*. Cambridge, MA: Harvard University Press.
Fumerton, Richard. 1995. *Metaepistemology and Skepticism*. Totowa, NJ: Rowman & Littlefield.
Goldman, Alvin. 1999. "Internalism Exposed." *Journal of Philosophy* 96, no. 6, 271–293.
Greco, John. 2002. "How to Reid Moore." *Philosophical Quarterly* 52, no. 209, 544–563.
Greco, John. 2000. *Putting Skeptics in Their Place: The Nature of Skeptical Arguments and Their Role in Philosophical Argumentation*. Cambridge, UK: Cambridge University Press.

Greenough, Patrick, and Duncan Pritchard, ed. 2009. *Williamson on Knowledge*. New York: Oxford University Press.
Grice, Paul. 1989. *Studies in the Way of Words*. Cambridge, MA: Harvard University Press.
Helvétius, Claude Adrien. 1759. *De l'Esprit: Or, Essays on the Mind, and Its Several Faculties, Translated from the edition printed under the author's inspection*. London.
Hirsch, Eli. 2018. *Radical Skepticism and the Shadow of Doubt: A Philosophical Dialogue*. New York: Bloomsbury Publishing.
Hobbes, Thomas. 1647. "Third Set of Objections." *The Philosophical Writings of Descartes*. Volume II. Translated and edited by John Cottingham, Robert Stoothoff, and Dugald Murdoch, 121–137. Cambridge: Cambridge University Press, 1984.
Hobson, J. Allen. 1999. *Dreaming as Delirium*. Cambridge, MA: MIT University Press.
Hobson, J. Allen. 1988. *The Dreaming Brain*. New York: Basic Books.
Joyce, Jim. 2044. "Williamson on Evidence and Knowledge." *Philosophical Books* 45, no. 4, 296–305.
Kaplan, Mark. 2018. *Austin's Way with Skepticism*. Oxford: Oxford University Press.
Kaplan, Mark. 2011. "Tales of the Unknown: Austin and the Argument from Ignorance." In *The Philosophy of J.L. Austin*. Edited by Martin Gustafson and Richard Sørli, 51–77. Oxford: Oxford University Press.
Kelly, Thomas. 2005. "Moorean Facts and Belief Revision, Or Can the Skeptic Win?" *Philosophical Perspectives* 19, no. 1, 179–209.
Lawlor, Krista. 2015. "Replies to Leite, Turri, and Gerken." *Philosophy and Phenomenological Research* 90, no. 1, 235–255.
Lawlor, Krista. 2013. *Assurance: An Austinian View of Knowledge and Knowledge Claims*. Oxford: Oxford University Press.
Le Fébure, Guillaume-René. 1783. *Observations pratiques, rares et curieuses, sur divers accidents vénériens [et] autres qui leur sont relatifs: pour servir de supplément au Mémoire clinique sur les maladies vénériennes*. Utrecht: chez Barthélémy Wild.
Lear, Jonathan. 2011. *A Case for Irony (The Tanner Lectures on Human Values)*. Cambridge, MA: Harvard University Press.
Lehrer, Keith. 1978. "Why Not Skepticism?" In *Essays on Knowledge and Justification*. Edited by George Sortiros Pappas and Marshall Swain, 346–363. Ithaca, NY: Cornell University Press.
Leite, Adam. 2020. "Austin and the Scope of Our Knowledge," *International Journal for the Study of Skepticism* 12, no. 3, 195–206. doi: https://doi.org/10.1163/22105700-bja10005
Leite, Adam. 2019. "Skepticism and Epistemic Asymmetry." *Philosophical Issues* 29, no. 1), 184–197 (John Wiley & Sons).
Leite, Adam. 2018. "The Plain Inquirer's Plain Evidence Against the Global Skeptical Scenarios." *The International Journal for the Study of Skepticism* 8, no. 3, 208–222.
Leite, Adam. 2015. "Why Don't I Know I'm Not a Brain-in-a-Vat?" *Philosophy and Phenomenological Research* 90, no. 11, 205–213.
Leite, Adam. 2013. "But That's Not Evidence; It's Not Even True!" *Philosophical Quarterly* 63, no. 250, 81–104.
Leite, Adam. 2011a. "Austin, Dreams, and Skepticism." In *New Essays on the Philosophy of J.L. Austin*. Edited by Martin Gustafsson and Richard Sorli, 78–113. New York: Oxford University Press.
Leite, Adam. 2011b. "Immediate Warrant, Epistemic Responsibility, and Moorean Dogmatism." In *Reasons for Belief*. Edited by Andrew Reisner and Asbjørn Steglich-Petersen, 158–179. Cambridge: Cambridge University Press.

Leite, Adam. 2010. "How to Take Skepticism Seriously." *Philosophical Studies* 148, no. 1, 39–60.

Leite, Adam. 2008. "Believing One's Reasons Are Good." *Synthese* 161, no. 3, 419–441.

Leite, Adam. 2005. "Epistemological Externalism and the Project of Traditional Epistemology." *Philosophy and Phenomenological Research* 70, no. 3, 505–533.

Leite, Adam. 2004a. "Is Fallibility an Epistemological Shortcoming?" *Philosophical Quarterly* 54, no. 215, 232–251.

Leite, Adam. 2004b. "Skepticism, Closure, and Sensitivity (or Why the Closure Principle is Irrelevant to Skepticism)." Special issue, *Croatian Journal of Philosophy* 4, no. 12, 335–350.

Ludwig, Kirk. Unpublished. "Skepticism, Logical Independence, and Epistemic Priority." https://socrates.sitehost.iu.edu/papers/Skepticism,%20Logical%20Independence,%20and%20Epistemic%20Priority.htm

Lycan, William. 2007. "Moore's Anti-Skeptical Strategies." In *Themes from G.E. Moore: New Essays in Epistemology and Ethics*. Edited by Gary Seay and Susana Nuccetelli, 84–99. New York: Oxford University Press.

Maddy, Penelope. 2022. "Wittgenstein on Hinges." In *A Plea for Natural Philosophy and Other Essays*, 137–158. Oxford: Oxford University Press.

Maddy, Penelope. 2018. "Reply to Coliva, Leite, and Stroud." *International Journal for the Study of Skepticism* 8, no. 3, 231–244.

Maddy, Penelope. 2017. *What Do Philosophers Do? Skepticism and the Practice of Philosophy*. New York: Oxford University Press.

Maddy, Penelope. 2007. *Second Philosophy*. New York: Oxford University Press.

Malcolm, Norman. 1949. "Defending Common Sense." *Philosophical Review* 58, no. 3, 201–220.

Marušić, Berislav. 2016. "Asymmetry Arguments." *Philosophical Studies* 173, 1081–1102.

McDowell, John. 2011. *Perception as a Capacity for Knowledge*. Milwaukee, WI: Marquette University Press.

McDowell, John. 1995. "Knowledge and the Internal." *Philosophy and Phenomenological Research* 55, 877–893.

McDowell, John. 1982. "Criteria, Defeasibility, and Knowledge." *Proceedings of the British Academy* 68, 455–479.

McGinn, Marie. 1989. *Sense and Certainty*. Oxford: Basil Blackwell.

Moore, G.E. 1993a. "Certainty." In his *Philosophical Papers*. London: George, Allen and Unwin, 1959, 226–251. Reprinted in Moore, *Selected Writings*, 171–196. Page references are to the *Selected Writings*.

Moore, G.E. 1993b. "A Defence of Common Sense." In *Contemporary British Philosophy* (2nd series). Edited by J.H. Muirhead. London: George, Allen and Unwin, 1925. Reprinted in Moore, *Selected Writings*, 106–133. Page references are to the *Selected Writings*.

Moore, G.E. 1993c. "Four Forms of Scepticism." In his *Philosophical Papers*. London: George, Allen and Unwin, 1959, 196–225. Reprinted in Moore, *Selected Writings*, 196–226. Page references are to the *Selected Writings*.

Moore, G.E. 1993d. "Proof of an External World." *Proceedings of the British Academy* 25, no. 5, 273–300. Reprinted in Moore, *Selected Writings*, 147–170. Page references are to the *Selected Writings*.

Moore, G.E. 1993e. *Selected Writings*. Edited by Thomas Baldwin. New York: Routledge.

Moore, G.E. 1992. "Autobiography." In *The Philosophy of G.E. Moore*. Edited by Paul Arthur Schilpp, 3–39. La Salle, IL: Open Court.
Moore, G.E. 1959. *Philosophical Papers*. London: George, Allen & Unwin.
Moore, G.E. 1953. *Some Main Problems of Philosophy*. London: George Allen & Unwin. Chapter 6 reprinted as "Hume's Theory Examined" in Moore, *Selected Writings*, 59–78.
Moore, G.E. 1922. "Some Judgments of Perception." *Proceedings of the Aristotelian Society* 19 (1918): 1–29. Reprinted in *Philosophical Studies*, 220–252. London: Routledge & K. Paul, 1922.
Neta, Ram. 2007. "Fixing the Transmission: The New Mooreans." In *Themes From G.E. Moore: New Essays in Epistemology and Ethics*, edited by Susana Nuccetelli and Gary Seay, 62–83. Oxford: Oxford University Press.
Neta, Ram. 2002. "S Knows That P." *Nous* 36, no. 4, 663–681.
Nozick, R. 1981. *Philosophical Explanations*. Cambridge, MA: Harvard University Press.
Price, H.H. 1932. *Perception*. London: Methuen & Co. Ltd.
Pritchard, Duncan. 2016. *Epistemic Angst: Radical Skepticism and the Groundlessness of our Believing*. Princeton, NJ: Princeton University Press.
Pritchard, Duncan. 2012. *Epistemological Disjunctivism*. Oxford: Oxford University Press.
Pritchard, Duncan. 2005. *Epistemic Luck*. New York: Oxford University Press.
Pryor, Jim. 2014. "Is There Immediate Justification?" In *Contemporary Debates in Epistemology*. 2nd ed. Edited by Matthias Steup, John Turri, and Ernest Sosa, 181–205. Malden, MA: John Wiley & Sons.
Pryor, Jim. 2012. "When Warrant Transmits." In *Mind, Meaning & Knowledge: Themes from the Philosophy of Crispin Wright*. Edited by Annalisa Coliva, 269–303. New York: Oxford University Press.
Pryor, Jim. 2004. "What's Wrong with Moore's Argument?" *Philosophical Issues* 14, no. 1, 349–378.
Pryor, Jim. 2000. "The Skeptic and the Dogmatist." *Nous* 34, no. 4, 517–549.
Reichenbach, Hans. 1952. "The Experiential Element in Knowledge." *Philosophical Review* 61, no. 2, 147–159.
Rescorla, Michael. 2009. "Shifting the Burden of Proof?" *Philosophical Quarterly* 59, no. 234, 86–109.
Silins, Nicholas. 2005. "Deception and Evidence." *Philosophical Perspectives* 19, no. 1, 375–404.
Sosa, Ernest. 2009. *Reflective Knowledge*. New York: Oxford University Press.
Sosa, Ernest. 2007. *A Virtue Epistemology: Apt Belief and Reflective Knowledge*. Volume I. New York: Oxford University Press.
Sosa, Ernest. 2005. "Dreams and Philosophy." *Proceedings and Addresses of the American Philosophical Association* 79, 7–18.
Sosa, Ernest. 2002. "Tracking, Knowledge, and Competence." In *The Oxford Handbook of Epistemology*. Edited by Paul K. Moser, 264–286. Oxford: Oxford University Press.
Sosa, Ernest. 1999. "How to Defeat Opposition to Moore." *Philosophical Perspectives* 13, 141–153.
Sosa, Ernest. 1994. "Philosophical Scepticism and Epistemic Circularity." *Proceedings of the Aristotelian Society, Supplementary* 68, 263–307.
Spire, Arnaud. 2012. "Descartes, travail intellectuel et recherche de la verité," https://www.gauchemip.org/spip.php?article15072.
Strawson, P.F. 1957. "Professor Ayer's 'The Problem of Knowledge.'" *Philosophy* 32, no. 123, 302–314.

Stroud, Barry. 2018. "Comments on Penelope Maddy's *What Do Philosophers Do?*" *International Journal for the Study of Skepticism* 8, no. 3, 223–230.
Stroud, Barry. 2015. "Perceptual Knowledge and the Primacy of Judgment." *Journal of the American Philosophical Association* 1, no. 3, 385–395.
Stroud, Barry. 2011. "Seeing What Is So." In *Perception, Causation, and Objectivity*. Edited by J. Roessler, H. Lerman, and N. Eilan, 92–102. New York: Oxford University Press.
Stroud, Barry. 2002. "Understanding Human Knowledge in General." In *Understanding Human Knowledge: Philosophical Essays*, 99–121. Oxford: Oxford University Press.
Stroud, Barry. 1999. "Radical Interpretation and Philosophical Skepticism." In *The Philosophy of Donald Davidson*. Edited by Lewis Hahn, 139–161. Chicago: Open Court.
Stroud, Barry. 1984. *The Significance of Philosophical Scepticism*. Oxford: Clarendon Press.
Stroud, Barry. 1977. *Hume*. New York: Routledge.
Tenaillon, Nicolas. 2013. "Faites dans L'évidence." *Philosophie Magazine*. May 29, 2013. https://www.philomag.com/articles/faites-dans-levidence.
Thomson, Judith Jarvis. 1964. "Reasons and Reasoning." In *Philosophy in America*. Edited by Max Black, 282–303. Ithaca, NY: Cornell University Press.
Wedgwood, Ralph. 2002. "Internalism Explained." *Philosophy and Phenomenological Research* 65, no. 2, 349–369.
Williams, Bernard. 2005. *Descartes: The Project of Pure Enquiry*. New York: Routledge.
Williams, Michael. 2001. *Problems of Knowledge*. Oxford: Oxford University Press.
Williams, Michael. 1996. *Unnatural Doubts*. Princeton, NJ: Princeton University Press.
Williamson, Timothy. 2013. "Gettier Cases in Epistemic Logic." *Inquiry* 56, no. 1, 1–14.
Williamson, Timothy. 2000. *Knowledge and Its Limits*. New York: Oxford University Press.
Wittgenstein, Ludwig. 2009. *Philosophical Investigations*. 4th edition. Revised by P.M.S. Hacker and Joachim Schulte. Translated by G.E.M. Anscombe, P.M.S. Hacker, and Joachim Schulte. Malden, MA: Blackwell Publishing Ltd.
Wittgenstein, Ludwig. 1969. *On Certainty*. Translated and edited by G.E.M. Anscombe and G.H. von Wright. Oxford: Blackwell.
Wright, Crispin. 2007. "The Perils of Dogmatism." In *Themes from G.E. Moore: New Essays in Epistemology and Ethics*. Edited by Susana Nuccetelli and Gary Seay, 25–48. New York: Oxford University Press.
Wright, Crispin. 2004a. "Wittgensteinian Certainties." In *Wittgenstein and Scepticism*. Edited by Denis McManus, 22–55. New York: Routledge.
Wright, Crispin. 2004b. "Warrant for Nothing (and Foundations for Free)." *Aristotelian Society Supplemental* 78, no. 1, 167–212.
Wright, Crispin. 2004c. "Scepticism, Certainty, Moore, and Wittgenstein." In *Wittgenstein's Lasting Significance*. Edited by Max Kölbel and Bernhard Weiss, 228–248. London: Routledge.
Wright, Crispin. 2003. "Some Reflections on the Acquisition of Warrant by Inference." In *New Essays on Semantic Externalism and Self-Knowledge*. Edited by Susana Nuccetelli, 57–77. Cambridge, MA: MIT Press.
Wright, Crispin. 2002. "(Anti-)Sceptics Simple and Subtle: G.E. Moore and John McDowell." *Philosophy and Phenomenological Research* 65, no. 2, 330–348.
Wright, Crispin. 1985. "Facts and Certainty." *Proceedings of the British Academy* 71, 429–472.

Index

For the benefit of digital users, indexed terms that span two pages (e.g., 52–53) may, on occasion, appear on only one of those pages.

accessibility asymmetry, 160–63, 164–72, 173–79, 181, 184–85
Alston, William, 150, 151
American pragmatism, 15
analytic philosophy, 4–5, 14, 15, 330
argument from ignorance, 97–98, 99, 100, 110–12
   epistemic priority requirement and, 113–14, 117
   Evil Demon Hypothesis and, 112, 117
   ordinary, pre-philosophical position and, 99, 100
   of Pritchard, 101–3, 115
Austin, J.L., 4–5, 15, 120
   on alternative possibilities, objections involving, 66–70, 69n.19, 222–23
   on circumstance-dependent matters, 90, 92–94
   on dreaming, 56, 57–65, 59n.4, 61–62nn.9–10, 63n.13, 73–85
   on epistemic priority, 70–75, 80, 88–89, 91–92, 93–94
   on evidence, 63–64, 68, 69, 72, 76, 78–79, 93–94, 146, 157–58, 192
   on external world skepticism, 85–92, 97
   on Global Epistemic Priority Thesis, 263–64
   Moore and, 15, 56, 94, 97, 101, 102–3, 208, 221, 319–20, 324–25
   on ordinary, pre-philosophical position, 56, 65–85, 94
   "Other Minds" by, 65–68, 71, 76–77
   Sense and Sensibilia by, 57–58, 60, 60n.6, 61n.9, 70–71, 263–64
   Stroud and, 88–89, 90, 91–92
Austinian Empirical Argument, 78–85
Austin's Claim, 74–75, 94, 157–58
Ayer, A.J., 59, 261, 264, 267

begging the question, 105
belief revision, 29, 296–301
Berkeley, George, 15
Bonjour, Laurence, 92, 128, 277, 324
brain-in-a-vat scenario, 4, 5, 41–42, 102, 103–4
Bridges, Jason, 230–31, 235–36

Cartesian demands, skeptical hypotheses and, 136–39, 150, 153
Cartesian reconstruction of empirical knowledge, 261–62
Cavell, Stanley, 54, 319–23, 324, 325
"Certainty" (Moore), 28–29, 32–33
Children of Brunettes Hypothesis, 121–22, 131, 138–39, 311
   detached rational re-evaluation of, 152–53, 154
   epistemic asymmetry and, 145, 146–48, 156–57
   epistemic circularity and, 148–49, 150–51
   evidence and, 139–42, 143–44, 145, 146–50, 151–53, 154, 155
   Maddy on, 138–41, 145, 152–53
   Plain Inquirer on, 139–42, 144, 145, 146–47, 149, 151–53, 155
   rational support and, 196–97
Chisholm, Roderick, 123–24, 251, 261, 262–63, 264, 266, 267–75, 278–79, 280
Chisholm's contrast and claim, 269–72
Clarke, Thomson, 43–44
closure-based skeptical arguments, 110–11, 117–18, 221–25
ClosureKK Principle, 193–94
ClosureRK, 101, 115–16
Coliva, Annalisa, 231–32

common sense, 15, 18–19, 22, 24–25, 32, 34, 211
comparative judgment, 30–32
competent deduction, 115–17, 193–94, 195–96, 198
Conee, Earl, 22, 29–30, 31, 108n.7
critical epistemic reassessment, 40, 43–44, 46, 47–48, 100

"Defence of Common Sense, A" (Moore), 32–33, 34
Descartes, René, 7–8, 45, 124, 125, 155, 273–74
　Cartesian demands, skeptical hypotheses and, 136–39
　Cartesian reconstruction of empirical knowledge, 261–62
　on dreams and dreaming, 56, 63
　Evil Demon Hypothesis of, 99, 133–34, 135n.3, 136, 156, 157–59, 256
　on sensory perception, 230, 237–38
　Stroud on, 230
detached rational evaluation, 152–55
dialectical justificatory regresses, 277–87
disjunctivism, 15, 99, 101, 230, 231
dreams and dreaming
　Austin on, 56, 57–65, 59n.4, 61–62nn.9–10, 63n.13, 73–85
　Descartes on, 56, 63
　evidence and, 63–64, 78–80, 82–83, 84–85, 86–87
　external world skepticism and, 85–91
　Hobbes on, 63–64, 64n.14
　lucid dreaming, 62
　Maddy on, 139, 142–43

empirical background assumptions and beliefs, 74–75, 91, 93–94
empirical background information, 76, 82–83, 91–92, 233, 234, 259
empirical background knowledge, 65, 232–33, 234, 236–37, 253–54
empirical justification, 17–18, 27–28, 247
empirical knowledge, 261–62, 264, 268–69
epistemic assessment
　critical epistemic reassessment, 40, 43–44, 46, 47–48, 100
　general, 40–43, 45, 46, 47, 48–55, 92, 207
　principles and procedures of, 45–46, 47, 48–54, 207, 317, 318, 321, 322–23
epistemic asymmetry, 145–48, 152, 224, 305
　accessibility asymmetry, 160–63, 164–72, 173–79, 181, 184–85
　evidence and, 145–48, 156–57, 212
　Evil Demon Hypothesis and, 145, 147, 156–57, 179–80, 181, 183
　external world skepticism and, 160, 187
　knowledge asymmetry, 160, 162–64, 163n.8, 165, 179
　Moorean anti-skeptical project and, 156, 186, 187
　Plain Inquirer on, 152, 156–57
　position-to-know asymmetry, 160, 164–65, 179
　Williamson on, 157, 167, 184–85, 187
epistemic basing relation, 244–46, 248–50, 251–52, 253–54, 287
epistemic circularity, 148–52, 254
epistemic closure, 110–13, 110n.10, 115–16, 117–18
epistemic priority, 70–75, 117–18, 120. See also global epistemic priority thesis
　Austin on, 70–75, 80, 88–89, 91–92, 93–94
　evidence, reliability objections and, 71–72, 73
　Evil Demon Hypothesis and, 113–14, 115, 117
epistemic rationality, 125, 231–32
epistemic responsibility, 124
epistemological disjunctivism, 15, 99, 101, 231
epistemological imagination, 90–91, 243–46
epistemological theory and theorizing
　external world skepticism and, 22–23, 329–30
　Moore, Stroud and, 43–48
　Moore and, 22, 25–26, 29–30, 36, 41
　ordinary, pre-philosophical position and, 189–90, 236, 311–12, 327–30
　ordinary epistemic life and, 17–18, 20
　on sensory perception, 232, 236–37

skepticism and, 3–13, 17, 20, 29–30
substantial, 22, 25–26, 29–30
evidence, 219–21
  alternative possibilities objections and, 66–67, 68, 69
  Austinian Empirical Argument and, 79–80, 82–83, 84–85
  Austin on, 63–64, 68, 69, 72, 76, 78–79, 93–94, 146, 157–58, 192
  Children of Brunettes Hypothesis and, 139–42, 143–44, 145, 146–50, 151–53, 154, 155
  Chisolm on, 272–75
  current epistemic situation and, 139–44
  in detached rational evaluation, 152–55
  dreaming and, 63–64, 78–80, 82–83, 84–85, 86–87
  epistemic asymmetry and, 145–48, 156–57, 212
  epistemic circularity, reliability of sense perception and, 148–52
  Evil Demon Hypothesis and, 106–10, 122–23, 129, 132, 137–38, 139–40, 142, 144, 145, 149–50, 151–52, 154, 155, 159, 213–14, 256, 260–61, 301–7
  experiential, 306, 307–8, 311–12
  in folk-psychological explanations of belief formation, 298–301
  Global Epistemic Priority Thesis and, 234–35, 258–61, 265, 266–67, 272–76, 296, 304, 307–9, 311–12
  limitations on, 229, 236, 309
  ordinary, pre-philosophical position and, 219–20, 241, 254, 265, 274, 276, 279–80, 302, 309, 318–19
  ordinary epistemic commitments and, 130, 276
  from ordinary epistemic practice, 258–61
  Plain Inquirer on, 146–47, 148, 149–50, 151–53, 154, 155, 156–58
  reflectively accessible, 123, 125, 130, 140–41, 316
  reliability objections, epistemic priority and, 71–72, 73
  sensory, 216–17, 234, 236, 237–38, 255, 258
  sensory experience and, 148–52, 236, 305–6
  subjective conscious experience and, 207–8, 212–13, 216
  Williamson on, 275–76
evidential asymmetry, 160, 183–87, 260–61, 303–4, 305
evidential fundamentality, 270–72
evidential relations, 70, 83, 159, 169, 172, 178, 243–44, 270–71
Evil Demon Hypothesis, 4, 5, 27, 41–42, 99–100, 102, 103–4, 224
  accessibility asymmetry and, 165–66, 167, 169, 169n.12, 170–72, 178–79
  argument from ignorance and, 112, 117
  of Descartes, 99, 133–34, 135n.3, 136, 156, 157–59, 256
  detached rational re-evaluation of, 154
  epistemic asymmetry and, 145, 147, 156–57, 179–80, 181, 183
  epistemic circularity, reliability of sense perception and, 150–51
  epistemic closure and, 111–13, 116
  epistemic priority requirement and, 113–14, 115, 117
  evidence and, 106–10, 122–23, 129, 132, 137–38, 139–40, 142, 144, 145, 149–50, 151–52, 154, 155, 159, 213–14, 256, 260–61, 301–7
  evidential asymmetry and, 303–4
  general reliability-based priority requirement and, 119–22
  Global Epistemic Priority Thesis and, 301–3, 304, 305, 306, 307
  knowledge asymmetry and, 165
  Lawlor on, 224
  Maddy on, 132, 134–36, 138–40, 145, 152, 157–58, 165–66, 180
  Moorean anti-skeptical project on, 156
  New Evil Demon Hypothesis, 126–28, 260–61, 301–7
  ordinary epistemic commitments and, 303–5
  Plain Inquirer on, 134–35, 135nn.3–4, 136, 137–38, 139–40, 142, 144, 145, 151–53
  Pritchard on, 192, 194, 195
  Pryor on, 199, 201n.4, 201–2n.7, 202, 206–7
  rationally grounded knowledge and, 116–17, 191–92

Evil Demon Hypothesis (*cont.*)
  skeptical reliability-based priority requirement and, 120–21
  SPK on, 199, 201–2n.7, 202
  Wright on, 205–7, 213–14
experiential evidence, 306, 307–8, 311–12
external world skepticism, 3, 6–7, 9, 13, 317–18. *See also* Evil Demon Hypothesis
  Austin on, 85–92, 97
  Cavell on, 322, 323
  dream argument for, 85–91
  epistemic asymmetry and, 160, 187
  epistemological theory and, 22–23, 329–30
  general epistemic assessment on, 46
  Moore on, 17, 19–20, 21–22, 23–27, 28–29, 29n.6, 37, 44–45, 49–50, 85–86, 97, 156, 203–4, 328
  Pryor on, 27–29
  Stroud on, 86–87
  Wright on, 203–10, 212

fallibilism, 3–4, 50, 61–62, 134, 185n.17
Feldman, Richard, 108n.7, 330–31
Firth, Roderick, 250, 261–62, 263, 264
folk-psychological explanation, 296–301
foundationalism, 24, 236, 265, 272, 277, 288–89, 304
"Four Forms of Skepticism" (Moore), 21–22, 23–24, 32–33, 44
Fumerton, Richard, 277, 288–89

general epistemic assessment, 40–43, 44, 45, 46, 47, 48–55, 92, 207
general reliability-related priority requirement, 72–73, 119–22
Global Epistemic Priority Thesis, 241–42
  Chisolm and, 261, 262–63, 264, 266, 267–75
  concerns and objections, 238–54
  demand for, 324–25
  dialectical regress as argument for, 277–87
  in early-to-mid twentieth century epistemology, 261–67, 276, 296
  evidence and, 234–35, 258–61, 265, 266–67, 272–76, 296, 304, 307–9, 311–12

  Evil Demon Hypothesis and, 301–3, 304, 305, 306, 307
  explanation of error and, 301–7
  key components, 257
  ordinary, pre-philosophical position and, 255, 256–57, 258, 266–67, 276, 277, 285–87, 295–96, 305, 309–12, 325
  ordinary epistemic practice and, 258–61, 281–82, 307
  orthogonal issues, 264–67
  rational belief formation, folk-psychological explanation and, 296–301
  regress arguments and, 277–94
  on sensory experience in knowledge of the world, 234–35, 238–54, 264, 265
  structural regress as argument for, 287–94
Goodman, Nelson, 15
Greco, John, 9, 23–25, 26–27
Grice, Paul, 51–52

hinge commitments and hinge propositions, 101, 190, 192–93, 194–96, 197, 198
Hobbes, Thomas, 63–64, 64n.14, 272–73, 272–73n.8
Hume, David, 17–18, 34

immediate justification, 290–93, 293n.2
independent grounds, 71–72, 85, 88–89, 119–20, 121, 201–2, 212, 291
inferential justification, 288
information-dependence skeptical arguments, 202–21
interlocutor-deviance, 282–85
internalism, 123–29, 296–99

justification, 123, 124, 125–26, 207–8
  empirical, 17–18, 27–28, 247
  inferential, 288
  mediate, 290–93, 293n.2
justificational architecture of perceptual claims, 208–9, 236
justificatory order, 70–71, 289–90, 291–93
justificatory regresses, 277, 281–82, 287, 288–89, 296

dialectical, 277–87
    ordinary epistemic practice and, 279–82, 286
    structural, 277, 287–94

Kaplan, Mark, 47n.1
Kelly, Thomas, 29, 34–35
knowledge asymmetry, 160, 162–64, 163n.8, 165, 179

Lawlor, Krista, 189
    on closure-based skeptical arguments, 221–25
    on information-dependence, 214–21
    on Leite, 215, 218–21, 222, 224–25
    on Moore, 218
    on ordinary, pre-philosophical commitments, 218–19
    on Wright, 211, 214–21
Leite, Adam, 215, 218–21, 222, 224–25
Lewis, C.I., 261, 264
Locke, John, 15
Ludwig, Kirk, 135n.3, 167n.10, 302n.5
Lycan, William, 30–31

Maddy, Penelope, 15, 130–31, 132. *See also* Plain Inquirer, The
    accessibility asymmetry and, 165–66
    on Children of Brunettes Hypothesis, 138–41, 145, 152–53
    on current epistemic situation and evidence, 139–44
    on detached rational evaluation, 152–55
    on dreaming, 139, 142–43
    on epistemic asymmetry and evidence, 145–48, 156–57
    on epistemic circularity and sense perception, 148–52
    on Evil Demon Hypothesis, 132, 134–36, 138–40, 145, 152, 157–58, 165–66, 180
    on skeptical hypotheses and Cartesian demands, 136–39
    Wittgenstein and, 191
manifest truths, 34–35, 324–25, 326–27
McDowell, John, 231
mediate justification, 290–93, 293n.2
metaphysical disjunctivism, 230
metaphysics of perception, 230
Moore, G.E., 4, 8–9, 13, 14–15, 242
    analytic philosophy and, 15
    Austin and, 15, 56, 94, 97, 101, 102–3, 208, 221, 319–20, 324–25
    "Certainty" by, 28–29, 32–33
    on common sense, 18–19, 25, 32, 34
    on comparative judgment, 31–32
    contemporary epistemology and, 20, 21–32
    "A Defence of Common Sense" by, 32–33, 34
    epistemological theory and, 22, 25–26, 29–30, 36, 41, 43–48
    epistemology of, 32–37
    on external world skepticism, 17, 19–20, 21–22, 23–27, 28–29, 29n.6, 37, 44–45, 49–50, 85–86, 97, 156, 203–4, 328
    Feldman on, 330–31
    "Four Forms of Skepticism" by, 21–22, 23–24, 32–33, 44
    Greco on, 23–25, 26–27
    Kelly and, 29, 34–35
    Lawlor on, 218
    Lycan and, 30
    Maddy and, 133
    on ordinary, pre-philosophical position, 21, 27, 30–31, 32–37, 38–40, 44, 45–47, 48, 51–52, 56, 86, 156, 204–5, 209–10, 232, 311, 315
    on ordinary epistemic commitments, 18–20, 21, 32–34, 38–39, 44
    on ordinary life, 17
    particularism of, 34–35
    "Proof of an External World" by, 21–22, 23–24, 25–26, 27, 28–29, 28n.5, 44–45, 203–4, 252–53
    on proof *versus* perception, 24–26
    on propositions, 32, 33
    Pryor and, 28–29, 29n.6, 215
    "Some Judgments of Perception" by, 31–32
    Some Main Problems of Philosophy by, 34–35
    Stroud and, 40, 41–42, 43–49, 51–52, 54, 229
    Wright on, 203–10, 212–13, 215, 216–18, 229, 252–53

Moorean anti-skeptical project, 156–58, 186, 187
Moorean Dogmatist approach to empirical justification, 27
Moorean facts, 29
mutual dependence, 73–74, 240, 243, 244, 253–54
"Myth of the Given, The" (Chisholm), 262–63

New Evil Demon Hypothesis, 126–28, 260–61, 301–7
noninferentially justified beliefs, 288–89
Nozick, Robert, 7–8, 63n.13, 106, 165, 179

On Certainty (Wittgenstein), 146, 190
ordinary, pre-philosophical position, 17–18, 25, 52–53, 130, 221, 315–19, 325–27
 argument from ignorance and, 99, 100
 Austin on, 56, 65–85, 94
 Cavell and, 319–23
 epistemological theory and, 189–90, 236, 311–12, 327–30
 evidence and, 219–20, 241, 254, 265, 274, 276, 279–80, 302, 309, 318–19
 folk-psychological explanations and, 298–99
 Global Epistemic Priority Thesis and, 255, 256–57, 258, 266–67, 276, 277, 285–87, 295–96, 305, 309–12, 325
 Moore on, 21, 27, 30–31, 32–37, 38–40, 44, 45–47, 48, 51–52, 56, 86, 156, 204–5, 209–10, 232, 311, 315
 principles and procedures of epistemic assessment and, 45–46, 47, 48–54, 207, 317, 318, 321, 322–23
 rationally grounded knowledge and, 101, 102, 103–4
 regress and, 246, 287
 sensory perception and, 230, 232–38, 240, 255
 Stroud on conditions of knowledge and, 51–52
 über hinge proposition and, 193
 underdetermination argument and, 99–100, 103–4

 Wright on, 204–5, 209–11, 212–13, 214, 216–17
ordinary claims to know, 19, 42, 52n.2
ordinary epistemic commitments, 9, 10–11, 12–13, 14, 50, 53–54, 104, 275, 277, 294
 Austin on, 65–85
 Chisholm's contrast and, 271–72
 evidence and, 130, 276
 Evil Demon Hypothesis and, 303–5
 general epistemic assessment and, 41–42, 207
 Lawlor on, 218–19
 Moore on, 18–20, 21, 32–34, 38–39, 44
 of ordinary epistemic practices, 9, 10, 65–85, 190, 246, 248, 249, 254, 289–90, 303–4, 310, 311–12
 reflectively accessible reasons and, 128
 Stroud on, 41–42
ordinary epistemic life, 4, 7–8, 10–11, 12, 13, 14–15, 36–37, 46, 49–50
 epistemological theorizing and, 17–18, 20
 evidence and, 229
 Stroud on conditions of knowledge and, 51–52
ordinary epistemic practice, 19, 70, 123–25, 246–52
 commitments of, 9, 10, 65–85, 190, 246, 248, 249, 254, 289–90, 303–4, 310, 311–12
 evidence from, 258–61
 evidential asymmetry and, 303–4
 Global Epistemic Priority Thesis and, 258–61, 281–82, 307
 justificatory regress and, 279–82, 286
ordinary life and science, 6–7, 10, 16, 17, 60–61, 127–28, 139, 318–19, 327
"Other Minds" (Austin), 65–68, 71, 76–77

perceptual justification, Pryor's theory of, 27–28
Philosophical Investigations (Wittgenstein), 7, 189, 315
Plain Inquirer, the
 on Children of Brunettes Hypothesis, 139–42, 144, 145, 146–47, 149, 151–53, 155

detached rational re-evaluation by, 152–53, 154, 155
on epistemic asymmetry, 152, 156–57
on epistemic circularity, 149, 150, 151
on evidence, 146–47, 148, 149–50, 151–53, 154, 155, 156–58
on Evil Demon Hypothesis, 134–35, 135nn.3–4, 136, 137–38, 139–40, 142, 144, 145, 151–53
global skeptical scenarios and, 133–36, 139–40, 150–51
on project of evaluation and improvement, 152–53
reliability of sense perception and, 148–51
position-to-know asymmetry, 160, 164–65, 179
Price, H.H., 266
Pritchard, Duncan, 102n.4
  argument from ignorance of, 101–3, 115
  epistemological disjunctivism of, 101, 231
  on Evil Demon Hypothesis, 192, 194, 195
  hinge commitment and hinge proposition, 101, 190, 192–93, 194–96, 197, 198
  on rationally grounded knowledge and rational support, 189, 190–98
  underdetermination argument of, 103–4
  Wittgenstein and, 190, 191–92, 193
private language argument, 4–5
"Proof of an External World" (Moore), 21–22, 23–24, 25–26, 27, 28–29, 28n.5, 44–45, 203–4, 252–53
Pryor, Jim, 8–9, 28–29, 130, 169n.12, 189, 328–29
  on Evil Demon Hypothesis, 199, 201n.4, 201–2n.7, 202, 206–7
  Global Epistemic Priority Thesis and, 263
  on mediate and immediate justification, 290–93, 293n.2
  Moore and, 28–29, 29n.6, 215
  on perceptual experience, 231
  on perceptual justification, 27–28
  skeptical principle of, 198–202

on SPK, 198–202
Wright and, 206–7, 216, 217–18

Quine, W.V.O., 15

rapprochement, 283, 284
rational belief formation, 296–301
rationally grounded knowledge, 101, 102–4, 115, 116–17, 189, 190–98
reasoned discourse, norms of, 282–85
reflectively accessible evidence, 123, 125, 130, 140–41, 316
reflectively accessible reasons and justifications, 125–26, 128
regresses, 242–52, 269. *See also* justificatory regress
Reichenbach, Hans, 264
Reid, Thomas, 23–25, 27
reliabilist foundationalism, 24
Rescorla, Michael, 282–85
Russell, Bertrand, 21–22, 44, 261, 264

self-justifying beliefs and claims, 268–69, 270–71
Sense and Sensibilia (Austin), 57–58, 60, 60n.6, 61n.9, 70–71, 263–64
sensitivity condition on knowledge, 106, 165, 179
sensory evidence, 216–17, 234, 236, 237–38, 255, 258
sensory perception
  Bridges on, 230–31, 235–36
  Descartes on, 230, 237–38
  epistemological theory on, 232, 236–37
  epistemology of, 229–32, 233
  evidence and, 148–52, 236, 305–6
  Global Epistemic Priority Thesis on knowledge of the world and, 234–35, 238–54, 264, 265
  in knowledge of the world, 230–32, 234–54, 255, 311
  metaphysics of, 230
  ordinary, pre-philosophical position and, 230, 232–38, 240, 255
  reliability of, 148–52
  Stroud on, 229, 230, 231, 242–43
Shaftesbury (Lord), 15
skeptical principle, of Pryor, 198–202

Skeptical Principle about Knowledge (SPK), 169n.12, 198–202, 201–2n.7
skeptical reliability-based priority requirement, 120–21
"Some Judgments of Perception" (Moore), 31–32
Some Main Problems of Philosophy (Moore), 34–35
speaker-immunity, 282–83, 284–85
SPK. *See* Skeptical Principle about Knowledge
Strawson, P.F., 267
Stroud, Barry, 17, 110–11, 111–12n.13, 256n.1, 324, 325
  Austin and, 88–89, 90, 91–92
  on conditions of knowledge, ordinary life and, 51–52
  on critical epistemic reassessment, 40, 43–44, 46, 47–48, 100
  on Descartes, 230
  on epistemic relation to world, 309–10
  on external world skepticism and dreaming, 86–89
  on general epistemic assessment, 40–43, 44, 45, 46, 47, 48–55, 92
  Moore and, 40, 41–42, 43–49, 51–52, 54, 229
  on sensory perception, 229, 230, 231, 242–43
structural justificatory regresses, 277, 287–94

Thomson, Judith Jarvis, 205–6

über hinge commitment and proposition, 192–93, 194–96, 197, 198
underdetermination argument, 99–100, 101, 103–4, 234–35

Warnock, G.J., 57–58
Wedgwood, Ralph, 296–98
What Do Philosophers Do? (Maddy), 15, 130–31, 132
Williams, Bernard, 163
Williams, Michael, 9
Williamson, Timothy, 106, 157, 167, 184–85, 187, 275–76
Wittgenstein, Ludwig, 4–5, 15, 56, 330
  On Certainty by, 146, 190
  Philosophical Investigations by, 7, 189, 315
  Pritchard and, 190, 191–92, 193
Wright, Crispin, 130, 189, 236
  on Evil Demon Hypothesis, 205–7, 213–14
  on external world skepticism, 203–10, 212
  I-II-III reasoning template of, 211–21
  information-dependence skeptical argument, 202–21
  Lawlor on, 211, 214–21
  Moore and, 203–10, 212–13, 215, 216–18, 229, 252–53
  on ordinary, pre-philosophical position, 204–5, 209–11, 212–13, 214, 216–17
  Pryor and, 206–7, 216, 217–18